ARCHAIC

AN ESSAY IN DECIPHERING PREHISTORY FROM
MEGALITHIC MONUMENTS, EARTHWORKS,
CUSTOMS, COINS, PLACE-NAMES, AND
FAERIE SUPERSTITIONS

BY

HAROLD BAYLEY

AUTHOR OF " THE SHAKESPEARE SYMPHONY," " A NEW LIGHT ON THE RENAISSANCE,"
" THE LOST LANGUAGE OF SYMBOLISM," ETC.

" One by one tiny fragments of testimony accumulate attesting such a survival and continuance of folk memory as few men of to-day have suspected."—JOHNSON

LONDON

CHAPMAN & HALL LTD.

11 HENRIETTA STREET

1919

Part 2

TO

W. L. GROVES

WHO HAS GREATLY AIDED ME

CONTENTS

IX.	BRIDE'S BAIRNS	455
X.	HAPPY ENGLAND	522
XI.	THE FAIR MAID	593
XII.	PETER'S ORCHARDS	663
XIII.	ENGLISH EDENS	710
XIV.	DOWN UNDER	764
XV.	CONCLUSIONS	832
	APPENDIX	871
	INDEX	877

"Of all the many thousands of earthworks of various kinds to be found in England, those about which anything is known are very few, those of which there remains nothing more to be known scarcely exist. Each individual example is in itself a new problem in history, chronology, ethnology, and anthropology; within every one lie the hidden possibilities of a revolution in knowledge. We are proud of a history of nearly twenty centuries: we have the materials for a history which goes back beyond that time to centuries as yet undated. The testimony of records carries the tale back to a certain point: beyond that point is only the testimony of archæology, and of all the manifold branches of archæology none is so practicable, so promising, yet so little explored, as that which is concerned with earthworks. Within them lie hidden all the secrets of time before history begins, and by their means only can that history be put into writing: they are the back numbers of the island's story, as yet unread, much less indexed."—A. HADRIAN ALLCROFT.

"It is a gain to science that it has at last been recognised that we cannot penetrate far back into man's history without appealing to more than one element in that history. Some day it will be recognised that we must appeal to *all* elements in that history."—GOMME.

"History bears and requires Authors of all sorts."—CAMDEN.

CHAPTER IX

BRIDE'S BAIRNS

"But, I do not know how it comes to pass, it is the unhappy fashion of our age to derive everything curious and valuable, whether the works of art or nature, from foreign countries: as if Providence had denied us both the genius and materials of art, and sent us everything that was precious, comfortable, and convenient, at second-hand only, and, as it were, by accident, from charity of our neighbours."—BORLASE (1754).

HOMER relates that the gods watched the progress of the siege of Troy from the far-celebrated Mount Ida in Asia Minor: there is another equally famous Mount Ida in Crete, at the foot of which lived a people known as the Idaei. With Homer's allusion to "spring-abounding Ida's lowest spurs," where wandered—

> . . . in the marshy mead
> Rejoicing with their foals three thousand mares,

may be connoted his reference to "Hyde's fertile vale,"[1] and there is little doubt that spring-abounding Idas and Hyde Parks were once as plentiful as Prestons, Silverdales, and Kingstons.

The name Ida is translated by the dictionaries as meaning *perfect happiness*, and Ada as *rich gift*: we have already seen that the ideal pair of Ireland were Great King Conn and Good Queen Eda, and that it was during the

[1] *Iliad*, Bk. XX., 434.

reign of these royal twain that Ibernia, " flowed with the pure lacteal produce of the dairy ".[1]

Hyde Park, now containing Rotten Row at Kensington, occupies the site of what figured in Domesday Book as the Manor of Hyde: the immediately adjacent Audley Streets render it possible that the locality was once known as Aud lea, or meadow, whence subsequent inhabitants derived their surname. Hyde Park is partly in Paddington, a name which the authorities decode into " town of the children of Paeda ". This Paeda is supposed to have been a King of Mercia, but he would hardly have been so prolific as to have peopled a town, and, considered in conjunction with the neighbouring Praed or *pere Aed* street, it is more likely that Paeda was Father Eda, the consort of Maida or Mother Eda, after whom the adjacent Maida Vale and Maida Hill seemingly took their title. By passing up Maida Vale one may traverse St. John's Wood, Brondesbury or Brimsbury, Kensal Green, Cuneburn, and eventually attain the commanding heights of Caen, or Ken wood, from whence may be surveyed not only " Hyde's fertile vale," situated on " spring-abounding Ida's lowest spurs," but a comprehensive sweep of greater London.

According to Tacitus " some say that the Jews were fugitives from the island of Crete,"[2] and he continues: " There is a famous mountain in Crete called Ida; the neighbouring tribe, the Idaei, came to be called Judaei by a barbarous lengthening of the national name ". Modern

[1] A King Cunedda figures in Welsh literature as the first native ruler of Wales, and tradition makes Cunedda a son of the daughter of Coel, probably the St. Helen who was the daughter of Old King Cole, and who figures as the London Great St. Helen and Little St. Helen: possibly, also, as the ancient London goddess Nehallenia = New Helen, Nelly = Ellen.

[2] *History*, Bk. V.

editors of Tacitus regard this statement as no doubt the invention of some Greek etymologer, but with reference to the Idaei they speak of this old Cretan race as "being regarded as a kind of mysterious half-supernatural beings to whom mankind were indebted for the discovery of iron and the art of working it".[1]

There is evidence of a similar idealism having once existed among the Britons and the Jews in the second Epistle of Monk Gildas to the following effect: "The Britons, contrary to all the world and hostile to Roman customs, not only in the mass but also in the tonsure, are with the Jews slaves to the shadows of things to come rather than to the truth".[2] By "truth" Gildas here of course means his own particular "doxy," and the salient point of his testimony is the assertion that practically alone in the world the British and the Jews were dreamy, immaterial, superstitious idealists. That the Idaeians of Crete, Candia, or Idaea were singularly pure or candid may be judged from the testimony of Sir Arthur Evans: "Religion entered at every turn, and it was, perhaps, owing to the religious control of art that among all the Minoan representations—now to be numbered by thousands—no single example of indecency has come to light".[3] Referring to British candour, Procopius affirms: "So highly rated is chastity among these barbarians that if even the bare mention of marriage occurs without its completion the maiden seems to lose her fair fame".[4]

This alleged purity of the British Maid is substantiated

---

[1] Church, A. J. and Brodribb, W. J., *The History of Tacitus*, 1873, p. 229.
[2] Quoted in *Celtic Britain*, Rhys, Sir J., p. 74.
[3] Address to British Association.
[4] Quoted in *The Veil of Isis*, Reade, W. W., p. 47.

by the words *prude* and *proud*, both of which like *pretty*, *purity*, and *pride*, are radically pure Ide. Skeat defines *prude* as a woman of affected modesty, and adds "see *prow*ess"; but prudery has little connection with prowess, and is it really necessary to assume that primitive prudery was "affected"? The Jewish JAH is translated by scholars as "pure Being"; the passionate adoration of purity is expressed in the prehistoric hymn quoted *ante* page 183, Hu the Mighty was pre-eminently pure, and it is thus likely that the ancient Pere, Jupiter, or Aubrey meant originally the *Pure*.

We have seen that Jupiter, the divine *Power*, was conceived indifferently as either a man or an immortal maid: a maid is a virgin, and the words *maid* or *mayde*, like Maida, is radically "Mother Ida". According to Skeat *maid* is related to Anglo-Saxon *magu*, a son or kinsman; and one may thus perhaps account for *brother*, *bruder*, or *frater*, as meaning originally the produce or progeny of the same *pere*—but not necessarily the same *pair*.

To St. Bride may be assigned not only the terms *bride* and bridegroom, or brideman; but likewise *breed* and *brood*. Skeat connects the latter with the German *bruhen* to scald, but a good mother does not scald her brood, and as St. Bride was known anciently as "The Presiding Care"; even although *bairn* is the same word as *burn*, we may assume that St. Bride did not burn her *brat*.

There is a Bridewell and a church of St. Bride in London, but to the modern Londoner this "greatest woman of the Celtic Church" is practically unknown. In Hibernia and the Hebrides, however, St. Bride yet lives, and in the words of a modern writer is "more real than the great names of history. They, pale shadows moving in an unreal world, have gone, but she abides. With each revolving year she flits across the Machar, and her tiny flowers burn golden among the short, green, turfy grass at her coming. Her herald, the Gillebrighde, the servant of Bride, calls its own name and hers among the shores, a message that the sea, the treasury of Mary, will soon yield its abundance to the fisher, haven-bound by the cold and stormy waters of winter. He sees St. Bride, the Foster Mother, but his keen vision penetrates a vista far beyond the ages when Imperial Rome held sway and, in that immemorial past, beholds her still. In the uncharted regions of the Celtic imagination, she abides unchanging, her eyes starlit, her raiment woven of fire and dew; her aureole the rainbow. To him she is older than the world of men, yet eternally young. She is beauty and purity and love, and time for her has no meaning. She is a ministering spirit, a flame of fire. It is she who touches with her finger the brow of the poet and breathes into his heart the inspiration of his song. She is born with the dawn, and passes into new loveliness when the sun sets in the wave. The night winds sing her lullaby, and little children hear the music of her voice and look into her answering eyes. Who and what, then, is St. Bride? She is Bridget of Kildare, but she is more. She is the daughter of Dagda, the goddess of the Brigantes; but she is more. She is the maid of Bethlehem, the tender Foster Mother; but she is more even than that. She is of the race of the immortals. She is the spirit and the genius of the Celtic people."[1]

St. Bride was known occasionally as St. Fraid, and Brigit, or Brigid, an alternative title of the Fair Ide, may be modernised into *Pure Good*. With her white wand

[1] Wilkie, James, *Saint Bride, the Greatest Woman of the Celtic Church*.

Brigit was said to breathe life into the mouth of dead Winter, impelling him to open his eyes to the tears, the smiles, the sighs, and the laughter of Spring, whence to Brid, or Bryth of the Brythons, may be assigned the word *breathe* ; and as Bride was represented by a sheaf of grain carried joyously from door to door, doubtless in her name we have the origin of *bread*.

The name Bradbury implies that many barrows were dedicated to Brad ; running into the river Rye of Kent is a river Brede, and as the young goddess of Crete was known to the Hellenes as Britomart, which means *sweet maiden*, we may equate Britomart with Britannia. At the village of Brede in Kent the seat now known as Brede Place is also known as the Giant's House, whence in all probability St. Bride was the maiden Giant, Gennet, or Jeanette.

In the province of Janina in Albania is the town of Berat, and the foundation of either this Berat or else the Beyrout of Canaan was ascribed by the Greek mythologists to a maiden named Berith or Beroë.

> Hail Beroë, fairest offering of the Nereids!
> Beroë all hail! thou root of life, thou boast
> Of Kings, thou nurse of cities with the world
> Coeval ; hail thou ever-favoured seat of Hermes . . .
> With Tethys and Oceanus coeval.
> But later poets feign that lovely Beroë
> Derived her birth from Venus and Adonis
> Soon as the infant saw the light with joy
> Old Ocean straight received her in his arms.
> And e'en the brute creation shared the pleasure.
> . . . In succeeding years
> A sacred town derived its mystic name
> From that fair child whose birth coeval was
> With the vast globe ; but rich Ausonia's sons
> The city call Berytus.[1]

---

[1] Nonnus, quoted from *A Dissertation on The Mysteries of the Cabiri*, Faber, G. S., vol. ii., p. 313.

The same poet repeatedly maintains that the age of the city of Beroë was equal to that of the world, and that it could boast an antiquity much greater than that of Tarsus, Thebes, or Sardis. The reference to Beroë or Berith as the ever-favoured seat of Hermes implies the customary equation of Britannia = Athene = Wisdom. The prehistoric car illustrated in the preceding chapter is reproduced from a stone in Perthshire or Perithshire, and in a description written in 1569 this stone was then designated the Thane Stone.[1] That this was an Athene stone is somewhat implied by the further details, " it had a cross at the head of it and a goddess next that in a cart, and two horses drawing her and horsemen under that, and footmen and dogs ". The Thanes of Scotland were probably the official representatives of Athene, or Wisdom, or Justice, and the dogs of the Thane Stone may be connoted with the Hounds of Diana or Britomart, and the greyhounds of the English Fairy Queen.

Athene is presumably the same as Ethne, the reputed mother of St. Columba, and also as Ieithon, the Keltic goddess of speech or *prat*ing, after whom Anwyl considers the river Ieithon in Radnorshire was named. This Welsh river-name may be connoted with the river Ythan in Scotland, and the legend IDA, found upon the reverse of some of the Ikenian coins of England, may be connoted with the place-name Odestone, or Odstone, implying seemingly a stone of Od, or Odin.

At Oddendale in Westmorland are the remains of a Druidic circle and traces of old British settlements: with the Thanestone may be connoted the carved example illustrated *ante*, page 381, from Dingwall, and also the

[1] Huyshe, W., *The Life of St. Columba*, p. 247.

decorated "Stone of the Fruitful Fairy," which exists in Ireland.[1]

The authorities think it possible that the river Idle—a tributary of the Trent—derived its name from being empty, vain, or useless; but it is more probable that this small stream was christened by the Idaeans, and that the resident Nymph or Fruitful Fairy was the idyll, or the idol, whom they idealised. It is not without significance that the starting point of the races at Uffington was Idles Bush: "As many as a dozen or more horses ran, and they started from Idle's Bush which wur a vine owld tharnin-tree in thay days—a very nice bush. They started from Idle's Bush as I tell 'ee sir, and raced up to the Rudge-way."[2] Doubtless there were also many other "Idles Bush's," perhaps at some time one in every Ideian town or neighbourhood: there is seemingly one notable survival at Ilstrye or *Ideles*tree, now Elstree near St. Albans.

That the Idaean ideal was Athene is implied by the adjective *ethnic*. The word *ethic* which means, "relating to morals," is connected by Skeat with *sitte*, the German for custom: there is, however, no seeming connection between German custom and the Idyllic.[3]

---

[1] Canon ffrench, *Prehistoric Faith and Worship*, p. 56.

[2] Hughes, T., *The Scouring of the White Horse*, p. 111.

[3] Apart from recent experiences and the records of the Saxon invaders of this country, one may connote the candid maxims of the Frederick upon whom the German nation has thought proper to confer the sobriquet of "Great," *e.g.* :—

"It was the genius of successive rulers of our race to be guided only by self-interest, ambition, and the instinct of self-preservation."

"When Prussia shall have made her fortune, she will be able to give herself the air of good-faith and of constancy which is only suitable for great States or small Sovereigns."

The early followers of Britomart are universally described as an industrious and peaceful people who made their conquests in arts and commerce: to them not only was ascribed the discovery of iron and the working of it, but the Cretan treatment of bronze proves that the Idaeans were

"As for war, it is a profession in which the smallest scruple would spoil everything."

"Nothing exercises a greater tyranny over the spirit and heart than religion. . . . Do we wish to make a treaty with a Power? If we only remember that we are Christians all is lost, we shall always be duped."

"Do not blush at making alliances with the sole object of reaping advantage for yourself. Do not commit the vulgar fault of not abandoning them when you believe it to be to your advantage to do so; and, above all, ever follow this maxim that to despoil your neighbours is to take from them the means of doing you harm."

In the eyes of the stupid and unappreciative Britons the Saxons were "swine," and the "loathest of all things," *vide* Layamon's *Brut*, *e.g.*: "Lo! where here before us the heathen hounds, who slew our ancestors with their wicked crafts; and they are to us in land *loathest of all things*. Now march we to them, and starkly lay on them, and avenge worthily our kindred, and our realm, and avenge the mickle shame by which they have disgraced us, that they over the waves should have come to Dartmouth. And all they are forsworn, and all they shall be destroyed; they shall be all put to death, with the Lord's assistance! March we now forward, fast together"—(Everyman's Library, p. 195).

"The Saxons set out across the water, until their sails were lost to sight. I know not what was their hope, nor the name of him who put it in their mind, but they turned their boats, and passed through the channel between England and Normandy. With sail and oar they came to the land of Devon, casting anchor in the haven of Totnes. The heathen breathed out threatenings and slaughter against the folk of the country. They poured forth from their ships, and scattered themselves abroad amongst the people, searching out arms and raiment, firing homesteads and slaying Christian men. They passed to and fro about the country, carrying off all they found beneath their hands. Not only did they rob the hind of his weapon, but they slew him on his hearth with his own knife. Thus throughout Somerset and a great part of Dorset, these pirates spoiled and ravaged at their pleasure, finding none to hinder them at their task"—(*Ibid.*, p. 47).

consummate bronzesmiths. In Crete, according to Sir Arthur Evans, "new and refined crafts were developed, some of them like inlaid metal-work unsurpassed in any age or country".

That the Britons were expert blacksmiths is evident not merely from their chariot wheels, but also from the superb examples of bronze art-craft, found notably in the Thames. For the sum of one shilling the reader may obtain *A Guide to the Antiquities of the Iron Age*, published by the British Museum, in which invaluable volume two wonderful examples of prehistoric ironmongery are illustrated in colour. One of these, a bronze shield discovered at Battersea, is rightly described by Romilly Allen, as "about the most beautiful surviving piece of late Celtic metal-work". The Celts, as this same authority observes, had already become expert workers in metal before the close of the Bronze Age; they could make beautiful hollow castings for the chapes of their sword sheaths; they could beat out bronze into thin plates and rivet them together sufficiently well to form water-tight cauldrons; they could ornament their circular bronze shields and golden diadems with repoussé patterns, consisting of corrugations and rows of raised bosses; and they were not unacquainted with the art of engraving on metal.[1]

Not only were the Britons expert in ordinary metal-work but they are believed to have *invented* the art of enamelled-inlay. Writing in the third century of the present era, an oft-quoted Greek observed: "They say that the barbarians who live in Ocean pour colours on heated bronze and that they adhere, become as hard as stone, and preserve the designs that are made in them".

[1] Allen J. Romilly, *Celtic Art in Pagan and Christian Times*, p. 130.

It is admitted that nowhere was greater success attained by this art of the early Iron Age than in Britain, and as Sir Hercules Read rightly maintains: "There are solid reasons for supposing this particular style to have been confined to this country".[1] The art of enamelling was of course practised elsewhere, particularly at Bibracte in Gaul, long before the Roman Conquest, but in the opinion of Dr. Anderson, the Bibracte enamels are the work of mere dabblers in the art compared with the British examples: the home of the art was Britain, and the style of the patterns, as well as the associations in which the objects decorated with it were found, demonstrate with certainty that it had reached its highest stage of indigenous development before it came in contact with the Roman culture.[2] The evidence of the bronze spear-head points to the same remarkable conclusions as the evidence of enamelled bronze, and in the opinion of the latest and best authorities, from its first inception throughout the whole progress of its evolution the spear-head of the United Kingdom has a character of its own, one quite different from those found elsewhere. In no part of the world did the spear-head attain such perfection of form and fabric as it did in these islands, and the old-fashioned notion that bronze weapons were imported from abroad is now hopelessly discredited. "Why, then," ask the authors of *The Origin, Evolution, and Classification of the Bronze Spear-Head*,[3] "may not a bronze culture have had its birth in our country where it ultimately attained a development scarcely equalled,

---

[1] *A Guide to the Antiquities of the Iron Age*, p. 89.
[2] Quoted by J. Romilly Allen, in *Celtic Art*, p. 138.
[3] Rev. Wm. Greenwell and Parker Brewis, *Archæologia*, vol. lxi., pp. 439, 472 (1909).

certainly not surpassed, by that in any other part of the world?"

One of the distinctions of the British spear-head is a certain variety of tang, of which the only parallel has been found in one of the early settlements at Troy. Forms also, somewhat similar, have been discovered in the Islands of the Ægean sea, and in the Terramara deposits of Northern Italy, but it is the considered opinion of Canon Greenwell and Parker Brewis, that whatever may be the true explanation of the history of the general development of a bronze culture in Great Britain and Ireland, "there can be no doubt whatever that the spear-head in its origin, progress, and final consummation was an indigenous product of those two countries, and was manufactured within their limits apart from any controlling influence from outside".[1]

The magnificent bronze shield and *bric a brac* found in London were thus presumably made there, and it is not improbable that the principal smitheries were situated either at Smithfield in the East, or Smithfield in the West in the ward of Farringdon or Farendone.

Stow in his *London* uses the word *fereno* to denote an ironmonger, in old French *feron* meant a smith, and wherever the ancient ferenos or smiths were settled probably became known as *Farindones* or *fereno towns*. Stow mentions several eminent goldsmiths named Farendone; from *feron*, the authorities derive the surname Fearon, which may be seen over a shop-front near Farringdon Street to-day.

Modern Farringdon Street leads from Smithfield or

---

[1] Rev. Wm. Greenwell and Parker Brewis, *Archæologia*, vol. lxi., p. 4.

Smithy field[1] to Blackfriars, and it may be suggested that the original Black Friars were literally freres or brethren, who forged with industrious ferocity at their fires and furnaces. Without impropriety the early fearons might have adopted as their motto *Semper virens*: smiting in smithies is smutty work, and all these terms are no doubt interrelated, but not, I think, in the sense which Skeat supposes them, *viz.*: " Smite, *to fling*. The original sense was to smear or rub over. 'To rub over,' seems to have been a sarcastic expression for 'to beat'; we find *well anoynted*—well beaten."

The word *bronze* was derived, it is said, from Brundusinum or Brindisi, a town which was famous for its bronze workers. Brindisi is almost opposite Berat in Epirus; the smith or *faber* is proverbially *burly*, *i.e.*, *bur* like or *brawny*, and it is curious that the terms *brass*, *brasier*, *burnish*, *bronze*, etc., should all similarly point to Bru or Brut. With St. Bride or St. Brigit, who in one of her three aspects was represented as a smith, may be connoted *bright*, and with Bress, the Consort of Brigit, may be connoted *brass*. And as Bride was alternatively known as Fraid, doubtless to this form of the name may be assigned *fer*, *fire*, *fry*, *frizzle*, *furnace*, *forge*, *fierce*, *ferocious*, and *force*.

That the island of Bru or Barri in South Wales was a reputed home of the burly *faber*, *feuber*, or Fire Father, is to be inferred from the statement of Giraldus Cambrensis, that "in a rock near the entrance of the island there is a small cavity to which if the ear is applied a noise is heard like that of smiths at work, the blowing of the bellows, strokes of the hammers, grinding of tools and roaring of

---

[1] The standard supposition that Smithfield is a corruption of *smooth field* may or may not be well founded.

furnaces ".[1] It is supposed that Barri island owes its name to a certain St. Baroc, the remains of whose chapel once stood there: that St. Baroc was Al Borak, the White Horse or *brok*, upon whom every good Mussalman hopes eventually to ride, is implied by the story that St. Baroc borrowed a friend's horse and rode miraculously across the sea from Pembrokeshire to Ireland.

On the coast between Pembroke and Tenby is Manor*beer*, known anciently as Maenor Pyrr, that is, says Giraldus, " the mansion of Pyrrus, who also possessed the island of Chaldey, which the Welsh call Inys Pyrr, or the island of Pyrrus ". But the editor of Giraldus considers that a much more natural and congenial conjecture may be made in supposing Maenor Pyrr to be derived from *Maenor* a *Manor*, and Pyrr, the plural of Por, a lord. I have already suggested a possible connection between the numerous *pre* stones and Pyrrha, the first lady who created mankind out of stones.

Near Fore Street, in the ward of Farringdon by Smithfield, will be found Whitecross Street, Redcross Street, and Cowcross Street: the last of these three cross streets by which was "Jews Garden," may be connoted with the Geecross of elsewhere. The district is mentioned by Stow as famous for its coachbuilders, and there is no more reason to assume that the word *coach* (French *coche*) was derived from Kocsi, a town in Hungary, than to suppose that the first coach was a cockney production and came from Chick Lane or from Cock Lane, both of which neighbour the Cowcross district in Smithfield. The supposition that the *gig* or *coach* (the words are radically the same) was primarily a vehicle used in the festivals to Gog

[1] Bohn's ed., p. 382.

the *High High,* or *Mighty Mighty,* is strengthened by the testimony of the solar chariot illustrated *ante,* page 405.

Not only were the British famed from the dawn of history[1] for their car-driving but from the evidence of

---

[1] The psychology of Homer's description of the Vulcan menage is curiously suggestive of a modern visit to the village blacksmith :—

> "Him swelt'ring at his forge she found, intent
> On forming twenty tripods, which should stand
> The wall surrounding of his well-built house,
> The silver-footed Queen approach'd the house.
> Charis, the skilful artist's wedded wife,
> Beheld her coming, and advanc'd to meet ;
> And, as her hand she clasp'd, address'd her thus :
>   'Say, Thetis of the flowing robe, belov'd
> And honour'd, whence this visit to our house,
> An unaccustom'd guest ? but come thou in,
> That I may welcome thee with honour due.'
>   Thus, as she spoke, the goddess led her in,
> And on a seat with silver studs adorn'd,
> Fair, richly wrought, a footstool at her feet,
> She bade her sit ; then thus to Vulcan call'd ;
>   'Haste hither, Vulcan ; Thetis asks thine aid.'
>   Whom answer'd thus the skill'd artificer :
>   'An honour'd and a venerated guest
> Our house contains ; who sav'd me once from woe,
> Then thou the hospitable rites perform,
> While I my bellows and my tools lay by.'
> He said, and from the anvil rear'd upright
> His massive strength ; and as he limp'd along,
> His tott'ring knees were bow'd beneath his weight.
> The bellows from the fire he next withdrew,
> And in a silver casket plac'd his tools ;
> Then with a sponge his brows and lusty arms
> He wip'd, and sturdy neck and hairy chest.
> He donn'd his robe, and took his weighty staff ;
> Then through the door with halting step he pass'd ;
>   . . . with halting gait,

sepulchral chariots and sepulchral harness the authorities are of opinion that the fighting car was long retained by the Kelts, " and its presence in the Yorkshire graves seems to show that it persisted in Britain longer than elsewhere ".[1]

Somewhere in the Smithfield district originally existed what Stow mentions as Radwell, and this well of the Redcross, or Ruddy rood, may be connoted with the Rood Lane a mile or so more eastward. Between Rood Lane and Red Cross Street is Lothbury: the suffix *bury* (as in Lothbury, and Aldermanbury) is held by Stow, and also by Camden, to mean a Court of Justice, and this definition accords precisely with the theory that the barrow was originally the seat of Justice. At Lothbury the noise or *bruit* made by the burly fabers was so vexatious that Stow seriously defines the place-name *Loth*bury as indicating a *loath*some locality.[2] The supposition that Cow-

> Pass'd to a gorgeous chair by Thetis' side,
> And, as her hand he clasp'd, address'd her thus:
> ' Say Thetis, of the flowing robe, belov'd
> And honour'd, whence this visit to our house,
> An unaccustom'd guest? say what thy will,
> And, if within my pow'r esteem it done.' "
>
> *Iliad,* Bk. XVIII., p. 420-80.

[1] British Museum, *A Guide to the Antiquities of the Early Iron Age,* p. 54.

[2] " Antiquities to be noted therein are: First the street of Lothberie, Lathberie, or Loadberie (for by all these names have I read it), took the name (as it seemeth) of berie, or court of old time there kept, but by whom is grown out of memory. This street is possessed for the most part by founders, that cast candlesticks, chafing-dishes, spice mortars, and such like copper or laton works and do afterward turn them with the foot, and not with the wheel, to make them smooth and bright with turning and scrating (as some do term it), making a loathsome noise to the by-passers that have not been used to the like, and therefore by them disdainfully called Lothberie."—*London* (Ev. Lib.), p. 248.

cross Street, Jews Garden, and the Redcross or Ruddy rood site were primarily in the occupation of men of Troy or Droia may possibly be strengthened by the fact that here was a *Tre*mill brook, and the seat of a Sir Drew Drury. The parish church of Blackfriars is St. Andrews, there is another St. Andrews within a bow-shot of Smithfield, and that the "drews" were a skilled family is obvious from the fact that the name Drew is defined as Teutonic *skilful*. Both Scandinavians and Germans possess the Trojan tradition; the All Father of Scandinavia was named *Borr*, Thor, the Hammer God, was assigned to Troy, and in Teutonic mythology there figure two celestial Smith-brethren named Sindre and Brok.

The cradle of the Cretan Zeus is assigned sometimes not to Mount Ida but to the neighbouring Mount Juktas which is described as an extraordinary "cone". When the Cretan script is deciphered it will probably transpire that Mount Juktas was associated with Juk, Jock, or Jack, and the name may be connected with *jokul*, the generic term in Scandinavia for a snow-covered or white-crowned height. Jack is seemingly the same word as the Hebrew Isaac, which is defined as meaning *laughter*: Jack may thus probably be equated with *joke* and *jokul* with *chuckle*, all of which symptoms are the offspring of *joy* or *gaiety*. To *kyg*, an obsolete adjective meaning *lively*—and thus evidently a variant of *agog*—are assigned by our authorities the surnames Keach, Ketch, Kedge, and Gedge. In connection with *kyg* Prof. Weekley quotes the line—

Kygge or joly, *jocundus*.

Among the gewgaws found in the sacred shrines of Juktas are numerous bijou gigs, or coaches, all no doubt once very *juju*, or sacred.

To appreciate the outlook of the "half-supernatural" Idaeans one may find a partial key in the words of Aratus: "Let us begin with *Zeus*, let us always call upon and laud his name; all the network of interwending roads and all the busy markets of mankind are full of *Zeus*, and all the paths and fair havens of the sea, and everywhere our hope is in *Zeus* for we are also his children".[1]

Stow mentions the firmly-rooted tradition that the Cathedral of St. Paul stands upon the site of an ancient shrine to Jupiter. It may be merely coincidence that close to St. Paul's once stood an Ypres Hall:[2] in the immediate vicinity of Old St. Paul's used also to exist a so-called Pardon Churchyard, perhaps an implication that Ludgate Hill was once known as *Par dun* or *Par Hill*. That "Pardon" was equivalent to "Pradon" is evident from the fact that modern Dumbarton was originally *Dun Brettan*, or the Briton's Fort. The slope leading from the Southern side of St. Paul's or Pardon Churchyard, is still named Peter's Hill, and in view of the Jupiter tradition it is not altogether unlikely that Peter's Hill was originally *eu Peter's* Hill, synonymously *Pere dun*. The surname Pardon may still be found in this Godliman Street neighbourhood, where in Stow's time stood not only Burley House, but likewise Blacksmiths Hall. A funeral *pyre* is a fire; a *phare* is a lighthouse, and the intense purity of Bride's fire, phare, or pyre is implied by the fact that it was not suffered to be blown by human breath but by bellows only. From time immemorial the Fire of Bride was tended by nineteen holy maids, each of whom had the care of the Fire for one night in turn: on the twentieth night the nineteenth maid, having piled wood upon the fire,

[1] *Phenomena*, p. xvii. [2] Stow, *London*, p. 221.

said: "Brigit, take charge of your own fire, for this night belongs to you". The tale ends that ever on the twentieth morning the fire had been miraculously preserved.[1]

The patron saint of engineers is Barbara or Varvara, the sacred pyre of Bride was maintained within a circle or periphery of stakes and brushwood, and close at hand were certain very beautiful meadows called St. Bridget's pastures, in which no plough was ever suffered to turn a furrow. The words *mead* and *meadow* are the same as *maid* and *maida*, whence it seems to follow that all meadows were dedicated to Bride, the pretty Lady of the Kine. Homer's "fertile vale of Hyde," and the Londoner's Hyde Park, were alike probably idealised and sacred meadows corresponding to the Irish Mag-Ithe or Plains of Ith; it is not unlikely that all *heaths* were dedicated to *Ith*. To the Scandinavian Ith or Ida Plains we find an ancient poet thus referring: "I behold Earth rise again with its evergreen forests out of the deep . . . the Anses meet on Ida Plain, they talk of the mighty earth serpent, and remember the great decrees, and the ancient mysteries of the unknown God". After foretelling a time when "All sorrows shall be healed and Balder shall come back," the poet continues: "Then shall Hœni choose the rods of divination aright, and the sons of the *Twin Brethren* shall inhabit the wide world of the winds".[2]

In Fig. 26ᶜ—an Etrurian bucket—two diminutive Twin Brethren are being held by the *Bona Dea*—a winged Ange or Anse—who is surmounted by the symbolic cockle or coquille. The fact that this bucket was found at Offida renders it possible that the mother here represented was

[1] *Giraldus Cambrensis*, p. 97.
[2] *Cf.* Rhys, Sir J., *Celtic Heathendom*, p. 613.

known to the craftsman who portrayed her as *Offi divine*, otherwise Hipha, Eve, or Good Iva. It will be noticed

Fig. 266.—Etruscan Bucket, Offida, Picenum. From *A Guide to the Antiquities of the Early Iron Age*, p. 17.

that the child on the right is white, that on the left black, and I have elsewhere drawn attention to many other emblems in which two A's, Alphas, Alifs, or Elves were similarly portrayed, the one as white, the other as black.[1] The intention of the artist seems to have been to express the current philosophy of a Prime or Supreme supervising both good and evil, light and dark, or day and night. Pliny says that British women used to attend certain religious festivals with their nude bodies painted black like Ethiopians, and there is probably some close connection between this obscure function, and the fact that Diana of the Ephesians, the many-breasted All-mother of Life, was portrayed at times as white, at times as black. There must be a further connection between this black and white *Bona Dea*, and the fact that in the Lady Godiva processions near Coventry, which took place at the opening of the Great May Fair festival, there were two Godivas, one of whom was the natural colour but the other was dyed black.[2]

The *Bona Dea* of Egypt, like the figure on the Etrurian bucket, was represented holding in her arms two children, one white and one black; and the two circles at Avebury, lying within the larger Avereberie or periphery, were probably representative of Day and Night circled by all-embracing and eternal Time.

The Twin Brethren or Gemini are most popularly known as Castor and Pollux, and the propitious figures of these heavenly Twins were carved frequently upon the *prows* of ancient ships. The phosphorescent stars or Will-o-the-wisps, which during storms sometimes light upon the masts of ships, used to be known as St. Elmo's Fires: St. Elmo is obviously St. Alma or St. All Mother, and the St. Helen

[1] *Cf. A New Light on the Renaissance* and *The Lost Language of Symbolism*.
[2] Windle, B. C. A., *Life in Early Britain*, p. 116.

with whom she is identified is seemingly St. Alone. It

FIG. 267.—From *Ancient Pagan and Modern Christian Symbolism* (Inman, C. W.)

was believed that two stars were propitious, but that a solitary one boded bad luck: according to Pliny a single

St. Elmo's fire was called Helen, "but the two they call Castor and Pollux, and invoke them as gods".

The appearance of the will-o-the-wisps, Castor and Pollux, was held to be an argument that the tempest was caused by "a sulphurous spirit rarefying and violently moving the clouds, for the cause of the fire is a sulphurous and bituminous matter driven downwards by the impetuous motion of the air and kindled by much agitation". I quote this passage as justifying the suggestion that *sulphur*—the yellow and fiery—is radically *phur*, and that *brimstone*, or *brenstoon*, as Wyclif has it, may be the stone of Brim or Bren, which burns.

The identification of Castor and Pollux with stars or *asters*, enables us to equate Castor as the White god or Day god, for *dextra*, the Latin for right, is *de castra*, *i.e.*, *good great astra*. The white child in Fig. 266 is that on the *right* hand of the *Bona Dea*: that Pollux was the dark, *sinister*, *sinistra*, or left-hand power, is somewhat confirmed by the fact that the Celtic Pwll was the Pluto or deity of the underworld. Possibly the Latin *castra*, meaning a fort, originated from the idea that Castor was the heroic Invictus who has developed into St. Michael and St. George. The *sin* of *sinister* may possibly be the Gaelic *sen*, meaning senile, and the implication follows that the dark twin was the old in contradistinction to the new god.

The French for nightmare is *cauche*mar, the French for left is *gauche*, and it is the left-hand mairy, or fairy, in Fig. 266 which is the shady one. Not only does *gauche* mean *left*, but it also implies awkward, uncanny, and inept, whence it is to be feared that the Gooches, the Goodges, and their affiliated tribes were originally "Blackfriars," and followers of the Black God. I have already suggested that the Gogs were unpopular among the Greeks, and the intensity of their feeling is seemingly reflected by the Greek adjective *kakos* [1] (the English *gagga?*), which means evil, dirty, or unpleasant.

Castor and Pollux, or the Fires of St. Helen, were known along the shores of the Mediterranean as St. Telmo's Fires, the word Telmo being seemingly *t Elmo* or Good Alma. By the Italians they are known as the Fires of St. Peter and St. Nicholas; Peter here corresponding probably to the *auburn* Aubrey, and Nicholas to "Old Nick".

It was fabled that Castor and Pollux were alike immortal, that like day and night they periodically died, but that whenever one of the brothers expired the other was restored to life, thus sharing immortality between them. "There was," says Duncan, "an allusion to this tradition in the Roman horse-races, where a single rider galloped round the course mounted on one horse while he held another by the rein." [2] This ceremony becomes more interesting when we find that the cauchemar, the nightmare, or the blackmare used in England to be known as the "ephialtes".[3] That this ill-omened *hipha*, or hobby, was ill-boding Helena, seems somewhat to be confirmed by the custom in Cumberland of allotting to servants the years' allowance for horse-meat on St. Helen's, Eline's, or Elyn's day.[4] It is believed that horse meat is now taboo in Britain, because the eating of horse was so persistently denounced by Christianity as a heathen rite.

[1] Cacus figures in mythology as a huge giant, the son of Vulcan, and the stealer of Hercules' oxen.

[2] Duncan, T., *The Religions of Profane Antiquity*, p. 59.

[3] Hazlitt, W. Carew, *Faith and Folklore*, vol. i., p. 210.

[4] A trace of the old sacrificial eating?

Fig. 268.—British Altar. By kind permission of the authorities of the British Museum.

[To face page 479.

I have shown elsewhere some of the innumerable forms under which the fires of Elmo, or the heavenly Twain, were represented. In England it is evident that a pair of horses served as one form of expression, for among the treasures at the British Museum is an article which is thus described : " Bronze plate representing an altar decorated with blue, green, and red sunk enamels, and evidently unfinished, hence native work of the fourth or fifth century. Found in the river Thames, 1847 ". The principal decoration of this bijou altar—significantly 7 inches high—is two winged steeds supporting a demijohn, vase, or phial, the handles of which, in the form of $S\mathcal{Z}$, are detached from the vase, but are emerging flame-like from the supporters' heads. The fact of these steeds appearing upon an "altar" is evidence of their sacred character, and one finds apparently the same two beasts delineated on a bucket, *vide* Fig. 270. This so termed "barbaric production," discovered in an Aylesford gravel pit belonging to a gentleman curiously named Wagon, is attributed to the first century B.C., and has been compared unfavourably with the Etruscan bucket reproduced on page 474. The authorities of the British Museum comment upon it as follows : " The effect of barbaric imitation during two or three centuries may be appreciated by comparing the Etruscan *cista* of the *fourth century*, with the Aylesford bucket of the *first century* B.C. The first thing to be noticed is the absence from the latter of the heavy solid castings that form the feet and handle-attachments of the classica specimen. Such work was beyond the range of the British artificer, who was never successful with the human or animal form, but there is an evident desire to reproduce the salient features of the prototype. The solid uppermost band of the Etruscan specimen is represented by a thin embossed strip at Aylesford, while the classical motives

Fig. 269.—Bronze-mounted bucket, Aylesford. From *A Guide to Antiquities of the Early Iron Age* (B.M.).

Fig. 270.—Embossed frieze of bucket, Aylesford. From *A Guide to Antiquities of the Early Iron Age* (B.M.).

are woefully caricatured. Minor analogies are noticed later, but the degradation of the ornament may fitly be dwelt on here as showing the limitations, and at the same time the originality of the native craftsman."

I confess myself unable either to appreciate or dwell upon the alleged degradation of this design, or the woeful inadequacy of the craftmanship. The bold execution of the spirals proves that the British artist—had such been his intent—could without difficulty have delineated a copybook horse: what, however, he was seemingly aiming at was a facsimile of the heraldic and symbolic beasts which our coins prove were the cherished insignia of the country, and these "deplorable abortions" I am persuaded were no more barbarous or unsuccessful than the grotesque lions and other fantastics which figure in the Royal Arms to-day.

In all probability the Aylesford bucket was made in the neighbourhood where it was found, for at Aylesford used to stand a celebrated "White Horse Stone". The attendant local legend—that anyone who rode a beast of this description was killed on or about the spot[1]—is seemingly a folk-memory of the time when the severe penalty for riding a white mare was death.[2] The place-name Aylesbury is derived by the authorities from *bury*, a fortified place of, and *Aegil*, the Sun-archer of Teutonic mythology: the head-dress of the face constituting the hinge of the Aylesford bucket consists of two circles which correspond in idea with the two children in the arms of the Etruscan hinge. That the bucket was originally a sacerdotal and sacred vessel is implied not only by the word but by the ancient custom thus recorded: "First on a pillar was placed a perch on the sharp prickled back whereof stood this idol

---

[1] Gomme, L., *Folklore as an Historic Science*, p. 43.
[2] See Johnson, W., *Byways of British Archæology*. "Among the Saxons only a high priest might lawfully ride a mare," p. 436.

... in his left hand he held up a wheel, and in his right he carried a pail of water wherein were flowers and fruits".[1] I have elsewhere reproduced several emblems of Jupiter and Athene each seated on a "sharp prickled back," *i.e.*, a *broccus*, saw, or zigzag, symbolic of the shaggy solar rays.

There is nothing decadent or seriously wrong with the drawing of the steeds delineated in Figs. 271 and 272, although the "what-not" proceeding from the mouth of the Geho is somewhat perplexing. This is seemingly a ribbon or a chain, and like the perfect chain surrounding our

FIGS. 271 to 273.—British. From Akerman.

SOLIDO coins, and the chain which will be noted upon the Trojan spindle whorl illustrated on page 583, was probably intended to portray what the ancients termed Jupiter's Chain: "All things," says Marcus Aurelius, "are connected together by a sacred chain, and there is not one link in it which is not allied with the whole chain, for all things have been so blended together as to form a perfect whole, on which the symmetry of the universe depends. There is but one world, and it comprehends everything; one God endued with ubiquity; one eternal matter; and one law, which is the Reason common to all intelligent creatures."

[1] Faber, G. S., *The Mysteries of the Cabiri*, i., 220.

A chain of pearls is proceeding from the mouth of the little figure which appears on some of the Channel Island coins, *vide* the DRUCCA example herewith: students of fairy-tale are familiar with the story of a Maid out of whose mouth, whenso'er she opened it fell jewels, and that this fairy Maid was Reason is implied by the present day compliment in the East, "Allah! you are a wise man, you spit pearls." The DRUCCA coin is officially described as a "female figure standing to the left, her right hand holding

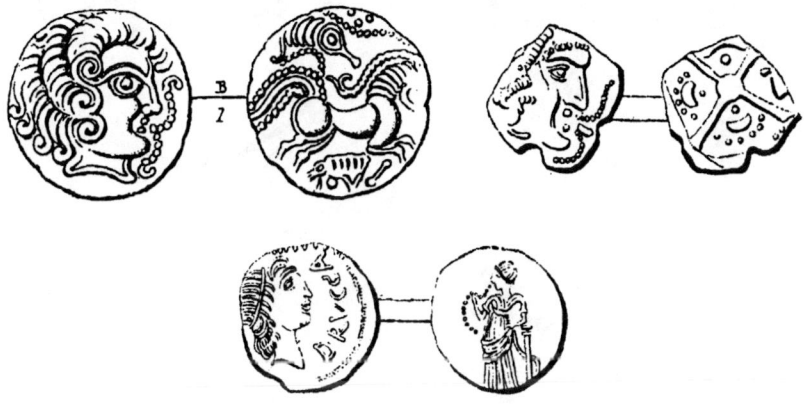

FIGS. 274 to 276.—British. From Evans, and from Barthelemy.

a serpent (?)" and it is quite likely that the serpent or symbol of Wisdom was intended by the artist. There is no question about the serpents in the Tyrian coin here illustrated, where on either side of the Maiden they are represented with almost precisely the same S2 form as the S2 proceeding from the mouths of the two steeds on the British "altar". In the latter case the centre is a vase or demijohn, in the former the centre is a Maid or Virgin. Without a doubt this BER virgin is Beroë or Berith, the *pherepolis* of Beyrout: in Fig. 278 the two serpents are associated with a phare, fire, or pyre; from the mouth of the British "Jupiters," illustrated in Figs. 274 and 275, the same two serpentine flames or S's are emerging.

The word BER, as has been seen, is equivalent to Vir, and in all probability the word *virgin* originally carried the same meaning as *burgeon*. That old Lydgate, the monk

FIGS. 277 and 278.—From *Ancient Pagan and Modern Christian Symbolism* (Inman, C. W.).

of *Bery*, knew all about Vera and how she made the buds to burgeon is obvious from his lines :—

> Mightie Flora Goddesse of fresh flowers
> Which clothed hath the soyle in lustie greene,
> Made buds spring with her sweet showers
> By influence of the sunne-shine
> To doe pleasannce of intent full cleane,
> Unto the States which now sit here
> Hath *Vere* down sent her own daughter deare.

It is evident that Vere is here the equivalent of Proserpine, the Maid who was condemned to spend one-half her time in Hades, and that "Verray" was occasionally noxious is implied by the old sense attributed to this word of *nightmare*, *e.g.*, Chaucer :—

[IX.] BRIDE'S BAIRNS 485

Lord Jesus Christ and Seynte Benedykte
Bless this house from every wikked wight
Fro nyghte's *verray*, etc.

FIG. 279.—Bas Relievo on the Portal of the Temple of Montmorillon in France. From *Antiquities of Cornwall* (Borlase).

Some authorities connoted this word *verray* with Werra, a Sclavonic deity, and the connection is probably well

486 ARCHAIC ENGLAND [CHAP.

founded: the Cornish Furry dance was also termed the Flora dance.

The name Proserpine is seemingly akin to Pure Serpent —the same Serpent, perhaps, whose form is represented *in extenso* at Avebury: the *Bona Dea* of Crete was figured

Fig. 280.—The Church as a Dove with Six Wings. A Franco-German Miniature of the XI. Cent. From *Christian Iconography* (Didron).

holding serpents and the nude figure on the left of Fig. 279 has been ingeniously, and, I think, rightly interpreted by Borlase as Truth, or Vera. It was doubtless some such similar emblem as originated the ridiculous story that St. Christine of Tyre was "tortured" by having live serpents placed at her breasts: "The two asps hung at her breasts and did her no harm, and the two adders wound them about her neck and licked up her sweat."[1] Not only is this suffering Christine assigned to Tyre (in Italy), but she is said to have been enclosed in a certain *tower* and to have been set upon a burning *tour* or wheel. Christine is the feminine of Christ, and that Christ was identified with *Sophia* or Wisdom is obvious from the design herewith.

The Sicilian coins of Janus depicted Columba or the Dove, and the same symbol of the Cretan, Epheia, Britomart, Athene, or Rhea figures in the hand of the Elf on

Fig. 281.—Jesus Christ as Saint Sophia. Miniature of Lyons, XII. Cent. From *Christian Iconography* (Didron).

page 627, and on the reverse of other British coins illustrated on the same page. The Dove is the acknowledged symbol of the Holy Ghost, yet the symbolists depicted even the immaculate Dove as duplex: the six wings of the parti-coloured Columba have in all probability an ultimate connection with the six beneficent world-supervisors of the Persian philosophy.

In the Christian emblem below, the Holy Ghost is represented as a Child floating on the Waters of Chaos between the circles of Day and Night, and that the Supreme was the Parent alike of both Good and Evil is expressed

[1] *Golden Legend*, iv., 96.

in the verse: "I form the light and create darkness; I make peace and create evil. I, the Lord, do all these things." The preceding sentence runs: "There is none beside me. I am the Lord and there is none else."[1] That

Fig. 282.—The Holy Ghost, as a Child, Floating on the Waters. From a Miniature of the XIV. Cent. From *Christian Iconography* (Didron).

this idea was prevalent among the Druids of the west is strongly to be inferred from an ancient chant still current among the Bretons, which begins—

Beautiful child of the Druid, answer me right well.
   What wouldst thou that I should sing?
Sing to me the series of number one, that I may learn it this very day.

[1] Is. xlv. 7.

There is no series for one, for One is Necessity alone.
The father of death, there is nothing before and nothing after.[1]

The *Magna Mater* of Fig. 266 might thus appropriately have been known as Fate, Destiny, Necessity, or Fortune. *Fortuna* is radically *for*, and with the Fortunes or fates may be connoted the English fairies known as Portunes. The Portunes are said to be peculiar to England, and are

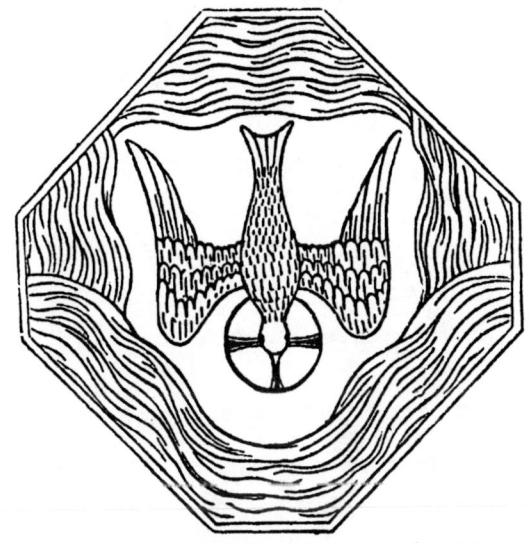

Fig. 283.—From *Christian Iconography* (Didron).

known by the French as Neptunes: the English Portunes are represented as diminutive little people who, "if anything is to be carried into the house, or any laborious work to be done, lend a hand and finish it sooner than any man could".[2] A jocular and amiable little people who loved to warm themselves at the fire.

Among the heathen chants of the Spanish peasantry is one in which the number One stands for the wheel of

[1] Quoted from Eckenstein, Miss Lena, *Comparative Studies in Nursery Rhymes*, p. 153.
[2] Keightley, *Fairy Mythology*, p. 285.

Fortune, and the number six "for the loves you hold". These six loves may be connoted with the six pinions of the Dove illustrated on page 486, and that Janus of the Dove was regarded as the Chaos, Ghost, or Cause is obvious from the words which are put into his mouth by Ovid: "The ancients called me Chaos (for I am the original substance). Observe, how I can unfold the deeds of past times. This lucid air, and the three other bodies which remain, fire, water, and earth, formed one heap.[1] As soon as this mass was liberated from the strife of its own discordant association, it sought new abodes. Fire flew upwards: air occupied the next position, and earth and water, forming the land and sea, filled the middle space. Then I, who was a globe, and formless, assumed a countenance and limbs worthy of a god. Even now, as a slight indication of my primitive appearance, my front and back are the same."

In the mouth of Fig. 283 is the wheel of the four quarters, and variants of this wheel-cross form the design of a very large percentage of English coins: I here use the word English in preference to British as "there was no native coinage either in Scotland, Wales, or Ireland": in England alone have prehistoric British coins been found,[2] and in England alone apparently were they coined. Somewhat the same conclusions are indicated by the wheel-cross which is peculiar to Wales, Cornwall, and the Isle of Man: neither in Scotland or Ireland does the circular form exist.[3]

Among the seals of Crete there has been found one figuring a ship and two half-moons: it has been supposed that this token signified that the devotee had ventured on

---

[1] The "one heap" of chaos was illustrated *ante*, p. 224.
[2] Allen F. Romilly, *Celtic Art*, p. 78.   [3] *Ibid.*, p. 188.

a two months' voyage and signalised the successful exploit by the fabrication of an *ex voto;* but if the subject in

FIG. 284.—Cretan Seal.

FIG. 285.—British. From *English Coins and Tokens* (Jewitt & Head).

FIG. 286.—British. From Evans.

question actually represents a material vessel one may question whether the mariner could successfully have negotiated even a two hours' trip. The pair of crescents which figure so frequently on the wheel-cross coins of Britain probably implied the twin lily-white maids of Druidic folk-song, and the superstitions in connection with this symbol of the two *sickles*—the word is essentially the same as *cycle*, Greek *kuklos*—seem in Anglesea or Mona even to linger yet.[1] Among sepulchral offerings found in a prehistoric barrow near Bridlington or Burlington, were " two pieces of flint chipped into the form of crescents,"[2] and it is possible that Ida the Flame bearer, whose name is popularly connected with *flame bearer* or Flamborough Head, was not the Anglian chieftain, but the divine Ida, Head, or Flame to whom all Forelands and Headlands were dedicated. With Bridlington or Burlington may be connoted the fact that this town of the children of Brid is situated in the Deira district, which was occupied by the

---

[1] The following letter appeared in *Folklore* of June 29, 1918:—

"Twenty-five years ago an old man in one of the parishes of Anglesey invariably bore or rather wore a sickle over his neck—in the fields, and on the road, wherever he went. He was rather reticent as to the reason why he wore it, but he clearly gave his questioner to understand that it was a protection against evil spirits. This custom is known in Welsh as '*gwisgo'r gorthrwm*,' which literally means 'wearing the oppression'. *Gorthrwm* = *gor*, an intensifying affix = *super*, and *trwm* = heavy, so that the phrase perhaps would be more correctly rendered 'wearing the overweight'. It is not easy to see the connection between the practice and the idea either of overweight or oppression; still, that was the phrase in common use.

"For a similar reason, that is, protection from evil spirits during the hours of the night, it was and is a custom to place two scythes archwise over the entrance-side of the wainscot bed found in many of the older cottages of Anglesey. It is difficult to find evidence of the existence of this practice to-day as the old people no doubt feel that it is contrary to their prevailing religious belief and will not confess their faith in the efficacy of a 'pagan' rite which they are yet loth to abandon.

"R. GWYNEDON DAVIES."

[2] Wright T., *Essays on Arch. Subjects*, i., 26.

Parisii : this name is by some authorities believed to be only a corruption of that of the Frisii, originally settlers from the opposite coast of Friesland.

The Etruscan name for Juno was Cupra, which may be connoted with Cabira, one of the titles of Venus, also with Cabura, the name of a fountain in Mesopotamia wherein Juno was said to bathe himself. The mysterious deities known as the Cabiri are described as " mystic divinities (? Phœnician origin) worshipped in various parts of the ancient world. The meaning of their name, their character, and nature are quite uncertain ".[1] Faber, in his *Dissertation on the Mysteries of the Cabiri*, states that the Cabiri were the same as the Abiri :[2] in Hebrew *Cabirim* means the Mighty Ones, and there is seemingly little doubt that Cabiri was originally *great abiri*. In Candia or Talchinea, the Cabiri were worshipped as the Telchines, and as *chin* or *khan* meant in Asia Minor Priest as well as King, and as the offices of Priest and King were anciently affiliated, the term *talchin* (which as we have seen was applied to St. Patrick) meant seemingly *tall* or *chief King-Priest*. The custom of Priest-Kings adopting the style and titles of their divinities renders it probable that the historical Telchins worshipped an archetypal Talchin. The original Telchins are described by Diodorus, as first inhabiting Rhodes, and the Colossus of Rhodes was probably an image of the divine *Tall King* or *Chief King*.

It is related that Rhea entrusted the infant Neptune to the care of the Telchines who were children of the sea, and that the child sea-god was reared by them in conjunction with Caphira or Cabira, the daughter of Oceanus. As

---

[1] Smith, W., *A Smaller Classical Dictionary*.
[2] Vol. i., p. 210.

Faber observes: "Caphira is evidently a mere variation of Cabira," and he translates Cabira as *Great Goddess*: in view of the evidence already adduced one might likewise translate it Great *Power*, Great *Pyre*, or Great *Phairy*. The Cabiri are often equated with the Dioscuri or Great *Pair*, and these Twain were not infrequently expressed symbolically by Twin circles.

The emblem of the double disc, "barnacle," or "spectacle ornament" is found most frequently in Scotland where it is attributed to the Picts: sometimes the discs are undecorated, others are elaborated by a zigzag or zed,

FIG. 287.—Mykenian.   FIG. 288.—Cretan.   FIG. 289.—Scotch. From *Myths of Crete and Prehellenic Europe* (Mackenzie, D. A.).

which apparently signified the Central and sustaining *Power*, Fire, or Force. Figs. 287 and 288 from Crete represent the discs transfixed by a *broca* or spike and the winged ange or angel with a wand—the magic rod or wand which invariably denoted Power—may be designated King Eros. In Scotland the central *brocco, i.e.*, skewer, shoot, or stalk is found sprouting into what one might term *broccoli*, and in Fig. 291 the dotted eyes, wheels, or paps are elaborated into sevens which possibly may have symbolised the seven gifts of the Holy Spirit. Notable examples of this disc ornament occur at Doo Cave in Fife, and as the Scotch refer to a Dovecote as "Doocot," it may be suggested that

Doo Cave was a Dove Cave sacred to the *deux,* or *duo,* or Dieu. Other well-known specimens are found on a so-called "Brodie" stone and on the Inchbrayock stone in Forfarshire. Forfar, I have already suggested, was a land of St. Varvary: Overkirkhope, where the symbol also occurs, was presumably the hope or hill of Over, or *uber,* Church, and Ferriby,[1] in Lincolnshire, where the emblem is again found, was in all probability a *by* or abode of Ferri. The

Figs. 290 to 292.—Scotch. From *Archaic Sculpturings* (Mann, L. M.).

name Cupar may be connoted with Cupra—the Juno of Etruria—and Inchbrayock is radically Bray or Brock.

Sometimes the discs—which might be termed *Brick a Brack* or, Bride's Bairns—are centred by what looks like a tree (French *arbre*) or, in comparison with Fig. 295, from the catacombs, might be an anchor: it has no doubt rightly been assumed that this and similar carvings symbolised the Tree of Life with Adam and Eve on either hand. According to a recent writer: "The symbol group of a man and woman on either side of a tree with a serpent at times introduced is of pre-Christian origin. The figures narrowly

[1] Domesday Ferebi, "probably dwelling of the *comrade* or partner". Do the authorities mean *friend?*

considered as Adam and Eve and broadly as the human family are accompanied by the Tree which stands for Knowledge, and the serpent which represents Wisdom.

FIGS. 293 and 294.—From *Archaic Sculpturings* (Mann, L. M.).

This old world-wide symbol seems to crop up in Pictland twisted and changed in a curious fashion."[1] One of these fantastic forms is, I think, the feathered elphin or *antennaed* solar face of Fig. 293.

FIG. 295.—From *Christian Iconography* (Didron).

Among the ancients the word *Eva*, not only denoted *life*, but it also meant *serpent*: the jumbled traditions of the Hebrews associated Eve and the Serpent unfavourably, but according to an early sect of Gnostic Christians known as the Ophites, *i.e.*, *Evites*, or "Serpentites," the Serpent of

[1] Mann, L., *Archaic Sculpturings*, p. 30.

Genesis was a personification of the Good principle, who instructed Eve in all the learning of the world which has descended to us. There is frequent mention in the Old Testament of a people called the Hivites or Hevites, so called because, like the Christian Ophites, they were wor-

FIG. 296.—From *A Dictionary of Non-Classical Mythology* (Edwardes an Spence).

shippers of the serpent. We meet again with Eff the serpent in F the fifth letter of the alphabet: this letter, according to Dr. Isaac Taylor, was formed originally like a horned or sacred serpent, and the two strokes of our F are the surviving traces of the two horns.[1]

The term Hivites is sometimes interpreted to mean

[1] *Cf. The Alphabet*, i., 12.

Midlanders, which seems reasonable as they lived in the middle of Canaan. In connection with these serpent-worshipping Midlanders or Hivites it is significant that not only is the English Avebury described as being "situated in the very centre or heart of our country,"[1] but that it is geographically the very nave or bogel of the surrounding neighbourhood.

Eva is in all probability the source of the word *ivy*, German *epheu*, for the evergreen ivy is notoriously a long-lived plant, and even by the early Christian Church[2] Ivy was accepted as the emblem of life and immortality. As immortality was the primary dogma of the Druids, hence perhaps why they and their co-worshippers decked themselves with wreaths of this undying and seemingly immortal plant.[3] The figure of the Græco-Egyptian "Jupiter," known as Serapis, appears (supported by the Twins) surrounded by an ivy wreath, and that the ancient Jews ivy-decked themselves like the British on festival occasions is evident from the words of Tacitus: "Their priests it is true made use of fifes and cymbals: they were crowned with wreaths of ivy, and a vine wrought in gold was seen in their temple".[4] The leaf on the British VIRI coin here illustrated has been

Fig. 297.—British. From Akerman.

---

[1] Lord Avebury. Preface to *A Guide to Avebury*, p. 5.

[2] Durandus, *Rationale*.

[3] "Ruddy was the sea-beach and the circular revolution was performed by the attendance of the white bands in graceful extravagance when the assembled trains were assembled in dancing and singing in cadence with garlands and ivy branches on the brow."—*Cf.* Davies, E. *Mythology of British Druids.*

[4] *History*, V., 5.

held to be a vine " which does not appear to have been

Fig. 298.—Thrones.—Fiery Two-winged Wheels. From Didron.

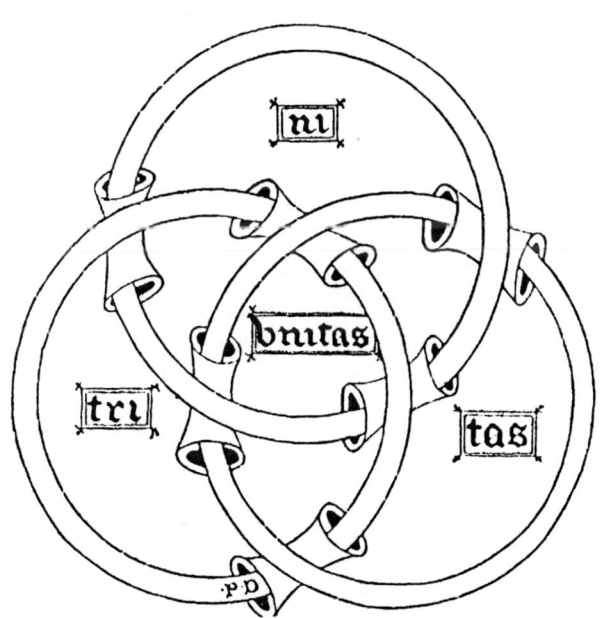

Fig. 299.—The Trinity under the Form of Three Circles. From a French Miniature of the close of the XIII. Cent. From Didron.

borrowed from any Roman coin," but, continues Sir John Evans, " whether this was an original type to signify the fertility of the soil in respect of vines or adapted from some other source it is hard to say ".[1] If the device be a Vine leaf it probably symbolised the True Vine; if a fig leaf it undoubtedly was the sign of Maggie Figgy, the Mother of Millions, and the Ovary of Everything: the Sunday before Easter used to be known as Fig Sunday, and on this occasion figs were eaten in large quantities.

Fig. 300.—French MS., XIII. Cent. From Didron.

From Aubrey's plan of the Overton circle constituting the head of the serpent at Avebury, it will be seen that the neck was carefully modelled, and that a pair of barrows appeared at the mouth (see *ante*, page 335). This head of the Eve or serpent was a stone circle distant about a mile from the larger peripheries, and the whole design covered upwards of two miles of country. As already noted the serpent was the symbol of immortality and rejuvenes-

[1] *Ancient British Coins*, p. 173.

cence, because it periodically sloughed its skin and reappeared in one more beautiful.

That the two and the three circles were taken over intact

FIG. 301.—From *Ancient Pagan and Modern Christian Symbolism* (Inman, C. W.).[1]

by Christianity is evident from the emblems illustrated on p. 499, and that the French possessed the tradition of Good Eva or the Good Serpent is manifest from Fig. 300.

[1] "Copied by Higgins, *Anacalypsis*, on the authority of Dubois, who states (vol. iii., p. 39), that it was found on a stone in a church in France, where it had been kept religiously for six hundred years. Dubois regards it as wholly astrological, and as having no reference to the story told in Genesis."

502   ARCHAIC ENGLAND   [CHA.

The Iberian inscription around Fig. 301—a French example—has not been deciphered, but it is sufficiently evident that the emblem represents the Iberian Jupiter with Juno and the Tree of Life.

The Jews or Judeans of to-day are known indifferently as either Jews or Hebrews, and it would seem that Jou was

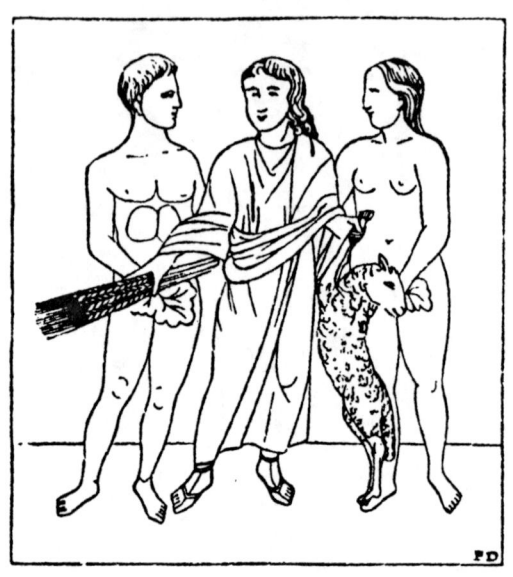

Fig. 302.—God the Father, without a Nimbus and Beardless, Condemning Adam to Till the Ground and Eve to Spin the Wool. From *Christian Iconography* (Didron).

"Hebrew," or, as the Italians write the word, Ebrea: the French for Jew is *juif*, evidently the same title as Jove or Jehovah.

In Fig. 302, Jehovah is rather surprisingly represented as a *puer* or boy: as already mentioned, the Eros of Etruria was named Epeur, and it is possible that the London church of St. Peter le Poor—which stood in Brode Street next Pawlet or Little Paul House—was originally a shrine of Jupiter the *puer*, or Jupiter the Boy.[1]

In the design now under consideration the Family consists of three—the Almighty and Adam and Eve—but frequently the holy group consists of five, the additional two probably being Cain and Abel, Cain who slew his brother Abel, being obviously Night or Evil. In the emblems here illustrated which are defined by Briquet as "cars"; four

FIGS. 303 to 306.—Mediæval Paper Marks. From *Les Filigranes* (Briquet, C. M.).

cycles are supported by a broca or spike, constituting the mystic five. In Jewish mysticism the Chariot of Jehovah, or Yahve, was regarded as "a kind of mystic way leading up to the final goal of the soul".[2]

The number of the Cabiri was indeterminate, and there is a probability that the sacerdotal Solar Chariot of the Cabiri, whether four or two-wheeled, originated the term

---

[1] It is quite improbable that there was any foundation for Stow's surmise that the epithet Poor was applied to the parish of St. Peter in Brode Street, "for a difference from others of that name, sometimes peradventure a poor parish". It is, however, possible that the church was dedicated to Peter the Hermit, *i.e.*, the poor Peter.

[2] *Cf.* Abelson, J., *Jewish Mysticism*, p. 34.

cabriolet, whence our modern cab. I have elsewhere reproduced two pillars bearing the legend CAB, and we might assume that the two-wheeled vehicle illustrated, *ante*, page 454, represented a cab were it not for the official etymology of *cabriolet*. This term, we are told, is from *cabriole*, a caper, leap of a goat, "from its supposed lightness".[1] I have never observed a cab either skipping like a ram, or capering like a goat; and in the days before springs the alleged skittishness of the cab must have been even less marked. In any case the particular vehicle illustrated *ante*, page 454, cannot with propriety be termed "a caperer," for it is reproduced by the editor of Adamnan's *Life of Columba*, as being no doubt the type of car in which the Saint, even without his lynch pins, successfully drove a sedate and undeviating course.

The goat or *caper* was a familiar emblem of *Jupiter*, and our words *kid* and *goat* are doubtless the German *gott*: the horns and the hoofs of the Solar goat—see *ante*, page 361—are perpetuated in the current notions of "Old Nick," and in many parts of Europe Saints Nicholas and Michael are equated ;[2] hence there is very little doubt that these two once occupied the position of the two Cabiri, Nick or *Nixy* being *nox* or night, and Michael—Light or Day.

The Gaulish coin here illustrated is described by Akerman, as "Two goats (?) on their hind legs face to face ;

---

[1] *Cf.* also Brachet A., *Ety. Dictionary of French Language*: "A two-wheeled carriage which being light *leaps* up". Had our authorities been considering *phaeton*, this definition might have passed muster. Although Skeat connects *phaeton* with the Solar Charioteer he nevertheless connotes *phantom*. Why?

[2] Blackie, C., *Place-names*, p. 137.

the whole within a beaded circle": on the reverse is a hog, and some other animal represented with a *broccus*, or saw on its back. As this is a coin of the people inhabiting Agedincum Senonum (now Sens), the revolving twain are probably *gedin*—either *goats*, *kids*, or *gods*, and the baroque animal with the *broccus* on its back may be identified with a *boar*. There is not much evidence in this coin, which was found at *Brettenham*, Norfolk, of "degradation" from the Macedonian stater illustrated *ante*, page 394, nevertheless, Sir John Evans sturdily maintains: "the degeneration of the head of Apollo into two boars and a wheel, impossible as it may at first appear, is in fact but a com-

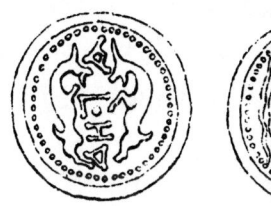

Fig. 307.—Gaulish. From Akerman.

paratively easy transition when once the head has been reduced into a form of regular pattern".[1]

The Meigle in Perthshire, where the two-wheeled barrow or barouche was inscribed on the Thane stone, may be equated with St. Michael, and upon another stone at the same Meigle there occurs a carving which is defined as a group of four men placed in svastika form, one hand of each man holding the foot of the other. The author of *Archaic Sculpturings* describes this attitude as indicating the unbreakable character of the association of each figure with its neighbours, and expresses the opinion: "This elaborate variant of the symbol seems to symbolise aptly

[1] *Coins of the Ancient Britons*, p. 121.

the four quarters of the earth, each quarter being represented by a man. The four quarters make a complete circle, and therefore all humanity, through love and affinity, should join from the four parts and form one inseparable bond of brotherhood."[1]

The wheel of *Fortune* was sometimes represented by *four* kings, one on each quadrant, and this emblem was used not only as an inn-sign, but also in churches, notably in Norfolk—the land of the Ikeni. The authors of *A History of Signboards* cite continental examples surviving at Sienna, and in San Zeno at Verona. The wheels of San Zeno, Sienna, or Verona may be connoted with the Sceatta wheel-coin figured in No. 39 of page 364 *ante*, and with the seemingly revolving seals on the coin here illustrated.[2] The Sceatta four beasts connected by astral spokes are probably intended to denote seals, the phoca or seal having, as we have seen (*ante*, page 224), been associated

FIG. 308.—British. From Evans.

---

[1] P. 28.

[2] It is a miracle that this and the other coins illustrated on page 364 did not go into the dustbin. The official estimate of their value and interest is expressed in the following reference from Hawkin's *Silver Coins of England*, p. 17:—

" After the final departure of the Romans, about the year 450, the history of the coinage is involved in much obscurity; the coins of that people would of course continue in circulation long after the people themselves had quitted the shores, and it is not improbable that the rude and uncouth pieces, which are imitations of their money, and *are scarce because they are rejected from all cabinets and thrown away as soon as discovered*, may have been struck during the interval between the Romans and Saxons."

The italics are mine, and comment would be inadequate. Happily, in despite of " the practised numismatist," Time, which antiquates and hath an art to make dust of all things, hath yet spared these minor monuments.

with Chaos or Cause. In all probability the *phoca* was a token of the Phocean Greeks who founded Marseilles: the phoca was pre-eminently associated with *Pro*teus, and in the *Faroe* Islands they have a curious idea that seals are the soldiers of *Pharaoh* who was drowned in the sea. Pharaoh, or *Peraa*, as the Egyptian wrote it, was doubtless the representative Priest-King of Phra, the Egyptian Sungod, and the drowning of Pharaoh in the Red Sea was probably once a phairy-tale based on the blood-red demise of a summer sun sinking beneath the watery horizon.

On Midsummer Day in England children used to chant—

> Barnaby Bright, Barnaby Bright,
> The longest day and the shortest night,

whence it would appear that Barnaby was the *auburn*[1] divinity who was further connected with the burnie bee, ladybird, or "Heaven's little chicken". The rhyme—

> Burnie bee, Burnie bee, fly away home
> Your house is on fire, your children will burn,

is supposed by Mannhardt to have been a charm intended to speed the sun across the dangers of sunset, in other words, the house on fire, or welkin of the West.

The name Barnabas or Barnaby is defined as meaning *son of the master* or *son of comfort*; Bernher is explained as *lord of many children*, and hence it would seem that St. Barnaby may be modernised into Bairnsfather. In this connection the British Bryanstones may be connoted with the Irish Bernesbeg and with "The Stone of the Fruitful Fairy". Bertram is defined by the authorities as meaning *fair and pure*, and Ferdy or Ferdinand, the

---

[1] Auburn hair is golden-red—hence I am able to recognise only a remote comparison with *alburnum*, the white sap wood or inner bark of trees.

Spanish equivalent of this name, may be connoted with the English Faraday.

The surname Barry, with which presumably may be equated variants such as Berry and Bray, is translated as being Celtic for *good marksman*: the Cretans were famed archers, and the archery of the English yeomen was in its time perhaps not less famous. If Barry meant *good marksman*, it is to be inferred that the archetypal Barry

FIG. 309.—Jehovah, as the God of Battles. Italian Miniature, close of the XII. Cent. From *Christian Iconography* (Didron).

FIG. 310.—Emblem of the Deity. *Nineveh* (Layard).

was Jou, Jupiter, or Jehovah as here represented, and as there is no known etymology for *yeoman*, it may be that the original *yeomen* were like the Barrys, " good marksmen ". The Greeks portrayed Apollo, and the Tyrians Adad, as a Sovereign Archer, and as the lord of an unerring bow. The name Adad is seemingly ad-ad, a duplication of Ad probably once meaning *Head Head*, or *Haut Haut*,[1]

---

[1] " We also find Adad numbered among the gods whom the Syrians worshipped; nevertheless we find but little concerning him, and that little obscure and unsatisfactory, either in ancient or modern writers. Macrobius

and the Celtic *dad* or *tad* is presumably a corroded form of Adad. The famous archer Robin Hood, now generally accepted as a myth survival, will be considered later; meanwhile it may here be noted that the authorities derive the surnames Taddy, Addy, Adkin, Aitkin, etc., from *Adam*. One may connote Adkin or Little Ad with Hudkin, a Dutch and German elf akin to Robin Goodfellow: "Hudkin is a very familiar devil, who will do nobody hurt, except he receive injury; but he cannot abide that, nor yet be mocked. He talketh with men friendly, sometimes visibly, sometimes invisibly. There go as many tales upon this Hudkin in some parts of Germany as there did in England on Robin Goodfellow."[1] To this Hud the Leicestershire place-name Odestone or Odstone near Twycross—*query* Two or Twa cross—may be due.

I have suggested that the word *bosom* or *bosen*, was originally the plural of *boss*, whence it is probable that the name Barnebas meant the Bairn, Boss, or teat. The word *bosse* was also used to denote a fountain or gush, and the Boss Alley, which is still standing near St. Paul's, may mark either the site of a spring, or more probably of what was known as St. Paul's Stump. As late as 1714 the porters of Billingsgate used to invite the passer-by to *buss* or kiss Paul's Stump; if he complied they gave him a name, and he was

---

says, "The Assyrians, or rather the Syrians, give the name Adad to the god whom they worship, as *the highest* or greatest," and adds that the signification of this name is the One or the Only. This writer also gives us clearly to understand that the Syrians adored the sun under this name; at least, the surname Adad, which was given to the sun by the natives of Heliopolis, makes them appear as one and the same."—Christmas, H. Rev., *Universal Mythology*, p. 119.

[1] *Discourse concerning Devils*, annexed to *The Discovery of Witchcraft*, Reginald Scot. i., chap. xxi.

compelled to choose a godfather: if he refused to conform to the custom he was lifted up and bumped heavily against the stump. This must have been the relic of an extremely ancient formality, and it is not unlikely that the Church of Boston in Norfolk covers the site of a similar stump: Boston, originally *Icken*hoe, a haw or hill of Icken, is situated in what was once the territory of the Ikeni, and its church tower to this day is known as " Boston Stump ". At Boskenna (*bos* or abode of *ikenna?*) in the parish of St. Buryan, Cornwall, is a stone circle, and a cromlech " thought to have been the seat of an arch Druid ". The chief street of Boston is named Burgate, there is a Burgate at Canterbury near which are Bossenden Woods, and Bysing Wood.

In the West of England the numerous *bos-* prefixes generally mean *abode:* one of the earliest abodes was the beehive hut, which was essentially a boss.

At Porlock (Somerset) is Bossington Beacon ; there is a Bossington near Broughton, and a Bosley at Prestbury, Cheshire. In the immediate proximity of Bosse Alley, London, Stow mentions a Brickels Lane, and there still remains a Brick Hill, Brooks Wharf, and Broken Wharf. It is not improbable that the river Walbrook which did *not* run around the *walls* of London but passed immediately through the heart of the city was named after Brook or Alberick, or Oberon : in any case the generic terms *burn*, *brook*, and *bourne* (Gothic *brunna*, a spring or well), have to be accounted for, and we may seemingly watch them forming at the English river Brue, and at least two English bournes, burns, or brooks known as Barrow.

We have already considered the pair of military saints famous at Byzantium or St. Michael's Town : in the neighbourhood of Macclesfield, Cheshire, is a Bosley: the Bosmere district in Cumberland includes a Mickfield, in view of which it becomes interesting to note, near Old Jewry, in London, the parish church of St. Michael, called St. Michael at Bassings hall. With Michael at Bassings hall may be connoted St. Michael of Guernsey, an island once divided into two great fiefs, of which one was the property of Anchetil Vicomte du *Bessin*. The bussing of St. Paul's Stump or the Bosse of Billingsgate had evidently its parallel in the Fief du Bessin, for Miss Carey in her account of the Chevauchee of St. Michael observes that, "the one traditional dance connected with all our old festivals and merry-makings has always been the one known as *A mon beau Laurier*, where the dancers join hands and whirl round, curtsey, and kiss a central object".[1]

We may reasonably assume that John Barton, who is mentioned by Stow as a great benefactor to the church of St. Michael, was either John Briton, or John of some particular Barton, possibly of the neighbouring Pardon Churchyard. The adjacent Bosse Alley is next *Huggen* Lane, wherein is the Church of All Hallows, and running past the church of St. Michael at Bassings hall is another *Hugan* Lane. *Gyne*, as in gynæcology, is Greek for *woman*, whence the *gyne* or *queen* of the Ikenian *Icken*hoe or Boston Stump, may have meant simply woman, maiden, *queen*, or "a flaunting extravagant *quean*". Somewhat east from the Sun tavern,[2] on the north side of this Michael's church, is Mayden Lane, "now so called," says Stow, "but of old time Ingene Lane, or Ing Lane":

[1] *Folklore*, xxv., 4, p. 426.

[2] "The Sun and Moon have been considered as signs of pagan origin, typifying Apollo and Diana," *History of Signboards*, p. 496.

"down lower," he continues, "is Silver Street (I think of Silversmiths dwelling there)". It has been seen that Silver Streets are ubiquitous in England, and as this Silver Street is in the immediate proximity of Adle Street and Ladle Lane, there is some presumption that Silver was here the Leda, or Lady, or Ideal, by whom it was said that Jupiter in the form of a swan became the Parent of the Heavenly twins or Fairbairns. We have considered the sign of the Swan with two necks as found near Goswell Road, and the neighbouring *Goose* Lane, Wind*goose* Lane, Pente*cost* Lane, and *Chis*well Street are all in this connection interesting. I have already suggested that Angus, Aengus, or Oengus, the pre-Celtic divinity of New Grange, meant *ancient goose*: Oengus was alternatively known as Sen-gann or Old Gann, connected with whom were two young Ganns who were described sometimes as the sons of Old Gann, sometimes as his father. In the opinion of Prof. Macalister Oengus, *alias* Dagda mor, the Great Good Fire, *alias* Sengann, "was not originally *son* of the two youths, but *father* of the two youths, and he thus falls into line with other storm gods as the parent of Dioscuri." [1]

There is little doubt that Aengus, the *ancient goose*, the Father of St. Bride, was Sengann the Old Gander, and in connection with St. Michael's goose it is noteworthy that Sinann, the Goddess of the Shannon, was alternatively entitled Macha. Mr. Westropp informs [2] us that Sengann was the god of the Ganganoi who inhabited Connaught, hence no doubt he was the same as Great King Conn, and Sinann was the same as Good Queen Eda.

At the north end of London Bridge stands Old Swan

---

[1] *Proc. of Royal Irish Acad.*, xxxiv., c. 10-11, pp. 318, 320.
[2] *Ibid.*, c. 8, p. 159.

Pier, upon the site of which was once Ebgate, an ancient water-gate. "In place of this gate," says Stow, " is now a narrow passage to the Thames called Ebgate Lane, but more commonly the Old Swan." *Eb*gate may be connoted with the neighbouring Abchurch Lane, where still stands what Stow termed " the parish church of St. Marie *Ab*church, *Ape*church, or *Up*church, as I have read it," and this same root seemingly occurs in the Upwell of St. Olave *Up*well distant only a few hundred yards. This spot accurately marks the *hub* of ancient London, and there is here still standing the once-famous London stone: " some have imagined," says Stow, " the same to be set up by one John, or Thomas Londonstone, dwelling there against, but more likely it is that such men have taken name of the stone than the stone of them ".

There is little doubt that London stone, where oaths were sworn and proclamations posted, was the Perry stone of the men who made the six main roads or tribal tracks which centred there, of which great wheel *Ab*church formed seemingly the *hob* or *hub*. Abchurch was in all probability originally a church of Hob, and it may aptly be described as one of the many primitive *abbeys* : there is an Ibstone at Wallingford, which the modern authorities—like the " John Londonstone" theorists of Stow's time—urge, was probably Ipa's stone: there is an Ipsley at Redditch, assumed to be either *aspentree meadow* or perhaps *Aeppas mead*. Ipstones at Cheadle, we are told, "may be from a man as above"; of Hipswell in Yorkshire Mr. Johnston concludes, " there is no name at all likely here, so this must be well at the hipple or little heap ". But as Hipswell figures in Leland as *Ipre*swell, is there any absolute *must* about the "hipple," and is it not possible that Ipres or

514   ARCHAIC ENGLAND   [CHAP.

Hipswell may have been dedicated to the same *hipha* or *hip*, the Prime Parent of our Hip! Hip! Hip! who was alternatively the Ypre of Ypres Hall and Upwell by Abchurch? At Halifax there is a *Hipper*holme which appeared in Domesday as *Huperun*, and here the authorities are really and seriously nonplussed. "It seems hard to explain Huper or Hipper. There is nothing like it in *Onom*, unless it be Hygebeort or Hubert; but it may be a dissimilated form of *hipple, hupple*, and mean 'at the little heaps'."[1]

Let us quit these imaginary "little heaps" and consider the position at the Halifax Hipperholme, or Huperun. The church here occupied the site of an ancient hermitage said to have been dedicated to St. John the Baptist, the Father of hermits, and to have possessed as a sacred relic the alleged true face of St. John: my authority continues that this attracted great numbers of pilgrims who "approached by four ways, which afterwards formed the main town thoroughfares concentrating at the parish church; and it is supposed to have given rise to the name Halifax, either in the sense of *Holy Face* with reference to the face of St. John, or in the sense of *Holy ways* with reference to the four roads, the word *fax* being Old Norman French for *highways*".[2] More recent authorities have compared the word with Carfax at Oxford, which is said to mean Holy fork, or Holy road, converging as in a fork. The roads at Carfax constitute a four-limbed cross; Oxenford used to be considered "the admeasured centre of the whole island";[3] it was alternatively known as Rhydy-

---

[1] Johnston, Rev. J. B., *The Place-names of England and Wales*, p. 304.
[2] Wilson, J. M., *Imperial Gazetteer of England and Wales*, i., 839.
[3] Herbert, A., *Cyclops Christianus*, p. 93.

chain, whence I do not think that Rhydychain meant a ford for oxen, but more probably either *Rood King*, or *Ruddy King*.

In 1190 Halifax was referred to as Haliflex, upon which the Rev. J. B. Johnston comments: "the *l* seems to be a scribe's error, and *flex* must be *feax*. Holy flax would make no sense. In Domesday it seems to be called Feslei, can the *fes* be *feax* too?" In view of the cruciform streets of Chichester, of our cruciform rood or rota coins, and of the four rivers supposed by all authorities to flow to the four quarters out of Paradise, is it not possible that

FIG. 311.—From *The Cross: Heathen and Christian* (Brock, M.).

four-quartered Haliflex was a fay's lea or meadow, whose founders built their "abbey"[1] in the true-face form of the *Holy Flux* or Fount, the *ain* or flow of living water? Four *ains* or eyes are clearly exhibited on the emblems here illustrated, which show the four-quartered sacramental buns or brioches, whence the modern Good Friday bun has descended.

It was a prevalent notion among our earliest historians that "In such estimation was Britain held by its inhabitants, that they made in it four roads from end to end, which were placed under the King's protection to the intent that no one should dare to make an attack upon his enemy on these roads".[2] These four great roads, dating from

---

[1] In Ireland an "abbey" is a cell or hermitage.
[2] *Cf.* Guest, Dr., *Origines Celticæ*, ii., 223.

Fig. 312.—Roman roads. From *A New Description of England and Wales* (Anon. 1724).

the time of King Belinus, and supposedly running from sea to sea, were probably mythical, but in view of the sanctity of public highways and the King's Peace which was enforced thereon, it is not improbable that numerous "Holloways"—now supposed to mean hollow or sunk ways—were originally and actually *holy ways.*

The Punjaub is so named because it is watered not by four but by five rivers, and that five streams possessed a mystic significance in British mythology is evident from the story of Cormac's voyage to the Land of Paradise or Promise.[1] "Palaces of bronze and houses of white silver, thatched with white bird's wings are there. Then he sees in the garth a shining fountain with five streams flowing out of it, and the hosts in turn a-drinking its water."[2]

It has been recently pointed out that the Celtic conception of Paradise "offers the closest parallel to the Chinese," whence it is significant to find that in the Chinese "Abyss of Assembly" there were supposed to lie five fairy islands of entrancing beauty, which were inhabited by spirit-like beings termed *shên jên*.[3] I have in my possession a

---

[1] The name Cormac is defined as meaning *son of a chariot*. Is it to be assumed that the followers of Great Cormac understood a physical road car?

[2] Wentz., W. Y. E., *The Fairy Faith in Celtic Countries*, p. 341.

[3] "The inhabitants are called *shên jên*, spirit-like beings, a term hardly synonymous with *hsien*, though the description of them is consistent with the recognised characteristics of *hsien*. The passage runs as follows: 'Far away on the Isle of Ku-shê there dwell spirit-like beings whose flesh is [smooth] as ice and [white] as snow, and whose demeanour is as gentle and unassertive as that of a young girl. They eat not of the Five Grains, but live on air and dew. They ride upon the clouds with flying dragons for their teams, and roam beyond the Four Seas. The *shên* influences that pervade that isle preserve all creatures from petty maladies and mortal ills, and ensure abundant crops every year.'"—Yetts, Major W. Perceval, *Folklore*, XXX., i., p. 89.

Chinese temple-ornament consisting of a blue porcelain broccus of five rays or peaks, which, like the five fundamental cones of the Etruscan tomb (*ante*, p. 237), in all probability represent the five bergs or islands of the blessed. The inner circle of Stonehenge consisted of five upstanding trilithons of which the stones came—by popular repute—from Ireland. Among the Irish divinities mentioned by Mr. Westropp is not only the gracious Aine who was worshipped by five Firbolg tribes, but also an old god who kindled five streams of magic fire from which his sons—the fathers of the Delbna tribes—all sprang.[1]

It will be remembered that the Avebury district is the boss, gush, or spring of five rivers, and Avebury or Abury was almost without doubt another "abbey" or *bri* of Ab on similar lines to the six-spoked *hub*, *hob*, or *boss* of Abchurch, Londonstone. It is difficult to believe that the six roads meeting at Abchurch arranged themselves so symmetrically by chance, and it is still more difficult to attribute them to the Roman Legions.

As Mr. Johnson has pointed out there is a current supposition, seemingly well based, that some of the supposedly Roman roads represent older trackways, straightened and adapted for rougher usage.[2] That London stone at Abchurch was the hub, navel or *bogel* of the Cantian British roads may be further implied by the immediately adjacent *Buckle*sbury, now corrupted into Bucklersbury. Parts of the Ichnield Way—notably at Broadway—are known as Buckle Street, the term *buckle* here being seemingly used in the sense of Bogle or Bogie. It is always the custom of a later race to attribute any great work of unknown

---

[1] *Proc. Roy. Irish Acad.*, xxxiv., c. 8, p. 135.
[2] *Folk Memory*, p. 339.

origin to Bogle or the Devil, *e.g.*, the Devil's Dyke, and innumerable other instances.

Ichnos in Greek means *track, ichneia* a *tracking;* whence the immemorial British track known as the *Ichnield* Way may reasonably be connoted with the ancient Via *Egnatio* near Berat in Albania. That Albion, like Albania, possessed very serviceable ways before the advent of any Romans is clear from Cæsar's *Commentaries.* After mentioning the British rearguard—" about 4000 charioteers only being left "—Cæsar continues : " and when our cavalry for the sake of plundering and ravaging the more freely scattered themselves among the fields, he (Cassivelaunus) used to send out charioteers from the woods by *all the well-known roads* and paths, and to the great danger of our horse engage with them, and this source of fear hindered them from straggling very extensively ".[1]

It has been seen that the Welsh tracks by which the armies marched to battle were known as Elen's Ways, whence possibly six such Elen's Ways concentrated in the heart of London, which I have already suggested was an Elen's dun. In French forests radiating pathways, known as *etoiles* or stars, were frequent, and served the most utilitarian purpose of guiding hunters to a central Hub or trysting-place.

One of the marvels which impress explorers in Crete is the excellence of the ancient Candian roads. According to Tacitus the British, under Boudicca, chiefly Cantii, Cangians, and Ikeni, " brought into the field an incredible multitude ".[2] The density of the British population in ancient times is indicated by the extent of prehistoric

---

[1] *De B. Gallico*, v., 19.   [2] *Annals*, xxxiv.

reliques, whereas the Roman invaders were never numerically more than a negligible fraction. It is now admitted by historians that Roman civilisation did not succeed in striking the same deep roots in British soil as it did into the nationality of Gaul or Spain. "For one thing, the numbers both of Roman veterans and of Romanised Britons remained comparatively small; for another, beyond the Severn and beyond the Humber lay the multitudes of the un-Romanised tribes, held down only by the terror of the Roman arms, and always ready to rise and overwhelm the alien culture."[1]

Commenting upon the Icknield Way, Dr. Guest remarks the lack upon its course of any Roman relics, a want, however, which, as he says, is amply compensated for by the many objects, mostly of British antiquity, which crowd upon us as we journey westward—by the tumuli and "camps" which show themselves on right and left—by the six gigantic earthworks which in the intervals of eighty miles were raised at widely different periods to bar progress along this now deserted thoroughfare.[2] In a similar strain Mr. Johnson writes of the Pilgrim's Way in Surrey: "To my thinking, the strongest argument for the prehistoric way lies in the plea expressed by the grim old earthworks and silent barrows which stud its course, and by the numerous relics dug up here and there, relics of which we may rest assured not one-half has been put on record."[3]

Tacitus pictures a Briton as reasoning to himself "compute the number of men born in freedom and the Roman invaders are but a handfull".[4] Is it in these circumstances

---

[1] Hearnshaw, F. J. C., *England in the Making*, p. 22.
[2] *Origines Celticæ*, ii., 240.   [3] *Folk Memory*, p. 349.   [4] *Agricola*, xv.

likely that the Roman handful troubled to construct six great arteries or main roads centring to London stone?

The Romans ran military roads from castra to castra, but in Roman eyes London was merely "à place not dignified with the name of a colony, but the chief residence of merchants and the great mart of trade and commerce".[1]

Holloway Road, in London, implies, I think, at least one *Holy Way*, and there seems to me a probability that London stone was a primitive Jupiterstone, yprestone, preston, pray stone, or phairy stone, similar to the holy centre-stone of sacred Athens: "Look upon the dance, Olympians; send us the grace of Victory, ye gods who come to the heart of our city, where many feet are treading and incense streams: in sacred Athens come to the holy centre-stone".

[1] Tacitus, *Annals*, xxxiii.

CHAPTER X

HAPPY ENGLAND

"In the old time every Wood and Grove, Field and Meadow, Hill and Cave, Sea and River, was tenanted by tribes and communities of the great Fairy Family, and at least one of its members was a resident in every House and Homestead where the kindly virtues of charity and hospitality were practised and cherished. This was the faith of our forefathers—a graceful, trustful faith, peopling the whole earth with beings whose mission was to watch over and protect all helpless and innocent things, to encourage the good, to comfort the forlorn, to punish the wicked, and to thwart and subdue the overbearing."—ANON, *The Fairy Family*, 1857.

"It is very much better to believe in a number of gods than in none at all."—W. B. YEATS.

IT is generally supposed that the site of London has been in continuous occupation since that remote period when the flint-knappers chipped their implements at Gray's Inn, and the pile-dwelling communities, whose traces have been found in the neighbourhood of London Stone, drove their first stakes into the surrounding marshes. Not only are there in London the material evidences of antediluvian occupation, but the fact remains that in the city of London there are more survivals from past history than can be found within the compass of any other British city, or of any other area in Britain."[1]

Sir Laurence Gomme assigns some importance to the place-name "Britaine Street"—now "Little Britain"—where, according to Stow, the Earls of Britain were lodged,

[1] Gomme, Sir L., *London*, p. 74.

but it is probable that in *Up*well, *Eb*gate, *Ab*church, *Ape*church or *Up*church, we may identify relics of an infinitely greater antiquity.

When Cæsar paid his flying visit to these islands he learned at the mouth of the Thames that what he terms an *oppidum* or stronghold of the British was not far distant, and that a considerable number of men and cattle were there assembled. As it has been maintained that London was the stronghold here referred to, the term *oppidum* may possibly have been a British word, Cæsar's testimony being: "*The Britons apply* the name of *oppidum* to any woodland spot difficult to access, and fortified with a rampart and trench to which they are in the habit of resorting in order to escape a hostile raid".[1] That the *dum* of *oppidum* was equivalent to *dun* is manifest from the place-name Dumbarton, which was originally Dunbrettan.

In view of the natural situation of St. Alban's there is a growing opinion among archæologists that London, and not St. Alban's, was the stronghold which stood the shock of Roman conquest when Cæsar took the *oppidum* of Cassivellaunus.

The inscriptions EP, EPPI, and IPPI figure frequently on British coins, and there were probably local hobby stones, hobby towns, and *oppi duns* in the tribal centre of every settlement of hobby-horse worshippers. In Durham is Hoppyland Park, near Bridgewater is Hopstone, near Yarmouth is Hopton, and Hopwells; and Hopwood's, Happy Valley's, Hope Dale's, Hope Point's, Hopgreen's, Hippesley's and Apsley's may be found in numerous directions. It is noteworthy that none of these terms can have had

[1] *De bello Gallico*, v., 21.

any relation to the hop plant, for the word *hops* is not recorded until the fifteenth century; nor, speaking generally, have they any direct connection with *hope*, meaning "the point of the low land mounting the hill whence the top can be seen ".[1]

The word *hope*, meaning expectation, is in Danish *haab*, in German *hoffe* : Hopwood, near Hopton, is at Alvechurch (Elf Church ?), apart from which straw one would be justified in the assumption that Hop, Hob, or Hoph, where it occurs in place-names, had originally reference to Hob-with-a-canstick, *alias* Hop-o'-my-Thumb. The Hebrew expression for the witch of Endor, consulted by King Saul, is *ob* or *oub*, but in Deuteronomy xviii. 11, the term *oph* is used to denote a familiar spirit.[2] As we find a reference in Shakespeare to " urchins, *ouphes*, and fairies," the English ouphes would seem to have been one of the orders of the Elphin realm : the authorities equate it with *alph* or *alp*, and the word has probably survived in the decadence of Kipling's " muddied *oaf* ".

Offa, the proper name, is translated by the dictionaries as meaning *mild*, *gentle* : it is further remarkable that the root *oph*, *op*, or *ob*, is very usually associated with things diminutive and small. In Welsh *of* or *ov* means " atoms, first principles " ;[3] in French *œuf*, in Latin *ova*, means an egg ; the little egg-like berry of the hawthorn is termed a *hip* ; to *ebb* is to diminish, and in S.W. Wiltshire is " a *small* river," named the Ebbe. Hob, with his flickering candlestick, or the homely Hob crouching on the hob, seems rarely to have been thought of otherwise than as the

---

[1] Blackie, C., *Dictionary of Place-names*, p. 21.
[2] Garnier, Col., *The Worship of the Dead*, p. 240.
[3] Thomas, J., *Brit. Antiquissima*, p. 108.

child Elf, such as that superscribed EP upon the British coin here illustrated: yet to the *u*biquitous Hob may no doubt be assigned *up*, which means aloft or overhead, and *hoop*, the symbol of the Sun or Eye of Heaven.

FIG. 313.—British. From Akermann.

Within and all around the *oppida* the military and sacerdotal hubbub was undoubtedly at times uproarious, and the vociferation used on these occasions may account for the word *hubbub*,[1] a term which according to Skeat was "imitative". This authority adds to his conjecture: "formerly also *whoobub*, a confused noise. Hubbub was confused with *hoop-hoop*, re-duplication of *hoop* and *whoobub* with *whoop-hoop*." But even had our ancestors mingled *hip! hip!* in their muddled minds even then the confusion would have been excusable.

Ope, when occurring in proper-names such as Panope or Europe, is usually translated Eye—thus, Panope as *Universal Eye*, and Europa as *Broad Eye*. The small red eye-like or optical berries of the hawthorn are termed

---

[1] The choral music of the Teutons did not create a favourable impression on the mind of Tacitus, *vide* his account of a primitive Hymn of Hate: "The Germans abound with rude strains of verse, the reciters of which, in the language of the country, are called Bards. With this barbarous poetry they inflame their minds with ardour in the day of action, and prognosticate the event from the impression which it happens to make on the minds of the soldiers, who grow terrible to the enemy, or despair of success, as the war-song produces an animated or a feeble sound. Nor can their manner of chanting this savage prelude be called the tone of human organs: it is rather a furious uproar; a wild chorus of military virtue. The vociferation used upon these occasions is uncouth and harsh, at intervals interrupted by the application of their bucklers to their mouths, and by the repercussion bursting out with redoubled force."—*Germania*, I., iii., p. 313.

hips or haws, and it is probable that once upon a time the hips were deemed the elphin eyes of Hob, the Ubiquitous or Everywhere. In India the favourite bead in rosaries is the seed named *rudraksha*, which means "the Eye of the god Rudra or S'iva": Rudra, or the *ruddy one*, is the Hub or centre of the Hindoo pantheon, and S'iva, his more familiar name (now understood to mean "kindly, gracious, or propitious") is more radically "dear little Iva or Ipha". In India millions of S'eva stones are still worshipped, and the *rudraksha* seeds or Eyes of S'iva are generally cut with eleven facets,[1] evidently symbolising the eleven Beings which are said to have sprung from the dual personalities —male and female—of the Creative Principle.

Epine, the French for thorn, is ultimately akin to Hobany, and *hip* may evidently be equated with the friendly Hob. According to Bryant Hip or Hipha was a title of the Phœnician Prime Parent, and it is probable that our *Hip! Hip! Hip!*—the parallel of the Alban *Albani! Albani!*—long antedated the *Hurrah!*

The Hobdays and the Abdys of Albion may be connoted with *Good Hob*, and that this Robin Goodfellow or benevolent elf was the personification of shrewdness and cunning is implied by *apt* and in*ept*, and that happy little Hob was considered to be pretty is implied by *hübsch*, the Teutonic for *pretty*: the word *pretty* is essentially *British*, and the piratical habits of the early British are brought home to them by the word *pirate*. We shall, however, subsequently see that *pirates* originally meant "attempters" or men who *tried*.

The surname Hepburn argues the existence at some

[1] Blackman, Winifred S., *The Rosary in Magic and Religion*, Folklore, xxiv., 4.

time of a Hep bourne or brook; in Northumberland is Hepborne or Haybourne, which the authorities suppose meant "burn, brook, with the hips, the fruit of the wild rose": but hips must always have been as ubiquitous and plentiful as sparrows. In Yorkshire is Hepworth, anciently written Heppeword, and this is confidently interpreted as meaning *Farm of Heppo*: in view, however, of our hobby-horse festivals, it is equally probable that in the Hepbourne the Kelpie, the water horse, or *hippa* was believed to lurk, and one may question the historic reality of farmer Heppo.

The hobby horse was principally associated with the festivals of May-Day, but it also figured at Yule Tide. On Christmas Eve either a wooden horse head or a horse's skull was decked with ribbons and carried from door to door on the summit of a pole supported by a man cloaked with a sheet: this figure was known as "Old Hob":[1] in Welsh *hap* means fortune—either good or bad.

Apparently the last recorded instance of the Hobby-Horse dance occurred at Abbot's Bromley, on which occasion a man carrying the image of a horse between his legs, and armed with a bow and arrow (the emblems of Barry the Sovereign Archer), played the part of Hobby: with him were six companions wearing reindeer heads (the emblems of the Dayspring) who danced the hey and other ancient dances. Tollett supposes the famous hobby horse to be the King of the May "though he now appears as a juggler and a buffoon with a crimson foot-cloth fretted with gold, the golden bit, the purple bridle, and studded with gold, the man's purple mantle with a golden border which is latticed with purple, his golden crown, purple cap with a red feather, and with a golden knop".[2]

[1] Wright, E. M., *Rustic Speech and Folklore*, p. 303.
[2] *Cf.* Hazlitt, W. Carew, *Faiths and Folklore*, i., p. 314.

A *knop* or *knob* means a boss, protuberance, or rosebud —originally, of course, a wild rosebud which precedes the hip—and it is probably the same word as the CUNOB which

FIGS. 314 to 317.—British. From Akerman.

occurs so frequently in British coins. In Fig. 314 CUNOB occurs alone, and I am not sure that Figs. 315 and 318 should not be read ELINI CUNOB. The knob figured not only on our Hobby Horse, but also as a symbol on the

FIG. 318.—British. From Camden.

FIG. 319 —Head Dress of the King (N.W. Palace Nimroud). From *Nineveh* (Layard).

head-dress of Tyrian kings, and there is very little doubt that the charming small figure on the obverse of CUNOB ELINI is intended for King Ob, or Ep. There is a Knap Hill at Avebury, a Knapton in Yorkshire, and a Knapwell in Suffolk: Knebworth in Herts was Chenepenorde in Domesday, and the imaginary farmer Cnapa or Cnebba, to whom these place-names are assigned, may be equated with the afore-mentioned farmer Heppo of Hepworth.

Knaves Castle (Lichfield), now a small mound—a *heap?* —is ascribed to "*cnafa*, a boy or servant, later a knave, a rogue": Cupid is a notorious little rogue, nevertheless, proverbially Love makes the world go round, and constitutes its nave, navel, hub, or boss: with *snob* Skeat connotes *snopp*, meaning a boy or anything *stumpy*.

In course of time like *boss*, Dutch *baas*, *knob* seems to have been applied generally to mean a lord or master, and the Londoner who takes an agreeable interest in the "nobs"[1] (and occasional *snobs*) riding in Hyde Park is possibly following an ancestral custom dating from the time when the Ring was originally constructed. Apsley House, now standing at the east end of Rotten Row, occupies the site of the park ranger's lodge, the Ranger was a highly important personage, and it is not improbable that the site of Apsley House was once known as Ap's lea or meadow. The immediately adjacent Stanhope Gate and Stanhope Street, or Stanhope in Durham, may mark the site of a stone hippa or horse similar to the famous stone

---

[1] Cockney dialect is closely akin to Kentish, and abounds in venerable verbal relics: "The stranger enters, but he nonetheless pays his toll; he does not leave any mark on London, but London leaves an indelible stamp upon him. The children of the foreigner, the children of the Yorkshireman or Lancastrian, belong in speech neither to Yorkshire nor Lancashire, they become more Cockney than the Cockneys; and even the alien voices of the east end, notably less musical than those of our own people, take on the tones of London's ancient speech."—MacBride, Mackenzie, *London's Dialect, An Ancient form of English Speech, with a Note on the Dialects of the North of England, and the Midlands and Scotland*, p. 8.

horse in Brittany upon which—I believe to this day—
women superstitiously seat themselves with the same pur-

Fig. 320.—La Venus de Quinipily, near Baud Morbihan, Brittany. From
Symbolism of the East and West (Aynsley, Mrs. Murray).

pose as they sit upon the Brahan stone in Ireland : Bryanstone Square in London is not more than a mile from
Stanhope Street and Apsley House.

The Breton statue of Quinipily may be deemed a portrait

of *holy Queen Ip*, and Gwennap, near Redruth, where is a famous amphitheatre, was probably a Queen Hip lea or seat of the same Queen's worship.

Gwen Ap was presumably the same as Queen Aph or Godiva, the Lady of the White Horse, and Godrevy on the opposite side of St. Ives Bay may be equated with *Good rhi Evy*, or Good Queen Evie. A few miles from Liskeard there is a village named St. Ive, which the natives pronounce *St. Eve*: the more western, better-known Saint Ive's, is mentioned in a document of 1546 as " Seynt Iysse," and what apparently is this same dedication reappears at a place four miles west of Wadebridge termed St. Issey. "Whose name is it," inquires W. C. Borlase, " that the parish of St. Issey bears ? " He suggests somewhat wildly that it may be the same as Elidius, corrupted to Liddy, Ide, or Idgy, endeavouring to prove that this Elidius is the same as the great Welsh Teilo.

It would be simpler and more reasonable to assume that St. Issey is a trifling corruption of "Eseye," which was one of the titles of the old British Mother of Life. The goddess Esseye—alternatively and better known as Keridwen—is described by Owen in his *Cambrian Biography* as " a female personage, in the mythology of the Britons considered as *the first of womankind*, having nearly the same attributes with Venus, in whom are personified the generative powers ".

With Eseye and with St. Issey, *alias* St. Ive, may be connoted the deserted town of Hesy in Judea: on the mound now known as Tell el Hesy, or the hill town of Hesy, the remains of at least eight super-imposed prehistoric cities have been excavated, and among the discoveries on this site was a limestone lampstand subscribed on the base APHEBAL.[1] The winged maiden found at the same time is essentially Cretan, and it is not an unreasonable assumption that on this *Aphe* fragment of pottery

FIG. 321.—From *A Mound of Many Cities* (Bliss, J. B.).

from Hesy we have a contemporary portrait of the Candian Aphaia or Britomart, *alias* Hesy, or St. Issy, or St. Ive: the British Eseye was alternatively known as Cendwen.

FIG. 322.—From *A Mound of Many Cities* (Bliss, J. B.).

The British built their *oppida* not infrequently in the form of an eye or optic, and also of an oeuf, ova, or egg. The perfect symmetry of these designs point conclusively to the probability that the earthworks were not mere strongholds scratched together anyhow for mere defence: the British burial places or barrows were similarly either circular or oval, and that the Scotch dun illustrated in Fig. 324 was British, is implied not only by its name Boreland-

[1] Bliss, J. B., *A Mound of Many Cities or Tell el Hesy Excavated.*

Mote, but by its existence at a place named Parton,

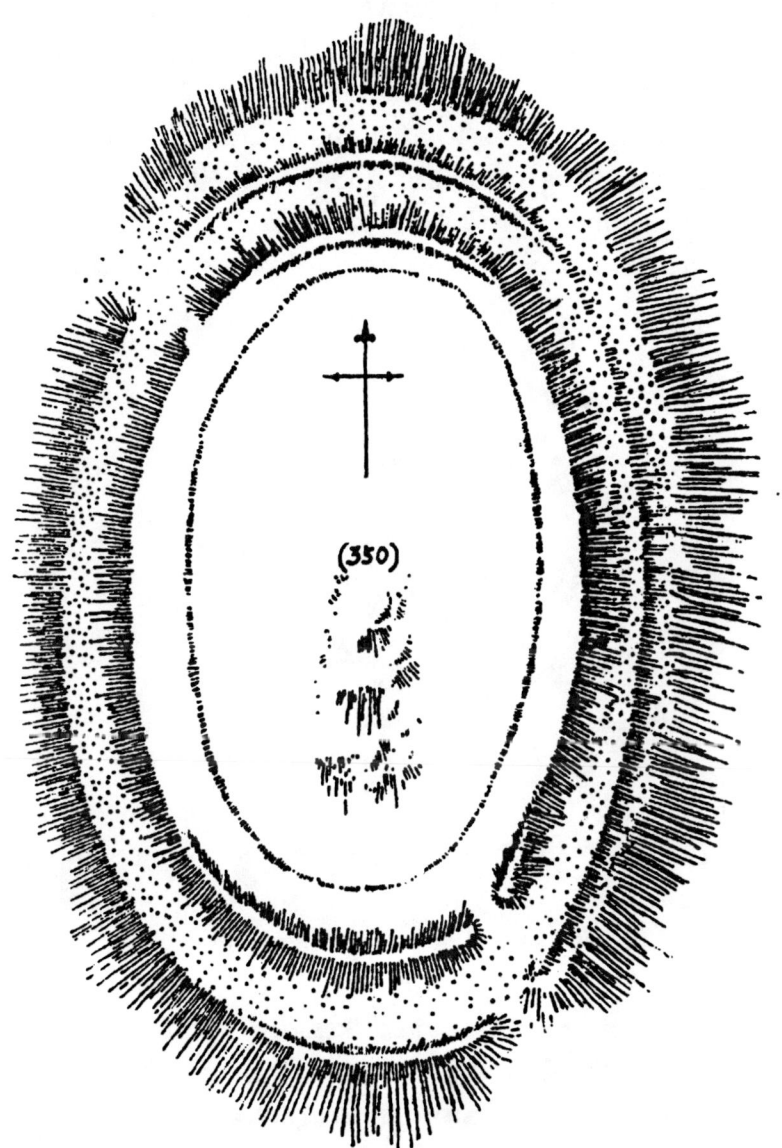

Fig. 323.—From *The Motes of Kirkcudbrightshire* (Coles, F. R.). (Scot. Antiq. Scot.).

this word, like the Barton of Dumbarton, no doubt signifying Dun Brettan or Briton.

Egypt was known as "The Land of the Eye":[1] the amulet of the All-seeing Eye was perhaps even more popular in Egypt than in Etruria, and the mysterious and unaccountable objects called "spindle whorls," which occur so profusely in British tombs, and which also have been found in countless numbers underneath Troy, were probably Eye amulets, rudely representative of the human iris. The Trojan examples here illustrated are conspicu-

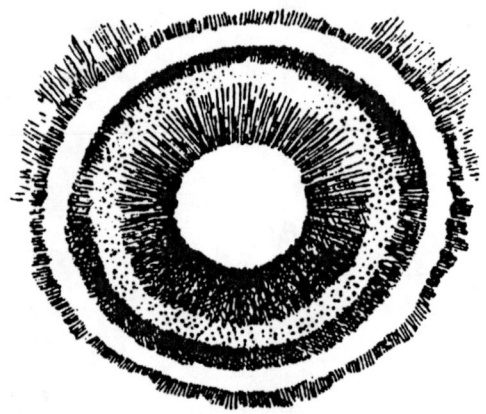

Fig. 324.—From *The Motes of Kirkcudbrightshire* (Coles, F. R.). (Soc. Antiq. Scot.)

ously decorated with the British *Broad* Arrow, which is said to have been the symbol of the Awen or Holy Spirit. In their accounts of the traditional symbols, speech, letters, and signs of Britain, according to their preservation by means of memory, voice, and usages of the Chair and Gorsedd, the Welsh Bards asserted that the three strokes of the Broad Arrow or bardic hieroglyph for God originated from three diverging rays of light seen descending towards the earth. Out of these three strokes were constituted all

---

[1] I was unaware of this rather corroborative evidence when I put forward the suggestion five years ago that *Egypt* was radically *ypte* or *Good Eye*.

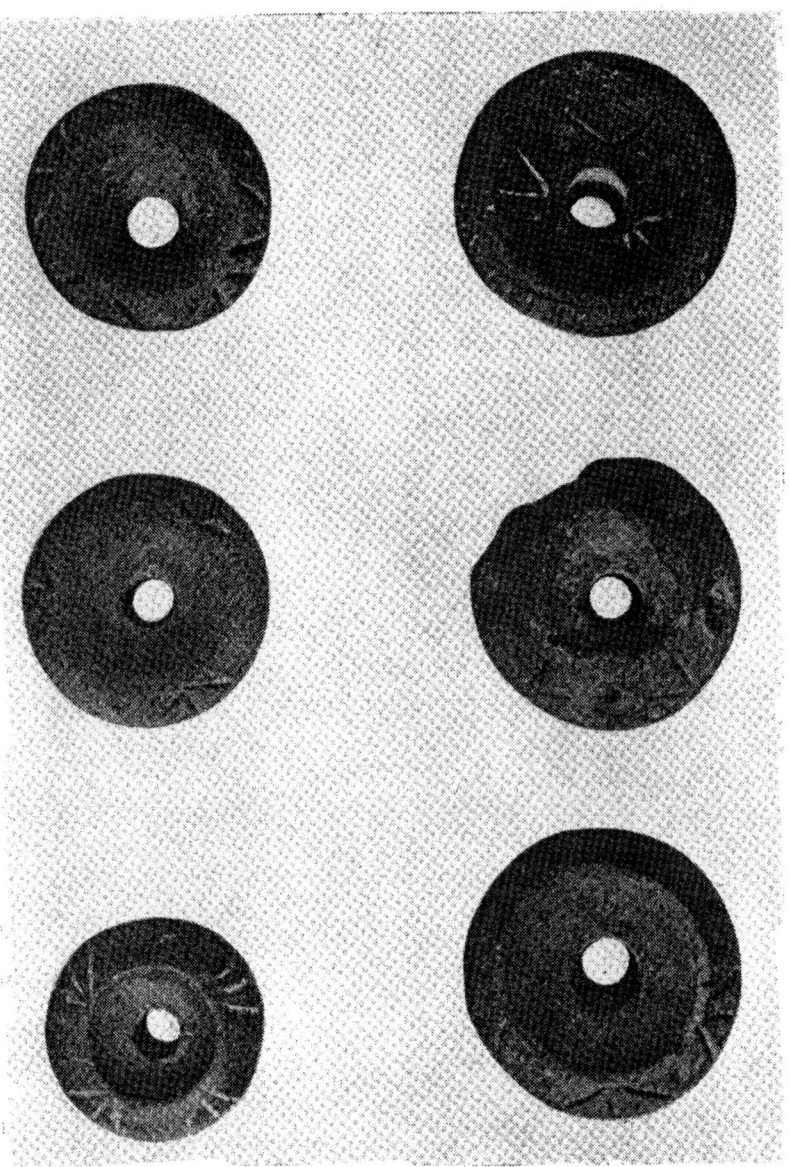

Fig. 325.—"Spindle-whorls" from Troy. From *Prehistoric London* (Gordon, E. O.).

[*To face page* 534.

the letters of the bardic alphabet, the three strokes ╱ │ ╲ reading in these characters respectively 0 1 0, and thus spelling the mystic OHIO or YEW; hence it would seem that this never-to-be-pronounced Name [1] was a faerie conception originating in the mind of some primitive poet philosophising from a cloud-encumbered sunrise or sunset. According to tradition there were five ages of letters: "The first was the age of the three letters, which above all represented the Name of God, and which were a sign of Goodness and Truth, and Understanding and Equity, of whatsoever kind they might be".[2] On these rays, it is said, were inscribed every kind and variety of Science and Knowledge, and on His return to Heaven the Almighty Architect is described as—

> Followed with acclamation, and the sound
> Symphonious of ten thousand harps that tun'd
> Angelic harmonies.

The philosophers of Egypt believed that the universe was created by the pronunciation of the divine name; similarly the British bards taught that: "The universe is matter as ordered and systematised by the intelligence of God. It was created by God's pronouncing His own name —at the sound of which light and the heavens sprang into existence. The name of God is itself a creative power. What in itself that name is, is known to God only. All music or natural melody is a faint and broken echo of the creative name."[3]

Everywhere and in everything the Druids recognised this celestial Trinity: not only did their Hierarchy consist of three orders, *i.e.*, Druids, Bards, and Seers, each group

---

[1] The Iberians and Jews also possessed a never-to-be-uttered sacred Name.
[2] *Barddas*, p. 95.   [3] *Ibid.*, p. 251.

being again subdivided into three, but also, as we have seen, they uttered their Triads or aphorisms in triple form. There is little doubt that the same idea animated the Persian philosophy of Good Thought, Good Deed, Good Word, and Micah's triple exordium: "Do justly, love mercy, walk humbly". The bards say distinctly: "The three mystic letters signify the three attributes of God, namely, Love, Knowledge, and Truth, and it is out of these three that justice springs, and without one of the three there can be no justice".[1]

This is a simpler philosophy than the incomprehensibilities of the Athanasian Creed,[2] and it was seemingly drilled with such living and abiding force into the minds of the Folk, that even to-day the Druidic Litanies or Chants of the Creed still persist. Throughout Italy and Sicily the Chant of the Creed is known as The Twelve Words of Verita or Truth, and it is generally put into the mouth of the popular Saint Nicholas of *Bari*.[3] The Sicilian or Hyperean festival of the Bara has already been noted *ante*, p. 320.

---

[1] *Barddas*, p. 23.

[2] As also was the Bardic conception of God, summed up in the Triad:—

"Three things which God cannot but be; whatever perfect
Goodness ought to be; whatever perfect
Goodness would desire to be; and whatever perfect
Goodness can be."

Again—

"There is nothing beautiful but what is just;
There is nothing just but *love*;
There is no love but God."

And thus it ends. Tydain, the Father of Awen, sang it, says the Book of Sion Cent (*Barddas*, p. 219).

[3] Eckenstein, L., *Comparative Studies in Nursery Rhymes*, p. 146.

The British chant quoted *ante*, page 373, continues: "What will be our three boys"? "What will be our four"? five? six? and onwards up to twelve, but always the refrain is—

> My only ain she walks alane
> And ever mair has dune, boys.

In Irish mythology we are told that the Triad similarly "infected everything," hence Trinities such as Oendia

Fig. 326.—St. John. From *Christian Iconography* (Didron).

Fig. 327.—Christ, with a Nimbus of Three Clusters of Rays. Miniature of the XVI. Cent. MS. of the Bib. Royale. *Ibid*.

(the one god), Caindea (the gentle god), and Trendia (the mighty god): other accounts specify the three children of the Boyne goddess, as Tear Bringer, Smile Bringer, and Sleep Bringer: the word *sleep* is in all probability a corruption of *sil Eep*.

Among the Trojan "spindle whorls" some are decorated with four awens, corresponding seemingly to the Four Kings of the Wheel of Fortune; others with three groups constituting a total of nine strokes. As each ray represented a form of Truth, the number nine—which as already noted is invariably true to itself—was essentially the symbol of Truth, and that this idea was absorbed by Christianity is obvious from representations such as Figs. 326 and 327.

At Sancreed in Cornwall—supposedly a dedication to the holy Creed—there is a remarkable "cross" which is

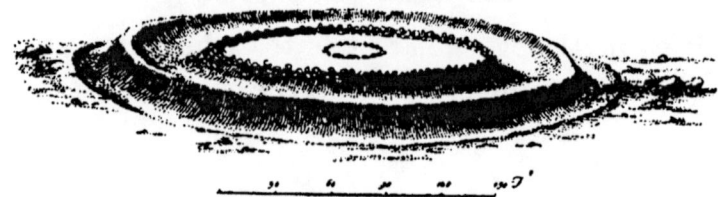

Fig. 329.—Caerbrân Castle in Sancred. From *Antiquities of Cornwall* (Borlase).

actually a holed stone on a shank:[1] and in the same parish is a "castle" which was once evidently a very perfect Eye. In the Scilly Islands, lying within a stone circle, is what might be a millstone with a square hole in its centre: this Borlase ranks among the holed stones of Cornwall, and that it was a symbol of the Great Eye is a reasonable

Figs. 330 and 331.—British. From Evans.

inference from the name Salla Key where it is still lying. We have seen the symbolic Eye on the Kio coin illustrated *ante*, page 253; the word *eye* pronounced frequently *oy* and *ee*, is the same as the *hey* of *Heydays* and the Shepherds' Dance or *Hey*, hence in all probability Salla Key or Salakee Downs[2] were originally sacred to the festivals of *Sala*

---

[1] Illustrated on page opposite.

[2] This name appears on maps sometimes as Salla Key, sometimes as Salakee.

FIG. 328.—"Cross" at Sancreed (Cornwall). From *The Cornish Riviera* (Stone, J. Harris).

To face page 538.

Kee, *i.e.*, silly, innocent, or happy, *'Kee* or *Great Eye*. The old plural of *eye* was *eyen* or *een*, and it is not unlikely that the primeval Ian, John, or Sinjohn, was worshipped as the joint Sun and Moon, or Eyes of Day and Night. On the hobby-horse coins here illustrated, the body consists of two curiously conspicuous circles or *eyen*, possibly representing the *awen*.

> My only *ane* she walks alane
> And ever mair has dune, boys.

On Salla Key Downs is Inisidgen Hill, which takes its name from an opposite island: in old MSS. this appears as *Enys au geon*, which the authorities assume meant "Island of St. John". *Geon*, however, was the Cornish for *giant;* on Salla Key Downs is "Giant's Castle," and close at hand is the Giant's Chair: this is a solid stone worked into the form of an arm-chair: "It looks like a work of art rather than nature, and, according to tradition, it was here the Arch Druid was wont to sit and watch the rising Sun".[1] The neighbouring island of Great Ganilly was thus in all probability sacred to *Geon*, the Great King, or Queen Holy.

The Saints' days, heydays, and holidays of our predecessors seem to have been so numerous that the wonder is that there was ever any time to work: apparently from such evidence as the Bean-setting dance, even the ancient sowing was accomplished to the measure of a song, and the festivities in connection with old Harvest Homes are too multifarious and familiar to need comment.

The attitude of the clergy towards these ancient festivals seems to have been uniform and consistent.

---

[1] Tonkin, J. C., *Lyonesse*, p. 38.

> These teach that dancing is a Jezebel,
> And barley-break the ready way to hell;
> The morrice-idols, Whitsun-ales, can be
> But profane relics of a jubilee.[1]

One of the greatest difficulties of the English Church was to suppress the dancing which the populace—supported by immemorial custom—insisted upon maintaining, even within the churches and the churchyards. Even to-day English churches possess reindeer heads and other paraphernalia of archaic feasts, and in Paris, as recently as the seventeenth century, the clergy and singing boys might have been seen dancing at Easter in the churches.[2] In Cornwall on the road from Temple to Bradford Bridge is a stone circle known as The Trippet Stones, and doubtless many churches occupy the sites of similar places where from time immemorial the Folk tripped it jubilantly on jubilees: custom notoriously dies hard.

In the Eastern counties of England the two principal reapers were known as the Harvest Lord and Lady, who presided over the Hoppings, and other festivities of the season. Sometimes the Harvest Lady was known as the Hop Queen,[3] and this important potentate may be connoted with the harvest doll which, in Kent particularly, was termed the Ivy Girl. As Prof. Weekley connotes the surname Hoppe with Hobbs, Hobson, and Hopkins, we may infer from the name *Hopkin*son, there must once have been a Hop King as well as a Hop Queen, and the rôle of this English Hopkin was probably similar to that enacted by other Jack-in-Greens, King-of-the-Years, or Spirit-of-the-Years. The pomp and circumstance of the

---

[1] Randolph (1657). [2] Johnson, W., *Byways*, p. 185.
[3] Hazlitt, W. Carew, *Faiths and Folklore*, i., 309.

parallel of the Hopkin ceremony in Greece may be judged from the following particulars: "They wreathe," says Plato, "a pole of olive wood with laurel and various flowers. On the top is fitted a bronze globe from which they suspend smaller ones. Midway round the pole they place a lesser globe, binding it with purple fillets, but the end of the pole is decked with saffron. By the topmost globe they mean the sun, to which they actually compare Apollo. The globe beneath this is the moon; the smaller globes hung on are the stars and constellations, and the fillets are the course of the year, for they make them 365 in number. The Daphnephoria is headed by a boy, both whose parents are alive, and his nearest male relation carries the filleted pole. The Laurel-Bearer himself, who follows next, holds on to the laurel; he has his hair hanging loose, he wears a golden wreath, and he is dressed out in a splendid robe to his feet and he wears light shoes. There follows him a band of maidens holding out boughs before them, to enforce the supplication of the hymns."[1]

With this Greek festival of the Laurel-Bearer may be connoted the "one traditional dance connected with all our old festivals and merry makings" in Guernsey, and known as *A mon beau Laurier*. In this ceremony the dancers join hands, whirl round, curtsey, and kiss a central object, in later days either a man or a woman, but, in the opinion of Miss Carey, "perhaps originally either a sacred stone or a primeval altar".[2] Adulation of this character is calculated to create *snobs*, the word as we have seen being fundamentally connected with *stump*. I have already suggested a connection between the salutation *A*

---

[1] Quoted from Harrison, J., *Ancient Art and Ritual*, p. 188.
[2] *Folklore*, XXV., iv., p. 426.

mon beau Laurier and the kissing or bussing of Paul's stump at Billingsgate, which is situated almost immediately next Ebgate. On Mount Hube, in Jersey, have been found the remains of a supposed Druidic temple, and

FIG. 332.—From *The Everyday Book* (Hone, W.).

doubtless Mount *Hube*, like Apechurch or Abechurch, was a primitive Hopeton, *oppidum*, or Abbey.

The Hoop is a frequent inn sign generally associated with some additional symbol such as is implied in the familiar old signs, Swan-on-the-Hoop, Cock-on-the-Hoop, Crown-on-the-Hoop, Angel-on-the-Hoop, Falcon-on-the Hoop, and

Bunch-of-Grapes-on-the-Hoop.[1] That the hoop or circle was a sacred form need not be laboured, for the majority

Fig. 333.—From *The Everyday Book* (Hone, W.).

of our megalithic monuments are circular, and there is no doubt that these rude circles are not simply and solely

[1] Larwood and Hotten, *Hist. of Signboards*, p. 504.

"adjuncts of stone age burials," but were the primitive temples of the Hoop Lady or Fairy Queen. It was customary to represent the Hop Lady within hoops or wheels; and that the Virgin was regarded indifferently as either One, Two, Three or Four is clear from the indeterminate number of dolls which served on occasion as the idola or ideal. In Irish *oun* or *ain* means the cycle or course of the seasons, and the great Queen Anu or Aine who was regarded as the boss, hub, or centre of the Mighty Wheel may be equated with Una, the Fairy Queen.

The Druids are said to have considered it impious to enclose or cover their temples, presumably for the same reasons as prevailed among the Persians. These are explained by Cicero who tells us that in the expedition of Xerxes into Greece all the Grecian temples were destroyed at the instigation of the Magi because the Grecians were so impious as to enclose those gods within walls who ought to have all things around them open and free, their temple being the universal world. In Homer's time—

> On rough-hewn stones within the sacred cirque
> Convok'd the hoary sages sat.

and there is little doubt that similarly in these islands the priest-chiefs held their solemn and ceremonial sessions.

The word Druid is in disfavour among modern archæologists; nevertheless, apparently all over Britain the Druids were traditionally associated in the popular memory with megalithic monuments. Martin, in the relation of his Tour of the Hebrides, made in the middle of the eighteenth century, observes: "In the Western Islands where there are many, what are called by the common people *Druin Crunny*, that is Druids' Circles," and the same observer recounts: "I inquired of the inhabitants what tradition they had concerning these stones, and they told me it was a place appointed for worship in the time of heathenism, and that the chief Druid stood near the big stone in the centre from whence he addressed himself to the people that surrounded him ".[1]

There is presumptive and direct evidence that the stone circles of Britain served the combined uses of Temple, Sepulchre, Place of Assembly, and Law Court. The custom of choosing princes by nobles standing in a circle upon rocks, prevailed until comparatively recent times, and Edmund Spenser, writing in 1596 on the State of Ireland, thus described an installation ceremony: " One of the Lords arose and holding in his hand a white wand perfectly straight and without the slightest bend, he presented it to the chieftain-elect with the following words, ' Receive the emblematic wand of thy dignity, now let the unsullied whiteness and straightness of this wand be thy model in all thy acts, so that no calumnious tongue can expose the slightest stain on the purity of thy life, nor any favoured friend ever seduce thee from dealing out even-handed justice to all '." [2]

The white wand figuring in this ceremony is evidently the magic rod or fairy wand with which the Elphin Queen is conventionally equipped, and which was figured in the hand of the Cretan " Hob," *ante*, page 494.

Sometimes in lieu of a centre stone the circles contained stone chairs. Many of these old Druidic thrones have been broken up into gate-posts or horse-troughs, but

---

[1] *Cf.* Borlase, W., *Cornwall*, pp. 193, 201.

[2] One may connote this ceremony with the Bardic triad: " God is the measuring rod of all truth, all justice, and all goodness, therefore He is a yoke on all, and all are under it, and woe to him who shall violate it ".

several are still in existence, and some are decorated with a carving of two footprints. These two footprints were in all probability one of the innumerable forms in which the perennial Pair were represented, *vide* the Vedic invocation: "Like two lips speaking sweetly to the mouth, like two breasts feed us that we may live. Like two nostrils as guardians of the body, like two ears be inclined to listen to us. Like two hands holding our strength together ... like two hoofs rushing in quickly," etc.

In the British coin here illustrated the Giant Pair are featured as joint steeds: "Coming early like two heroes on their chariots ... ye bright ones every day come hither like two charioteers, O ye strong ones! Like two winds, like two streams your motion is eternal; like *two eyes*[1] come with your sight toward us! Like two hands most useful to the body; *like two feet* lead us towards wealth."[2]

Fig. 334.—British. From Akerman.

Occasionally the two footprints are found cut into simple rock: in Scotland the King of the Isles used to be crowned at Islay, standing on a stone with a deep impression on the top of it made on purpose to receive his feet. The meaning of the feet symbol in Britain is not known, but Scotch tradition maintained that it represented the size of the feet of Albany's first chieftain. On Adam's Peak in Ceylon (ancient *Tafrobani*) there is a super-sacred footprint which is still the goal of millions of devout pilgrims, and on referring to India where the foot emblem is familiar we find it explained as very ancient, and used by the Buddhists in

---

[1] See Fig. 331, p. 538.
[2] Quoted from *Science of Language*, Max Müller, p. 540.

remembrance of their great leader Buddha. In the tenth century a Hindu poet sang:—

> In my heart I place the feet
> The Golden feet of God.

and it would thus seem that the primeval Highlander anticipated by many centuries Longfellow's trite lines on great men, happily, however, before departing, graving the symbolic footprints of his "first Chieftain," not upon the sands of Time, but on the solid rocks.

The Ancients, believing that God was centred in His Universe, a point within a circle was a proper and expressive hieroglyph for Pan or All. The centre stone of the rock circles probably stood similarly for God, and the surrounding stones for the subsidiary Principalities and Powers thus symbolising the idea: "Thou art the Eternal One, in whom all order is centred; Lord of all things visible and invisible, Prince of mankind, Protector of the Universe".[1] A tallstone or a longstone is physically and objectively the figure one, 1.

If it were possible to track the subsidiary Powers of the Eternal One to their inception we should, I suspect, find them to have been personifications of Virtues, and this would seem to apply not merely to such familiar Trinities as Faith, Hope, and Charity; Good Thought, Good Deed, and Good Word, but to quartets, quintets, sextets, and septets such as the Seven Kings or Seven Gifts of the Holy Spirit, i.e., "Ye gifte of wisdome; ye gifte of pittie; ye gifte of strengthe; ye gifte of comfaite; ye gifte of understandinge; ye gifte of counyinge; ye gifte of dreede".

The Persian Trinity of Thought, Deed, and Word, is perfectly expressed in the three supposed Orders of the

---

[1] Sabean Litany attributed to Enoch.

Christian hierarchy. As stated in *The Golden Legend* these are—sovereign Love as touching the order of Seraphim, perfect Knowledge, and perpetual Fruition or usance. " There be some," continues De Voragine, " that overcome and dominate over all vices in themselves, and they by right be called of the world, gods among men." [1]

It is related of King Arthur that he carried a shield named Prydwen, and if the reader will trouble to count the dots ranged round the centre boss of the shield on page 120 the number will be found to be *eleven*. At Kingston on Thames, where the present market stone is believed to be the surviving centre-piece of a stone-circle, a brass ring ornamented with *eleven* bosses was discovered.[2] In Etruria *eleven* mystic shields were held in immense veneration :[3] it will further be noted that the majority of the wheatears on British and Celtiberian coins consist of *eleven* corns.

The word *eleven*, like its French equivalent *onze*, *ange*, or *angel*, points to the probability that for some reason eleven was essentially the number sacred to the *elven*, *anges*, or *onzes*. Elphinstone, a fairly common surname, implies the erstwhile existence of many Elphinstones : there is an Alphian rock in Yorkshire ; bronze urns have been excavated at Alphamstone in Essex, and the supposititious Aelfin, to whom the Alphington in Exeter is attributed, was far more probably Elphin.

The dimensions of many so-called longstones—whether solitary or in the centres of circles—point to the probability that menhirs or standing-stones were frequently and

---

[1] *G. L.*, v. 185, 195.
[2] Walford E., *Greater London*, vol. ii., p. 299.
[3] Dennis G., *Cities of Etruria*.

preferably 11 feet high. In Cornwall alone I have noted the following examples of which the measurements are extracted from *The Victoria County History*. The longstone at Trenuggo, Sancreed, now measures 11 feet 2 inches; that at Sithney 11 feet; that at Burras "about 10 feet," that at Parl 12 feet; and that at Bosava 10 feet. In the parish of St. Buryan the longstones standing at Pridden, Goon Rith, Boscawen Ros, and Trelew, now measure respectively 11 feet 6 inches, 10 feet 6 inches, 10 feet, and 10 feet 4 inches.

If one takes into account such casualties of time as weathering, washing away of subsoil, upcrop of undergrowth, subsidence, and other accidents, the preceding figures are somewhat presumptive that each of the monuments in question was originally designed to stand 11 feet high.

Frequently a circle of stones is designated The Nine Maids, or The Virgin Sisters, or The Merry Maidens. The Nine Maidens is suggestive of the Nine Muses, and of the nine notorious Druidesses, which dwelt upon the Island of Sein in Brittany. The Merry Maidens may be equated with the Fairy or Peri Maidens, and that this phairy theory holds good likewise in Spain is probable from the fact that at Pau there is a circle of nine stones called La Naou *Peyros*.[1]

"When we inquired," says Keightley, "after the fairy system in Spain, we were told that there was no such thing for that the Inquisition had long since eradicated such ideas." He adds, however, "we must express our doubt of the truth of this charge": I concur that not even the Inquisition was capable of carrying out such fundamental

---

[1] *Cornwall*, vol. i., 397; *Victoria County Histories*.

destruction as the obliteration of all peyros. Probably the old plural for peri or fairy was *peren* or *feren*, in which case the great Fernacre circle in the parish of St. Breward, Cornwall, was presumably the sacred eye or hoop of some considerable neighbourhood. About 160 feet eastward of Fernacre (which is one of the largest circles in Cornwall), and in line with the summit of *Brown* Willy (the highest hill in Cornwall) is a small erect stone. The neighbouring Row Tor (*Roi* Tor or *Rey* Tor?) rises due north of Fernacre circle, and as the editors of *Cornwall* point out: " If as might appear probable this very exact alignment north and south, east and west, was intentional, and part of a plan where Fernacre was the pivot of the whole, it is a curious feature that the three circles mentioned should have been so effectively hidden from each other by intervening hills ".[1]

The major portion of this district is the property of an Onslow family; there is an Onslow Gardens near Alvastone Place in Kensington, and there is a probability that every Alvastone, Elphinstone, or *Ons*low neighbourhood was believed to be inhabited by *Elven* or *Anges*: it is indeed due to this superstition that the relatively few megalithic monuments which still exist have escaped damnation, the destruction where it has actually occurred having been sometimes due to a deliberate and bigoted determination, " to brave ridiculous legends and superstitions ".[2] Naturally the prevalent and protective superstitions were fostered and encouraged by prehistoric thinkers for the reasons

---

[1] *Cornwall*, vol. i., 394 ; *Victoria County Histories*.

[2] Blackie's *Dictionary of Place-Names* defines Godmanham as follows: " the holy man's dwelling, the site of an idol temple destroyed under the preaching of Paulinus whose name it bears," p. 98.

doubtless quite rightly surmised by an eighteenth century archæologist who wrote: "But the truth of the story is, it was a burying place of the Britons before the calling in of the heathen sexton (*sic* query *Saxon*) into this Kingdom. And this fable invented by the Britons was to prevent the ripping up of the bones of their ancestors." The demise of similar fables under the corrosive influence of modern kultur, has involved the destruction of countless other stone-monuments, so that even of Cornwall, their natural home, Mr. T. Quiller Couch was constrained to write: "Within my remembrance the cromlech, the holy well, the way-side cross and inscribed stone, have gone before the utilitarian greed of the farmer and the road man, and the undeserved neglect of that hateful being, the *cui bono* man".

Parish Councils of to-day do not fear to commit vandalisms which private individuals in the past shrank from perpetrating.[1] A Welsh "Stonehenge" at Eithbed, Pembrokeshire, shown on large-scale Ordinance maps issued last century, has disappeared from the latest maps of the district, and a few years ago an archæologist who visited the site reported that the age-worn stones had been broken up to build ugly houses close by—"veritable monuments of shame".

In the Isle of *Pur*beck near *Bourne*mouth, *Brank*sea,

---

[1] "The year before last I went to Bodavon Mountain to take photographs of the cromlech that used to lie there. When I got there, however, I found the place absolutely bare, not a vestige of the cromlech remaining. On making inquiries, a road newly metalled was pointed out to me, and I was told that the cromlech had been used for that purpose. This was done despite the fact that many tons of loose stone are lying on the mountain-side close by."—Griffith, John E., *The Cromlechs of Anglesey and Carnarvon*, 1900.

*Bronk*sea (Bronk's *ea* or island) *Branks*ome and numerous other *Bron* place-names which imply that the district was once haunted by Oberon, is a barrow called Puckstone, and on the top of this barrow, now thrown down, is a megalith said to measure 10 feet 8 inches. In all probability this was once 11 feet long, and was the Puckstone or Elphinstone of that neighbourhood: near Anglesea at Llandudno is a famous longstone which again is *eleven* feet high.

In Glamorganshire there is a village known as Angel Town, and in Pembroke is Angle or Nangle: Adamnan, in his *Life of Columba*, records that the saint opened his books and "read them on the Hill of the Angels, where once on a time the citizens of the Heavenly Country were seen to descend to hold conversation with the blessed man". Upon this his editor comments: "this is the knoll called 'great fairies hill'. Not far away is the 'little fairies hill'. The fairies hills of pagan mythology became angels hills in the minds of the early Christian saints."[1] One may be permitted to question whether this metamorphosis really occurred, and whether the idea of Anges or Angles is not actually older than even the Onslows or *ange* lows. The Irish trinity of St. Patrick, St. Bride, and St. Columba, are said all to lie buried in one spot at Dunence, and the place-name *Dunence* seemingly implies that that site was an *on's low*, or *dun ange*. The term *angel* is now understood to mean radically a messenger, but the primary sense must have been deeper than this: in English *ingle*—as in inglenook—meant *fire*, and according to Skeat it also meant a darling or a paramour. Obviously *ingle* is here the same word as *angel*, and presumably the more primitive Englishman tactfully addressed his consort as "mine ingle".

[1] Huyshe, W., *Life of St. Columba*, p. 176.

The Gaelic and the Irish for fire is *aingeal* ; we have seen that the burnebee or ladybird was connected with fire, and that similarly St. Barneby's Day was associated with Barnebee *Bright* : hence the festival held at *Engle*wood, or *Ingle*wood (Cumberland) yearly on the day of St. Barnabas would appear to have been a primitive fire or *aingeal* ceremony. It is described as follows: "At Hesket in Cumberland yearly on St. Barnabas Day by the highway side under a Thorn tree according to the very ancient manner of holding assemblies in the open air, is kept the Court for the whole Forest of Englewood, the 'Englyssh wood' of the ballad of Adam Bel".[1]

Stonehenge used to be entitled Stonehengels, which may be modernised into the *Stone Angels*,[2] each stone presumably standing as a representative of one or other of the angelic hierarchy. When the Saxons met the British in friendly conference at Stonehenge—apparently even then the national centre—each Saxon chieftain treacherously carried a knife which at a given signal he plunged into the body of his unarmed, unsuspecting neighbour; subsequently, it is said, hanging the corpses of the British royalties on the cross rocks of Stonehenge: hence ever after this exhibition of Teutonic *realpolitik* Stonehenge has been assumed to mean the Hanging Stones, or Gallow Stones.[3] We find, however,

---

[1] Hazlitt, W. Carew, *Faiths and Folklore*, i., 210.

[2] "The metrical historian Hardyng twice employed but without explaining the appellation *stone Hengels*, 'which called is the Stone Hengles certayne'. This reads like *lapides Anglorum* or *lapides Angelorum*."— Herbert, A., *Cyclops Christianus*, p. 165.

[3] "Who would ween, in this worlds realm, that Hengest thought to deceive the king who had his daughter. For there is never any man, that men may not over-reach with treachery. They took an appointed day, that these people should come together with concord and with peace, in a plain

that Stonehenge was known as Sta*hengues* or *Estanges*, a plural form which may be connoted with Hengesdun or Hengston Hill in Cornwall: Stonehenge also appears under the form Senhange, which may have meant either *Old Ange* or *San Ange*, and as the priests of ancient cults almost invariably assumed the character and titles of their divinity it is probable that the Druids were once known as *Anges*. In Irish the word *aonge* is said to have meant

that was pleasant beside Ambresbury; the place was *Aelenge*; now hight it Stonehenge. There Hengest the traitor, either by word or by writ, made known to the king; that he would come with his forces, in honour of the king; but he would not bring in retinue but three hundred knights, the wisest men of all that he might find. And the king should bring as many on his side bold thanes, and who should be wisest of all that dwelt in Britain, with their good vestments, all without weapons, that no evil, should happen to them, through confidence of the weapons. Thus they it spake, and eft they it brake; for Hengest the traitor thus gan he teach his comrades, that each should take a long saex (knife), and lay be his shank, within his hose, where he it might hide. When they came together, the Saxons and Britons, then quoth Hengest, most deceitful of all knights: 'Hail be thou, lord king, each is to thee thy subject! If ever any of thy men hath weapon by his side, send it with friendship far from ourselves, and be we in amity, and speak we of concord; how we may with peace our lives live.' Thus the wicked man spake there to the Britons. Then answered Vortiger—here he was too unwary—' If here is any knight so wild, that hath weapon by his side, he shall lose the hand through his own brand, unless he soon send it hence'. Their weapons they sent away, then had they nought in hand; knights went upward, knights went downward, each spake with other as if he were his brother.

"When the Britons were mingled with the Saxons, then called Hengest of knights most treacherous: 'Take your saexes, my good warriors, and bravely bestir you and spare ye none!' Noble Britons were there, but they knew not of the speech, what the Saxish men said them between. They drew out the saexes, all aside; they smote on the right side, they smote on the left side; before and behind they laid them to the ground; all they slew that they came nigh; of the king's men there fell four hundred and five, woe was the king alive!"—Layamon, *Brut*.

magician or *sorcerer*, which is precisely the character assigned by popular opinion to the Druids. In *Rode hengenne*, another title of Stonehenge,[1] we have apparently the older plural hen*gen* with the adjectival *rood* or *ruddy*, whence Stonehenge would seem to have been a shrine of the Red Rood Anges.

FIG. 335.—Stonehenge. From *The Celtic Druids* (Higgens, G.).

As this monument was without doubt a national centre it is probable that as I have elsewhere suggested Stonehenge meant also the *Stone Hinge:* the word *cardinal* means radically hinge; the original Roman cardinals whose round red hats probably typified the ruddy sun, were the priests of Janus, who was entitled the Hinge, and there is no reason to suppose that the same idea was not equally current in England.

[1] *Cf.* Herbert, A., *Cyclops Christianias*, p. 163.

That the people of CARDIA associated their *angel* or *ange* with *cardo*, a *hinge* or *angle* is manifest from the coin illustrated in Fig. 336.

According to Prof. Weekley, "*Ing*, the name of a demigod, seems to have been early confused with the Christian *angel* in the prefix *Engel* common in German names, *e.g.*, Engelhardt anglicised as *Engleheart*. In Anglo-Saxon we find both *Ing* and *Ingel*. The modern name Ingoll represents Ingweald (Ingold) and *Inglett* is a diminutive of similar origin. The cheerful *Inglebright* is from Inglebeort. The simple *Ing* has given through Norse Ingwar the Scottish *Ivor*." [1] But is it not possible that Ivor never came through Ingwar, but was radically a synonym—*fairy* = *Ing*, or *fire* = *ingle*? Inga is a Scandinavian maiden-name, and if the Inge family—of gloomy repute—are unable to trace any cheerier origin it may be suggested that they came from the Isle of Man where the folk claim to be the descendants of fairies or anges: "The Manks confidently assert that the first inhabitants of their island were fairies, and that these little people have still their residence amongst them. They call them the 'Good people,' and say they live in wilds and forests, and mountains, and shun great cities because of the wickedness acted therein." [2]

As there is no known etymology for *inch* and *ounce* it is not improbable that these diminutive measures were connected with the popular idea of the *ange's* size and weight: Queen Mab, according to Shakespeare, was "no bigger than an agate stone on the forefinger of an alderman," and she weighed certainly not more than an ounce. The origin of

---

[1] *Surnames*, p. 31.
[2] *Cf.* Hazlitt, W. Carew, *Faith and Folklore*, ii., 389.

Queen Mab is supposedly Habundia, or La Dame Abonde, discussed in a preceding chapter, and there connoted with Eubonia, Hobany, and Hob: in Welsh Mab means *baby boy*, and the priests of this little king were known as the Mabinogi, whence the *Mabinogion*, or books of the Mabinogi.

Whether there is any reason to connect the three places in Ireland entitled Inchequin with the *Ange Queen*, or the Inchlaw (a hill in Fifeshire) with the Inch Queen Mab I have had no opportunity of inquiring.

The surnames Inch, Ince, and Ennis, are all usually connoted with *enys* or *ins*, the Celtic and evidently more primitive form of *ins*ula, an island, *ea* or *Eye*.

The Inge family may possibly have come from the Channel Islands or *insulæ*, where as we have seen the Ange Queen, presumably the Lady of the Isles or *inces*, was represented on the coinage, and the Lord of the Channel Isles seems to have been Pixtil or *Pixy tall*. That this *Pixy tall* was alternatively *ange tall* is possibly implied by the name Anchetil, borne by the Vicomte du Bessin who owned one of the two fiefs into which Guernsey was anciently divided. It will be remembered that in the ceremony of the Chevauchee de St. Michel, *eleven* Vavasseurs functioned in the festival; further, that the lance-bearer carried a wand $11\frac{1}{4}$ feet long. The Welsh form of the name *Michael* is *Mihangel*, and as Michael was the Leader of all angels, the *mi* of this British mihangel may be equated with the Irish *mo* which, as previously noted, meant *greatest*.

As Albion or *albi en*, is the equivalent to Elphin or *elven*, it is obvious that England—or *Inghilterra*, as some nations term it—is a synonym for Albion, in both cases the meaning being Land of the Elves or Angels. For some reason—possibly the Masonic idea of the right angle, rectitude, and square dealing—*angle* was connected with *angel*, and in the coin here illustrated the angel has her head fixed in a photographic pose by an angle. In Germany and Scandinavia, Engelland means the mystic land of unborn souls, and that the Angles who inhabited the banks of the *Elbe* (Latin *Alva*) believed not only in the existence of this spiritual Engelland, but also in the living existence of Alps, Elves, Anges, or Angels is a well-recognised fact. The Scandinavians traced their origin to a primal pair named Lif and Lifthraser: according to Rydberg it was the creed of the Teuton that on arriving with a good record at "the green worlds of the gods"; "Here he finds not only those with whom he became personally acquainted while on earth, but he may also visit and converse with ancestors from the beginning of time, and he may hear the history of his race, nay, the history of all past generations told by persons who were eye-witnesses".[1] The fate of the evil-living Teuton was believed to be far different, nevertheless, in sharp distinction to the Christian doctrine that all unbaptised children are lost souls, and that infants scarce a span in size might be seen crawling on the fiery floor of hell, even the "dull and creeping Saxon" held that every one who died in tender years was received into the care of a Being friendly to the young, who introduced them into the happy groves of immortality.

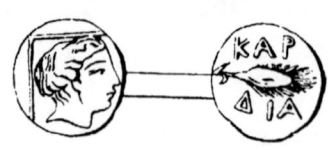

Fig. 336.—Greek. From Barthelemy.

The suggestion that the land of the Angels derived its

[1] *Teutonic Mythology*, Rydberg, p. 360.

title from the angelic superstitions of the inhabitants, may be connoted with seemingly a parallel case in Sweden, *i.e.*, the province of Elfland. According to Walter Scott this district "had probably its name from some remnant of ancient superstition":[1] during the witch-finding mania of the sixteenth century at one village alone in Elfland, upwards of 300 children "were found more or less perfect

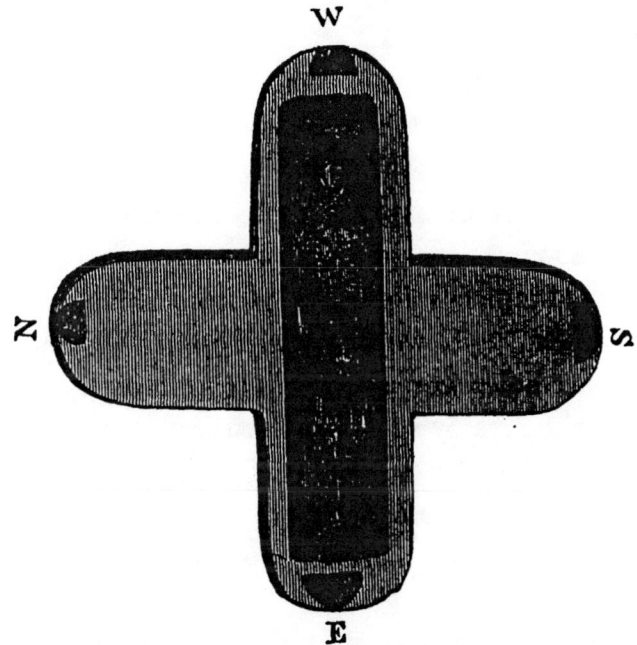

Fig. 337.—From *Essays on Archæological Subjects* (Wright, T.).

in a tale as full of impossible absurdities as ever was told round a nursery fire". Fifteen of these hapless little visionaries were led to death, and thirty-six were lashed weekly at the church doors for a whole year: an unprofitable "conspiracy" for the poor little "plotters"!

There figures in Teutonic mythology not only Lif the first parent, but also a divinity named Alf who is described

[1] *Demonology*, 177.

as young, but of a fine exterior, and of such remarkably white splendour that rays of light seemed to issue from his silvery locks. Whether the Anglo-Saxons, like the Germans, attributed any significance to *eleven* I do not know: if they did not the grave here illustrated which was found in the white chalk of Adisham, Kent, must be assigned to some other race. It is described by its excavator as follows: "The grave which was cut very neatly out of the rock chalk was full 5 feet deep; it was of the exact shape of a cross whose legs pointed very minutely to the four cardinal points of the compass; and *it was every way eleven feet long* and about 4 feet broad. At each extremity was a little cover or arched hole each about 12 inches broad, and about 14 inches high, all very neatly cut like so many little fireplaces for about a foot beyond the grave into the chalk."[1] It would seem possible that these crescentic corner holes were actually ingle nooks, and one may surmise a primitive lying-in-state with corner fires in lieu of candles. As the Saxons of the fifth and sixth centuries were notoriously in need of conversion to the Cross it is difficult to assign this crucial sepulchre to any of their tribes.

Whether Albion was ever known as Inghilterra or Ingland before the advent of the Angles from the Elbe need not be here discussed, but, at any rate, it seems highly unlikely that Anglesea, the sanctuary or Holyhead of British Druidism, derived its name from Teutonic invaders who can hardly have penetrated into that remote corner for long after their first friendly arrival. At the end of the second century Tertullian made the surprising and very puzzling statement: "Places in Britain hitherto un-

---

[1] *Cf.* Wright, T., *Essays on Archæological Subjects*, i., 120.

x.] HAPPY ENGLAND 561

visited by the Romans were subjected to Christianity ": [1] that the cross was not introduced by the Romans is obvious from the apparition of this emblem on our coinage one to two hundred years before the Roman invasion; the famous megalithic monument at Lewis in the Hebrides is cruciform, and the equally famed pyramid at New Grange is tunnelled in the form of a cross.

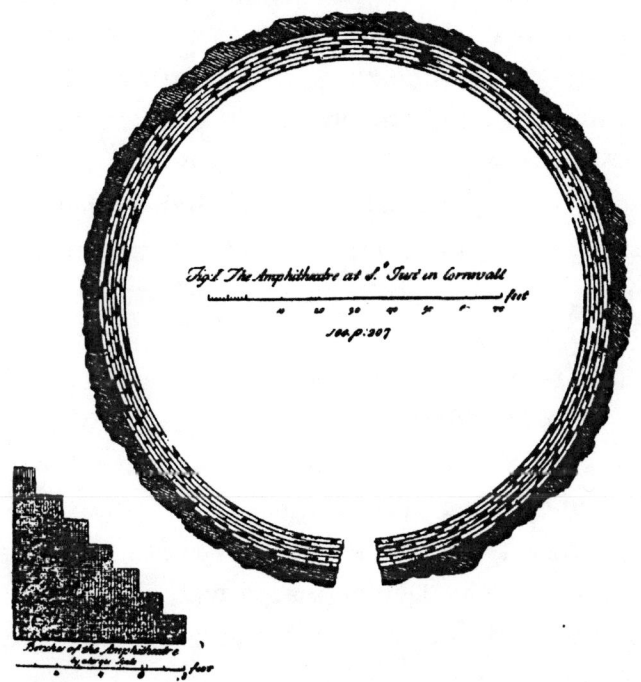

FIG. 338.—*Plan an Guare*, St. Just. From *Cornwall* (Borlase).

According to Pownal, New Grange was constructed by the Magi "or *Gaurs* as they were sometimes called": [2] Stonehenge or Stonehengels is referred to by the British Bards as Choir *Gawr*, a term which is of questioned origin: the largest stone circle in Ireland is that by Lough

---

[1] Davies, D., *The Ancient Celtic Church of Wales*, p. 14.
[2] *Cf. Sketches of Irish History*, anon., Dublin, 1844.

Gur ; the amphitheatre at St. Just is known as Plan an Guare or *Plain of Guare,* and the place-name *Gor*hambury or Verulam, where are the remains of a very perfect amphitheatre, suggests that this circle, as also that at Lough Gur, and Choir Gawr, was, like Bangor, a home, seat, or Gorsedd of the Gaurs or Aonges. Doubtless the *gaurs* of Britain like the *guru* or holy men of India, and the *augurs* of Rome, indulged in augury: in Hebrew *gor* means a congregation, and that the ancients congregated in and around stone circles choiring, and gyrating in a *gyre* or wheel, is evident from the statement of Diodorus Siculus, which is now very generally accepted as referring to Stonehenge or Choir Gawr. "The inhabitants [of Hyperborea] are great worshippers of Apollo to whom they sing many many hymns. To this god they have consecrated a large territory in the midst of which they have a magnificent round temple replenished with the richest offerings. Their very city is dedicated to him, and is full of musicians and players on various instruments who every day celebrate his benefits and perfections."

Among the superstitions of the British was the idyll that the music of the Druids' harps wafted the soul of the deceased into heaven: these harps were constructed with the same mysterious regard to the number three as characterised the whole of the magic or Druidic philosophy: the British harp was triangular, its strings were three, and its tuning keys were three-armed: it was thus essentially a harp of Tara. That the British were most admirable songsters and musicians is vouched for in numerous directions, and that Stonehenge was the Hinge of the national religion is evident from the fact that it is mentioned in a Welsh Triad as one of the "Three Great *Cors* of Britain in which there were 2400 saints, that is, there were 100 for every hour of the day and night, in rotation perpetuating the praise of God without intermission".[1] That similar *choirs* existed among the *gaurs* of ancient Ireland would appear from an incident recorded in the life of St. Columba: the popularity of this saint was, we are told, so great, even among the pagan Magi, that 1200 poets who were in Convention brought with them a poem in his praise: they sang this panegyric with music and chorus, " and a surpassing music it was"; indeed, so impressive was the effect that the saint felt a sudden emotion of complacency and gave way to temporary vanity.

The circle of St. Just was not only known as *Plan an guare*, but also as *Guirimir*, which has been assumed to be a contraction of *Guiri mirkl*, signifying in Cornish a *mirkl* or *miracle* play.[2] Doubtless not only Miracle Plays, but sports and interludes of every description were centred in the circles: that the Druids were competent and attractive entertainers is probable in view of the fact that the Arch Druid of Tara is shown as a leaping juggler with golden ear-clasps, and a speckled coat: he tosses swords and balls into the air " and like the buzzing of bees on a beautiful day is the motion of each passing the other".[3]

The circles were similarly the sites of athletic sports, duels, and other " martial challenges": the prize fight of yesterday was fought in a ring, and the ring still retains its popular hold. The Celts customarily banquetted in a circle with the most valiant chieftain occupying the post of honour in the centre.

[1] *Cf.* Gordon, E. O., *Prehistoric London, its Mounds and Circles*, p. 67.
[2] Borlase, *Cornwall*, p. 208.
[3] *Cf.* Bonwick, J., *Irish Druids*, p. 11.

We know from Cæsar that the Gauls who were "extremely devoted to superstitious rites," sent their young men to Britain for instruction in Druidic philosophy: we also know that it was customary when a war was declared to vow all captured treasures to the gods: "In many states you may see piles of these things heaped up in their consecrated spots, nor does it often happen that anyone disregarding the sanctity of the case dares either to secrete in his house things captured or take away those deposited: and the most severe punishment with torture has been established for such a deed".[1] As British customs "did not differ much" from those of Gaul it is thus almost a certainty that Stonehenge was for long periods a vast national treasure-house and Valhalla.

Notwithstanding the abundance of barrows, earthworks, and other evidences of prehistoric population it is probable that Salisbury Plain was always a green spot, and we are safe in assuming that Choir Gawr was the seat of Gorsedds. By immemorial law and custom the Gorsedd had always to be held on a green spot, in a conspicuous place in full view and hearing of country and aristocracy, in the face of the sun, the Eye of Light, and under the expansive freedom of the sky that all might see and hear. As *sedum* is the Latin for *seat*, and there seems to be some uncertainty as to what the term Gorsedd really meant, I may be permitted to throw out the suggestion that it was a Session, Seat, or Sitting of the Gaurs or Augurs: by Matthew Arnold the British Gorsedd is described as the "oldest educational institution in Europe," and moreover as an institution not known out of Britain.

Slightly over a mile from Stonehenge or Choir Gawr is

[1] *De Bello Gallico*, VI., x., 17.

the nearest village now known as Amesbury, originally written Ambrosbury or Ambresbury: here was the meeting-place of Synods even in historic times, and here was a monastery which is believed to have taken its name from Ambrosius Aurelius, a British chief. It is more probable that the monastery and the town were alike dedicated to the "Saint" Ambrose, particulars of whose life may be found in De Voragine's *Golden Legend*. According to this authority the name Ambrose may be said "of *ambor* in Greek which is to say as father of light, and *soir* that is a little child, that is a father of many sons by spiritual generations, clear and full of light". Or, says De Voragine, "Ambrose is said of a stone named *ambra* which is much sweet, oderant, and precious, and also it is much precious in the church". That amber was likewise precious in the eyes of the heathen is obvious from its frequent presence in prehistoric tombs, and from the vast estimation in which it was held by the Druids. Not only was the golden amber esteemed as an emblem of the golden sun, but its magical magnetic properties caused it to be valued by the ancients as even more precious than gold. There was also a poetic notion connecting amber and Apollo, thus expressed by a Greek poet:—

> The Celtic sages a tradition hold
> That every drop of amber was a tear
> Shed by Apollo when he fled from heaven
> For sorely did he weep and sorrowing passed
> Through many a doleful region till he reached
> The sacred Hyperboreans.[1]

It will be remembered that Salisbury Plain was sometimes known as Ellendown, with which name may be

---

[1] Quoted by Bryant from *Appollon Argonaut*, L. 4, V. 611.

connoted the statement of Pausanias that Olen the Hyperborean was the first prophet of Delphi.[1]

On turning to *The Golden Legend* we seem to get a memory of the Tears of Apollo in the statement that St. Ambrose was of such great compassion " that when any confessed to him his sin he wept so bitterly that he would make the sinner to weep". The sympathies of St. Ambrose, and his astonishing tendency to dissolve into tears, are again emphasised by the statement that he wept sore even when he heard of the demise of any bishop, "and when it was demanded of him why he wept for the death of good men for he ought better to make joy, because they went to Heaven," Ambrose made answer that he shed tears because it was so difficult to find any man to do well in such offices. The legend continues, "He was of so great stedfastness and so established in his purpose that he would not leave for dread nor for grief that might be done to him". In connection with this proverbial *constancy* it may be noted that at the village of *Constantine* there is a Longstone—the largest in Cornwall—measuring 20 feet high and known as Maen Amber, or the Amber Stone: this was apparently known also as Men *Perhen*, and was broken up into gateposts in 1764. In the same parish is a shaped stone which Borlase describes as "like the Greek letter omega, somewhat resembling a cap": from the illustration furnished by Borlase it is evident that this monument is a *knob* very carefully modelled and the measurements recorded, 30 feet in girth, *eleven* feet high,[2] imply that it was imminently an Elphinstone, Perhenstone, or Bryanstone. With this constantly

---

[1] *Cf.* Wilkes, Anna, *Ireland, Ur of the Chaldees*, p. 88.
[2] Borlase, *Antiquities of Cornwall*, p. 173.

recurrent combination of 30 and 11 feet, may here be connoted the measurements of the walls of Richborough or Rutupiæ: according to the locally-published *Short Account* " the north wall is the most perfect of the three that remain, 10 feet 8 inches in thickness and nearly 30 feet in height; the winding courses of tiles to the outer facing are in nearly their original state ".[1] The winding courses here mentioned consists of five rows of a red brick, and if one allows for inevitable *detritus* the original measurements of the quadrangle walls may reasonably be assumed as having been 30 × 11 feet: the solid mass of masonry upon which Rutupiæ's cross is superimposed reaches "downward about 30 feet from the surface". Four or five hundred yards from the castle and upon the very summit of the hill are the remains of an amphitheatre in the form of an egg measuring 200 × 160 feet. To this, the first *walled* amphitheatre discovered in the country, there were three entrances upon inclined planes, North, South, and West.

The first miracle recorded of St. Ambrose is to the effect that when an infant lying in the cradle a swarm of bees descended on his mouth; then they departed and flew up in the air so high that they might not be seen. Greek mythology relates that the infant Zeus was fed by bees in his cradle upon Mount Ida, and a variant of the same fairy-tale represents Zeus as feeding daily in Ambrosia—

> The blessed Gods those rocks Erratic call.
> Birds cannot pass them safe, no, not the doves
> Which his ambrosia bear to Father Jove.[2]

Ambrosia, the fabled food of the gods, appears to have been honey: it is said that the Amber stones were anointed with Ambrosia, hence it is significant to find in immediate

---

[1] p. 6.   [2] *Odyssey*, XII.

proximity to each other the place-names Honeycrock and Amberstone in Sussex. The Russians have an extraordinary idea that Ambrosia emanated from horses' heads,[1] and as there is a "Horse Eye Level" closely adjacent to the Sussex Honeycrock and Amberstone we may assume that the neighbouring Hailsham, supposed to mean "Home of Aela or Eile," was originally an Ellie or Elphin Home. Layamon refers to Stonehenge, "a plain that was pleasant besides Ambresbury," as Aelenge, which probably meant Ellie or Elphin meadow, for *ing* or *inge* was a synonym for meadow. The correct assumption may possibly be that all flowery meads were the recognised haunts of the anges or ingles: the fairy rings are usually found in meadows, and the poets feigned Proserpine in a meadow gathering flowers ere she was ravished below by Pluto: as late as 1788 an English poet expressed the current belief, "'Tis said the fairy people meet beneath the bracken shade on *mead* and hill".

Across the Sussex mead known as Horse Eye Level runs a "Snapsons Drove": Snap is a curious parental name and is here perhaps connected with Snave, a Kentish village, presumably associated with *San Aphe* or *San Ap*.[2] Not only was the hipha or hobby horse decorated with a knop or knob, but a radical feature of its performance seems to have been movable jaws with which by means of a string the actor snapped at all and sundry: were these snappers, I wonder, the origin of the Snapes and Snapsons? In view of the fact that the surname Leaper is authoritatively connoted with an entry in a fifteenth century account-

---

[1] Johnson, W., *Byways*, p. 440.

[2] As all our *Avons* are traced to Sanscrit *ap*, meaning water, one may here note the Old English word *snape*, meaning *a spring* in arable ground.

book: "To one that *leped* at Chestre 6s. 8d.," the suggestion may possibly be worth consideration.

In Sussex there are two Ambershams and an Amberley: in Hants is Amberwood. St. Ambrose is recorded to have been born in Rome, whence it is probable that he was the ancient divinity of *Umbria:* in Derbyshire there is a river Amber, and in Yorkshire a Humber, which the authorities regard as probably an aspirated form of *cumber*, "confluence". The magnetic properties of *amber*, which certainly cause a *humber* or confluence, may have originated this meaning; in any case *cumber* and *umber* are radically the same word. Probably Humberstones and Amberstones will be found on further inquiry to be as plentiful as Prestons or Peri stones: there is a Humberstone in Lincolnshire, another at Leicester, near Bicester is Ambrosden, and at Epping Forest is Ambresbury. This Epping Ambresbury, known alternatively as Ambers' Banks, is admittedly a British *oppidum:* the remains cover 12 acres of ground and are situated on the highest plateau in the forest. As there is an Ambergate near *Bux*ton it is noteworthy that Ambers' Banks in Epping are adjacent to Beak Hill, Buckhurst Hill, and High Beech Green. I have already connoted Puck or Bogie with the beech tree, and it is probable that Fairmead Plain by High Beech Green was the Fairy mead where once the pixies gathered: close by is Bury Wood, and there is no doubt the neighbourhood of Epping and Upton was always very British.

In old English *amber* or *omber* meant a pitcher—query a honey-crock[1]—whence the authorities translate the

---

[1] In the mediæval *Story of Asenath*, the Angel who describes himself as "Prince of the House of God and Captain of His Host," and was thus presumably Michael, says to Asenath: "Look within thine *Aumbrey*, and

570   ARCHAIC ENGLAND   [CHAP.

various Amberleys as *meadow of the pitcher*, and Ambergate, near Buxton, as "probably pitcher road". The Amber Hill near Boston, we are told, "will be from Old English *amber* from its shape," but as it is extremely unusual to find hills in the form of a pitcher this etymology seems questionable. At the Wiltshire Ambresbury there is a Mount Ambrosius at the foot of which, according to local tradition, used to exist a college of Druidesses,[1] in which connection it is noteworthy that just as Silbury Hill is distant about a mile from the Avebury Circle, so Mount Ambrosius is equally distant from Choir Gawr.

FIG. 339.—A Persian King, adorned with a Pyramidal Flamboyant Nimbus. Persian Manuscript, Bibliothèque Royale. From *Christian Iconography* (Didron).

To Amber may be assigned the words *umpire* and *empire;* Oberon, the lovely child, is haply described as the *Emperor* of Fairyland, whence also no doubt he was the lord and master of the *Empyrean*. When dealing elsewhere with the word *amber* I suggested that it meant radically *Sun Father*,[2] and

thou shall find withal to furnish thy table". Then she hastened thereto and found "a store of Virgin honey, white as snow of sweetest savour". The archangel tells Asenath that "all whom Penitence bringeth before Him shall eat of this honey gathered by the bees of Paradise, from the dew of the roses of Heaven, and those who eat thereof shall never see death but shall live for evermore."—*Aucassin and Nicolette and other Mediæval Romances*, p. 209 (Everyman's Library).

[1] Gordon, A. O., *Prehistoric London*, p. 66.   [2] *Lost Language*, ii., 141.

there are episodes in the life of St. Ambrose which support this interpretation, *e.g.*, "it happened that an enchanter called devils to him and sent them to St. Ambrose for

Fig. 340.—The Divine Triplicity, Contained within the Unity. From a German Engraving of the XVI. Cent. From *Christian Iconography* (Didron).

to annoy and grieve him, but the devils returned and said that they might not approach to his gate because there was a great fire all about his house". Among the Persians it was customary to halo their divinities, not with a circle but with a pyre or pyramid of fire, and in all probability to the *auburn* Auberon the Emperor of the Empyrean may be assigned not only *burn* and *brand*, but also *bran* in the sense of bran new. That St. Ambrose was Barnaby Bright or the White god of day is implied by the anecdote "a fire in the manner of a shield covered his head, and entered into his mouth: then became his face as white as any snow, and anon it came again to his first form".[1] The basis of this story would seem to have been a picture representing Ambrose with fire not entering into, but *emerging from*, his mouth and forming a surrounding halo "in the manner of a shield". *Embers* now mean ashes, and the Ember Days of Christianity probably trace backward to the immemorial times of prehistoric fire-worship. At Parton, near Salisbury, one meets with the curious surname Godber: and doubtless inquiry would establish a connection between this Godber of Parton and Godfrey.

The weekly fair at Ambresbury used to be held on *Fri*day; the maid Freya, to whom Friday owes its name, was evidently *Fire Eye;* the Latin *feriæ* were the hey-days or holidays dedicated to some fairy. Fairs were held customarily on the festival of the local saint, frequently even to-day within ancient earthworks: the most famous Midsummer Fair used to be that held at *Barnwell:* Feronia, the ancient Italian divinity at whose festival a great fair was held, and the first-fruits of the field offered, is, as has been shown, equivalent to Beronia or Oberon.

According to Borlase there is in Anglesea "a horse-shoe 22 paces in diameter called Brangwyn or Supreme court; it lies in a place called Tre'r Drew or Druids' Town".[2] Stonehenge consists of a circle enclosing a horse-shoe or

---

[1] *Golden Legend*, iii., 117. [2] *Cornwall*, p. 207.

x.] HAPPY ENGLAND 573

hoof—the footprint and sign of Hipha the White Mare, or Ephialtes the Night Mare, and a variant of this idea is expressed in the circle enclosing a triangle as exhibited

Fig. 341.—God, Beardless, either the Son or the Father. French Miniature of the XI. Cent. From *Christian Iconography* (Didron).

in the Christian emblem on p. 571. That Christianity did not always conceive the All Father as the Ancient of Days is evident from Fig. 341, where the central Power is de-

Fig. 342.—British. From Evans.

picted within the *writhings* of what is seemingly an acanthus *wreath:* the CUNOB fairy on the British coin illustrated *ante*, page 528, is extending what is either a ball of fire or else a wreath. The word *wraith*, meaning apparition, is connoted by Skeat with an Icelandic term meaning " a pile of stones to warn a wayfarer," hence this *heap* may be connoted with *rath* the Irish, and *rhaith* the Welsh, for a fairy dun or hill. Skeat further connotes *wraith* with the Norwegian word *vardyvle*, meaning " a guardian or attendant spirit seen to follow or precede one," and he suggests that *vardyvle* meant *ward evil*. Certainly the *wraiths* who haunted the raths were supposed to ward off evil, and the giant Wreath,[1] who was popularly associated with Port*reath* near *Redruth*, was in all probability the same *wraith* that originated the place-name Cape Wrath. In Welsh a speech is called *ar raith* or on the mound, hence we may link *rh*etoric to this idea, and assume that the raths were the seats of public eloquence as we know they were.

As wreath means a circle it is no doubt the same word as *rota*, a wheel, and Rodehengenne or Stonehengels may have meant the Wheel Angels. The cruciform *rath*, illustrated *ante*, page 55, is pre-eminently a *rota*, and in Fig. 343 Christ is represented in a circle supported by four somewhat unaerial Evangelists or Angels.

Mount Ida in Phrygia was the reputed seat of the *Dactyli*, a word which means *fingers*, and these mysterious Powers were sometimes identified with the Cabiri. The Dactyli, or *fingers*, are described as fabulous beings to whom the discovery of iron and the art of working it by means of fire was ascribed, and as the philosophy of Phairie is always grounded upon some childishly simple basis, it is probable that the Elphin eleven in its elementary sense represented the ten fingers controlled by Emperor Brain.

[1] Hunt, J., *Popular Romances of the West of England*, p. 76.

The digits are magic little workmen who level mountains and rear palaces at the bidding of their lord and master Brain: the word *digit*, French *doight*, is in fact *Good god*, and *dactyli* is the same word plus a final *yli*.

In *Folklore as an Historical Science* Sir Laurence Gomme lays some stress upon a tale which is common alike to Britain and Brittany, and is therefore supposed to be of earlier date than the separation of Britons and

Fig. 343.—Christ with a Plain Nimbus, Ascending to Heaven in a Circular Aureole. Carving in Wood of the XIV. Cent. From Evans.

Bretons. This tale which centres at London, is to the effect that a countryman once upon a time dreamed there was a priceless treasure hidden at London Bridge: he therefore started on a quest to London where on arrival he was observed loitering and was interrogated by a bystander. On learning the purpose of his trip the Cockney laughed heartily at such simplicity, and jestingly related how he himself had also dreamed a dream to the effect that there was treasure buried in the countryman's own village. On his return home the rustic, thinking the matter over, decided to dig where the cockney had facetiously indicated, whereupon to his astonishment he actually found a pot containing treasure. On the first pot unearthed was an inscription reading—

> Look lower, where this stood
> Is another twice as good.

Encouraged he dug again, whereupon to his greater astonishment he found a second pot bearing the same inscription: again he dug and found a third pot even yet more valuable. This fabulously ancient tale is notably identified with Upsall in Yorkshire; it is, we are told, " a constant tradition of the neighbourhood, and the identical bush yet exists (or did in 1860) beneath which the treasure was found; a *bur*tree or elder ".[1] Upsall was originally written Upeshale and Hupsale (primarily Ap's Hall ?) and the idea is a happy one, for in mythology it is undeniably true that the deeper one delves the richer proves the treasure trove. In suggesting that eleven may have been the number of the ten digits guided and controlled by the Brain one may thus not only remark the injunction to the Jews : " Thou shalt make curtains of goatshair to be a covering upon the tabernacle : *eleven* curtains shalt thou make,"[2] but one may note also the probable elucidation of this Hebrew symbolism :—

> Shall any gazer see with mortal eyes
> Or any searcher know by mortal mind :
> Veil after veil will lift, but there must be
> Veil upon veil behind.[3]

Assuming that in the simplest sense the elphin eleven were the ten digits and the Brain, one may compare with

---

[1] P. 20. [2] Exod. xxvi. 7. [3] Arnold, E., *Light of Asia*.

this combination the ten Powers or qualities which according to the Cabala emanated from "The Most Ancient One". "He has given existence to all things. He made ten lights spring forth from His midst, lights which shone with the forms which they had borrowed from Him and which shed everywhere the light of a brilliant day. The Ancient One, the most Hidden of the hidden, is a high beacon, and we know Him only by His lights which illuminate our eyes so abundantly. His Holy Name is no other thing than these lights."[1]

According to *The Golden Legend* the Emperor of Constantinople applied to St. Ambrose to receive the sacred mysteries, and that Ambrose was Vera or Truth is hinted by the testimony of the Emperor. "I have found a man of *truth*, my master Ambrose, and such a man ought to be a bishop." The word *bishop*, Anglo-Saxon *biscop*, supposed to mean *overseer*, is like the Greek *episcopus*, radically *op*, an *eye*.[2] Egyptian archæologists tell us that in Egypt the Coptic Land of the Great Optic, even the very games had a religious significance ; whence there was probably some ethical idea behind the British "jingling match by eleven blind-folded men and one unmasked and hung with bells". This joyous and diverting *jeu* is mentioned as part of the sports-programme at the celebrated Scouring of the White Horse: we have already noted the blind-folded Little Leaf Man, led blind Amor-like from house to house, also the *Blind* Man who is said to have sat for *eleven* years in the

[1] *Cf.* Abelson, J., *Jewish Mysticism*, p. 137.
[2] The Bryan of popular ballad seems to have been famed for the casting of his glad eye :—

" Bryan he was tall and strong
Right blithsome rolled his een."
—*Percy Reliques*, i., 276.

578   ARCHAIC ENGLAND   [CHAP.

Church of St. Maur (or Amour?), and among other sports at the Scouring, eleven enters again into an account of chasing the fore wheel of a wagon down the hill slope. The trundling of a fiery wheel—which doubtless took place at the several British Trendle Hills—is a well-known feature of European solar ceremonies: the greater interest of the Scouring item is perhaps in the number of competitors: "*eleven* on 'em started and amongst 'em a sweep-chimley and a millard [milord], and the millard tripped up the sweep-chimley and made the zoot fly a good 'un—the wheel ran pretty nigh down to the springs that time".[1]

FIGS. 344 and 345.—British. From Akerman and Evans.

The Jewish conception of The Most Ancient One, the most Hidden of the hidden, reappears in Jupiter Ammon, whose sobriquet of Ammon meant *the hidden one*: "Verily, Thou art a God that hidest Thyself". In England the game of *Hide and Seek* used to be known as *Hooper's Hide*,[2] and this curious connection between Jupiter, the Hidden one, and *Hooper's Hide* somewhat strengthens my earlier surmise that Hooper = Iupiter.

In the opinion of Sir John Evans "there can be little doubt" of the head upon the obverse of Fig. 344 being intended for Jupiter Ammon;[3] in Cornish Blind Man's Hide and Seek, the players used to shout "Vesey, vasey vum: *Buckaboo* has come!"[4]

[1] Hughes, T., *Scouring the White Horse*, p. 110.
[2] Taylor, J., *The Devil's Pulpit*, ii., 297.   [3] P. 344.
[4] Courtney, Miss M. L., *Cornish Feasts and Folklore*, p. 175.

If as now suggested the wheel and the "spindle whorl" were alike symbols of the Eye of Heaven, it is equally probable that the amber, and many other variety of bead, was also a talismanic eyeball:[1] among grave deposits the blue bead was very popular, assumedly for the reason that blue was the colour of heaven. Large quantities of blue "whorls" were discovered by Schliemann[2] at Mykenæ, and among the many varieties of beads found in Britain one in particular is described as "of a Prussian Blue colour

FIG. 346.—Glass Beads, England and Ireland. From *A Guide to the Antiquities of the Early Iron Age* (B.M.).

with three circular grooves round the circumference, filled with white paste".[3] This design of three circles reappears in Fig. 347 taken from the base of a British Incense-cup; likewise in a group of rock sculpturings (Fig. 348) found at Kirkmabreck in Kirkcudbrightshire. Mr. Ludovic Mann, who sees traces of astronomical intention in this sculpture, writes: "If the pre-historic peoples of Scotland and indeed Europe had this conception, then the Universe to their mind would consist of eleven units, namely, the

---

[1] Among the Maoris potent powers were supposed to reside in the human eye. "When a warrior slew a chief, he immediately gouged out his eyes and swallowed them, the *atua tonga*, or divinity, being supposed to reside in that organ; thus he not only killed the body, but also possessed himself of the soul of his enemy, and consequently the more chiefs he slew, the greater did his divinity become."—Taylor, R., *Te Ika A Maui, or New Zealand and its Inhabitants*.

[2] *Mykenæ*, p. 77.

[3] B.M., *Guide to the Early Iron Age*, p. 107.

nine celestial bodies already referred to, and the Central Fire and the 'Counter-Earth'. Very probably they knew also of elliptical motions. Oddly enough the cult of eleven units (which I detected some fifteen years ago) representing the universe can be discerned in the art of the late Neolithic and Bronze Ages in Scotland and over a much wider area. For example, in nearly all the cases of Scottish

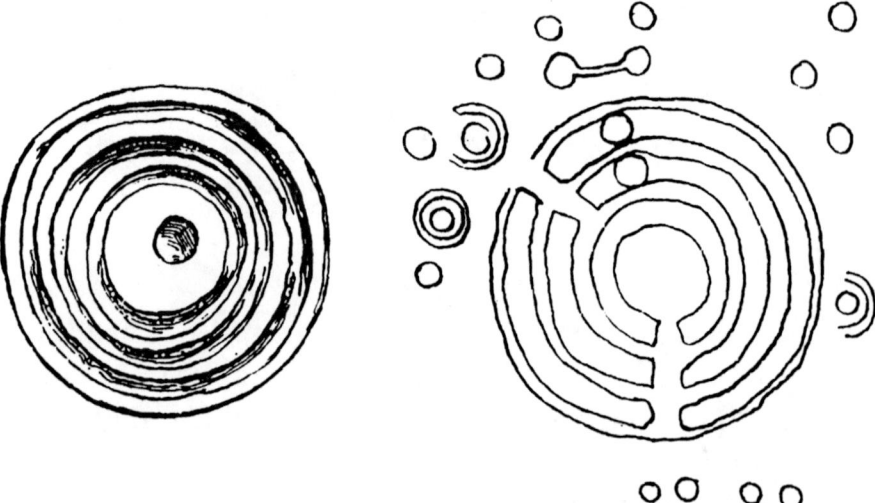

Fig. 347.—From *A Guide to the Antiquities of the Bronze Age* (B.M.).

Fig. 348.—From *Archaic Sculpturings* (L. Mann).

necklaces of beads of the Bronze Age which have survived intact, it will be found that they consist of a number of beads which is eleven or a multiple of eleven. I have, for example, a fine Bronze Age necklace from Wigtownshire consisting of 187 beads (that is of 17 × 11) and a triangular centre piece. The same curious recurrence of the number and its multiples can often be detected in the number of standing stones in a circle, in the number of stones placed in slightly converging rows found in Caithness, Sutherland, some parts of England, Wales, and in Brittany. The number eleven is occasionally involved in the Bronze Age pottery decorations, and in the patterns on certain ornaments and relics of the Bronze Age. . . . The Cult of eleven seems to survive in the numerous names of Allah, who was known by ninety-nine names, and hence it is invariably the case that the Mahommedan has a necklace consisting of either eleven or a multiple of eleven beads but not exceeding ninety-nine, as he is supposed to repeat one of the names for each bead which he tells."[1]

We have seen that the *rudraksha* or eye of the god S'iva seeds are usually eleven faceted, and my surmise that the whorls of Troy were universal Eyes is further implied by the group here illustrated. According to Thomas, our British Troy Towns or Caer Troiau were originally astronomical observatories, and he derives the word *troiau* from the verb *troi* to *turn*, or from *tro* signifying a *flux of time* :—[2]

> By ceaseless actions all that is subsists;
> Constant rotation of th' unwearied wheel
> That Nature rides upon, maintains her health,
> Her beauty and fertility. She dreads
> An instant's pause and lives but while she moves.

The Trojan whorls are unquestionably *tyres* or *tours*, and the notion of an eye is in some instances clearly imparted to them by radiations which resemble those of the *iris*. The wavy lines of No. 1835 and 1840 probably denote water or the spirit, in No. 1847 the "Jupiter chain" of our SOLIDO coin reappears; the astral specks on 1841 and 1844 may be connoted with the stars and planets, and in 1833 the sense of rolling or movement is clearly indicated.

[1] *Archaic Sculpturings*, p. 23.   [2] *Britannia Antiquissima*, p. 50.

582 ARCHAIC ENGLAND [CHAP.

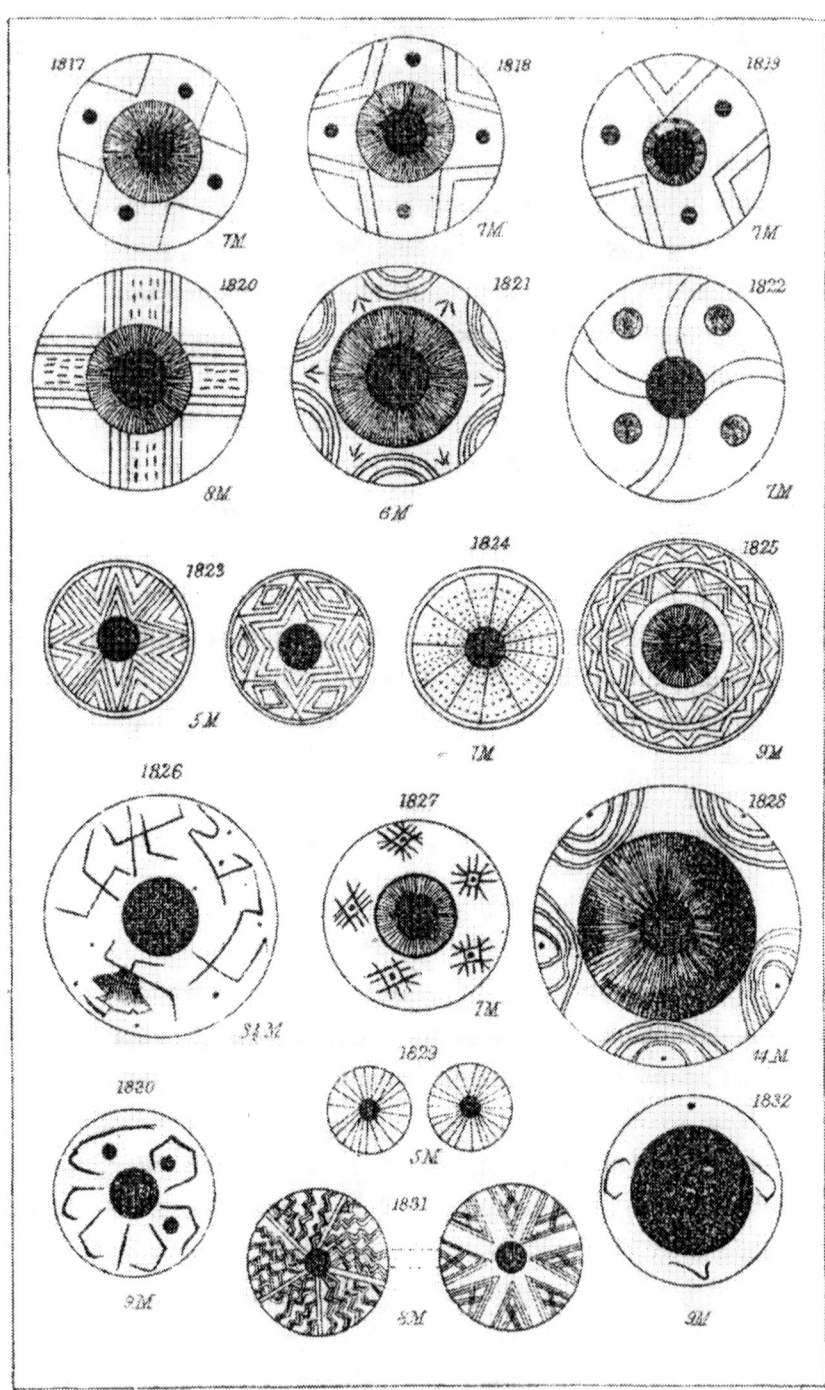

FIG. 349.—Specimen Patterns of Whorls Dug up at Troy. From *Ilios* (Schliemann).

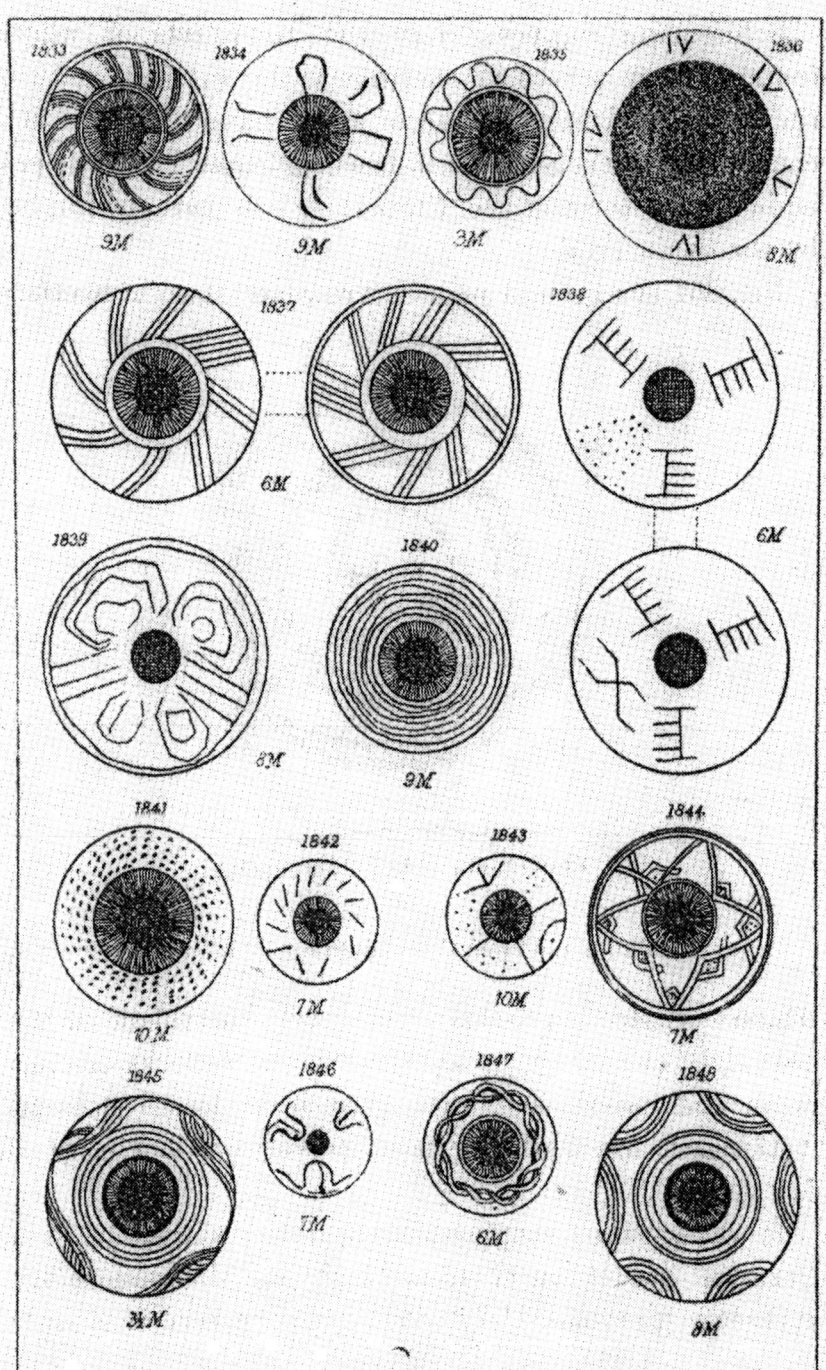

Fig. 350.—Specimen Patterns of Whorls Dug up at Troy. From *Ilios* (Schliemann).

Schliemann supposes that the thousands of whorls found in Troy served as offerings to the tutelary deity of the city, *i.e.*, Athene: some of them have the form of a cone, or of two cones base to base, and that Troy was preeminently a town of the Eternal Eye is perhaps implied by the name Troie.

Fig. 351 is a ground plan of Trowdale Mote in Scotland

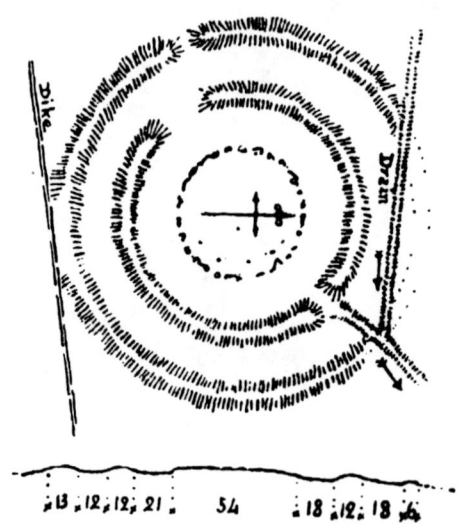

Fig. 351.—From Proceedings Soc. Ant. Scot.

which, situated on a high and lonely marshland within near sight of nothing but a few swelling hillocks amongst reeds and mosses and water, has been described as the "strangest, most solitary, most prehistoric looking of all our motes".[1]

It was popularly supposed that all the witches of West Cornwall used to meet at midnight on Midsummer Eve at Trewa (pronounced *Troway*) in the parish of Zennor,

[1] Coles, F. R., *The Motes of Kirkcudbrightshire*, p. 151.

and around the dying fires renewed their vows to the Devil, their master. In this wild Zennor (supposedly *holy land*) district is a witch's rock which if touched nine times at midnight reputedly brought good luck.

The "Troy Town" of Welsh children is the Hopscotch of our London pavements; at one time every English village seems to have possessed its maze (or Drayton ?), and that the mazes were the haunts of fairies is well known :—

> . . . the yellow skirted fays
> Fly after the night steeds
> Leaving their moon-loved maze.

In *A Midsummer-Night's Dream* Titania laments :—

> The nine men's morris is filled up with mud
> And the quaint mazes in the wanton green
> For lack of tread are indistinguishable.

At St. Martha's Church near Guildford, facing Newlands Corner are the remains of an earthwork maze close by the churchyard, and within this maze used to be held the country sports.[1] We shall consider some extraordinarily quaint mazes and Troy Towns in a subsequent chapter, but meanwhile it may here be noted that in the Scilly Islands (which the Greeks entitled Hesperides) is a monument thus described : " Close to the edge of the cliff is a curious enclosure called Troy Town, taking its name from the Troy of ancient history; the streets of ancient Troy were so constructed that an enemy, once within the gates, could not find his way out again. The enclosure has an outer circle of white pebbles placed on the turf, with an opening at one point, supposed to represent the walls and gate of Troy. Within this there are several rows of stones;

[1] Johnson, W., *Byways*, p. 195.

the spaces between them represent the streets. It presents quite a maze, and but few who enter can find their way out again without crossing one of the boundary lines. It is not known when or by whom it was constructed, but it has from time to time been restored by the islanders."[1]

This Troy Town is situated on *Camper*dizil Point; in the same neighbourhood is Carn *Himbra* Point, and *Himbrian*, *Kymbrian*, or *Cambrian* influences are seemingly much evident in this district, as doubtless they also were at Comberton[2] famous for its maze.

At the very centre, eye, or *San Troy* of St. Mary's Island is situated Holy Vale, and here also are the place-names Maypole, Burrow, and Content. It has already been suggested that Bru or Burrow was originally *pure Hu* or *pere Hu*, Hu being, as will be remembered, the traditional Leader of the Kymbri into these islands, and the first of the Three National Pillars of Britain: the chief town of St. Mary's is Hugh Town, and running through Holy Vale is what is described as a paved way (in wonderful preservation) known as the Old Roman Road, formerly supposed to be the main-way to Hugh Town. One may be allowed to question whether the Legions of Imperial Rome ever troubled to construct so fine a causeway in so insignificant an island; or if so, for what reason? The houses of Holy Vale are embowered in trees of larger growth than those elsewhere in the neighbourhood: they "complete a picture of great calm and repose," and that this Holy Vale was anciently an *abri* is fairly self-evident apart from the interesting place-name *Burrow*, and the neighbouring Bur Point.

[1] *Lyonesse, a Handbook for the Isles of Scilly*, p. 70.
[2] The Cambridgeshire Comberton is situated on the Bourn brook: there is also a Great and Little Comberton underlying Bredon Hill in the Pershore district of Worcester.

The Romans entitled the Scillies *Sillinæ Insulæ*: I have already suggested they were a seat of the Selli; we have met with Selene in connection with St. Levan's, and it is not improbable that the deity of *Sillinæ Insulæ* was Selene, Helena, or Luna. The Silus stone from the ruined chapel of St. Helen's at Helenium or Land's End (Cape Cornwall) has been already noted: the most ancient building in all the *Sillinæ Insulæ* or the Scillies is the ruined chapel on St. Helen's of which the northern aisle now measures 12 feet wide and 19 feet 6 inches long. As the Hellenes usually had ideas underlying all their measurements it is probable that the 19 feet 6 inches was primarily 19 feet, for nineteen was a highly mystic Hellenic number. Of the Hyperboreans Diodorus states: "They say, moreover, that Apollo once in nineteen years comes into the island in which space of time the stars perform their courses and return to the same points, and therefore the Greeks call the revolutions of nineteen years the Great Year". Nineteen nuns tended the sacred fire of St. Bridget, and according to some observers the inmost circle of Stonehenge consisted of nineteen "Blue Stones".[1] These nineteen Stone Hengles may be connoted with the nineteen ruined huts on the summit of Ingleborough in Yorkshire: the summit of Ingleborough is a plateau of about a mile in circuit and hereupon are "vestiges of an ancient British camp of about 15 acres inclosing traces of *nineteen* ancient *horseshoe shaped* huts".[2]

As the word *ingle*, meaning *fire*, is not found until 1508 the authorities are unable to interpret Ingleborough as meaning Fire hill, although without doubt it served as a

[1] The term "Bluestone" in the West of England meant *holy stone*.
[2] Wilson, J. G., *Imperial Gazetteer*.

Beacon: the same etymological difficulty likewise confronts them at Ingleby Cross, Inglesham, numerous Ingletons, and at Ingestre. We have seen that Inglewood was known as Englysshe Wood;[1] in Somerset is Combe English, and in the Scillies is English Island Hill: 500 yards from this English Hill is a stone circle embracing an upright stone the end of which is 18 inches square.

Fig. 352.—Stonehenge Restored. From *Our Ancient Monuments* (Kains-Jackson).

Eighteen courtiers were assigned to the *ange* Oberon: the megalith Long Meg is described as a square unhewn freestone column 15 feet in circumference by 18 feet high, and there is no doubt that eighteen or twice nine possessed at one time some significance. I suspect that the double nine stood for the Twain, each of which was reckoned as nine or True: on the top of Hellingy Downs in the Scillies

[1] On the tip-top of Highgate Hill is now standing an *Englefield* House immediately adjacent to an *Angel* Inn.

is a barrow covered with large stones *nine* feet long, and built upon a mound which is surrounded by inner and outer rows of stone.[1]

On Salakee Downs there is a monolith resting on a large flat rock, on three projections situated at a distance of *eighteen* inches from one another and each having a diameter of about 2 inches:[2] this is known as the Druid's throne, and about 5 yards to the east are two more upright rocks of similar size and shape named the Twin Sisters.[3] The Twin Sisters of Biddenden, whose name was Preston, were associated with five pieces of ground known as the Bread and Cheese Lands, in which connection it is interesting to find that near English Island Hill is Chapel *Brow*, constituting the eastern point of a deep bay known by the curious name of Bread and Cheese Cove.[4] In connection with Biddenden we connoted Pope's Hall and Bubhurst; it is thus noteworthy that near Bread and Cheese Cove is a Bab's Carn, and a large sea cavern known as Pope's Hole.

In Germany and Scandinavia the stone circles are known not as Merry Maidens, but as Adam's Dances. Close to Troy Town on St. Agnes in the Scillies are two rocks known as Adam and Eve: these are described as *nine* feet high with a space about *nine* inches between them: "Here, too, is the Nag's Head, which is the most curious rock to be met with on the islands; it has a remote resemblance to the head of a horse, and would seem to have been at one time an object of worship, being surrounded by a circle of stones".[5]

On the lower slopes of Hellingy are the remains of a

[1] *Lyonesse*, p. 41. [2] *Ibid*, p. 39. [3] *Ibid.*, p. 39.
[4] *Ibid.*, p. 79. [5] *Ibid.*, p. 73.

primitive village, and the foundations of many circular huts: among these foundations have been found a considerable quantity of crude pottery, and an ancient handmill which the authorities assign to about 2000 B.C. We have seen that the goddesses of Celtdom were known as the *Mairæ*, *Matronæ*, *Matres*, or *Matræ* (the mothers): further, that the Welsh for Mary is Fair, whence the assumption becomes pressing that the "Saint" Mary of the Scillies was primarily the Merry Fairy. The author of *The English Language* points out that in Old English *merry* meant originally no more than "agreeable, pleasing". Heaven and Jerusalem were described by old poets as "merry" places; and the word had supposedly no more than this signification in the phrase "Merry England," into which we read a more modern interpretation.[1] That the Scillies were permeated with the Fairy Faith is sufficiently obvious; at Hugh Town we find the ubiquitous Silver Street, and the neighbouring Holvear Hill was not improbably holy to Vera.

Near the Island of St. Helen's is a group of rocks marked upon the map as Golden Ball Bar; near by is an islet named Foreman. The farthest sentinel of the Scillies is an islet named the Bishop, now famous to all sea-farers for its *phare*. It is quite certain that no human Bishop would ever have selected as his residence an abode so horribly exposed, whence it is more likely that the Bishop here commemorated was the Burnebishop or Boy Bishop whose ceremonies were maintained until recent years, notably and particularly at Cambrai. In England it is curious to find the Lady-bird or Burnie Bee equated with a Bishop, yet it was so; and hence the rhyme:—

[1] P. 142.

Bishop, Bishop Burnebee, tell me when my wedding will be,
Fly to the east, fly to the west,
Fly to them that I love best.

In connection with the Island of St. *Agnes* it may be noted that *ignis* is the Latin for *fire*, whence it is possible that the islets, Big Smith and Little Smith, Burnt Island and Monglow, all had some relation to the Fieryman, Fairy Man, or Foreman : it is also possible that the neighbouring Camperdizil Point is connected with *deiseul*, the Scotch ejaculation, and with *dazzle*. Troy Town in St. Agnes is almost environed by Smith Sound, and this curious combination of names points seemingly to some connection between the Cambers and the metal smiths.[1]

It will be remembered that Agnes was a title of the Papesse Jeanne, who was said to have come from Engelheim or *Angel's Home :* in Germany the Lady Bird used to be known as the Lady Mary's Key-bearer, and exhorted to fly to Engelland : " Insect of Mary, fly away, fly away, to Engelland. Engelland is locked, its key is broken." [2] Sometimes the invocation ran : " Gold chafer up and away to thy high storey to thy Mother Anne, who gives thee *bread and cheese.* 'Tis better than bitter death." [3]

Thanks to an uncultured and tenacious love of Phairie, the keys of rural Engelland have not yet been broken, nor happily is Engelland locked. Our history books tell us of

---

[1] Writing *not* in connection with either Monglow or Camperdizil Miss Gordon observes : " We may conjure up the scene where the watery stretches reflected in molten gold the ' pillars of fire ' symbolising the presence of God ; we seem to behold the reverend forms of the white clad Druids revolving in the mystic ' Deasil ' dance from East to West around the glowing pile, and so following the course of the Sun, the image of the Deity ".— *Prehistoric London,* p. 72.

[2] Eckenstein, L., *Comp. St. Nursery Rhymes,* p. 97.   [3] P. 98.

a splendid pun[1] perpetrated by a Bishop of many centuries ago: noticing some captured English children in the market-place at Rome, he woefully exclaimed that had they been baptised then would they have been *non Angli sed angeli*. Has this episcopal pleasantry been overrated? or was the good Bishop punning unconsciously deeper than he intended?

[1] Skeat believed *pun* meant something *punched* out of shape. Is it not more probably connected with the Hebrew *pun* meaning *dubious?*

CHAPTER XI

THE FAIR MAID

"We could not blot out from English poetry its visions of the fairyland without a sense of irreparable loss. No other literature save that of Greece alone can vie with ours in its pictures of the land of fantasy and glamour, or has brought back from that mysterious realm of unfading beauty treasures of more exquisite and enduring charm."—ALFRED NUTT.

"We have already shown how long and how faithfully the Gaelic and Welsh peasants clung to their old gods in spite of all the efforts of the clerics to explain them as ancient kings, or transform them into wonder-working saints, or to ban them as demons of Hell."—CHARLES SQUIRE.

IN the preceding chapter it was shown that the number eleven was for some reason peculiarly identified with the Elven, or Elves: in Germany eleven seems to have carried a somewhat similar significance, for on the eleventh day of the eleventh month was always inaugurated the Carnival season which was celebrated by weekly festivities which increased in mirthful intensity until Shrove Tuesday.[1] Commenting upon this custom it has been pointed out that "The fates seem to have displayed a remarkable sense of artistry in decreeing that the Great War should cease at the moment when it did, for the hostilities came to an end at the 11th hour of the 11th day of the 11th month".[2]

Etymologists connect the word Fate with fay; the expression *fate* is radically *good fay*, and it is merely a matter of choice whether Fate or the Fates be regarded as

---

[1] *The Evening Standard*, 12th Nov., 1918. [2] *Ibid.*

Three or as One: moreover the aspect of Fate, whether grim or beautiful, differs invariably to the same extent as that of the two fairy mothers which Kingsley introduces into *The Water Babies,* the delicious Lady Doasyouwouldbedoneby and the forbidding Mrs. Bedonebyasyoudid.

The Greek *Moirae* or Fates were represented as either three austere maidens or as three aged hags: the Celtic *mairae*, of which Rice Holmes observes that "no deities were nearer to the hearts of Celtic peasants," were repre-

Fig. 353.—Printer's Ornament (English, 1724).

sented in groups of three; their aspect was that of gentle, serious, motherly women holding new-born infants in their hands, or bearing fruits and flowers in their laps; and many offerings were made to them by country folk in gratitude for their care of farm, and flock, and home.[1]

In the Etrurian bucket illustrated on page 474, the Magna Mater or Fate was represented with two children, one white the other black: in the emblems herewith the supporting Pair are depicted as two Amoretti, and the Central Fire, Force, or Tryamour is portrayed by three hearts blazing with the fire of Charity. There is indeed no doubt that the Three Charities, Three Graces, and Three Fates were merely presentations of the one unchanging

[1] *Ancient Britain*, p. 283.

central and everlasting Fire, Phare, or Force. Among the Latins the Moirae were termed Parcae, and seemingly all mythologies represent the Great Pyre, Phare, or Fairy as at times a Fury. In Britain Keridwen—whose name the authorities state meant *perpetual love*—appears very notably as a Fury, and on certain British coins she is similarly depicted. What were the circumstances which caused the moneyers of the period to concentrate such anguish into

FIG. 354.—Printer's Ornament (English, 1724).

the physiognomy of the pherepolis it would be interesting to know: the fact remains that they did so, yet we find what obviously is the same fiery-locked figure with an expression unmistakably serene.

Tradition seems to have preserved the memory of the Virgin Mary as one of the Three Greek Moirae or Three Celtic Mairae or Spinners, for according to an apocryphal gospel Mary was one of the spinsters of the Temple Veil: "And the High priest said; choose for me by lot who shall spin the gold and the white and fine linen, and the blue and the scarlet, and the true purple. And the

Figs. 355 to 358.—British.

true purple and the scarlet fell to the lot of Mary, and she took them and went away to her house."[1] The purple heart-shaped mulberry in Greek is *moria*, and the Athenian

[1] *Cf.* Stoughton, Rev. J., *Golden Legends of the Olden Time*, p. 9.

XI.] THE FAIR MAID 597

district known as Moria is supposed to have been so named from its similitude to a mulberry leaf. In Cornwall the scarlet-berried holly is known as Aunt Mary's Tree, and as

FIG. 359.—Mary, in an Oval Aureole, Intersected by Another, also Oval, but of smaller size. Miniature of the X. Cent. From *Christian Iconography* (Didron).

aunt in the West of England was a title applied in general to *old* women, it is evident that Aunt Mary of the Holly Tree must have been differentiated from the little Maid of Bethlehem. According to *The Golden Legend* St. Mary died at the age of seventy-two, a number of which the significance has been partially noted, and she was reputed to have been fifteen years of age when she gave birth to the Saviour of the World: the number fifteen is again connected with St. Mary in the miracle thus recorded of her early childhood: "And when the circle of three years was rolled round, and the time of her weaning was fulfilled, they brought the Virgin to the Temple of the Lord with offerings. Now there were round the temple according to the fifteen Psalms of Degrees, fifteen steps going up."[1] Up these mystic fifteen steps we are told that the new-weaned child miraculously walked unaided.

The New Testament refers to three Marys; in the design overleaf the figure might well represent Fate, and that there was once a Great and a Little Mary is somewhat implied by the fact that in Jerusalem adjoining the church of St. Mary was "another church of St. Mary called the Little":[2] that there was also at one time a White Mary and a Black Mary is indubitable from the numerous Black Virgins which still exist in continental churches. Even the glorious Diana of Ephesus was, as has been seen, at times represented as black: the name Ephesus, where the Magna Mater was pre-eminently worshipped, is radically Ephe, and that Godiva of Coventry was alternatively associated with night is clear from the fact that the Godiva procession at a village near Coventry included two Godivas, one white, the other black.[3]

Near King's Cross, London, in the ward of Farendone, used to exist a spring known as Black Mary's Hole: this name was popularly supposed to have originated from a

---

[1] *Cf*, Stoughton, Rev. J., *Golden Legends of the Olden Time*, p. 5.
[2] Wright, T., *Travels in the East*, p. 39.
[3] Windle, Sir B. C. A., *Life in Early Britain*, p. 116.

negro woman who kept a black cow and used to draw water from the spring, but tradition also said that it was originally the Blessed Mary's Well, and that this having fallen into disrepute at the time of the Reformation the less attractive cognomen was adopted.[1]

The immense antiquity of human occupation of this site is indicated by the fact that opposite Black Mary's Hole there was found at the end of the seventeenth cen-

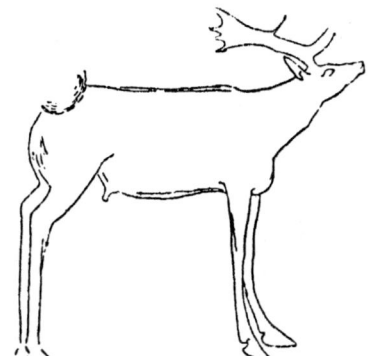 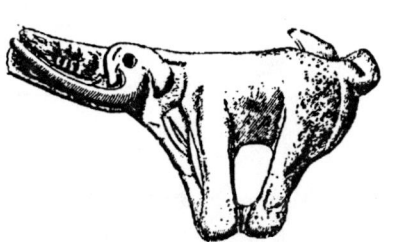

FIG. 360.—Engraving on Pebble, Montastruc, Bruniquel. FIG. 361.—Dagger-handle in form of mammoth, Bruniquel.

From *A Guide to the Antiquities of the Stone Age* (B.M.).

tury a pear-shaped flint instrument in the company of bones of some species of elephant: after lying unappreciated for many years the tool in question has since been recognised as a piece of human handiwork, and may fairly claim to be the first of its kind recorded in this or any other country.[2] That the contemporaries of the mammoth were no mean artists is proved by the Bruniquel objects—particularly the engraving on pebble—here illustrated: not only does the elephant figure on our prehistoric coinage,

[1] Mitton, G. E., *Clerkenwell*, p. 79.
[2] B.M., *Guide to Antiquities of Stone Age*, p. 26.

but it is also found carved on upwards of a hundred stones in Scotland and notably upon a broch at *Brechin* in Forfarshire. Such was the skill of the Brigantian flintworkers who were settled around Burlington or Bridlington (Yorkshire, anciently *Deira*) that they successfully fabricated small fish-hooks out of flint, a feat forcing one to endorse the dictum of T. Quiller Couch : " This is a matter not unconnected with our present subject, as the hand which fashioned so skilfully the barbed arrow-head of flint, and the polished hammer-axes may be fairly associated with a brain of high capabilities ".[1]

We have seen that in Scandinavia Mara—doubtless

Fig. 362.—Probable Restoration of Dagger with Mammoth Handle. From *A Guide to the Antiquities of the Stone Age* (B.M).

Black Mary—was a ghastly spectre associated with the Night *Mare :* to this Black Mary may perhaps be assigned *mar*, meaning to injure or destroy, and probably also *morose, morbid*, and *murder*. We again get the equation *mar* = Mary in *marrjan* the old German for *mar*, for *marrjan* is equivalent to the name Marian which is merely another form of Mary. The Maid Marian who figured in our May-day festivities in association with the sovereign archer Robin Hood, was obviously not the marrer nor the morose Mary but the Merry Lady of the Morris Dance, *alias* the gentle Maiden Vere or daughter deare of Flora. To White Mary or Mary the Weaver of the scarlet and true purple, may be assigned *mere*, meaning true and also *merry, mirth*,

[1] *Holy Wells of Cornwall.*

and *marry*: to Black Mary may be assigned *myrrh* or *mar*, meaning bitterness, and it is characteristic of the morose tendency of clericalism that it is to this root that the authorities attribute the Mary of Merry England.

The association of the May-fair or Fairy Mother with fifteen, and merriment is pointed by the custom that the great fair which used to be held in the Mayfair district of London began on May 1 and lasted for fifteen days: this fair, we are told, was " not for trade and merchandise, but for musick, showes, drinking, gaming, raffling, lotteries, stage plays, and drolls ".[1] That the Mayfair district was once dedicated to Holy Vera is possible from Oliver's Mount, the site of which, now known as Mount Street, is believed to mark a fort erected by Oliver Cromwell. We have noted an Oliver's Castle at Avebury or Avereberie, hence it becomes interesting to find an Avery Row in northern Mayfair, and an Avery Farm Row in Little Ebury Street. The term Ebury is supposed to mark the site of a Saxon *ea burgh* or *island fort*, an assumption which may be correct: at the time of Domesday there existed here a manor of Ebury, and that this neighbourhood was an *abri* or sanctuary dedicated to Bur or Bru is hinted in the neighbouring place-names *Bru*ton Street (adjoining Avery Row, which is equivalent to Abery Row), *Bour*don Street, *Bur*ton Street, and *Bur*wood Place. Among the charities of Mayfair is one derived from a benefactor named Abourne: we have noticed that the tradition of the neighbourhood is that Kensington Gardens were the haunt of Oberon's fair daughter, and I have already ventured the suggestion that Bryanstone Square— by which is Brawn Street—marks the site of a Brawn,

---

[1] Mitton, G. E., *Mayfair*, p. 1.

Bryan, Obreon, or Oberon Street. Northwards lies Brondesbury or Bromesbury: at Bromley in Kent the parish church was dedicated to St. Blaze, and the local fair used to be held on St. Blaze's Day,[1] and that the Broom or *planta genista* was sacred to the primal Blaze is further pointed by the ancient custom of firing broom-bushes on 1st May—the Mayfair's day.[2] In Cornwall furze used to be hung at the door on Mayday morning: at Bramham or Brimham Rocks in Yorkshire the custom of making a blaze on the eve of the Summer Solstice prevailed until the year 1786.[3] By Bromesbury or Brondesbury is Primrose Hill, which was also known as Barrow Hill: there are, however, no traces of a barrow on this still virgin soil which was probably merely a brownlow, brinsley, or brinsmead, unmarked except by fairy bush or stone.[4] The French for primrose is primevere, and that the Mayfair was the Prime and Princess of *all* meads is implied by Herrick's lines:—

> Come with the Spring-time forth, fair Maid, and be
> This year again the Meadow's Deity.
> Yet ere ye enter, give us leave to set
> Upon your head this flowry coronet;
> To make this neat distinction from the rest,
> You are *the Prime*, and Princesse of the feast:
> To which with *silver* feet lead you the way,
> While sweet-breath'd nymphs attend you on this day.
> This is your houre; and best you may command,
> Since you are Lady of this fairie land.
> Full mirth wait on you, and such mirth as shall
> Cherish the cheek, but make none blush at all.

[1] Walford, E., *Greater London*.
[2] Bonwick, E., *Irish Druids*, p. 208.
[3] Hardwick, C., *Traditions, Superstitions, and Folklore*, p. 34.
[4] The surname Brinsmead still survives in the Primrose Hill neighbourhood.

With the "silver feet" of the Meadow Maid may be connoted the curious custom of the London Merrymaids thus described by a French visitor to England in the time of Charles II.: "On the first of May, and the five or six days following, all the pretty young country girls, that serve the town with milk, dress themselves up very neatly and borrow abundance of silver plate whereof they make a pyramid which they adorn with ribbons and flowers, and carry upon their heads instead of their common milk-pails."[1] That this pyramid or pyre of silver represented a crown or halo is further implied by an engraving of the eighteenth century depicting a fiddler and two milk-maids dancing, one of the maids having on her head a silver plate. It is probable that this symbolised the moon, and that the second dancer represented the sun, the twain standing for the Heavenly Pair, or the Powers of Day and Night.

In Ireland there is little doubt that St. Mary was bracketed inextricably with St. Bride, whence the bardic assertion:—

> There are *two* holy virgins in heaven
> By whom may I be guarded
> Mary and St. Brighed.[2]

In a Latin Hymn Brighid—"the Mary of the Gael"—is startlingly acclaimed as the Magna Mater or Very Queen of Heaven:—

Brighid who is esteemed the Queen of the true God
Averred herself to be *Christ's Mother*, and made herself such by words and deeds.[3]

At Kildare where the circular pyreum assuredly symbolised the central Fire, the servants of Bride were known

---

[1] *Faiths and Folklore*, ii., 401.
[2] Herbert, A., *Cyclops Christianus*, p. 114.   [3] *Ibid.*, p. 114.

indeterminately as either Maolbrighde or Maolmuire, *i.e.*, servants of Brighde, or servants of Muire, and it is probable that *Muire*, the Gaelic form of Mary, was radically *mother ire*, the word *ire* being no doubt the same as *ur*, an Aryan radical meaning *fire*, whence *ar*son, *ar*dent, etc. The circular pyreum of Bride or Brighit the Bright, may be compared with the "round church of St. Mary" in Gethsemane : here the Virgin was said to have been born, and on the round church in question containing her sepulchre it was fabled that " the rain never falls although there is no roof above it ".[1] This circular church of St. Mary was thus like the circular hedge of St. Bride open to the skies, and it is highly probable that the word Mary, Mory, Maree, etc., sometimes meant *mor*, *mawr*, or *Big* Eye. The golden centre or Bull's Eye will be subsequently considered, meanwhile it is relevant to *Mor eye* to point out that less than 200 years ago it was customary to sacrifice a bull on 25th August—a most ardent period of the year—to the god Mowrie and his " devilians " on the Scotch island of Inis Maree, evidently Mowrie's island.[2] At other times and in other districts, Mowrie, Muire, or Mary was no doubt equated with the Celtic Saints Amary and Omer : the surviving words *amor*, *amour*, pointing logically to the conclusion that *love* was Mary's predominant characteristic. There is no radical distinction between *amour* and *humour*, both words probably enshrining the adjectival *eu*, meaning soft, gentle, pleasing, and propitious : humour is merriment. A notable connection with Mary and *amour* is found in Germany where Mother Mary is alternately Mother Ross or Rose : not only is the rose the symbol of *amour*, but the word *rose* is evidently a corrosion of *Eros*,

[1] *Travels in the East*, p. 28. [2] Donnelly, I., *Atlantis*, p. 428.

the Greek title of Cupid or Amor. Miss Eckenstein states: "I have come across Mother Ross in our own [English] chapbook literature,"[1] whence it becomes significant to find that Myrrha, the Virgin Mother of the Phrygian Adonis, was the consort of a divine Smith, or Hammer-god named Kinyras. The word Kinyras may thus reason-

Fig. 363.—From *Cities of Etruria* (Dennis, G.).

Fig. 364.—From *Ancient Pagan and Modern Christian Symbolism* (Inman, C.W.).

ably be modernised into King Eros, and it is not unlikely that inquiries at Ross, Kinross, and Delginross would elicit a connection between these places and the God of Love.

The authorities are slovenly content to equate Mary with Maria, Muire, Marion, etc., assigning all these variations without distinction to *mara*, or bitterness: with regard to Maria, however, it may be suspected that this

[1] *Comparative Studies in Nursery Rhymes*, p. 82.

form is more probably to be referred to Mother Rhea, and more radically to *ma rhi*, *i.e.*, Mother Queen, Lady, or Princess. That the word was used as generic term for Good Mother or Pure Mother is implied by its almost universal employment: thus not only was Adonis said to be the son of Myrrha, but Hermes was likewise said to be the child of Maia or Myrrha. The Mother of the Siamese Saviour was entitled Maya Maria, *i.e.*, the Great Mary; the Mother of Buddha was Maya; Maia was a Roman Flower goddess, and it is generally accepted that *May*, the month of the Flower goddess, is an Anglicised form of Maia.

Fig. 365.—Maya, the Hindoo Goddess, with a Cruciform Nimbus. Hindostan Iconography. From *Ancient Pagan and Modern Christian Symbolism* (Inman, C.W.).

The *earliest known* allusion to the morris dance occurs in the church records of Kingston-on-Thames, where the morris dancers used to dance in the parish church.[1] There are in Britain not less than forty or fifty Kingstons, three Kingsburys, four Kentons, seven Kingstons, one Kenstone, and four Kingstones: all these may have been the towns or seats of tribal Kings, but under what names were they known before Kings settled there? It is highly improbable that

[1] Walford, E., *Greater London*, ii., 305.

royal residences were planted in previously uninhabited spots, and it is more likely that our Kings were crowned and associated with already sacred sites where stood a royal and super-sacred stone analogous to the Scotch *Johnstone*. This was certainly the case at Kingston-on-Thames where there still stands in the market-place the holy stone on which our ancient Kings were crowned: near by is *Can*bury Park, and it would not surprise me if the original barrow or mound of *Can* were still standing there. The surname Lovekyn, which appears very prominently in Kingston records, may be connoted with the adjective *kind*, and it is probable that Moreford, the ancient name of Kingston-on-Thames, did not—as is supposed—mean *big ford*, but Amor or Mary ford. In Spain and Portugal (Iberia) the name Maria is bestowed indiscriminately upon men and women: that the same indistinction existed in connection with St. Marine may be inferred from the statement in *The Golden Legend*: "St. Marine was a noble virgin, and was *one only* daughter to her father who changed the habit of his daughter so that she seemed and was taken for his son and not a woman".[1]

If the Mary of the Marigolds or "winking marybuds," which "gin to ope their golden eyes," was Mary or Big Eye, it may also be surmised that San Marino was the darling of the Mariners, and was the chief Mary-maid, Merro-maid or Mermaid: although the New Testament does not associate the Virgin Mary with *mare* the sea, amongst her titles are "Myrhh of the Sea," "Lady of the Sea," and "Star of the Sea". At St. Mary's in the Scillies, in the neighbourhood of Silver Street, is a castle

[1] iii., 226.

known as Stella Maria: this castle is "built with salient angles resembling the rays of a star," and Pelistry Bay on the opposite side of the islet was thus presumably sacred to Belle Istry, the Beautiful Istar or Star. It has often been supposed that Start Point was named after Astarte, and there is every probability that the various rivers Stour, including the Kentish Great Stour and Little Stour, were also attributed to Istar or Esther. The Greek version of the Book of *Esther*—a varient of Istar—contains the remarkable passage, "A little fountain became a river, and there was light, and the sun, and much water": in the neighbourhood of the Kentish Stour is Eastry; in Essex there is a Good Easter and a High Easter, and in Wilts and Somerset are Eastertowns. In England the sun was popularly supposed to dance at Eastertide, and *in Britain alone* is the Easter festival known under this name: the ancient Germans worshipped a Virgin-mother named Ostara, whose image was common in their consecrated forests.

What is described as the "camp" surrounding St. Albans is called the Oyster Hills, and amid the much water of the Thames Valley is an Osterley or Oesterley. On the Oyster Hills at St. Albans was an hospice for infirm women, dedicated to St. Mary de Pree, the word *pree* here being probably *pre*, the French for a meadow—but Verulam may have been *pre land*, for in ancient times it was known alternatively as Vrolan or *B*rolan.[1] The Oesterley or Oester meadow in the Thames Valley, sometimes written Awsterley, was obviously common ground, for when Sir Thomas Gresham enclosed it his new park palings were rudely torn down and burnt by the populace, much to the

[1] *A New Description of England*, p. 112.

offence of Queen Elizabeth who was staying in the place at the time. Notwithstanding the royal displeasure, complaints were laid against Gresham "by sundry poor men for having enclosed certain common ground to the prejudice of the poor".

Next Osterley is Brentford, where once stood "the Priory of the Holy Angels in the Marshlands": other accounts state that this organisation was a "friary, hospital, or fraternity of the Nine holy orders of Angels". With this holy Nine may be connoted the Nine Men's Morrice and the favourite Mayday pageant of "the Nine Worthies". As *w* and *v* were always interchangeable we may safely identify the "worthies" with the "virtues," and I am unable to follow the official connection between *worth* and *verse:* there is no immediate or necessary relation between them. The Danish for *worth* is *vorde*, the Swedish is *varda*, and there is thus little doubt that *worthy* and *virtue* are one and the same word. In *Love's Labour's Lost* Constable Dull expresses his willingness to "make one in a dance or so, or I will play the tabor to the Worthies and let them dance the Hey".

Osterley is on the river Brent, which sprang from a pond "vulgarly called Brown's Well,"[1] whence it is probable that the Brent vulgarly derived its name from Oberon, the All *Parent*. Brentford was the capital of Middlesex; numerous pre-historic relics have been found there, and that it was a site of immemorial importance is testified by its ancient name of Breninford, supposed to mean King's Road or Way. But bren*en* is the plural of bren—a Prince or King, and two fairy Princes or two fairy

---

[1] *A New Description of England*, p. 118.

Kings were traditionally and proverbially associated with the place. In Cowper's *Task* occur the lines :—

> United yet divided twain at once
> So sit two kings of Brentford on one throne.

Prior, in his *Alma*, refers to the two Kings as being "discreet and wise," and it is probable that in Buckingham's *The Rehearsal*, of which the scene is laid at Brentford, we have further scraps of genuine and authentic tradition. *The Rehearsal* introduces us to two true Kings and two usurpers: the true Kings who are represented as being very fond of one another come on to the stage hand-in-hand, and are generally seen *smelling at one rose or one nosegay*. Imagining themselves being plotted against, one says to the other :—

> Then spite of Fate we'll thus combined stand
> And like true brothers still walk hand in hand.

Driven from their throne by usurpers, nevertheless, towards the end of the play, "the two right Kings of Brentford descend in the clouds singing in white garments, and three fiddlers sitting before them in green". Adjacent to Brentford is the village of Twickenham where at the parish church used to prevail a custom of giving away on Easter Day the divided fragments of two great cakes.[1] This apparently innocuous ceremony was, however, in 1645 deemed to be a superstitious relic and was accordingly suppressed. We have seen that charity-cakes were distributed at Biddenden in commemoration of the Twin Sisters; we have also seen that St. Michael was associated with a great cake named after him, hence it is exceedingly probable that Twickenham of the Two Easter Cakes was

[1] Walford, E., *Greater London*, i., 77.

a seat of the Two or Twa Kings who survived in the traditions of the neighbouring Breninford or King's Ford.

That the Two or Twa Kings of Twickenham were associated with Two Fires is suggested by the alternative name Twi*ttan*ham: in Celtic *tan* meant fire, and the term has survived in *tan*dsticker, *i.e.*, fire-sticks, or matches: it has also survived in *tinder*, "anything for kindling fires from

FIGS. 366 to 370.—British. From Akerman.

a spark," and in *etincelle*, the French for spark. In Etruria Jupiter was known as Tino or Tin, and on the British Star-hero coin here illustrated the legend reads TIN: the town of Tolentino, with which one of the St. Nicholas's was associated in combination with a star, was probably a shrine of Tall Ancient Tino; in modern Greece Tino is a contracted form of Constantine. The Bel*tan* or Bel*tein* fires were frequently in pairs or twins, and there is a saying still current in Ireland—" I am between Bels fires," meaning "I am on the horns of a dilemma". The Dioscuri or Two Kings were always associated with fires or stars: they were the *beau-ideal* warriors or War Boys, and to them was probably sacred the "Warboy's Wood" in Huntingdon, where on May Day the poor used to go "sticking" or gathering fuel. The Dioscuri occur frequently on Roman coins, and it will be noticed that the British Warboy is often represented with a star, and with the palm branch of Invictus. On the assumption of the Blessed Virgin Mary it is said that an angel appeared before her bearing "a bough of the palm of paradise—and the palm shone by right great clearness and was like to a green rod whose leaves shone like to the morrow star".[1] There is very little doubt that the mysterious fish-bone, fern-leaf, spike, ear of corn, or backbone, which figures so frequently among the "what-nots" of our ancient coinage represented the green and magic rod of Paradise.

Fig. 371.—Star or Bush (MS., circa 1425). From *The History of Signboards* (Larwood & Hotten).

At Twickenham is Bushey Park, which is assumed to have derived its name from the bushes in which it abounded: for some reason our ancestors combined their Bush and Star inn-signs into one, *vide* the design herewith: we have already traced a connection between *bougie* —a candle, and the *Bôgie* whose habitation was the brakes and bushes: whence it is not unlikely that Bushey Park derived its title from the Elphin fires, Will o-the-wisps, or bougies which must have danced nightly when Twickenham was little better than a swamp. The Rev. J. B. Johnston decodes Bushey into "Byssa's" isle or penin-

[1] *Golden Legend*, iv., p. 235.

sula, and it is not improbable that Bushey in Hertfordshire bears the same interpretation, only I do not think that the supposititious Byssa, Bissei, or Bisi was an Anglo-Saxon. That "Bisi" was Bogie or Puck is perhaps implied further by the place-name Den*bies* facing Boxhill: we have already noted in this district Bagdon, Pigdon, Bookham, and Pixham, whence Denbies, situated on the brow of Pigdon or Bagdon, suggests that here seemingly was the actual Bissei's den. The supposititious Bissei assigned to Bushey may be connoted with the giant Bosow who dwelt by repute on Buzza's Hill just beyond Hugh Town, St. Mary's. According to Miss Courtney the Cornish family of Bosow are traceable to the giant of Buzza's Hill.[1] Presumably to Puck or Bog, are similarly traceable the common surnames Begg, Bog, etc.

By the Italians the phosphorescent lights or bougies of St. Elmo are known not as Castor and Pollux, but as the fires of St. Peter and St. Nicholas: the name Nicholas is considered to mean "Victory of the People"; in Greek *nike* means *victory :* we have seen that in Russia Nicholas was equated with St. Michael, in face of which facts it is presumptive that St. Nicholas was Invictus, or the Unconquerable. In London, at Paternoster Lane used to stand "the fair parish church of St. Michael called Paternoster,"[2] and that St. Nicholas was originally "Our Father" or Paternoster is implied by the corporate seal of Yarmouth : this represents St. Nicholas supported on either side by angels, and bears the inscription *O Pastor Vere Tibi Subjectis Miserere.* It must surely have savoured of heresy to hail the supposed Nicholas of Patara in Lycia as *O Pastor Vere*, unless in popular estimation

---

[1] *Cornish Feasts and Folklore*, p. 114.   [2] Stow, p. 217.

St. Nicholas was actually the Great Pastor or True Feeder: that Nicholas was indeterminately either the Father or the Mother is deducible from the fact that in Scotland the name Nicholas is commonly bestowed on girls.

In France and Italy prayers are addressed to Great St. Nicholas, and it is probable that there was always a Nichol and a Nicolette or *nucleus*: we are told that St. Nicholas, whose mother's name was Joanna, was born at Patara, and that he became the Bishop of Myra: on his fete day the proper offering was a cock, and that Nicholas or Invictus was the chanteur or Chanticleer, is implied by the statement: "St. Nicholas went abroad in most part in London singing after the old fashion, and was received with many people into their houses, and had much good cheer, as ever they had in many places": on Christmas Eve St. Nicholas still wanders among the children, notwithstanding the sixteenth century censure—"thus tender minds to worship saints and wicked things are taught".

Nicholas is an extended form of Nike, Nick, or Neck, and the frequent juxtaposition of St. Nicholas and St. George is an implication that these Two Kings were once the Heavenly Twins. We have already noted an Eleven Stone at Trenuggo—the *abode of Nuggo*? and there is a likelihood that Nuggo or Nike was there worshipped as One and Only, the *Unique*: that he was Lord of the Harvests is implied by the fabrication of a harvest doll or Neck. According to Skeat *neck* originally meant the nape or knop of the neck; it would thus seem that *neck*—Old English *nekke*—was a synonym for knob or knop. In Cornwall Neck-day was the great day of the year, when the Neck was "cried"[1] and suspended in the ingle nook until the following year: in the words of an old Cornishwoman: "There were Neck cakes, much feasting and dancing all the evening. Another great day was Guldise day when the corn was drawn: Guldise cakes and a lump of pease-pudding for every one."[2]

Near London Stone is the Church of St. Nicholas Cole Abbey, and at Old Jewry stood St. Mary Cole Church: it is not unlikely that this latter was originally dedicated to Old King Cole, the father of the lovely Helen and the Merry Old Soul whose three fiddlers may be connoted with the three green fiddlers of the Kings of Brentford. The great bowl of Cole, the *ghoul* of other ages, may be equated with the *cauldron* or *calix* of the Pastor Vere: the British word for *cauldron* was *pair*, and the Druidic bards speak with great enthusiasm of "their cauldron," "the cauldron of Britannia," "the cauldron of Lady Keridwen," etc. This cauldron was identified with the Stone circles, and the Bardic poets also speak of a mysterious *pair dadeni* which is understood to mean "the cauldron of new birth or rejuvenescence".[3] The old artists seemingly represented the Virtues as emerging from this cauldron as three naked boys or Amoretti, for it is said that St. Nicholas revived three murdered children who had been pickled in brine by a wicked inn-keeper who had run short of bacon. This miracle is his well-known emblem, and the murder story by which the authorities accounted for the picture is probably as silly and brutal an afterthought as the horrid "tortures"

---

[1] In some parts this ceremony was known as "crying the Mare": in Wales the horse of the guise or goose dancers was known as Mari Lhwyd.

[2] Mrs. George of Sennen Cove.

[3] Irvine, C., *St. Brighid and her Times*, p. 6.

and protracted dolours of other saints. Nevertheless some ghoulish and horrible practices seem to have accompanied the worship of the cauldron, and the author of *Druidism Exhumed* reproduces a Scotch sculpture of a cauldron out of which protruding human legs are waving ominously in the air.

St. Nicholas of Bari is portrayed resuscitating three youths from three tubs: that Nicholas was radically the Prince of Peace is implied, however, from the exclamation "Nic'las!" which among children is equivalent to "fainites": the sign of truce or fainites is to cross the two fore-fingers into the form of the *treus* or cross.

St. Nicholas is the unquestioned patron of all children, and in the past bands of lads, terming themselves St. Nicholas' Clerks or St. Nicholas' Knights, added considerably to the conviviality of the cities. Apparently at all abbeys once existed the custom of installing upon St. Nicholas' Day a Boy Bishop who was generally a choir or singing boy: this so-called Bearn Bishop or Barnebishop was decked, according to one account, in "a myter of cloth and gold with *two knopps* of silver gilt and enamelled," and a study of the customs prevailing at this amazing festival of the Holy Innocent leaves little doubt that the Barnebishop personified the conception of the Pastor Vere in the aspect of a lad or "knave". The connection between *knop* and *knave* has already been traced, and the "two knopps" of the episcopal knave or bairnbishop presumably symbolised the *bren* or breasts of Pastor Vere, the celestial Parent: it has already been suggested that the knops on Figs. 30 to 38 (p. 149) represented the Eyes or Breasts of the All Mighty.

In Irish *ab* meant *father* or *lord*, and in all probability

St. Abb's Head, supposedly named after a Bishop Ebba, was once a seat of Knebba worship: that Cunobe was the Mighty Muse, singing like St. Nicholas after the old fashion, is evident from the British coin illustrated on page 305, a sad example of carelessness, declension, and degradation from the Macedonian Philippus.

The festival of the Burniebishop was commemorated with conspicuous pomp at Cambrai, and there is reason to think that this amazing institution was one of Cambrian origin: so fast and furious was the accompanying merriment that the custom was inevitably suppressed. The only Manor in the town of Brentford is that of Burston or Boston, whence it is probable that Brentford grew up around a primeval Bur stone or "Denbies". That the place was famous for its merriment and joviality is sufficiently evidenced by the fact that in former times the parish rates "were mainly supported by the profits of public sports and diversions especially at Whitsuntide".[1]

According to *The Rehearsal* when the True Kings or Two Kings, accompanied by their retinue of three green-clad fiddlers, descended from the clouds, a dance was then performed: "an ancient dance of right belonging to the Kings of Brentford, but since derived with a little alteration to the Inns of Court". On referring to the famous pageants of the Inns of Court we find that the chief character was the Lord of Misrule, known otherwise as the King of Cockneys or Prince of Purpool. We have seen that the Hobby Horse was clad in purple, and that Mary was weaver of the true purple—a combination of true blue and scarlet. The authorities connote *purple*, French *purpre*, with the Greek *porphureos*, "an epithet of the surging

---

[1] *Greater London*, l., p. 40.

sea," and they ally it with the Sanscrit *bhur*, meaning *to be active*. The cockney, and very active Prince of Purpool or Portypool was conspicuously celebrated at Gray's Inn which occupies the site of the ancient Manor of *Poripool*, and the ritual—condemned and suppressed by the Puritans as " popish, diabolical, and antechristian "—seems invariably to have started by a fire or phare lighted in the hall: this at any rate was the custom and status with which the students at St. John's, Oxford, opened the proceedings on All Hallows' Eve.

The Druidic Bards allude to their sacred pyreum, or fire-circle, as a *pair dadeni*, and that a furious Fire or Phare was the object of their devotion is obvious from hymns such as—

> Let burst forth ungentle
> The horse-paced ardent fire!
> Him we worship above the earth,
> Fire, fire, low murmuring in its dawn,
> High above our inspiration,
> Above every spirit
> Great is thy terribleness.[1]

Pourpre or *purple*, the royal or imperial colour, was doubtless associated with the Fire of Fires, and the connection between this word and *porphureos* must, I think, be sought in the idea of *pyre furious* or *fire furious*, rather than any epithet of the surging sea. The Welsh for purple is *porffor*.

Either within or immediately adjacent to the Manor of Poripool or Purpool were some famous springs named Bagnigge Wells: at the corner of Bathhurst Street, Paddington, was a second Bagnigge Wells, and the river

---

[1] Quoted, *St. Brighid and her Times*, p. 7.

Fleet used also at one time to be known as the Bagnigge. This ubiquitous Bagnigge was in all probability *Big Nigge* or Big Nicky—

> Know you the Nixies gay and fair?
> Their eyes are black and green their hair,
> They lurk in sedgy shores.

The fairy Nokke, Neck, or Nickel, is said to have been a great musician who sat upon the water's edge and played a golden harp, the harmony of which operated on all nature:[1] sometimes he is represented as a complete horse who could be made to work at the plough if a bridle of particular kind were used: he is also represented as half man and half horse, as an aged man with a long beard, as a handsome young man, and as a pretty little boy with golden hair and scarlet cap. That Big Nigge once haunted the Bagnigge Wells is implied by the attendant legend of Black Mary, Black Mary's Hole being the entrance, or immediately adjacent, to one of the Bagnigge springs: similarly, as has been noted, Peg Powler, and Peg this or that, haunted the streams of Lancashire.

We have seen that Keightley surmised the word *pixy* to be the endearing diminutive *sy* added to Puck, whence, as in Nancy, Betsy, Dixie, and so forth, Nixy may similarly be considered as *dear little Nick*. In Suffolk, the fairies are known as farisees, seemingly, *dear little fairies*, and our ancestors seem to have possessed a pronounced partiality for similar diminutives: we find them alluding to the Blood of the Lambkin, an expression which Adamnan's editors remark as "a bold instance of the Celtic diminutive of endearment so characteristic of Adamnan's style":

[1] Keightley, I., *F. M.*, pp. 139-49.

they add : "Throughout Adamnan's work, diminutives are constantly used, and these in most cases are used in a sense of endearment difficult to convey in English, perfectly natural as they are in the mouth of the kindly and warm-hearted Irish saint. In the present case Dr. Reeves thinks the diminutives may indicate the poorness of the animals from the little there was to feed them upon."[1] As the traditions of Fairyland give no hint for the assumption of any rationing or food-shortage it seems hardly necessary to consider either the pixies, the farisees, or the nixies as either half-starved or even impoverished.

In Scandinavia and Germany the nixies are known as the nisses, and they there correspond to the brownies of Scotland: according to Grimm the word *nisse* is "Nicls, Niclsen, *i.e.*, Nicolaus, Niclas, a common name in Germany and the North, which is also contracted to Klas, Claas"; but as *k* seems invariably to soften into *ch*, and again into *s*, it is a perfectly straight road from Nikke to Nisse, and the adjective *nice* is an eloquent testimonial to the Nisses' character. Some Nisses were doubtless *nice*, others were obviously nasty, noxious, and nocturnal: the Nis of Jutland is in Friesland called Puk, and also Niss-Puk, Nise-Bok, and Niss-Kuk: the *Kuk* of this last mentioned may be connoted with the fact that the customary offering to St. Nicholas was a cock—the symbol of the Awakener—and as St. Nicholas was so intimately connected with Patara, the cock of St. Peter is no doubt related to the legend.

St. Nicholas, or Santa Claus, customarily travels by night: the nixies were black-eyed; Old Nick was always painted black; *nox*, or night, is the same word as nixy; and *nigel*, *night*, or *nicht* all imply blackness. According

[1] Huyshe, W., *Life of Columba*, p. 129.

to Cæsar: "all the Gauls assert that they are descended from the god Dis, and say that this tradition has been handed down by the Druids. For that reason they compute the divisions of every season not by the number of days but by nights; they keep birthdays, and the beginnings of months and years in such an order that the day follows the night."[1] The expressions fortnight, and sen'night thus not only perpetuate an idea of great antiquity but one which is philosophically sound: to our forerunners Night was no wise evil, but the beneficent Mother of a Myriad Stars: the fairies revelled in the dark, and in eyes of old "the vast blue night was murmurous with peris wings"[2].

The place-name Knightsbridge is probably a mis-spelling of Neyte, one of the three manors into which Kensington was once divided: the other two were Hyde and Ebury, and it is not unlikely that these once constituted a trinity —Hyde being the Head, Ebury the Brightness, and Neyte —Night. The Egyptian represented Nut, Naut, or Neith as a Mother Goddess with two children in her arms, one white the other black: to her were assigned the words: "I am what has been, what is, and what will be," and her worshippers declared: "She hath built up life from her own body". In Scandinavia Nat was the Mother of all the gods: she was said to be an awe-inspiring, adorable, noble, and beneficent being, and to have her home on the lower slopes of the Nida mountains: *nid* is the French for *nest*, and with Neyte may be connoted *nuit*, the French for *night*. That St. Neot was *le nuit* is implied by the tradition that the Church of St. Neot in Cornwall was built not only by night, but entirely by Neot himself who

---

[1] *De Bello Gallico*, p. 121.   [2] See Appendix B, p. 873.

drew the stones from a neighbouring quarry, aided only by the help of reindeer. These magic reindeer are obviously the animals of St. Nick, and it is evidently a memory of Little Nick that has survived in the tradition that St. Neot was a saint of very small stature—somewhere about 15 inches high.[1] With Mother *Nat* of Scandinavia, and Mother *Naut* or Neith of Egypt, may be connoted Nutria, a Virgin-Mother goddess of Etruria; a divine nurse with whose name may be connected *nutrix* (nurse) and *nutriment*.

St. Nicholas is the patron saint of seafarers and there are innumerable dedications to him at the seaside: that Nikke was Neptune is unquestionable, and connected with his name is doubtless *nicchio* the Italian for a shell. From *nicchio* comes our modern *niche*, which means a shell-like cavity or recess: in the British EPPI coin, illustrated on page 284, the marine monster may be described as a nikke, and the apparition of the nikke as a perfect horse might not ineptly be designated a *nag*.

I have elsewhere illustrated many representations of the Water-Mother, the Mary-Maid, the Mermaid, the Merrow-Maid, or as she is known in Brittany—Mary Morgan. The resident nymph or genius of the river Se*vern* was named Sa*brina;* the Welsh for the Severn is Ha*vren*, and thus it is evident that the radical of this river name is *brina, vren,* or *vern:* the British Druids recognised certain governing powers named *feraon: fern* was already noted as an Iberian word meaning *anything good*, whence it is probable that in Havren or Severn the affix *ha* or *se* was either the Greek *eu* or the British and Sanscrit *su*, both alike meaning the *soft, gentle, pleasing,* and *propitious.*

[1] *Cf.* Courtney, Miss M. E., *Cornish Feasts and Folklore*, p. 105.

> Sabrina fair,
>   Listen where thou art sitting
> Under the glassy, cool, translucent wave,
>   In twisted braids of lilies, knitting
> The loose train of thy amber-dropping hair.

In the neighbourhood of Bryanstone Square is Lissom Grove, a corruption of Lillestone Grove: here thus seemingly stood a stone sacred to the Lily or the All Holy, and the neighbouring church of St. Cyprian probably marks the local memory of a traditional *sy brian, Sabrina*, or *dear little brownie*.

Near Silchester, on the boundary line between Berks and Hants, is a large stone known as the Imp stone, and as this was formerly called the Nymph stone,[1] it is probable that in this instance the Imp stone was a contraction of Imper or Imber stone—the Imp being the Nymph of the amber-dropping hair. The Scandinavians believed that the steed of the Mother Goddess Nat produced from its mouth a froth, which consisted of honey-dew, and that from its bridle dropped the dews in the dales in the morning: the same idea attached to the steeds of the Valkyre, or War Maidens, from whose manes, when shaken, dew dropped into the deep dales, whence harvests among the people.[2]

Originally, *imp* meant a scion, a graft, or an offspring, a sprout, or sprig: *sprig, spright, spirit, spirt, sprout*, and *sprack* (an old English word meaning lively, perky, or pert), are all radically *pr*: in London the sparrow "was supposed to be the soul of a dead person";[3] in Kent, a

---

[1] Wilson, J., *Imperial Gazetteer*, i., 1042.
[2] Rydberg, V., *Teutonic Mythology*, p. 361.
[3] Windle, Sir B. C. A., *Life in Early Britain*, p. 63.

624 ARCHAIC ENGLAND [CHAP.

sparrow is termed a *sprug*, whence it would appear that this pert, perky, little bird was once a symbol of the sprightly sprout, sprite, or spirit.

Stow mentions that the fair parish church of St. Michael called Paternoster when new built, was made a college of St. Spirit and St. Mary. All birds in general were symbols of St. Spirit, but more particularly the Columba or Culver,[1] which was pre-eminently the emblem of Great Holy Vere: we have already illustrated a half white, half black, six-winged representation of this sacred sign of simplicity and love, and the six-winged angel here reproduced is, doubtless, another expression of the far-spread idea:—

Fig. 372.—Six-winged angel holding lance, wings crossed on breast, arrayed in robe and mantle. (From Didron.)

> The embodied spirit has a thousand heads,
> A thousand eyes, a thousand feet, around
> On every side, enveloping the earth,
> Yet filling space no larger than a span.
> He is himself this very universe;
> He is whatever is, has been, and shall be;
> He is the lord of immortality.[2]

It is difficult to conceive any filthiness or evil of the dove, yet the hagiologists mention "a foul dove or black culver," which is said to have flown around the head of a

---

[1] The *cul* of *culver* or *culfre* and *columba* was probably the Irish *Kil*: hence the *umba* of *columba* may be connoted with *imp*.

[2] Rig-Veda (mandala X, 90).

certain holy Father named Nonnon.[1] We may connote this Nonnon with Nonna or Non, the reputed mother of St. David, for of St. David, we are told, his birth was heralded by angels thirty years before the event, and that among other miracles (such as restoring sight to the blind), doves settled on his shoulders. Dave or Davy is the same word as dove; in Welsh *dof* means *gentle*, and it is more probable that the gentle dove derived its title from this word than as officially surmised from the Anglo-Saxon *dufan*, "to plunge into". According to Skeat, *dove* means literally *diver*, but doves neither dive nor plunge into anything: they have not even a diving flight. The Welsh are known familiarly as Taffys, and the Church of Llan-*daff* is supposed to mean Church on the River Taff: it is more probable that Llandaff was a shrine of the Holy Dove, and that David with the doves upon his shoulder was a personification of the Holy Spirit or Wisdom. *Non* is the Latin for *not*, and the black dove associated with Nonnon or *not not* was no doubt a representation of that *Negation*, non-existence or inscrutable void, which existed before the world was, and is otherwise termed Chaos or Cause. That Wisdom or the Holy Spirit was conceived as the primal and inscrutable *Darkness*, is evident from the statement in *The Wisdom of Solomon*: "For God loveth none but him that dwelleth with Wisdom. For she is more beautiful than the sun, and above all the orders of stars: being compared with the light *she is found before it*."

The Nonnon of whom "it seemed that a foul dove or black culver flew about him whilst he was at Mass at the altar" was said to be the Bishop of Heliopolis, *i.e.*, the city

[1] *Golden Legend*, v., 235.

of the Sun, and he comes under notice in connection with St. Pelagienne—" said of *pelagus* which is as much to say as the *sea* ". The interpretation further placed upon St. Pelagienne is that " she was the sea of iniquity, and the flood of sins, but she plunged after into the sea of tears and washed her in the flood of baptism ". That poor Pelagienne was the Water Mother of Mary Morgan is implied further by the fragment of autobiography—" I have been called from my birth Pelagienne, but for the

FIGS. 373 to 376.—Greek. From Barthelemy.

pomp of my clothing men call me Margaret " :[1] we have seen that Pope Joanna of Engelheim was also called Margaret, whence it is to be suspected that although it is true that *pelagus* meant *the sea* St. Pelagienne was primarily the *Bella* or beautiful *Jeanne, i.e.*, Mary Morgan or Morgiana.

On the coins of King *Janus* of Sicily there figured a dove ; *jonah, yuneh*, or *Ione* are the Hebrew and Greek terms for dove ; the Ionian Greeks were worshippers of the dove, and the consociation of St. Columbe Kille or the " little

[1] *Golden Legend*, v., 236.

dove of the church " with the Hebridean island of Iona is presumptive evidence of the worship of the dove in Iona. In the Rhodian Greek coins here illustrated the reverse

Fig. 377.—British. From Akerman.

Fig. 378.—British. From Evans.

represents the rhoda or rose of Rhodes, and the obverse head may be connoted with the story of St. Davy with the dove settled on his shoulder: that the dove was also an

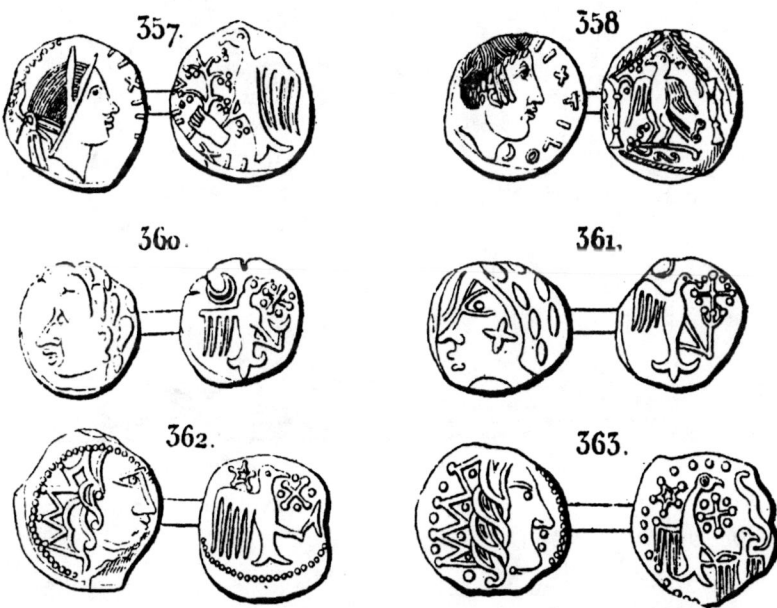

Figs. 379 to 384.—British (Channel Islands). From Barthelemy.

English emblem is obvious from the British coins, Figs. 377 to 384; the dove will also be found frequently introduced on the contemned *sceattae* illustrated *ante*, page 364.

Among the golden treasures unearthed by Schliemann

at Mykenae was a miniature "model of a temple" on which are seated two pigeons with uplifted wings:[1] among the curious and interesting happenings which occurred during

Fig. 385.—The Father, Represented as Slightly Different to the Son. French Miniature of the Close of the XIII. Cent. From *Christian Iconography* (Didron).

the childhood of the Virgin Mary it is recorded that "Mary was in the Temple of the Lord as if she were a dove that dwelt there, and she received food as from the hand of an angel": Fig. 380 appears to illustrate this dove dwelling in a Temple. The legend continues that when the Holy

[1] Mykenae, p. 267.

Virgin attained the age of twelve years the Angel of the Lord caused an assembly of all the widowers each of whom was ordained to bring with him his rod: the High Priest then took these rods and prayed over them, but there came no sign: at last Joseph took his rod " and behold a dove came out of the rod and flew upon Joseph's head ".[1] It is said by Lucian that in the most sacred part of the temple of Hieropolis, the holy city of Syria, were three

FIG. 386.—The Divine Dove, in a Radiating Aureole. From a French Miniature of the XV. Cent. From *Christian Iconography* (Didron).

figures of which the centre one had a golden dove upon its head: not only was no name given to this, but the priests said nothing concerning its origin or form, calling it simply "The sign": according to the British Bards— "To Addav came the sign. It was taught by Alpha, and it was the earliest polished melody of Holy God, and by a wise mouth it was canticled." There is little doubt that the descending dove with wings outstretched was a variant of the three rays or Broad Arrow, that the *awen* was the

[1] Stoughton, Dr. J., *Golden Legends of the Olden Time*, p. 9.

Fig. 387.—From *Christian Iconography* (Didron).

Fig. 388.—God the Father, with a Bi-Triangular Nimbus; God the Son, with a Circular Nimbus; God the Holy Ghost, without a Nimbus, and within an Aureole. (Fresco at Mount Athos.) From *Christian Iconography* (Didron).

XI.]   THE FAIR MAID   631

FIG. 389.—The Three Divine Persons, Adorned with the Cruciform Nimbus. Miniature of the close of the XIII. Cent. MS. in the Bibliothèque Royale. From *Christian Iconography* (Didron).

FIG. 390.—God the Father, and God the Son, with Features Exactly Identical. French Miniature of the commencement of the XIII. Cent. From *Christian Iconography* (Didron).

632   ARCHAIC ENGLAND   [CHAP.

Iona, and that this same idea was conveyed by the Three *ains*, or *eyen*, Eyes, Golden Balls, or pawnbroker's sign. It is recorded of St. Nicholas of Bari, the patron saint of pawnbrokers, that immediately he was born he stood up in the basin in which he was being washed and remained with hands clasped, and uplifted eyes, for two hours: in later life he became wealthy, and threw into a window on three successive nights a bag of gold as a dowry for three impoverished and sore-tempted maidens. In commemoration of these three bags of gold St. Nicholas became the patron saint of pawnbrokers whose sign of the Three Golden Balls is a conversion of the three anonymous gifts.

Fig. 391.—From Barthelemy.   Fig. 392.—British (Channel Islands). From Barthelemy.

In Hebrew the Three Apples, Eyes, or Golden Balls are called *ains* or fountains of living water, and to this day in Wales a spring of water is called in Welsh the Eye of the Fountain or the Water Spring. It will be remembered that the sister of St. Nonna, and therefore the aunt of St. Davy, was denominated Gwen of the Three Breasts, *Tierbron*, or three breasts, may be connoted with three-eyed Thor, and the combination of Eyes and Sprigs is conspicuously noticeable in Fig. 39, page 364: one will also note the head of No. 49 on the same plate.

The Three Holy Children on the reverse of Fig. 391

—a Byzantine coin—are presumably the offspring of St. Michael *alias* Nichol on the obverse: the arms of Cornwall consist of fifteen golden balls called *besants*; the county motto is One and All. Of St. Nicholas of Tolentino who became a friar at the age of *eleven*, we are told that a star rested over his altar and preceded him when he walked, and he is represented in Art with a lily in his hand—the symbol of his pure life—and a star over his head: that Nicolette was identified with the Little Star or Stella Maris is clear from Troubadour *chansons*, such as the following from that small classic *Aucassin and Nicolette*—

> Little Star I gaze upon,
> Sweetly drawing to the moon,
> In such golden haunt is set
> Love, and bright-haired Nicolette.
> God hath taken from our war
> Beauty, like a shining star.
> Ah, to reach her, though I fell
> From her Heaven to my Hell.
> Who were worthy such a thing,
> Were he emperor or king?
> Still you shine, oh, perfect Star,
> Beyond, afar.

It is impossible to say whether the three-eyed elphin faces illustrated *ante*, page 381, are asters, marguerites, marigolds, or suns: in the centre of one of them is a heart, and without doubt they one and all symbolised the Great Amour or Margret. During excavations at Jerusalem in 1871, the symbol of Three Balls was discovered under the Temple of King Solomon on Mount Moriah: this temple was circular, and it is probable that the name Moriah meant originally Moreye or Big Eye. That the three cavities in question were once ains or eyes is implied by the explorer's statement: "Within this recess are three cylindrical holes

5¼ inches in diameter, the lines joining their centres forming the sides of an equilateral triangle. Below this appears once to have been a basin to collect the water, but whatever has been there, it has been violently removed . . .

Fig. 393.—From *The Recovery of Jerusalem* (Wilson and Warren).

there can be little doubt that this is an ancient overflow from the Birket Israil."[1] It is probable that the measure of these three cup-like holes was once 5 inches, and that the resultant fifteen had some original connection with the fifteen besants or basins of Byzantine Britain.

[1] Wilson and Warren, *The Recovery of Jerusalem*, i., 166.

XI.] THE FAIR MAID 635

With the *brook Birket Israil* at Mount Moriah may be connoted the neighbouring "large pool called El Burak": the existence on Mount Moriah of subterranean cisterns or basins known as Solomon's Stables renders it probable that El Burak was El Borak, the fabulous white steed upon which the faithful Mussulman expects one day to ride. The Eyes of the British broks or nags here illustrated are

FIGS. 394 to 396.—British. From Evans.

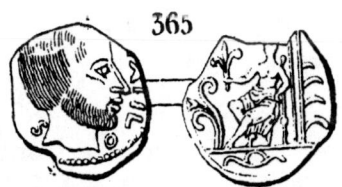

FIG. 397.—British Channel (Islands). From Barthelemy.

curiously prominent, and in Fig. 396 the *eleven*-eared wheat sprig is springing from a trefoil: with the lily surmounting the CUNO steed may be connoted the two stars or morrow stars which frequently decorate this triune emblem of Good Deed, Good Thought, Good Word: they may be seen to-day on the badges of those little Knights of To-morrow, the Boy Scouts.

The lily appears in the hand of the PIXTILOS figure here

illustrated, and among the Pictish emblems found on the vitrified fort at Anwath in Scotland is the puckish design illustrated on page 496, Fig. 293. This was probably a purely symbolic and elementary form of the dolorous and pensive St. John which Christianity figured with a pair of marigolds or marguerites in lieu of feathers or antennae.

Accompanying the Pictish inscription in question were the elaborate barnacles or spectacles reproduced *ante*, page 495: in Crete the barnacles, as illustrated on page 494, are found humanised by a small winged figure holding a wand, and the general effect of the two circles when superimposed is that of the figure 8. The nine-rayed ABRACAX lion as portrayed by the Gnostics, and doubtless a variant of Abracadabra, has its serpentine body twined into an 8; on a Longstone in Brittany there is a figure holding an 8 tipped staff, and the same emblem will be noticed on the coins of the Longostaliti, a *Gaul*-ish people who seemingly were so ghoulish as to venerate a *cal*ix or *caul*dron: from the *pair dadeni* or cauldron of renaissance represented on these astral coins it will be noticed there are emerging two stars and other interesting nicknacks. The locks of hair on the astral figure represented on the coins of Marseilles—a city founded by a colony of Phocean Greeks from Ionia—number exactly eight: in Scotland we have traced the memory of eight ancient hags, the Mothers of the World: in Valencia we have noted the procession of eight

Fig. 398.—From *Christian Iconography* (Didron).

XI.]　　　　　　　THE FAIR MAID　　　　　　　637

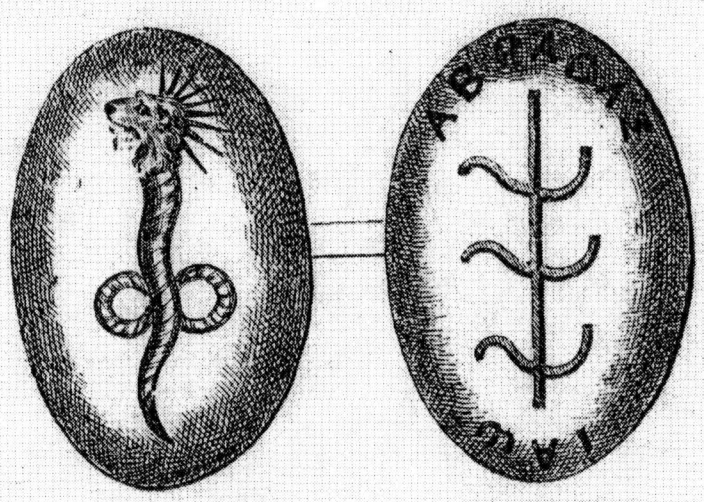

Fig. 399.—From *An Essay on Ancient Gems* (Walsh, R.).

Fig. 400.—Gaulish. From Akerman.

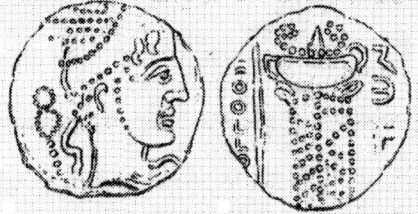

Figs. 401 and 402.—Gaulish. From Akerman.

638 ARCHAIC ENGLAND [CHAP.

Fig. 403.—From *Symbolism of the East and West* (Aynsley, Mrs. Murray).

scrupulously coiffured Giants, and there is very little doubt that the eight survivors of the Flood,[1] by whom the world

[1] Noah, Shem, Ham, Japhet, and their respective wives.

XI.] THE FAIR MAID 639

was re-peopled, is a re-statement of the same idea of the Gods of the four quarters and their Consorts. In connection with the Ogdoad or Octet of eight gods one may connote the curious erection which once decorated the London Guildhall, the seat of Gogmagog :[1] here, " on each side of the flight of steps was an *octangular* turreted gallery, balustraded, having an office in each, appropriated to the

Fig. 404.—English Eighteenth Century Printer's Ornament.

hallkeeper: these galleries assumed the appearance of arbours from being each surrounded by six palm-trees in ironwork, the foliage of which gave support to a large balcony, having in front a clock (with three dials) elaborately ornamented, and underneath a representation of the Sun, resplendent with gilding; the clock frame was of oak.

[1] Gogmagog is also found at Uriconium, now Wroxeter, in Shropshire. Since suggesting a connection between Gog and Coggeshall in Essex, I find that Coggeshall was traditionally associated with a giant whose remains were said to have been found. *Cf.* Hardwick, C., *Traditions, Superstitions and Folklore,* p. 205.

At the angles were the cardinal virtues, and on the top a curious figure of Time with a young child in his arms." [1] At the village of *Thame*-on-Thames, which the authorities state meant *rest, quiet*, otherwise *tame* or kindly, gentle *Time*, there is a celebrated figure of St. Kitt, *alias* Father Time, with the little figure of New Time or *Change* upon his shoulder. In Etruria a parallel idea would seem to have been current, for Mrs. Hamilton Gray describes an Etruscan work of art inscribed " Isis nourishing Horus, or Truth teaching Time ".[2] It is most unusual to find the Twins depicted as old men, or Bald ones with the mystic Lock of Horus on their foreheads, but in the eighteenth-century emblem here reproduced the intention of the deviser is unmistakable, and the central Sun is supported by two Times.

In a cave situated at the cross roads at Royston in Hertfordshire, there is the figure of St. Kitt beneath which are apparently eight other figures : these are assumedly " other saints," but the Christian Church does not assign any singular pre-eminence to St. Christopher, and the decorators of the Royston Cave evidently regarded St. Kitt as the Supreme One or God Himself. It is abundantly evident that to our ancestors Kit or Kate was God, Giant, Jeyantt,[3] or Good John : that he was deemed the deity of the ocean is obvious from instances where the water in which he stands is full of crabs, dolphins, and other ocean creatures. I have suggested that Christopher was a representation of *dad* or Death carrying the soul over the river of Death, *i.e.*, " Dowdy " with the spriggan on his back. Among sailors Death is known familiarly as " Old Nick," " Old

---

[1] Thornbury, W., *Old and New London*, i., 386.
[2] *Sepulchres of Ancient Etruria*, p. 16.
[3] The civic giant of Salisbury is named Christopher.

FIG. 405.—St. Christopher. From Royston Cave.

[*To face page* 640.

Davy," or "Davy Jones," and in Cornwall they have a curious and inexplicable saying: "as ancient as the Flood of Dava". I think this Dava must have been the genius of the rivers Dove, Taff and Tavy.

That Kit was connected with the eight of the Cretan Eros figure is further implied by the fact that on the summit of a lofty hill near Royston or Roystone there is, or was, a "hollow oval". The length of this prehistoric monument was stated in 1856 as about 31 feet (originally 33 ?) and its breadth about 22 feet. "Within this bank are two circular excavations meeting together in the middle and nearly forming the figure eight. Both excavations descend by concentric and contracting rings to the walls which form the sides of the chambers."[1] From this description the monument would appear to be identical in design with the 8-in-an-oval emblem here illustrated, a mediæval paper-mark traceable to the Italian town of St. Donino. Examples of twin earthwork circles forming the figure 8 are not unknown in Ireland.

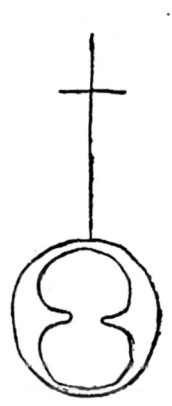

FIG. 406.—Mediæval Paper mark. From *Les Filigranes* (Briquet, C. M.).

At Royston, which, as we shall see, was the Lady Roesia's town, is a place called Cocken Hatch, but whether this is the site of the eight-form monument in question, I am unaware: in the megalithic stone illustrated on p. 638 the Cadi is not only holding an 8 on the tip of his *caduceus*, but he has also a *cadet* or little son by the hand: *cadi* is Arabic for a *judge*, and in Wales the Cadi no doubt acted as the final judge. In Celtic the word *cad* meant war, an

[1] *Archæologia*, from *The Gentleman's Magazine*, vol. i., p. 124.

implication that in one of his aspects Ked or St. Kitt was the ever-victorious Michael or the all-conquering Nike: there is a Berkshire ballad extant, in which the word *caddling*, meaning fighting, is employed, yet caddling is the same word as *cuddling*. In Scotland, *caddie* means a messenger or errand boy: Mercury or Hermes was the Messenger of the Gods: among the Greeks, Iris was the Messenger, and Iris was unquestionably the Turkish Orus or St. George. In Arabia, St. George is known as El Khoudr, and it is believed that El Khoudr is not yet dead, but still flies round and round the world: in a subsequent chapter it will be shown that Orus is the same as Horus the Egyptian dragon-slayer; hence Giggras, another of St. George's titles, may be resolved into Mighty Mighty Horus or Eros, and it is possible that the Pictish town of Delginross should read *Tall King Eros*.

The eleven rows of rocks at Carnac extend, it is said, for *eight* miles, and at the neighbouring Er-lanic are two megalithic circles, one dipping into the sea, the other submerged in deep water: according to Baring-Gould, these two rings are juxtaposed, forming an 8, and lie on the south-east of the island; the first circle consists of 180 stones (twice *nine*), but several are fallen, and it can only be seen complete when the tide is out; one stone is 16 feet high; the second circle can be seen only at low tide.[1]

It is probable that the measurements of the Venus de Quinipily, illustrated on p. 530, are not without significance: the statue stands upon a pedestal, 9 feet high, and the figure itself rises 8 feet high.[2] With eight may be further connoted the eastern teaching of the "Noble Eightfold

---

[1] *Brittany*, p. 232.

[2] Aynsley, Mrs. Murray, *Symbolism of the East and West*, p. 87.

Path," and also the belief of Western Freemasonry as stated in Mackey's *Lexicon of Freemasonry* : " Eight was esteemed as the first cube (2 × 2 × 2), and signified friendship, prudence, counsel, and justice. It designated the primitive Law of Nature, which supposes all men to be equal." The root of *eight, octave,* and *octet* or *ogdoad* is *Og*, the primeval giant, who, as we have seen, was reputed to have waded alongside the ark with its eight primordial passengers.

When flourishing, the megalithic monument at Carnac must have dwarfed our dual-circled, two-mile shrine at Avebury: "The labour of its erection," to quote from Deane, "may be imagined from the fact that it originally consisted of eleven rows of stones, about 10,000 in number, of which more than 300 averaged from 15 to 17 feet in height, and from 16 to 20 or 30 feet in girth; one stone even measuring 42 feet in circumference ".

One of the commonest of sepulchral finds in Brittany is the stone axe, sometimes banded in alternate stripes of black and white: the axe was pre-eminently a Cretan emblem, and my suggestion that the Carnac stones were originally erected to the honour of St. Ursula and the 11,000 Virgins is somewhat strengthened by the coincidence that the London Church of St. Mary Axe was closely and curiously identified with the legend. According to Stow : " In St. Marie Street had ye of old time a parish church of St. Marie the Virgin, St. Ursula and the 11,000 Virgins, whose church was commonly called St. Marie at the Axe of the sign of an axe over against the east, and thereof on St. Marie Pellipar ". In view of the fact that the town of Ypres boasted an enormous collection of relics of the 11,000 Virgins, the title Pellipar may be reasonably resolved into *Belle power*: the Cretan axe or double axe symbolised almighty *power*.[1]

According to an Assyrian hymn, Istar, the immaculate great *Star*, the "Lady Ruler of the Host of Heaven," the "Lady of Ladies," "Goddess without peer," who shaped the lives of all mankind was the "Stately world-Queen sov'ran of the Sky".

> Adored art thou in every sacred place,
> In temples, holy dwellings, and in shrines.
> Where is thy name not lauded? Where thy will
> Unheeded, and thy images not made?[2]

In the caves or "fetish shrines" of Crete have been found rude figurines of the Mother and the Child, and it is probable that the pathetically crude bronze statuettes

---

[1] I have elsewhere reproduced examples of the double axe crossed into the form of an ex (X). Sir Walter Scott observes that in North Britain "it was no unusual thing to see females, from respect to their supposed views into futurity, and the degree of divine inspiration which was vouchsafed to them, arise to the degree of HAXA, or chief priestess, from which comes the word *Hexe*, now universally used for a witch". He adds: "It may be worth while to notice that the word Haxa is still used in Scotland in its sense of a druidess, or chief priestess, to distinguish the places where such females exercised their ritual. There is a species of small intrenchment on the western descent of the Eildon hills, which Mr. Milne, in his account of the parish of Melrose, drawn up about eighty years ago, says, was denominated *Bourjo*, a word of unknown derivation, by which the place is still known. Here a universal and subsisting tradition bore that human sacrifices were of yore offered, while the people assisting could behold the ceremony from the elevation of the glacis which slopes inward. With this place of sacrifice communicated a path, still discernible, called the *Haxellgate*, leading to a small glen or narrow valley called the *Haxellcleuch*—both which words are probably derived from the Haxa or chief priestess of the pagans" (*Letters on Demonology*). It may be suggested that the mysterious *bourjo* was an *abri* of pere Jo or Jupiter. The Scotch *jo* as in "John Anderson my Jo," now signifying *sweetheart*, presumably meant joy.

[2] *Cf.* McKenzie, Donald A., *Myths of Babylonia*, p. 18.

here illustrated represent the austere wielder of the wand of doom. Fig. 407 comes from Iberia where it was discovered in the vicinity of what was undoubtedly a shrine near the pass over the Sierra *Morena* at Despena *Perros*: Fig. 408 comes from the English village of Aust-on-Severn. The place-name Aust appears in Domesday as Austreclive,

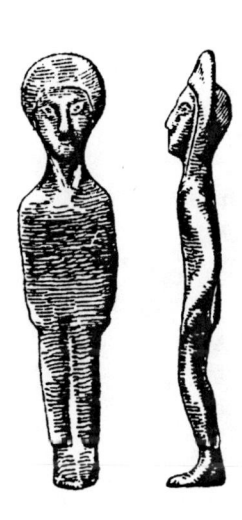
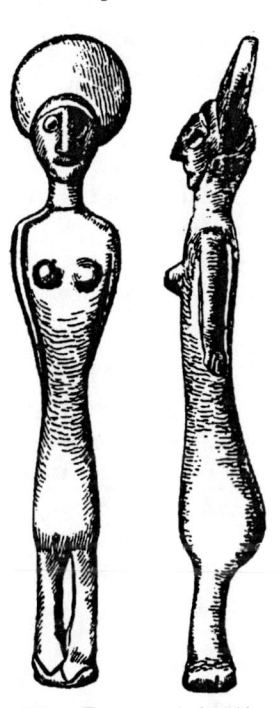

Fig. 407.—Bronze statuette, Despeña Perros.

Fig. 408.—Bronze statuette, Aust-on-Severn, Gloucs.

From *A Guide to the Antiquities of the Bronze Age* (B.M.).

and the authorities suppose it to have meant "not *East* as often thought, but the Roman Augusta": I doubt whether any Roman Augusta ever troubled to claim a mere cleeve, and it is more probable that Austreclive was a cleft or pass sacred to the austere Austre. There is an Austrey at Atherstone, an Austerfield at Bawtry, and an "Austrells" at Aldridge: this latter, which may be connoted with the

Oyster Hills round Verulam, the authorities assume to have meant "Austerhill, hill of the hearth, forge or furnace". That Istar was the mighty Hammer Smith is probable, for the archaic hymnist writes :—

> I thee adore—
> The gift of strength is thine for thou art strong.

In all likelihood the head-dress of our figurines was intended to denote the crescent moon for the same hymnist continues :—

> O Light divine,
> Gleaming in lofty splendour over the earth,
> Heroic daughter of the moon, O hear!
> O stately Queen,
> At thought of thee the world is filled with fear,
> The gods in heaven quake, and on the earth
> All spirits pause and all mankind bow down
> With reverence for thy name . . . O Lady Judge
> Thy ways are just and holy; thou dost gaze
> On sinners with compassion, and each morn
> Leadest the wayward to the rightful path.
> Now linger not, but come! O goddess fair.
> O Shepherdess of all, thou drawest nigh
> With feet unwearied.

I have suggested that the circle of Long Meg and her daughters originally embodying the idea of a Marygold, Marguerite, or Aster, was erected to the honour of St. Margaret the Peggy, or Pearl of Price, and it is possible that the oyster or producer of the pearl may have derived its name from Easter or Ostara: that Astarte was St. Margaret is obvious from the effigies herewith, and the connection is further pointed by the already noted fact that in the neighbourhood of St. Margaret's, Westminster, there prevailed traditions of a Giantess named Long Meg. This powerful Maiden was evidently Margaret or Invicta, on the War-path, her pugilistic exploits being far-famed: it is particularly related that Long Meg distinguished herself in the wars at Bulloigne, whence it will probably prove that "Bulloigne" was associated with the War Maid whom the Romans termed Bellona, and that both Bulloigne and Bologna were originally shrines of Bello gina, either the *Beautiful Woman* or the *War Queen*.

FIG. 409.—St. Margaret. From Westminster Abbey. From *The Cross: Christian and Heathen* (Brock, M.).

FIG. 410.—Astarte, the Syrian Venus. From a Coin in the British Museum. From *The Cross: Christian and Heathen* (Brock, M.).

That Istar, "the heroic daughter of the moon," was Bellona or the Queen of War is clear from the invocation—

O hear!
Thou dost control our weapons and award
In battles fierce the Victory at will.
O crowned majestic Fate. Ishtar most high,
Who art exalted above all the gods,
Thou bringest lamentation; thou dost urge
With hostile hearts our brethren to the fray.
The gift of strength is thine for thou art strong,
Thy will is urgent brooking no delay.
Thy hand is violent, thou *queen of war*,
Girded with battle and enrobed with fear,
Thou sov'ran wealder of the wand of Doom,
The heavens and earth are under thy control.

There is very little doubt that the heroic Long Meg of Westminster was alternatively the Mary Ambree of old English ballad: in Ben Jonson's time apparently any remarkable virago was entitled a Mary Ambree, and the name seems to have been particularly associated with Ghent.[1] As the word Ambree is radically *bree*, it is curious to find John of Gaunt, who is associated with Kensington, also associated with Carn Brea in Cornwall: here, old John of Gaunt is believed to have been the last of the giants, and to have lived in a castle on the top of Carn Brea, whence in one stride he could pass to a neighbouring town four miles distant. The Heraldic Chain of SSS was known as John of Gaunt's chain: the symbol of SSS occurs frequently on Candian or Cretan monuments, and it is probable that John of Gaunt's chain was originally Jupiter's, or Brea's chain.[2]

The name Ghent, Gand, or Gaunt may be connoted not only with Kent or Cantium, and Candia or Crete, but also with Dr. Lardner's statement: "That the full moon was the chief feast among the ancient Spaniards is evident from the fact that *Agandia or Astartia* is the name for Sunday among the Basques".

We have already seen that Cain was identified with "the Man in the Moon," that *cann* was the Cornish for *full moon*, and we have connoted the fairy Kenna of Kensington with the New Moon: the old English *cain*,

[1] Mary Ambree
Who marched so free,
To the siege of Gaunt,
And death could not daunt
As the ballad doth vaunt.

[2] In Kirtlington Park (Oxon) was a Johnny Gaunt's pond in which his spirit was supposed to dwell. A large ash tree was also there known as Johnny Gaunt's tree.

meaning *fair* or bright, is clearly connected with *candid* and *candescent*. Kenna is the saint to whom the village of Keynsham on the Somersetshire Avon is dedicated, and St. Kenna is said there to have lived in the heart of a wood. To the north of Kensington lies St. John's Wood, and also the ancient seat named Caen or Ken Wood: this Ken Wood, which is on the heights of Highgate, and is higher than the summit of St. Paul's, commands a panoramic view of the metropolis that can nowhere else be matched. Akin to the words *ken, cunning*, and *canny*, is the Christian name Conan which is interpreted as being Celtic for *wisdom*. The Celtic names Kean and Kenny—no doubt akin to Coyne—meant *vast*, and in Cornish *ken* meant *pity*. On the river Taff there is a Llan*gain* of which the church is dedicated to St. Canna, and on the Welsh river Canna there is a Llan*ganna* or Llan*gan*: at Llan*daff* by Car*diff* is Canon's Park.

There is a celebrated well in Cornwall known as St. Kean's, St. Kayne's, St. Keyne's, or St. Kenna's, and the supposed peculiarity of this fountain is that it confers mastery or chieftianship upon whichever of a newly-wedded couple first drinks at it after marriage. St. Kayne or St. Kenna is also said to have visited St. Michael's Mount, and to have imparted the very same virtue to a stone seat situated dizzily on the height of the chapel tower: " whichever, man or wife, sits in this chair first *shall rule* through life ": this double tradition associating rule and mastery with St. Kayne makes it justifiable to equate the " Saint " with *kyn, princess* and with *khan* the *great Han* or King. There was a well at Chun Castle whose waters supposedly bestowed perpetual youth: *can*, meaning a drinking vessel, is the root of *canal, channel*, or *kennel*, meaning water course: we have already connoted the word *demijohn* or Dame Jeanne with the Cornish well termed Joan's Pitcher, and this root is seemingly responsible for *canopus*, the Egyptian and Greek term for the human-headed type of vase as illustrated on page 301. A writer in *Notes and Queries* for 3rd January, 1852, quotes the following song sung by children in South Wales on New Year's morning, *i.e.*, 1st January, when carrying a can of water newly drawn from the well :—

> Here we bring new water
>   From the well so clear,
> For to worship God with
>   The happy New Year.
> Sing levez dew, sing levez dew,
>   The water and the wine;
> The seven bright gold wires
>   And the bugles they do shine.
>
> Sing reign of Fair Maid
>   With gold upon her toe,
> Open you the west door,
>   And let the old Year go.
> Sing reign of Fair Maid
>   With gold upon her chin,
> Open you the east door,
>   And let the New Year in.

We have traced Maggie Figgy of St. Levan on her titanic chair supervising the surging waters of the ocean, and there is little doubt that the throne of St. Michael's was the corresponding seat of Micah, the Almighty King or Great One. The equation of Michael = Kayne may be connoted with the London Church now known as St. Nicholas *Acon*: this name appearing mysteriously in ancient documents as alternatively " Acun," " Hakoun," " Hakun," and " Achun " it is supposed may have denoted a benefactor of the building. In Cornish *ughan* or *aughan* meant *supreme ;* in Welsh *echen* meant *origins* or *sources*,[1] and as *Nicholas* is the same word as *nucleus* it is impossible now to say whether St. Nicholas Acon was a shrine of the *Great One* or of *echen* the little Nicholas or *nucleus*. Probably as figured at Royston where Kitt is bearing the Cadet or the small *chit* upon his shoulder, the two conceptions were concurrent: on the opposite side of the Royston Cave is figured St. Katherine, Kathleen, or Kate: Catarina means *the pure one*, but *catha* as in *catholic* also means the universal, and there is no doubt that St. Kathleen or Kate was a personification of the Queen of the Universe.

Cendwen or Keridwen, *alias* Ked, was represented by the British Bards as a mare, whale, or ark, whence emerged the universe: the story of Jonah and the whale is a variant of the Ark legend, and it is not without significance that the Hebridean island of Iona is identified as the locale of a miraculous "Whale of wondrous and immense size lifting itself up like a mountain floating on the surface".[2] Notwithstanding the forbidding aspect of this monster St. Columba's disciple quiets the fears of his companion by the assurance: "Go in peace; thy faith in Christ shall defend thee from this danger; I and that beast are under the power of God".

It has been seen that Night was not necessarily esteemed as evil, nor were the nether regions considered to be outside the radius of the Almighty: that Nicholas, Nixy, or Nox was the black or nether deity is obvious, yet without doubt he was the same conception as the Babylonish "exalted One of the nether world, Him of the radiant

[1] Herbert, A., *Cyclops*, p. 202. [2] *Life of Columba*, p. 40.

face, yea radiant; the exalted One of the nether world, Him of the dove-like voice, yea dove-like".[1]

That St. Margaret was the White Dove rather than the foul Culver is probable from her representation as the Dragon-slayer, and it is commonly accepted that this almost world-wide emblem denoted Light subduing Darkness, Day conquering Night, or Good overcoming Evil. But there is another legend of St. Margaret to the effect that the maid so meek and mild was swallowed by a Dragon: her cross, however, haply stuck in its throat, and the beast perforce let her free by incontinently bursting (date uncertain); in Art St. Margaret therefore appears as holding a cross and rising from a dragon, although as Voragine candidly admits—"the story is thought to be apocryphal". We have seen that Magus or the Wandering Jew was credited with the feat of wriggling out of a post—" and they saw that he was no other than a beardless youth and fair faced": that the adventure of Maggie was the counterpart to that of Magus is rendered probable by the fact that St. Margaret's birth is assigned to Antioch, a city which was alternatively known as Jonah. With Jonah or Iona may be connoted the British Aeon—

> Aeon hath seen age after age in long succession,
> But like a serpent which has cast its skin,
> Rose to new life in youthful vigour strong.

In Calmet's *Biblical Dictionary* there is illustrated a medal of ancient Corinth representing an old man in a state of decrepitude entering a whale, but on the same medal the old man renewed is shown to have come out of the same fish in a state of infancy.

Among the Greeks Apollo or the Sun was represented as

[1] *Cf.* Mackenzie, D. A., *Myths of Babylonia*, p. 86.

riding on a dolphin's back: the word *dolphin* is connected with *delphus*, the womb, and doubtless also with *Delphi*, the great centre of Apollo worship and the legendary navel of the Universe. Alpha has been noted as the British name of Noah's wife, and it is probable that Delphi meant at one time the Divine Alpha or Elf: in the Iberian coin here illustrated (origin uncertain) the little Elf or spriggan is equipped with a cross; in the coin of Carteia (Spain) the inscription XIDD probably corresponds to the name which the British Bards wrote—" Ked ".

In India the Ark or Leviathan of Life is represented as half horse or half mare, and among the Phœnicians the

FIGS. 411 and 412.—Iberian. From Akermann.

word *hipha* denoted both *mare* and *ship:* in Britain the *Magna Mater*, Ked, was figured as the combination of an old giantess, a hen, a mare, and as a ship which set sail, lifted the Bard from the earth and swelled out like a ship upon the waters. Davies observes: " And that the ancient Britons actually did portray this character in the grotesque manner suggested by our Bard appears by several ancient British coins where we find a figure compounded of a bird, a boat, and a mare ". The coin to which Davies here refers is that illustrated on page 596, Fig. 356: that the Babylonians built their ships in the combined form of a mare and fish is clear from the illustration overleaf.

The most universal and generally understood emblem of

peace is a dove bearing in its beak an olive-branch,[1] or sprig, and this emblem is intimately associated with the

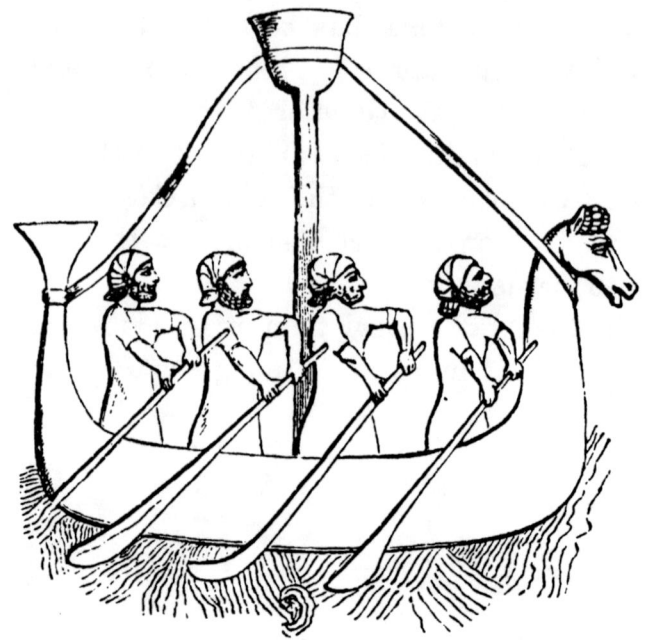

Fig. 413.—A Galley (Khorsabad). From *Nineveh* (Layard).

Figs. 414 and 415.—British (Channel Islands). From Barthelemy.

Ark: among the poems of the Welsh Bard Aneurin is the expectation—

> The crowned Babe will come like Iona
> Out of the belly of the whale; great will be his dignity.
> He will place every one according to his merits,
> He is the principal strong tower of the Kingdom.[2]

[1] There is a London church entitled " St. Nicholas Olave ".
[2] *Cf.* Morien, *Light of Britannia*, p. 67.

As Iona means dove, the culver on the hackney's back (Fig. 415) is evidently St. Columba, and the crowned Babe in Fig. 414 is in all probability that same "spriggan on Dowdy's back," or Elphin, as the British Bards speak so persistently and mysteriously of "liberating". In Egypt the spright is portrayed rising from a maculate or spotted beast, and in all these and parallel instances the emblem probably denoted rejuvenescence or new birth; either

Fig. 416. — From *The Correspondences of Egypt* (Odhler).

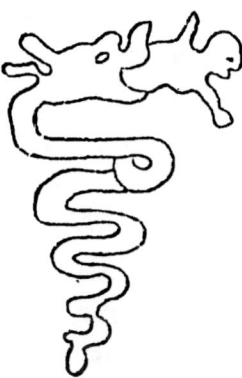

Fig. 417. — Mediæval Papermark. F·om *Les Filigranes* (Briquet, C. M.).

Spring *ex* Winter, Change *ex* Time, the Seen from the Unseen, Amor *ex* Nox, Visible from Invisible, or New from Old.

The eight parents from the Ark may be connoted with Aught from Naught, for *eight* is the same word as *aught* and *naught* is the same word as *night*, *nuit*, or *not* : *naughty* means evil, whence the legend of Amor being born from Nox or Night might perhaps have been sublimated into the idea of Good emerging even from things noxious or nugatory.[1] Yet in the Cox and Box like rule of Night and Day the all-conquering Nikky was no doubt regarded as *unique* : " Shining and vanishing in the beauteous circle of the Hours, dwelling at one time in gloomy Tartarus, at another elevating himself to Olympus giving ripeness to the fruits ": it is not unlikely that the ruddy *nectarine* was assigned to him, and similarly *nectar* the celestial drink of the gods, or *ambrosia* in a liquid form.

Of the universally recognised Dualism the black and white magpie was evidently an emblem, and the superstitions in connection with this bird are still potent. The Magpie is sometimes called Magot-pie, and Maggoty-pie, and for this etymology Skeat offers the following explanation : " Mag is short for Magot—French *Margot*, a familiar form of *Marguerite*, also used to denote a Magpie. This is from Latin *Margarita*, Greek *Margarites*, a pearl." There is no material connection between a pearl and a Magpie, but both objects were alike emblems of the same spiritual Power or Pair : between Margot and Istar the same equation is here found, for in Kent magpies were known popularly as *haggisters*.[2] Although I have deemed *hag* to mean *high* it will be remembered that in Greek *hagia* meant holy, whence haggister may well have been understood as *holy ister*.

Layamon in his *Brut* mentions that the Britons at the time of Hengist's invasion " Oft speak stilly and discourse with whispers of two young men that dwell far hence ; the one hight Uther the other Ambrosie ". Of these fabulous

---

[1] Skeat connotes *naughty* with " *na* not, *wiht* a whit, see no and whit " : it would thus seem to have been equivalent to *no white*, which is black or nocturnal.

[2] Hardwick, C., *Traditions, Superstitions, and Folklore*, p. 254.

Twain—the not altogether forgotten Two Kings of their ancestors—we may equate Uther with the *uter* or womb of Night and Aurelie Ambrosie with Aurora the Golden Sunburst.

It is probable that the Emporiae, some of whose elphin horse coins were reproduced on page 281, were worshippers of Aurelie Ambrosie or " St. Ambrose " of whom it will be remembered : " some said that they saw a star upon his body " : it is also not unlikely that our Mary Ambree or Fair Ambree was the daughter of Amber, the divine Umpire and the Emperor of the Empyrean. The ballad recalls :—

> There was none ever like Mary Ambree,
> Shee led upp her souldiers in battaile array
> 'Gainst three times theyr number by breake of the day ;
> Seven howers in skirmish continued shee,
> Was not this a brave bonny lasse, Mary Ambree ? [1]

The sex of this braw Maiden was disguised under a knight's panoply, and it was only when the fight was finished that her personality was revealed.

> No captain of England ; behold in your sight
> Two breasts in my bosome, and therefore no knight,
> No knight, sons of England, nor captain you see,
> But a poor simple lass called Mary Ambree.

If the reader will turn back to the Virago coins illustrated *ante*, p. 596, which I think represent *Ked* in the aspect of *Hecate*—the names are no doubt cognate—he will notice the pastoral crook of the little Shepherdess or Bishop of all souls, and there is little doubt that these figures depict

---

[1] The *seven* hours in skirmish are suggestive of the Fair maid with gold upon her toe :—

> The *seven* bright gold wires
> And the bugles they do shine,

ante, p. 650.

what a Welsh Bard termed "the winged genius of the splendid crosier".

Although Long Meg of Westminster was said to be a Virago, and was connected in popular opinion with "Bulloigne," it is not unlikely that Bulloigne· was a misconception of Bulinga; the ornamental water of what is now St. James' Park is a reconstruction of what was originally known as Bulinga Fen, and in that swamp it is probable that Kitty-with-her-canstick, *alias* Belinga the *Beautiful Angel*, was supposed to dwell. The name Bolingbroke implies the existence somewhere of a Bolinga's brook where Belle Inga might also probably have been seen "dancing to the cadence of the stream"; in Shropshire is an earthwork known as Billings Ring, and at Truro there is a Bolingey which is surmised to have meant "isle of the Bollings". These Bollings were presumably related to the Billings of Billingsgate and elsewhere,[1] and the Bellinge or Billing families were almost certainly connected with Billing, the race-hero of the Angles and Varnians. According to Rydberg the celestial Billing "represents the evening and the glow of twilight, and he is ruler of those regions of the world where the divinities of light find rest and peace": Billing was the divine defender of the Varnians or Varinians, which word, says Rydberg, "means 'defenders' and the protection here referred to can be none other than that given to the journey-

---

[1] Presumably Billingham River in Durham was a home of the Billings: there is a Billingley in Darfield parish, Yorkshire, a Billingsley in Bridgenorth, Salop: Billingbear in Berks is the seat of Lord Braybrook: Billingford *or Pirleston* belonged to a family named Burley: at Billington in Bradley parish, Staffs, is a commanding British camp known as Billington Bury. Billinge Hill, near Wigan, has a beacon on the top and commands a view of Ingleborough.

XI.] THE FAIR MAID 659

ing divinities of light when they have reached the Western horizon ".[1]

That Billing and the Ingles were connected with Barkshire, the county of the Vale of the White Horse or Brok, is implied by place-names such as Billingbare by Inglemeer Pond in the East, by Inkpen Beacon—originally Ingepenne or Hingepenne—in the South, and by Inglesham near

FIG. 418.—Adapted from the Salisbury Chapter Seal. From *The Cross: Christian and Pagan* (Brock, M.).

Fearnham and Farringdon in the West. Near Inglemeer is Shinfield and slightly westward is Sunning, which must once have been a place of uncanny sanctity for "it is amazing that so inconsiderable a village should have been the See of *eight* Bishops translated afterwards to Sherborn and at last to Salisbury."[2] The seal of Salisbury repre-

[1] *Teutonic Mythology.*
[2] *A New Description of England*, 1724, p. 61.

sents the Maiden of the Sun and Moon, and it is probable that the place-name Maidenhead, originally Madenheith, near Marlow (Domesday Merlawe—Mary low or hill ?) did not, as Skeat so aggressively assumes, mean a *hythe* or landing place for maidens, but Maiden*heath*, a heath or mead sacred to the braw Maiden.

With the Farens and the Varenians may be connoted the Cornish village of Trevarren or the abode of Varren : this is in the parish of St. Columb, where Columba the Dove is commemorated not as a man but as a Virgin Martyr. Many, if not all, Cornish villages had their so-called " Sentry field " and the Broad Sanctuary at St. Margaret's, Westminster, no doubt marks the site of some such sanctuary or city of refuge as will be considered in a following chapter. That St. Margaret the Meek or Long Meg was the *Bride* of the adjacent St. Peter is a reasonable inference, and it is probable that " Broad Sanctuary " was originally hers. According to *The Golden Legend* : " Margaret is Maid of a precious gem or ouche[1] that is named a Margaret. So the blessed Margaret was white by virginity, little by humility, and virtuous by operation. The virtue of this stone is said to be against effusion of blood, against passion of the heart, and to comfortation of the spirit." I am unable to trace any immediate connection between St. Margaret and the Dove, but an original relation is implied by the epithets which are bestowed by the Gaels to St. Columbkille of Iona who is entitled " The Precious Gem," " The Royal Bright Star," " The Meek," " The Wise," and " The Divine Branch who was in the yoke of the Pure Mysteries of God ". These are titles older than the worthy monk whose biography was written by Adamnan : they

[1] An *ouche* is a *bugle* : " the bugles they do shine ".

belong to the archetypal Columba or Culver. There is a river Columb in Devonshire upon which stands the town of Cullompton: in Kent is Reculver once a Royal town of which "the root is unknown, but the present form has been influenced by old English *culfre, culfer*, a culver-dove or wood-pigeon".

That St. Columba of Iona was both the White and the Black Culver is implied by his two names of Colum (dove) and Crimthain (wolf): that the great Night-dog or wolf was for some reason connected with the *nutrix* (*vide* the coin illustrated on page 364, and the Etrurian Romulus and Remus legend) is obvious, apart from the significance of the word *wolf* which is radically *olf*. Columbas' mother, we are told, was a certain royal Ethne, the *eleventh* in descent from Cathair Mor, a King of Leinster: Leinster was a *stadr, ster*, or place of the Laginenses, and that Columba was a personification of Young Lagin or the Little *Holy King* of Yule is implied (apart from much other evidence) in the story that one of his visitors "could by no means look upon his face, suffused as it was with a marvellous glow, and he immediately fled in great fear".

Among the Gaels the Little Holy King of Tir an Og, or the Land of the Young, was Angus Og or Angus the youthful: when discussing Angus (*excellent virtue*) in connection with the ancient goose and the cain goose I was unaware that the Greek for goose is *ken*. In the far-away Hebrides the men, women, and children of Barra and South Uist (or Aust?) still hold to a primitive faith in St. Columba, St. Bride, or St. Mary, and as a shealing hymn they sing the following astonishingly beautiful folk-song:—

> Thou, gentle Michael of the white steed,
> Who subdued the Dragon of blood,

For love of God and the Son of Mary
Spread over us thy wing, shield us all!
Spread over us thy wing, shield us all!

Mary, beloved! Mother of the White Lamb
Protect us, thou Virgin of nobleness,
Queen of Beauty! Shepherdess of the flocks!
Keep our cattle, surround us together,
Keep our cattle, surround us together.

Thou Columkille, the friendly, the kind,
In the name of the Father, the Son, and the Spirit Holy,
Through the Three-in-One, through the Three,
Encompass us, guard our procession,
Encompass us, guard our procession.

Thou Father! Thou Son! Thou Spirit Holy!
Be the Three-One with us day and night,
On the Machair plain, on the mountain ridge,
The Three-One is with us, with His arm around our head,
The Three-One is with us, with His arm around our head,

But the Boatmen of Barray sing for the last verse:—

Thou Father! Thou Son! Thou Spirit Holy!
Be the Three-One with us day and night,
And on the crested wave, or on the mountain side,
Our Mother is there, and Her arm is under our head,
Our Mother is there, and Her arm is under our head.[1]

[1] Quoted from *Adamnan's Life of Columba* (Huyshe, W.).

CHAPTER XII.

Peter's Orchards.

"But all the beauty of the pleasaunce drew its being from the song of the bird; for from his chant flowed love which gives its shadow to the tree, its healing to the simple, and its colour to the flower. Without that song the fountain would have ceased to spring, and the green garden become a little dry dust, for in its sweetness lay all their virtue."—*Provençal Fairy Tale.*

AMONG the relics preserved at the monastery of St. Nicholas of Bari is a club with which the saint, who is said to have become a friar at the age of *eleven*, was beaten by the devil: a club was the customary symbol of Hercules; the Celtic Hercules was, as has been seen, depicted as a baldhead leading a rout of laughter-loving followers by golden chains fastened to their ears, and as it was the habit of St. Nicholas-of-the-Club to wander abroad singing after the ancient fashion, one may be sure that Father Christmas is the lineal descendant of the British Ogmios or Mighty Muse, *alias* the Wandering Jew or Joy. That Bride "the gentle" was at times similarly equipped is obvious from a ceremony which in Scotland and the North of England used to prevail at Candlemas: "the mistress and servants of each family take a sheaf of oats and dress it up in woman's apparel, put it in a large basket and lay a wooden club by it, and this they call "Briid's Bed," and then the mistress and servants cry three times: "Briid is come, Briid is welcome"! This they do just before going to bed": another version of this custom records the cry as—"Bridget, Bridget, come is; thy bed is ready".

In an earlier chapter we connected Iupiter or Jupiter with Aubrey or Oberon, and that this roving Emperor of Phairie Land was familiar to the people of ancient Berkshire is implied not only by a river in that county termed the Auborn, but also by adjacent place-names such as Aberfield, Burfield, Purley, and Bray. Skeat connotes Bray (by Maidenhead) with "Old English *braw*, Mercian *breg*, an eyebrow," but what sensible or likely connection is supposed to exist between the town of Bray and an eyebrow I am unable to surmise: we have, however, considered the prehistoric "butterfly" or eyebrows, and it is not impossible that Bray was identified with this mysterious Epeur (Cupid) or Amoretto. The claims to ubiquity and antiquity put by the British poet into the mouth of Taliesin or *Radiant Brow*—the mystic child of Nine constituents [1]—

[1] Primary chief bard am I to Elphin,
And my original country is the region of the summer stars;
Idno and Heinin called me Merddin,
At length every king will call me Taliesin.

I was with my Lord in the highest sphere,
On the fall of Lucifer into the depth of hell
I have borne a banner before Alexander;
I know the names of the stars from north to south;
I have been on the galaxy at the throne of the Distributer;
I was in Canaan when Absalom was slain;
I conveyed the Divine Spirit to the level of the vale of Hebron;
I was in the court of Don before the birth of Gwdion.
I was instructor to Eli and Enoc;
I have been winged by the genius of the splendid crosier;
I have been loquacious prior to being gifted with speech;

is paralleled by the claims of Irish Ameurgin, likewise by the claims of Solomonic "Wisdom," and there is little doubt that the symbolic forms of the "Teacher to all Intelligences" are beyond all computation.

That Berkshire, the shire of the White Horse, was a seat of beroc or El Borak the White Horse is further implied by the name Berkshire: according to Camden this originated " some say from Beroc, a certain wood where box grew in great plenty"; according to others from a disbarked oak [*i.e.*, a *bare oak !*] to which when the state was in more than ordinary danger the inhabitants were wont to resort in ancient times to consult about their public affairs ".[1] Over-

> I was at the place of the crucifixion of the merciful Son of God;
> I have been three periods in the prison of Arianrod;
> I have been the chief director of the work of the tower on Nimrod
> I am a wonder whose origin is not known.
> I have been in Asia with Noah in the ark,
> I have seen the destruction of Sodom and Gomorra;
> I have been in India when Roma was built,
> I am now come here to the remnant of Troia.
>
> I have been with my Lord in the manger of the ass:
> I strengthened Moses through the water of Jordan;
> I have been in the firmament with Mary Magdalene;
> I have obtained the muse from the cauldron of Caridwen;
> I have been bard of the harp to Lleon or Lochlin,
> I have been on the White Hill, in the court of Cynvelyn,
> For a day and a year in stocks and fetters,
> I have suffered hunger for the Son of the Virgin,
> I have been fostered in the land of the Deity,
> I have been teacher to all intelligences,
> I am able to instruct the whole universe.
> I shall be until the day of doom on the face of the earth
> And it is not known whether my body is flesh or fish.

[1] *A New Description of England* (1724), p. 57.

looking Brockley in Kent is an Oak of Honor Hill, and probably around that ancient and possibly bare Oak the natives of old Brockley or Brock Meadow met in many a consultation.[1] At Coventry is Berkswell: Berkeleys are numerous, and that these sites were *abris* or sanctuaries is implied by the official definition of Great Berkhamstead, *i.e.*, " *Sheltered, home place,* or *fortified farm* ".

At St. Breock in Cornwall there is a pair of Longstones, one measuring 12 feet 4 inches, the other 8 feet, and in all probability at some time or other these pierres or petras were symbols of the phairy Pair who were the Parents and Protectors of the district. At St. Columb in Cornwall there is a Longstone known as " The Old Man ": now measuring 7 feet 6 inches, in all probability this stone was originally 8 feet high; it was also " once apparently surrounded by a small circle ".

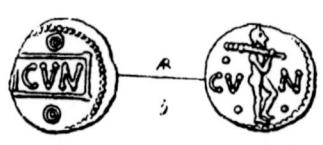

Fig. 419. — British. From Akerman.

In the British coin here illustrated the Old Man jogging along with a club is probably CUN the Great One, or the Aged One. The brow of Honor Oak ridge is known as Canonbie Lea, which may be resolved into the " meadow of the abode of King On ": from this commanding height one may contemplate all London lying in the valley; facing it are the highlands of Cuneburn, Kenwood, Caenwood, and St. John's Wood. London stone is situated in what is now termed Cannon Street—a supposed corruption of Candlewick Street: the greater probability is that the name is connected with the ancient Kenning or Watch Tower, known as a *burkenning*, which once occupied the

---

[1] *Braxfield* Road at modern Brockley may mark the site of this meadow.

site now marked by Tower Royal in Cannon Street: the ancient Cenyng Street by Mikelgate at York, or Eboracum—a city attributed to a King Ebrauc who will probably prove to be identical with Saint Breock—marked in all likelihood the site of a similar broch, burgkenning, barbican, or watch tower. One may account for ancient Candlewick by the supposition that this district was once occupied by a candle factory, or that it was the property of a supposititious Kendal, who was identical with the Brook, Brick, or Broken of the neighbouring Brook's wharf, Brickhill, and Broken wharf. At Kendal in Westmorland, situated on the river Can or Kent, around which we find Barnside, the river Burrow or Borrow, and Preston Hall, we find also a Birbeck, and the memories of a Lord Parr: this district was supposedly the home of the Concanni. The present site of Highbury Barn Tavern by Canonbury (London) was once occupied by a "camp" in what was known as Little St. John's Wood,[1] and as this part of London is not conspicuously "high," it is not improbable that Highbury was once an *abri*: in the immediate neighbourhood still exists Paradise Road, Paradise Passage, Aubert Park and a Calabria Road which may possibly mark the site of an original Kil abria. At Highbury is Canonbury Tower, whence tradition says an underground passage once extended to the *priory* of St. John's in Clerkenwell: from Highbury to the Angel at Islington there runs an Upper Street: *upper* is the Greek *hyper* meaning *over* (German *uber*), and that the celebrated "Angel" was originally a fairy or Bellinga, is somewhat implied by the neighbouring Fairbank Street—once a fairy bank?—and by Bookham Street—once a home of Bogie or Puck?

[1] Wilson, J., *Imperial Gazetteer*, i., 946.

From Canonbie Lea at Honor Oak, Brockley (London), one overlooks Peckham, Bickley, Beckenham, and Bellingham, the last named being decoded by the authorities into *home of Belling*.

We have noted the tradition at Brentford of Two Kings "united yet divided twain at once," yet there is also an extant ballad which commences—

> The noble king of Brentford
> Was old and very sick.

The Cornish hill of Godolphin was also known as Godolcan, and in view of the connection between Nicolas and eleven it may be assumed that this site was sacred either to Elphin, the *elven*, the Holy King, or the Old King. At Highbury is an Old Cock Tavern, and in Upper Street an Old Parr Inn: not improbably Old Parr was once the deity of " Upper " Street or " Highbury," and it is also not unlikely that the St. Peter of Westminster was similarly Old Parr, for according to *The History of Signboards*— "'The OLD MAN,' Market Place, Westminster, was probably intended for Old Parr, who was celebrated in ballads as 'The Olde, Olde, Very Olde Manne'. The token represents a bearded bust in profile, with a bare head.[1] In the reign of James I. it was the name of a tavern in the Strand, *otherwise called the Hercules Tavern*, and in the eighteenth century there were two coffee-houses, the one called 'the OLD MAN'S,' the other 'the YOUNG MAN'S' Coffee-house."[2]

If the Old, Old, Very Old Man were Peter the white-haired warden of the walls of Heaven it is obvious that the Young Man would be Pierrot: it is not by accident that white-faced Pierrot, or Peterkin, or Pedrolino, is garbed

---

[1] *Cf.* CUN, coin, *ante*, p. 666. [2] P. 494.

in white and wears a conical white cap, the legend that accounts for this curious costume being to the effect that years and years ago St. Peter and St. Joseph were once watching (from a burkenning?) over a wintry plain from the walls of Paradise, when they beheld what seemed a pink rose peering out from beneath the snow; but instead of being a rose it proved to be the face of a child, who St. Peter picked up in his arms, whereupon the snow and rime were transformed into an exquisite white garment. It was intended that the little Peter should remain unsullied, but, as it happened, the Boy, having wandered from Paradise, started playing Ring-o-Roses on a village green where a little girl tempted him to talk: then the trouble began, for Pierrot speckled his robe, and St. Peter was unable to allow him in again; but he gave him big black buttons and a merry heart, and there the story ends.[1]

In Pantomime—which has admittedly an ancestry of august antiquity—the counterpart to Pierrot is Columbine, or the Little Dove; doubtless the same Maiden as the Virgin Martyr of St. Columb, Cornwall: this parish is situated in what was termed "The Hundred of *Pydar*"; in Welsh Bibles Peter is rendered *Pedr*, and one of the Welsh bards refers to Stonehenge as "the melodious quaternion of Pedyr": in Cornwall there is also a Padstow or Petroxstowe, and there is no doubt that Peter, like Patrick, was the Supreme Padre or Parent. According to the native ancient ecclesiastical records of Wales known as the Iolo MSS., the native name of St. Patrick was Maenwyn, which means *stone sacred:* hence one may assume that the island of Battersea or Patrixeye was the abode of the padres who ministered at the neighbouring

---

[1] *Cf.* Pierrot's Family Tree. *T.P.'s Weekly*, 1st August, 1914.

shrine of St. Peter or petra, the Rock upon which the church of Christ is traditionally built.

At Patrixbourne in Kent was a seat known as Bifrons, once in the possession of a family named Cheyneys:[1] whether there be any connection between this estate named Bifrons and *Bifrons*, or *Two fronted*, a sobriquet applied to Janus, I am unaware: the connection Cheyneys—Bifrons —Patrixbourne is, however, the more curious inasmuch as they immediately neighbour a Bekesbourne, and on referring to Peckham we find that a so-termed Janus bifrons was unearthed there some centuries ago. The peculiarity of this Peckham Janus is that, unlike any other Janus-head I know, it obviously represents a Pater and Mater, and not two Paters, or a big and little Peter. The feminine of Janus is Jane or Iona, and at Iona in Scotland there existed prior to the Reformation when they were thrown into the sea, some remarkable *petræ*, to wit, three noble marble globes placed in three stone basins, which the inhabitants turned three times round according to the course of the sun:[2] these were known as *clacha brath* or Stones of Judgment.

Fig. 420. — From *A New Description of England* (1724).

Tradition connects St. Columba of Iona in the Hebrides with Loch Aber, or, as it was sometimes written, Loch Apor, and among the stories which the honest Adamnan received and recorded " nothing doubting from a certain religious, ancient priest," is one to the effect that Columba

[1] Wilson, J., *Imperial Gazetteer*, ii., 584.
[2] Toland, *History of Druids*, p. 356.

on a memorable occasion, turning aside to the nearest rock, prayed a little while on bended knees, and rising up after prayer blessed the brow of the same rock, from which thereupon water bubbled up and flowed forth abundantly. With the twelve-mouthed *petra* or rock of Moses which, according to Rabbinic tradition, followed the Israelites into the wilderness, may be connoted the rock-gushing fountain at Petrockstowe, Cornwall. That St. Patrick was Shony the Ocean-deity, to whom the Hebrideans used to pour out libations, is deducible from the legend that on the day of St. Patrick's festival the fish all rise from the sea, pass in procession before his altar, and then disappear. The personality of the great St. Patrick of the Paddys is so remarkably obscure that some hagiographers conclude there were seven persons known by that name; others distinguish three, and others recognise two, one of whom was known as "*Sen* Patrick," *i.e.*, the senile or senior Patrick : there is little doubt that the archetypal Patrick was represented indifferently as young and old and as either seven, three, two, or one : whence perhaps the perplexity and confusion of the hagiographers.

It is not improbable that the Orchard Street at Westminster may mark the site of a burial ground or "Peter's Orchard," similar to that which was uncovered in Wiltshire in 1852 : this was found on a farm at Seagry, one part of which had immemorially been known as "Peter's Orchard".[1] From generation to generation it had been handed down that in a certain field on this farm a church was built upon the site of an ancient *heathen* burial ground, and the persistence of the heathen tradition is seemingly

---

[1] *Cf.* Gomme, Sir L., *Folklore as an Historic Science*, pp. 43, 44.

presumptive evidence, not only of inestimable age, but of the memory of a pre-Christian Peter.

It may be assumed that "Peter's Orchard" was originally an apple orchard or an Avalon similar to the "Heaven's Walls," which were discovered some years ago near Royston: these "walls," immediately contiguous to the Icknield or Acnal Way, were merely some strips of unenclosed but cultivated land which in ancient deeds from time immemorial had been called "Heaven's Walls". Traditional awe attached to this spot, and village children were afraid to traverse it after dark, when it was said to be frequented by supernatural beings: in 1821 some labourers digging for gravel on this haunted spot inadvertently discovered a wall enclosing a rectangular space containing numerous deposits of sepulchral urns, and it then became clear that here was one of those plots of ground environed by walls to which the Romans gave the name of *ustrinum*.[1]

The old Welsh graveyards were frequently circular, and there is a notable example of this at Llanfairfechan: the Llanfair here means holy enclosure of Fair or Mairy, and it is probable that Fechan's round churchyard was a symbol of the Fire Ball or *Fay King*. At Fore in Ireland the Solar wheel figures notably at the church of "Saint" Fechan on an ancient doorway illustrated herewith. That the Latin *ustrinum* was associated with the Uster or Easter of resurrection is likely enough, for both Romans and Greeks had a practice of planting roses in their graveyards: as late as 1724 the inhabitants of Ockley or Aclea in Surrey had "a custom here, time immemorial, of planting rose trees in the graves, especially by the young men

[1] *Cf.* Gomme, Sir L., *Folklore as an Historic Science*, p. 44.

and maidens that have lost their lovers, and the churchyard is now full of them ".[1] That " The Walls of Heaven " by Royston was associated with roses is implied by the name Royston, which was evidently a rose-town, for it figures in old records as *Crux Roies*, *Croyrois*, and *Villa de*

Fig. 421.—From *The Age of the Saints* (Borlase, W. C.).

cruce Rosia. The expression " God's Acre " still survives, seemingly from that remote time when St. Kit of Royston, the pre-Christian " God," was worshipped at innumerable Godshills, Godstones, Gaddesdens, and Goodacres.

Tradition asserts that the abbey church of St. Peter's at Westminster occupies the site of a pagan temple to Apollo: the Etrurian form of Apollo was Aplu, and there is no

[1] *A New Description of England*, p. 65.

doubt that the sacred *apple* of the Druids was the symbol of the " rubicund, radiant Elphin " or Apollo. According to Malory, a certain Sir Patrise lies buried in Westminster, and this knight came to his untoward end by eating an apple, whereupon " suddenly he brast (burst) " :[1] from this parallel to the story of St. Margaret erupting from a dragon it is probable that Sir Patrise was the original patron of Westminster, or ancient Thorney Eye. Patera was a generic title borne by the ministers at Apollo's shrines, and as glorious Apollo was certainly the Shine, it is more than likely that Petersham Park at Sheen, where still stands a supposedly Roman *petra* or altar-stone, was a park or enclosure sacred to Peter, or, perhaps, to Patrise of the apple-bursting story.

The Romans applied the title Magonius to the Gaulish and British Apollo; sometimes St. Patrick is mentioned as Magounus, and it is probable that both these epithets are Latinised forms of the British name Magon : the Druidic Magon who figures in the traditions of Cumberland is in all probability the St. Mawgan whose church neighours that of the Maiden St. Columb in the Hundred of Pydar in Cornwall.

One of the principal towns in Westmorland is Appleby, which was known to the Romans as Abellaba : the Maiden Way of Westmorland traverses Appleby, starting from a place called Kirkby Thore, and here about 200 years ago was found the supposed " amulet or magical spell," illustrated in Fig. 422. The inscription upon the reverse is in Runic characters, which some authorities have read as THOR DEUS PATRIUS ; and if this be correct the effigy would seem to be that of the solar Sir Patrise, for ap-

---

[1] *Morte D'Arthur*, Bk. xviii, ch. viii.

parently the object in the right hand is an apple: there is little doubt that the great Pater figures at Patterdale, at Aspatria, and at the river Peterill, all of which are in this neighbourhood, and in all probability the Holy Patrise or Aspatria was represented by the culminating peak known as the "Old Man" of Coniston.

Some experts read the legend on Fig. 422 as THURGUT LUETIS, meaning "the face or effigies of the God Thor": according to others Thurgut was the name of the moneyer or mintmaster; according to yet others the coin was struck in honour of a Danish Admiral named Thurgut: where there is such acute diversity of opinion it is permissible to suggest that Thurgut—whose effigy is seemingly little suggestive of a sea-dog—was originally the *Three Good* or the *Three God*, for the figure's sceptre is tipped by the three circles of Good Thought, Good Deed, and Good Word. In Berkshire the country people, like the Germans with their *drei*, say *dree* instead of *three*, and thus it may be that the Apples Three, or the Apollos Three (for the ancients recognised Three Apollos—the celestial, the terrestrial, and the infernal) were worshipped at Apple*dre*, or Apple*dore* opposite Barnstable, and at Apple*dur* Comb or Apple*dur*well, a manor in the parish of Godshill, Isle of Wight.

FIG. 422.—From *A New Description of England*.

English "Appletons" are numerous, and at Derby is an Appletree which was originally Appletrefelde: it is known that this Apple-Tree-Field contained an apple-tree which was once the meeting place of the Hundred or Shire division, and it is probable that the two Apuldre's of Devon served a similar public use. As late as 1826 it was the custom, at Appleton in Cheshire, " at the time of the wake to clip and adorn an old hawthorn which till very lately stood in the middle of the town. This ceremony is called the bawming (dressing) of Appleton Thorn ".[1] Doubtless Appleton Thorn was originally held in the same estimation as the monument bushes of Ireland, which are found for the most part in the centre of road crossings. According to the anonymous author of *Irish Folklore*,[2] these ancient and solitary hawthorns are held in immense veneration, and it would be considered profanation to destroy them or even remove any of their branches: from these fairy and phooka-haunted sites, a lady dressed in a long flowing white robe was often supposed to issue, and "the former dapper elves are often seen hanging from or flitting amongst their branches". We have in an earlier chapter considered the connection between spikes and spooks, and it is obvious that the White Lady or Alpa of the white thorn or aubespine is the Banshee or Good Woman Shee:—

> She told them of the fairy-haunted land
> Away the other side of Brittany,
> Beyond the heaths, edged by the lonely sea;
> Of the deep forest-glades of Broce-liande,
> Through whose green boughs the golden sunshine creeps,
> Where Merlin,[3] *by the enchanted thorn-tree* sleeps.

In the forest of Breceliande—doubtless part of the fairy Hy Breasil—was a famed Fountain of Baranton or Beren-

---

[1] Hazlitt, W. Carew, *Faiths and Folklore*, i., 12.

[2] "Lageniensis," p. 86.

[3] Taliesin or *Radiant Brow* claims to have been Merlin.

don into which children threw tribute to the invocation, "Laugh, then, fountain of Berendon, and I will give thee a pin ".[1] The first pin was presumably a spine or thorn ; the first flower is the black-thorn ; on 1st January (the first day of the first month), people in the North of England used to construct a blackthorn globe and stand hand in hand in a circle round the fire chanting in a monotonous voice the words "Old Cider," prolonging each syllable to its utmost extent. I think that Old Cider must have been Thurgut, and that in all probability the initial *Ci* was *sy*, the ubiquitous endearing diminutive of pucksy, *pixie*, etc.

According to Maundeville, "white thorn hath many virtues ; for he that beareth a branch thereof upon him, no thunder nor tempest may hurt him ; and no evil spirit may enter in the house in which it is, or come to the place that it is in ": Maundeville refers to this magic thorn as the aubespine, which is possibly a corruption of *alba* thorn, or it may be of Hob's thorn. In modern French *aube* means the dawn.

---

[1] "All the old traditions which give an interest to the Forest continue to be current there. The Fairies, who are kind to children, are still reported to be seen in their white apparel upon the banks of the Fountain ; and the Fountain itself (whose waters are now considered salubrious) is still said to be possessed of its marvellous rain-producing properties. In seasons of drought the inhabitants of the surrounding parishes go to it in procession, headed by their *five* great banners, and their priests, ringing bells and chanting Psalms. On arriving at the Fountain, the Rector of the Canton dips the foot of the Cross into its waters, and it is sure to rain before a week elapses."

"Brecilien etait une de ces forets sacrees qu'habitaient les pretresses du druidisme dans le Gaule ; son nom et celui de sa vallee l'attesteraient a defaut d'autre temoignage ; les noms de lieux sont les plus surs garans des evenemens passés."—*Cf.* Notes on *The Mabinogion* (Everyman's Library), p. 383-90.

We have seen that there are some grounds for surmising that Brawn Street and Bryanstone Square (Marylebone) mark the site of a Branstone or fairy stone, in which connection it may be noted that until recently: "near this spot was a little cluster of cottages called 'Apple Village'":[1] in the same neighbourhood there are now standing to-day a Paradise Place, a Paradise Passage, and Great Barlow Street, which may quite possibly mark the site of an original *Bar low* or *Bar lea*. Apple Village was situated in what was once the Manor of Tyburn or Tyburnia: according to the "Confession" of St. Patrick the saint's grandfather came from "a village of Tabernia,"[2] and it is probable that the Tyburn brook, upon the delta of which stands St. Peter's (Westminster), was originally named after the Good Burn or Oberon of Bryanstone and the neighbouring Brawn Street. The word *tabernacle* is traceable to the same roots as *tavern*, French *auberge*, English *inn*.

Around the effigy of Thurgut will be noted either seven or eight M's: in mediæval symbolism the letter M stood usually for Mary; the parish church of Bryanstone Square is dedicated to St. Mary, and we find the Virgin very curiously associated with one or more apple-trees. According to the author of *St. Brighid and Her Times*: "Bardism offers nothing higher in zeal or deeper in doctrine than the *Avallenan*, or Song of the Apple-trees, by the Caledonian Bard, Merddin Wyllt. He describes his Avallenan as being one Apple-tree, the Avallen, but in another sense it was 147 apple-trees, that is, mystically (taking the sum of the digits, 1 4 7 equal 12), the sacred Druidic number.

---

[1] Mitton, G. E., *Hampstead and Marylebone*.
[2] Probably the Glamorganshire "Tabernae Amnis," now Bont y Von.

Thus in his usual repeated description of the Avallen as one apple-tree, he writes :—

> Sweet apple-tree! tree of no rumour,
> That growest by the stream, without overgrowing the circle.

Again, as 147 apple trees—

> Seven sweet apple-trees, and seven score
> Of equal age, equal height, equal length, equal bulk;
> Out of the bosom of mercy they sprung up.

Again—

> They who guard them are one curly-headed virgin.

In fairy-tale the apple figures as the giver of rejuvenescence and new life, in Celtic mythology it figures as the magic Silver Branch which corresponds to Virgil's Golden Bough. According to Irvine the word *bran* meant not only the Druidical system, but was likewise applied to individual Druids who were termed *brans*: I have already suggested that this "purely mystical and magical name" is our modern *brain*; according to all accounts the Druids were eminently men of brain, whence it is possible that the fairy-tale "Voyage of *Bran*" and the Voyage of St. Brandon were originally brainy inventions descriptive of a mental voyage of which any average brain is still capable. The Voyage of Bran relates how once upon a time Bran the son of Fearbal[1] heard strange music behind him, and so entrancing were the sounds that they lulled him into slumber: when he awoke there lay by his side a branch of silver so resplendent with white blossom that it was difficult to distinguish the flowers from the branch. With

---

[1] Fearbal or sometimes Fibal. The "Merry Devil" associated in popular tradition with Edmonton beyond Islington was known by the name of Peter Fabell: I think he was originally "the Angel," and that the names Fearbal or Fabell meant *Fairy or Fay Beautiful*.

this fairy talisman, which served not only as a passport but as food and drink, and as a maker of music so soothing that mortals who heard it forgot their woes and even ceased to grieve for their kinsmen whom the Banshee had taken, Bran voyaged to the Islands called Fortunate, wherein he perceived and heard many strange and beautiful things :—

> A branch of the Apple Tree from Emain
> I bring like those one knows;
> Twigs of white silver are on it,
> Crystal brows with blossoms.
>
> There is a distant isle
> Around which sea horses glisten :
> A fair course against the white swelling surge,
> Four feet uphold it.

In Wales on 1st January children used to carry from door to door a holly-decked apple into which were fixed three twigs—presumably an emblem of the Apple Island or Island of Apollo, supported on the three sweet notes of the Awen or creative Word. Into this tripod apple were stuck oats:[1] the effigy of St. Bride which used to be carried from door to door consisted of a sheaf of oats; in Anglo-Saxon *oat* was *ate*, plural *aten*, and it is evident that oats were peculiarly identified with the Maiden.

In Cormac's *Adventure in the Land of Promise* there again enters the magic Silver Branch, with three golden apples on it : " Delight and amusement to the full was it to listen to the music of that branch, for men sore wounded or women in childbed or folk in sickness would fall asleep, at the melody when that branch was shaken ". The Silver Branch which seems to have been sometimes that of the Apple, sometimes of the Whitethorn, corresponds to

---

[1] " Morien," *Light of Britannia*, p. 61.

the mistletoe or Three-berried and Three-leaved Golden Bough: until recent years a bunch of Mistletoe or "All Heal"—the essential emblem of Yule—used to be ceremoniously elevated to the proclamation of a general pardon at York or Ebor: it is still the symbol of an affectionate *cumber* or gathering together of kinsmen. King Camber is said to have been the son of Brutus; he was therefore, seemingly, the young St. Nicholas or the Little Crowned King, and in Cumberland the original signification of the "All Heal" would appear to have been traditionally preserved. In *Tales and Legends of the English Lakes* Mr. Wilson Armistead records that many strange tales are still associated with the Druidic stones, and in the course of one of these alleged authentic stories he prints the following Invocation :—

1st Bard. Being great who reigns alone,
    Veiled in clouds unseen unknown;
    Centre of the vast profound,
    Clouds of darkness close Thee round.

3rd Bard. Spirit who no birth has known,
    Springing from Thyself alone,
    We thy living emblem show
    In the mystic mistletoe,
    Springs and grows without a root,
    Yields without flowers its fruit;
    Seeks from earth no mother's care,
    Lives and blooms the child of air.

4th Bard. Thou dost Thy mystic circle trace
     Along the vaulted blue profound,
    And emblematic of Thy race
     We tread our mystic circle round.

Omnes. Shine upon us mighty God,
     Raise this drooping world of ours;
    Send from Thy divine abode
     Cheering sun and fruitful showers.

In view of the survival elsewhere of Druidic chants and creeds which are unquestionably ancient, it is quite possible that in the above we have a genuine relic of prehistoric belief: that the ideas expressed were actually held might without difficulty be proved from many scattered and independent sources: that Cumberland has clung with extraordinary tenacity to certain ancient forms is sufficiently evident from the fact that even to-day the shepherds of the *Borrow*dale district tell their sheep in the old British numerals, *yan, tyan, tethera, methera*,[1] etc.

The most famous of all English apple orchards was the Avalon of Somerset which as we have seen was encircled by the little river Brue: with Avalon is indissolubly associated the miraculous Glastonbury Thorn, and that Avalon[2] was essentially British and an *abri* of King Bru or Cynbro is implied by its alternative title of Bride Hay or Bride Eye: not only is St. Brighid said to have resided at Avalon or the Apple Island, but among the relics long faithfully preserved there were the blessed Virgin's scrip, necklace, distaff, and bell. The fact that the main streets of Avalon form a perfect cross may be connoted with Sir John Maundeville's statement that while on his travels in the East he was shown certain apples: " which they call apples of Paradise, and they are very sweet and of good savour. And though you cut them in ever so many slices

---

[1] I am inclined to think that the *eena deena dina dux* of childrens' games may be a similarly ancient survival.

[2] There was also an Aballo, now Avalon, in France: there is also near Dodona in Albania an Avlona or Valona. A correspondent of *The Westminster Gazette* points out that: " Valona is but a derivative of the Greek (both ancient and modern) *Balanos*. This is clearer still if you realise that the Greek *b* is (and no doubt in ancient days also was) pronounced like an English *v*: thus, *valanos*."

or parts across or end-wise, you will always find in the middle the figure of the holy cross."[1] That Royston, near the site of "Heaven's Walls," was identified with the Rood, Rhoda, or Rose Cross is evident from the ancient forms of the name Crux Roies (1220), Croyrois (1263), and Villa de Cruce Rosia (1298): legend connects the place with a certain Lady Roese, "about whom nothing is known," and probability may thus associate this mysterious Lady with Fair Rosamond or the Rose of the World. In the Middle Ages, The Garden of the Rose was merely another term for Eden, Paradise, Peter's Orchard, or Heaven's Walls, and the Lady of the Rose Garden was unquestionably the same as the Ruler of the Isles called Fortunate—

—a Queen
So beautiful that with one single beam
Of her great beauty, all the country round
Is rendered shining.

Some accounts state that the bride of Oberon was known as Esclairmond, a name which seemingly is one with *eclair monde* or "Light of the World".

We have seen that the surroundings of the Dane John at Canterbury are still known as Rodau's Town: the coins of the Rhodian Greeks were sometimes *rotae* or wheel crosses in the form of a rose, and there is little doubt that our British rota coins were intended to represent various conceptions of the Rose Garden, or Avalon, or the Apple Orchard: using another simile the British poets preached the same Ideal under the guise of the Round Table.[2] Fig.

---

[1] *Travels in the East*, p. 152.
[2] According to Malory: "Merlin made the Round Table in tokening of roundness of the world, for by the Round Table is the world signified by right, for all the world, Christian and heathen, repair unto the Round

179, (*ante*, p. 339) represented a rose combined with four sprigs or sprouts, and in Fig. 423 (British) the intention of the rhoda is clearly indicated: on the carved column illustrated on page 708 the rood is a *rhoda*, and my suggestion in an earlier chapter that "Radipole road," near London, may have marked the site of a rood pole is somewhat strengthened by the fact that Maypoles occasionally displayed St. George's red rood or the banner of England, and a white pennon or streamer emblazoned with a red cross terminating like the blade of a sword. Occasionally the poles were painted yellow and black in spiral lines,

Figs. 423 and 424.—British. From Akerman.

the original intention no doubt being representative of Night and Day.

> Alas poore Maypoles what should be the cause
> That you were almost banished from the earth?
> Who never were rebellious to the lawes,
> Your greatest crime was harmless honest mirth,
> What fell malignant spirit was there found
> To cast your tall Pyramids to ground?

The same poet[1] deplores the gone-for-ever time when—

> All the parish did in one combine
> To mount the rod of peace, and none withstood

Table; and when they are chosen to be of the fellowship of the Round Table they think them more blessed and more in worship than if they had gotten half the world; and ye have seen that they have lost their fathers and their mothers, and all their kin, and their wives and their children, for to be of your fellowship."—*Morte D'Arthur*, Book xiv. 11.

[1] Fenner, W., *Pasquils Palinodia*, 1619.

> When no capritious constables disturb them,
> Nor Justice of the peace did seek to curb them,
> Nor peevish puritan in rayling sort,
> Nor over-wise churchwarden spoyled the sport.

Overwise scholars have assumed that the Maypole was primarily and merely a phallic emblem; it was, however, more generally the simple symbol of justice and "the rod of peace": *rod*, *rood*, and *ruth* are of course variants of one and the same root.

Among, if not the prime of the May Day dances was one known popularly as Sellingers Round: here probably the *r* is an interpolation, and the immortal Sellinga was in all likelihood *sel inga* or the innocent and happy Ange of Islington :—

> To Islington and Hogsdon runnes the streame,
> Of giddie people to eate cakes and creame.

At the famous "Angel" of Islington manorial courts were held seemingly from a time immemorial: on a shop-front now facing it the curious surname Uglow may be seen to-day, and in view of the adjacent Agastone Road it is reasonable to assume that at Hogsdon, now spelt Hoxton, stood once an Hexe or Hag stone, perhaps also that the hill by the Angel was originally known as the *ug low* or Ug hill. We have noted that fairy rings were occasionally termed hag tracks, and that the Angel district was once associated with these evidences of the fairies is seemingly implied by a correspondent who wrote to *The Gentleman's Magazine* in 1792 as follows: "Having noticed a query relating to fairy rings having once been numerous in the meadow between Islington and Canonbury, and whether there were any at this time, and having never seen those extraordinary productions whether of Nature or of animals, curiosity led me on a late fine day to visit the above spot in search of them, but I was disappointed. There are none there now; the meadow above mentioned is intersected by paths on every side and trodden by man and beast." Man and beast have since converted these intersections into mean streets among which, however, still stand Fairbank and Bookham Streets.

The Maypole was generally a sprout and was no doubt

Fig. 425.—From *Christian Iconography* (Didron).

in this respect a proper representative of the "blossoming tree" referred to in a Gaelic Hymn in honour of St. Brighid—

> Be extinguished in us
> The flesh's evil, affections
> By this blossoming tree
> This Mother of Christ.

The May Queen was invariably selected as the fairest

and best dispositioned of the village maidens, and before being "set in an Arbour on a Holy Day" she was apparently carried on the shoulders of four men or "deacons":[1] assuredly these parochial deacons were personages of local importance, and they may possibly account for the place-name Maydeacon House which occurs at Patrixbourne, Kent, in conjunction with Kingston, Heart's Delight, Broome Park, and Barham. The word *deacon* is *Good King* or *Divine King*: we have seen that four kings figured frequently in the wheel of Fortune, and the ceremonious

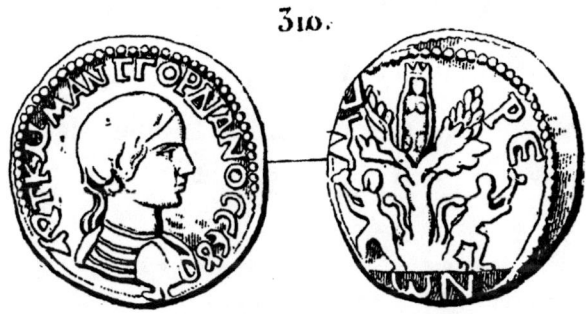

FIG. 426.—Cretan. From Barthelemy.

carrying by four deacons was not merely an idle village sport for it formed part of the ecclesiastical functions at the Vatican. An English traveller of some centuries ago speaking of the Pope and his attendant ceremonial, states that the representative of Peter was carried on the back of four deacons "after the maner of carrying whytepot queenes in Western May games":[2] the "Whytepot Queen" was no doubt representative of Dame Jeanne, the demijohn or Virgin, and the counterpart to Janus or St. Peter.

One of what Camden would have dubbed the sour kind of critics inquired in 1577: "What adoe make our young

---

[1] *Faiths and Folklore*, ii., 401.   [2] *Ibid.*, 402.

men at the time of May? Do they not use night-watchings to rob and steal yong trees out of other men's grounde, and bring them home into their parish with minstrels playing before? And when they have set it up they will deck it with floures and garlands and dance around, men and women together most unseemly and intolerable as I have proved before." The scenes around the Maypole ("this stinckyng idoll rather") were unquestionably sparkled by a generous provision of " ambrosia ":—

> From the golden cup they drink
> Nectar that the bees produce,
> Or the grapes ecstatic juice,
> Flushed with mirth and hope they burn.[1]

On that ever-memorable occasion at Stonehenge, when the Saxons massacred their unsuspecting hosts, a Bard relates that—

> The glad repository of the world was amply supplied.
> Well did Eideol prepare at *the spacious circle of the world*
> Harmony and gold and great horses and intoxicating mead.

The word *mead* implies that this celestial honey-brew was esteemed to be the drink of the Maid; *ale* as we know was ceremoniously brewed within churches, and was thus probably once a *holy* beverage drunk on *holy*-days: the words *beer* and *brew* will account for representations of the senior Selenus, as at times *inebriate*. The Fairy Queen, occasionally the "Sorceress of the ebon Throne," was esteemed to be the "Mother of wildly-working dreams"; Matthew Arnold happily describes the Celts as " drenched and intoxicated with fairy dew," and it seems to have a general tenet that the fairy people in their festal glee were sometimes inebriated by ambrosia:—

[1] Aneurin's *Gododin*.

> From golden flowers of each hue,
> Crystal white, or golden yellow,
> Purple, violet, red or blue,
> We drink the honey dew
> > Until we all get mellow,
> > Until we all get mellow.[1]

In the neighbourhood of Fair Head, Antrim, there is a whirlpool known as Brecan's Cauldron in connection with which one of St. Columba's miracles is recorded. That the Pure King or Paragon was also deemed to be "that brewer" or the Brew King of the mystic cauldron, is evident from the magic recipe of Taliesin, which includes among its alloy of ingredients "to be mixed when there is a calm dew falling," the liquor that bees have collected, and resin (amber?) and pleasant, precious silver, the ruddy gem and the grain from the ocean foam (the pearl or margaret?) :—

> And primroses and herbs
> And topmost sprigs of trees,
> Truly there shall be a puryfying tree,
> Fruitful in its increase.
> Some of it let that brewer boil
> Who is over the *five*-woods cauldron.

We have noted the five acres allotted to each Bard, five springs at Avebury, five fields at Biddenden, "five wells" at Doddington, five banners at the magic fountain of Berenton, and five fruits growing on a holy tree: the mystic meaning attached to five rivers was in all probability that which is thus stated in Cormac's *Adventure in the Land of Promise:* "The fountain which thou sawest with the five streams out of it is the fountain of Knowledge, and the streams are the five senses through which Knowledge is obtained. And no one will have Knowledge who

---

[1] *Cf.* "Laganiensis," *Irish Folklore,* p. 35.

drinketh not a draught out of the fountain itself and out of the streams." That Queen Wisdom was the Lady of the Isles called Fortunate, is explicitly stated by the poet who tells us that there not Fantasy but Reason ruled: he adds:—

> All this is held a fable: but who first
> Made and recited it, hath in this fable
> Shadowed a truth.[1]

From the group of so-called Sun and Fire Symbols here reproduced, it will be seen that the svastika or "Fare ye

FIG. 427.—Sun and Fire Symbols from Denmark of the later Bronze Age. From *Symbolism of the East and West* (Murray-Aynsley).

well" cross assumed multifarious forms: in Thrace, the emblem was evidently known as the *embria*, for there are in existence coins of the town of Mesembria, whereon the

---

[1] *Cf. New Light on Renaissance*, p. 169.

legend MESEMBRIA, meaning the (city of the) midday sun, is figured by the syllable MES, followed by the svastika as the equivalent of EMBRIA.[1]

The whirling bird-headed wheel on page 709 is a peculiarly interesting example of the British rood, or rota of ruth; as also is No. 40 of Fig. 201 (*ante*, p. 364) where the peacock is transformed into a svastika: the *pear*-shaped visage on the obverse of this coin may be connoted with the Scotch word *pearie*, meaning a pear-shaped spinning-top, and the seven *ains* or balls may be connoted with the statement of Maundeville, that he was shown seven springs which gushed out from a spot where once upon a time Jesus Christ had played with children.

No. 43 of the contemned sceattae (p. 364) evidently represents the legendary Bird of Fire, which, together with the peacock and the eagle, I have discussed elsewhere: this splendid and mysterious bird—as those familiar with Russian ballet are aware—came nightly to an apple-tree, but there is no reason to assume that the apple was its only or peculiar nourishment. The Mystic Boughs illustrated on page 627 (Figs. 379 to 384) may well have been the mistletoe or any other berried or fruit-bearing branch: in Fig. 397 (p. 635) the Maiden is holding what is seemingly a three-leaved lily, doubtless corresponding to the old English Judge's bough or wand, now discontinued, and only faintly remembered by a trifling nosegay.[2]

Symbolists are aware that in Christian and Pagan art, birds pecking at either fruit or flowers denote the souls of the blessed feeding upon the joys of Paradise: all winged things typified the Angels or celestial Intelligences who

---

[1] Birdwood, Sir G., preface to *Symbolism of East and West*, p. xvi.
[2] Hazlitt, W. Carew, *Faiths and Folklore*, ii., 402.

were deemed to flash like birds through the air, and the reader will not fail to note the angelic birds sitting in Queen Mary's tree (Fig. 425, p. 686).

There is a delicious story of a Little Bird in Irish folk-tale, and among the literature of the Trouveres or Troubadours, there is *A Lay of the Little Bird* which it is painful to curtail: it runs as follows: "Once upon a time, more than a hundred years ago, there lived a rich villein whose name I cannot now tell, who owned meadows and woods and waters, and all things which go to the making of a rich man. His manor was so fair and so delightsome that all the world did not contain its peer. My true story would seem to you but idle fable if I set its beauty before you, for verily I believe that never yet was built so strong a keep and so gracious a tower. A river flowed around this fair domain, and enclosed an orchard planted with all manner of fruitful trees. This sweet fief was builded by a certain knight, whose heir sold it to a villein; for thus pass baronies from hand to hand, and town and manor change their master, always falling from bad to worse. The orchard was fair beyond content. Herbs grew there of every fashion, more than I am able to name. But at least I can tell you that so sweet was the savour of roses and other flowers and simples, that sick persons, borne within that garden in a litter, walked forth sound and well for having passed the night in so lovely a place. Indeed, so smooth and level was the sward, so tall the trees, so various the fruit, that the cunning gardener must surely have been a magician, as appears by certain infallible proofs.

"Now in the middle of this great orchard sprang a fountain of clear, pure water. It boiled forth out of the ground, but was always colder than any marble. Tall trees stood about the well, and their leafy branches made a cool shadow there, even during the longest day of summer heat. Not a ray of the sun fell within that spot, though it were the month of May, so thick and close was the leafage. Of all these trees the fairest and the most pleasant was a pine. To this pine came a singing bird twice every day for ease of heart. Early in the morning he came, when monks chant their matins, and again in the evening, a little after vespers. He was smaller than a sparrow, but larger than a wren, and he sang so sweetly that neither lark, nor nightingale, nor blackbird, nay, nor siren even, was so grateful to the ear. He sang lays and ballads, and the newest refrain of the minstrel and the spinner at her wheel. Sweeter was his tune than harp or viol, and gayer than the country dance. No man had heard so marvellous a thing; for such was the virtue in his song that the saddest and the most dolent forgot to grieve whilst he listened to the tune, love flowered sweetly in his heart, and for a space he was rich and happy as any emperor or king, though but a burgess of the city, or a villein of the field. Yea, if that ditty had lasted 100 years, yet would he have stayed the century through to listen to so lovely a song, for it gave to every man whilst he hearkened, love, and riches, and his heart's desire. But all the beauty of the pleasaunce drew its being from the song of the bird; for from his chant flowed love which gives its shadow to the tree, its healing to the simple, and its colour to the flower. Without that song the fountain would have ceased to spring, and the green garden become a little dry dust, for in its sweetness lay all their virtue. The villein, who was lord of this domain, walked every day within his garden to hearken to the bird. On a certain morning he came to the well to bathe his face in the cold spring, and the bird, hidden close within the pine branches, poured out his full heart in a delightful lay, from which rich profit might be drawn. 'Listen,' chanted the bird in his own tongue, 'listen to my voice, oh, knight, and clerk, and layman, ye who concern yourselves with love, and suffer with its dolours: listen, also, ye maidens, fair and coy and gracious, who seek first the gifts and beauty of the world. I speak truth and do not lie. Closer should you cleave to God than to any earthly lover, right willingly should you seek His altar, more firmly should you hold to His commandment than to any mortal's pleasure. So you serve God and Love in such fashion, no harm can come to any, for God and Love are one. God loves sense and chivalry; and Love holds them not in despite. God hates pride and false seeming; and Love loveth loyalty. God praiseth honour and courtesy; and fair Love disdaineth them not. God lendeth His ear to prayer; neither doth Love refuse it her heart. God granteth largesse to the generous, but the grudging man, and the envious, the felon and the wrathful, doth he abhor. But courtesy and honour, good sense and loyalty, are the leal vassals of Love, and so you hold truly to them, God and the beauty of the world shall be added to you besides. Thus told the bird in his song'."[1]

It is not necessary to relate here the ill-treatment suffered by the bird which happily was full of guile, nor to describe its escape from the untoward fate destined for it by the villein.

In Figs. 428 to 430 are three remarkable British coins all of which seemingly represent a bird in song: it is not

---

[1] *Cf. Aucassin and Nicolette*, Everyman's Library.

improbable that the idea underlying these mystic forms is the same as what the Magi termed the *Honover* or Word, which is thus described: "The instrument employed by the Almighty, in giving an origin to these opposite principles, as well as in every subsequent creative act, was His Word. This sacred and mysterious agent, which in the Zendavesta is frequently mentioned under the appellations *Honover* and *I am*, is compared to those celestial birds which constantly keep watch over, the welfare of nature. Its attributes are ineffable light, perfect activity, unerring prescience. Its existence preceded the formation

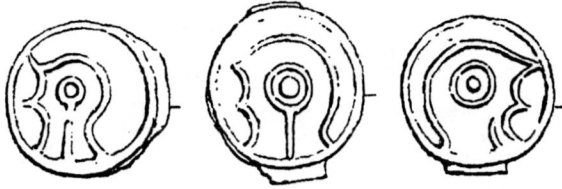

FIGS. 428 to 430.—British. From Evans.

of all things—it proceeds from the first eternal principal—it is the gift of God." [1]

The symbol of Hanover [2] was the White Horse and we have considered the same connection at Hiniver in Sussex: it is also a widely accepted verity that the White Horse—East and West—was the emblem of pure Reason or Intelligence; the Persian word for *good thought* was *humanah*, which is seemingly our *humane*, and if we read *Honover* as *ancient ver* the term may be equated in idea with *word* or *verbum*. The Rev. Professor Skeat derives

[1] Fraser, J. B., *Persia*, p. 129.

[2] At Looe in Cornwall the site of what was apparently the ancient forum or Fore street, is now known as "Hannafore". Opposite is St. George's Islet. The connection between George and Hanover suggests that St. George was probably the patron saint of Hanover.

the words *human* and *humane* from *humus* the ground, whence the Latin *homo*, a man, literally, "a creature of earth," but this is a definition which the pagan would have contemptuously set aside, for notwithstanding his perversity in bowing down to wood and stone he believed himself to be a creature of the sun and claimed: "my high descent from Jove Himself I boast".

We have seen that Jove, Jupiter, or Jou was in all probability Father *Joy*, and have suggested that the Wandering Jew was a personification of the same idea: it has also been surmised that Elisha—one of the alternative names of the Wanderer—meant radically Holy Jou: it is not improbable that the Shah or Padishah of Persia was similarly the supposed incarnation of this phairy *père*. The various well-authenticated apparitions of the Jew are quite possibly due to impersonations of the traditional figure, and two at least of these apparitions are mentioned as occurring in England: in one case the old man claiming to be the character wandered about ejaculating "Poor Joe alone"; in another "Poor John alone alone".[1] Both "Joe" and "John" are supposed by Brand to be corruptions of "Jew": the greater probability is that they were genuine British titles of the traditional Wanderer.

The exclamation of "alone alone" may be connoted with the so-called Allan apples which used to figure so prominently in Cornish festivities: these Allan apples doubtless bore some relation to the Celtic St. Allan: *haleine* means *breath*,[2] *elan* means fire or energy, and it is in further keeping with St. Allan that his name is translated as having meant *cheerful*.

[1] Hardwick, C., *Traditions, Superstitions, and Folklore*, p. 159.
[2] The *lungs* are the organs of *haleine*.

The festival of the Allan apple was essentially a cheery proceeding: two strips of wood were joined crosswise by a nail in the centre; at each of the four ends was stuck a lighted candle with large and rosy apples hung between. This construction was fastened to a beam or the ceiling of the kitchen, then made to revolve rapidly, and the players whose object was to catch the Allan apples in their mouths frequently instead had a taste of the candles.[1] Obviously this whirling firewheel was an emblem of Heol the Celtic Sun *wheel*, and as Newlyn is particularly mentioned as a site of the festival, we may equate St. Newlyna of Newlyn with the Noualen of Brittany, and further with the Goddess Nehellenia or New Helen of London. Nehellenia has seemingly also been traced at Tadcaster in Yorkshire where the local name Helen's Ford is supposed to be a corruption of the word Nehellenia:[2] Nelly, however, is no corruption but a variant of Ellen. The Goddess Nehallenia is usually sculptured with a hound by her side and in her lap is a basket of fruits "symbolising the fecundating power of the earth".[3] In old English *line* meant to fecundate or fertilise, and in Britain Allan may be considered as almost a generic term for rivers—the all fertilisers—for it occurs in the varying forms Allen, Alan, Alne, Ellen, Elan, Ilen, etc.: sometimes emphasis on the second syllable wears off the preliminary vowel, whence the river-names Len, Lyn, Leen, Lone, Lune, etc., are apparently traceable to the same cause as leads us to use *lone* as an alternative form of the word *alone*. The Extons Road, Jews Lane, and Paradise now found at King's Lynn point to the probability that King's Lynn (Domesday *Lena*,

---

[1] Courtney, Miss M. E., *Cornish Feasts*, p. 3.
[2] Johnson, W., *Folk Memory*, p. 212.   [3] *Cf. ibid.*, p. 211.

1100 *Lun*, 1314 Lenne [1]) was once a London and an Exton. The great red letter day in Lynn used to be the festival of Candlemas, and on that occasion the Mayor and Corporation attended by twelve decrepit old men, and a band of music, formerly opened a so-called court of Piepowder: on reference to the Cornish St. Allen it is agreeable to find that this saint " was the founder of St. Allen's Church in Powder". This Powder, sometimes written Pydar, is not shown on modern maps, but it was the title for a district or Hundred in Cornwall which contains the village of Par : it would appear to be almost a rule that the place-name

Fig. 431.—Sixteenth Century Printer's Ornament.

Peter should be closely associated with Allen, *e.g.*, Peterhead in Scotland, near Ellon, and Petrockstowe or Padstowe in Cornwall is near Helland on the river Allan.

In the emblem herewith the *alan* or cheery old Pater is associated like Nehelennia with the fruits of the earth, amongst which one may perhaps recognise *coddlins* and other varieties of Allan apple.

The Cornish Allantide was celebrated on the night of Hallow'een, and as Sir George Birdwood rightly remarks the English Arbor Day—if it be ever resuscitated—should be fixed on the first of November or old " Apple Fruit

[1] The authorities are perplexed by this place-name. "O.E. *Llynn* means usually a torrent running over a rock which does not exist here. Its later meaning, a pool, is not recorded until 1577 ".

Day," now All Hallows[1] or All Saint's Day, the Christian substitute for the Roman festival of Pomona ; also of the first day of the Celtic Feast of Shaman or Shony the Lord of Death. Shaman may in all probability be equated with Joe alone, and Shony with poor John alone alone: Shony, as has been seen, was an Hebridean ocean-deity, and the omniscient Oannes or John of Sancaniathon, the Phœnician historian, lived half his time in ocean: the Eros or Amoretto here illustrated from Kanauj may be connoted with Minnussinchen or the little Sinjohn of Tartary.

With the apple orchard Pomona or of the Pierre, Pere, or Pater Alone, the monocle and monarch of the universe, may be connoted the far-famed paradise of Prester or Presbyter *John* : this mythical priest-king is rendered sometimes as Preste *Cuan*, sometimes as *Un Khan* or John King-Priest, and sometimes as Ken Khan: he was clearly a personification of the King of Kings, and his marvellous Kingdom, which streamed with honey and was overflowing with milk, was evidently none other than Paradise or the Land of Heaven. " Mediæval credulity " believed that this so-called " Asiatic phantom," in whose country stood the Fountain of Youth and many other marvels, was attended by seven kings, twelve archbishops, and 365 counts: the seventy-two kings and their kingdoms said to be the tributaries of Prester John may be connoted with the

FIG. 432.—From Kanauj. From *Symbolism of the East and West* (Aynsley, Mrs. Murray).

---

[1] The Elsdale Street at Hackney which is found in close contact with Paradise Passage, Well Street, and Paragon Road may mark an original Elves or Ellie's Dale. Leading to " The Grove " is *Pigwell* Passage.

seventy-two dodecans of the Egyptian and Assyrian Zodiac: these seventy-two dodecans I have already connoted with the seventy-two stones constituting the circle of Long Meg. Facing the throne of Prester John—all of whose subjects were virtuous and happy—stood a wondrous mirror in which he saw everything that passed in all his vast dominions. The mirror or monocle of Prester John is obviously the speculum of Thoth, Taut, or Doddy, and I suspect that the seventy-two dodecans of the Egyptian and Chaldean Zodiac were the seventy-two Daddy Kings of Un Khan's Empire: none may take, nor touch, nor harm it—

> For the round of Morian Zeus has been its watcher from of old
> He beholds it and Athene thy own sea-grey eyes behold.[1]

The first written record of Preste Cuan figures in the chronicles of the Bishop of Freisingen (1145): the name Freisingen is radically *singen*: and it is quite probable that the Bungen Strasse at Hamelyn identified with the Pied Piper was actually the scene of a "Poor John, Alone, Alone," incident such as Brand thus describes: "I remember to have seen one of these impostors some years ago in the North of England, who made a very hermit-like appearance and went up and down the streets of Newcastle with a long train of boys at his heels muttering, 'Poor John alone, alone!' I thought he pronounced his name in a manner singularly plaintive,"[2] we have seen that the Wandering Jew was first recorded at St. Albans: the ancient name for Newcastle-on-Tyne—where he seems to have made his last recorded appearance—was *Pandon*. With the *panshen* or pope of Tartary may be connoted the probability that the rosy Allan apple of Newlyn was a

[1] *Ante*, p. 323. [2] *Cf.* Hardwick, C., *Trad. Super. and Folklore*, p. 159.

pippen : the parish of "Lynn or St. Margaret," not only includes the wards of Paradise and Jews Lane, but we find there also an Albion Place, and the curious name Guanock; modern Kings Lynn draws its water supply from a neighbouring *Gay* wood.

In the year 1165 a mysterious letter circulated in Europe emanating, it was claimed, from the great Preste Cuan, and setting forth the wonders and magnificence of his Kingdom: this epistle was turned into verse, sung all over Europe by the *trouveres*, and its claims to universal dominion taken so seriously by Pope Alexander that this *Pont*iff or *Ponti*fex [1] published in 1177 a counter-blast in which he maintained that the Christian professions of the mysterious Priest King were worse than worthless, unless he submitted to the spiritual claims of the See of Rome. There is little doubt that the popular Epistle of Prester John was the wily concoction of the Gnostic Trouveres or Merry Andrews, and that the unimaginative Pope who was so successfully stung into a reply, was no wise inferior in perception to the scholars of recent date who have located to their own satisfaction the mysterious Kingdom of Prester John in Tartary, in Asia Minor, or in Abyssinia: by the same peremptory and supercilious school of thought the Garden of Eden has been confidently placed in Mesopotamia, and the Irish paradise of Hy Breasil, "not unsuccessfully," identified with Labrador.

The probability is that every community attributed the Kingdom of Un Khan to its own immediate locality, and that like the land of the Pied Piper it was popularly supposed to be joining the town and close at hand. In the

[1] This word means evidently much more than, as supposed, *bridge builder.*

fifteenth century a hard-headed French traveller who had evidently fallen into the hands of some whimsical mystic, recorded: "There was also at *Pera* a Neapolitan, called Peter of Naples, with whom I was acquainted. He said he was married in the country of Prester John, and made many efforts to induce me to go thither with him. I questioned him much respecting this country, and he told me many things which I shall here insert, but I know not whether what he said be the truth, and shall not therefore warrant any part of it." Upon this honeymoon the archæologist, Thomas Wright, comments: "The manner in which our traveller here announces the relation of the Neapolitan shows how little he believed it; and in this his usual good sense does not forsake him. This recital is, in fact, but a tissue of absurd fables and revolting marvels, undeserving to be quoted, although they may generally be found in authors of those times. They are, therefore, here omitted: most of them, however, will be found in the narrative of John de Maundeville."[1]

We have seen that the Wandering Jew was alternatively termed Magus, a fact already connoted with the seventy-two stones of Long Meg, or Maggie: it was said that Un Khan was sprung from the ancient race of the Magi,[2] and

---

[1] The Rev. Baring-Gould quotes portions of this epistle in his *Curious Myths of the Middle Ages*, but its contents are evidently distasteful to him as he breaks off: "I may be spared further extracts from this extraordinary letter which proceeds to describe the church in which Prester John worships, by enumerating the precious stones of which it is constructed, and their special virtues": as a matter of fact, the account is an agreeable fairy-tale or fable which is no more extravagant than the account of the four-square, cubical, golden-streeted New Jerusalem attributed to the Revelations of St. John.

[2] Chambers' *Encyclopædia*, viii., 398.

I think that the solar circle at Shanagolden by Canons Island Abbey, on the Shannon in the country of the Ganganoi, was an *abri* of Ken Khan, Preste Cuan, or Un Khan.

The rath or dun of Shanid or Shenet, as illustrated *ante*, p. 55, has a pit in its centre which, says Mr. Westropp, "I can only suppose to have been the base of some timber structure": whether this central structure was originally a well, a tower, or a pole, it no doubt stood as a symbol of either the Tower of Salvation, the Well of Life, or the Tree of Knowledge. There is little doubt that this solar wheel or wheel of Good Fortune—which as will be remembered was occasionally depicted with four deacons or divine kings, a variant of the seventy-two dodecans—was akin to what British Bardism alluded to as "the melodious quaternion of Peter," or "the quadrangular delight of Peter, the great choir of the dominion":[1] it was also akin to the design on the Trojan whorl which Burnouf has described as the four epochs (quarters) of the month or year, and the holy sacrifice".[2]

The English earthwork illustrated in Fig. 433 (A) is known by the name of Pixie's Garden, and its form is doubtless that of one among many varieties of "the quadrangular delight of Peter". A pixy is an elf or *ouphe*, and the Pixie's Garden of *Uff*culme Down (Devon) may be connoted in idea with "Johanna's Garden" at St. Levans: Johanna, as we have seen, was associated with St. Levan (the home of Maggie Figgie), and in the words of Miss Courtney: "Not far from the parish of St. Levan is a small piece of ground—Johanna's Garden—which is fuller of weeds than of flowers".[3] I suspect that Johanna, like

---

[1] Guest, Dr., *Origines Celticæ*, ii., 182.
[2] *Cf.* Schliemann, *Troy.*   [3] *Cornish Feasts*, p. 76.

Pope Joan of Engelheim and Janicula, was the fabulous consort of Prester John or Un Khan.

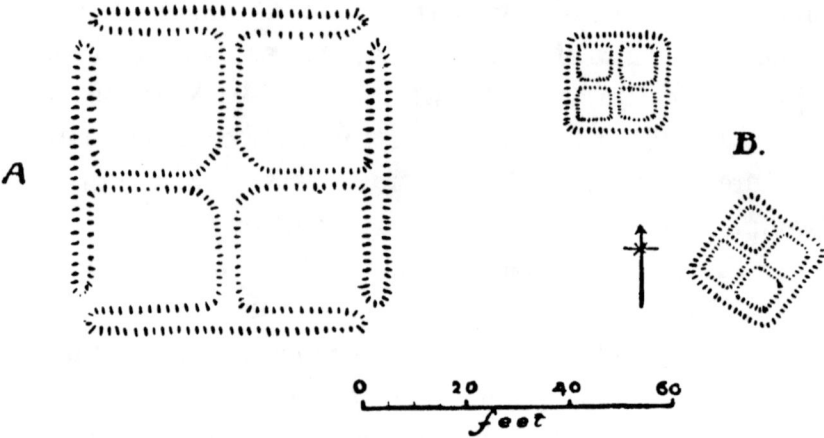

FIG. 433.—From *Earthwork of England* (A. Hadrian Allcroft).

Fig. 433 (B) represents two diminutive earthworks which once existed on Bray Down in *D*orsetshire: these little

FIG. 434.—From *Symbolism of the East and West* (Aynsley, Mrs. Murray)

Troytowns or variants of the quadrangular delight of Peter may be connoted with the obverse design of the Thorgut talisman found near Appleby and illustrated on page 675 : the two crescent moons may be connoted with two sickles still remembered in Mona, and the twice-eight crescents surrounding Fig. 434 which is copied from a mosaic pavement found at Gubbio, Italy.

The Pixie's Garden illustrated in Fig. 433 (A) obviously consists of four T's centred to one base and the elaborate svastika, illustrated in Fig. 435, is similarly distinguished by four concentric T's. The Kymbri or Cynbro customarily introduced the figure of a T into the thatch of their huts, and it is supposed that *ty*, the Welsh for a house or home, originated from this custom. We have seen that the Druids trained their super sacred oak tree (Hebrew *allon*) into the form of the T or Tau, which they inscribed Thau (*ante*, p. 393), and as *ty* in Celtic also meant *good*, the four T's surrounding the svastika of Fig. 435 would seem to be an implication of all surrounding beneficence, good luck, or *all bien*.

Fig. 435.— From *The Word in the Pattern* (Watts, Mrs. G. F.).

The Cynbro are believed to have made use of the T—Ezekiel's mark of election—as a magic preservative against fire and all other misfortunes, whence it is remarkable to find that even within living memory at *Camber*well by Peckham near London, the *chi*-shaped or ogee-shaped [1] angle irons, occasionally seen in old cottages, were believed to have been inserted "*in order to protect the house from fire* as well as from falling down".[2]

Commenting upon Fig. 435, which is taken from a Celtic

---

[1] *Cf. ante*, p. 345, Fig. 183, No. 10.
[2] Aynsley, Mrs. Murray, *Symbolism of the East and West*, p. 60.

706   ARCHAIC ENGLAND   [CHAP.

cross at Carew in Wales, Mrs. G. F. Watts observes: " This symbol was used by British Christians to signify the labyrinth or maze of life round which was sometimes written the words " God leadeth ".[1] Among the Latin races the Intreccia or Solomon's Knot, which consists frequently of three strands, is regarded as an emblem of the divine Being existent without beginning and without end—an unbroken

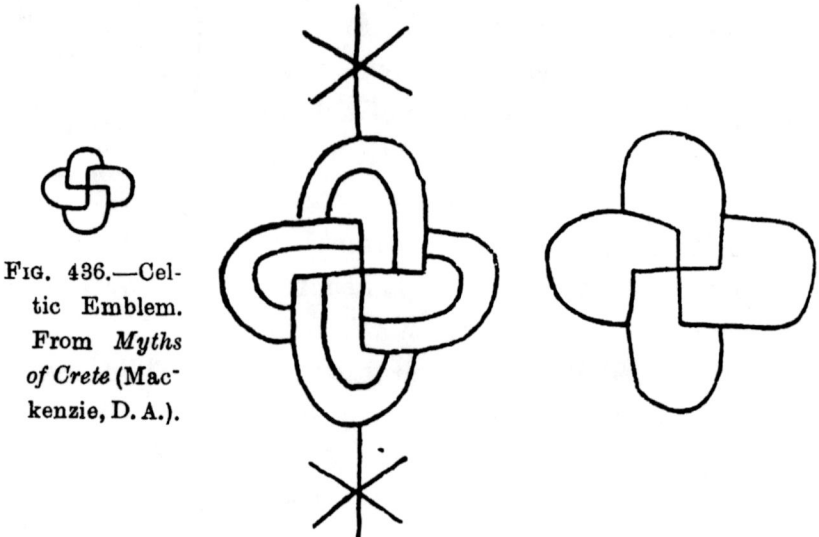

Fig. 436.—Celtic Emblem. From *Myths of Crete* (Mackenzie, D. A.).

Figs. 437 and 438.—Mediæval Papermarks. From *Les Filigranes* (Briquet, C. M.).

Unity: coiled often into the serpentine form of an S it decorates Celtic crosses and not infrequently into the centre of the maze is woven the *svastika* or Hammer of Thor. The word Svastika is described by oriental scholars as being composed of *svasti* and *ka*: according to the Dictionaries *svasti* means *welfare, health, prosperity, blessing, joy, happiness,* and *bliss*: in one sense *ka* (probably the *chi* χ) had the same meaning, but *ka* also meant " The Who,"

[1] *The Word in the Pattern.*

"The Inexplicable," "The Unknown," "The Chief God," "The Object of Worship," "The Lord of Creatures," "Water," "The Mind or Soul of the Universe".

In southern France—the Land of the Troubadours—the Solomon's Knot, as illustrated in Fig. 438, is alternatively known as *lacs d'amour*, or the knot of the Annunciation: this design consists, as will be noted, of a svastika extended into a rose or maze, and a precisely similar emblem is found in Albany. The title *lacs d'amour* or lakes of love, consociated with the synonymous knot of the Annunciation,

Fig. 439.—From *Troy* (Schliemann).

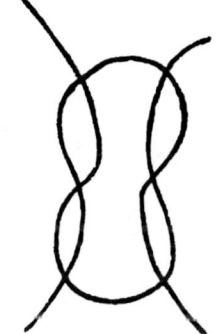

Figs. 440 and 441.—Mediæval Papermarks. From *Les Filigranes* (Briquet, C. M.).

is seemingly further confirmation of the equation *amour* = Mary: another form of knot is illustrated in Fig. 440, and this the reader will compare with Fig. 439, representing a terra-cotta tablet found by Schliemann at Troy.

It will be remembered that according to the Pierrot legend St. Peter looking out from the Walls of Heaven detected what he first took to be a rosebud in the snow: the name Piers, which like Pearce is a variant of Peter, is essentially *pieros*, either Father Rose or Father Eros. The rood or rhoda pierre here illustrated is a Rose cross, and is conspicuously decorated with intreccias, or Solomon's

708   ARCHAIC ENGLAND   [CHAP.

Knots: whether the inscription—which looks curiously Arabic—has ever been deciphered I am unable to say; it would, however, seem that the Andrew or Chi cross, which figures upon it, permits the connection of this Chooyvan rood with Choo or Jou.

The Carv'd Pillar or Monument call'd Maen y Chwyvan in Flintshire

FIG. 442.—From *A New Description of England* (Anon, 1724).

Among the whorls from Troy, Burnouf has deciphered objects which he describes as a wheel in motion; others as the *Rosa mystica*; others as the three stations of the Sun, or the three mountains. The Temple of Solomon was situated on Mount Moriah, one of the three holy hills of Hierosolyma, and it is probable that Meru, the paradise peak of Buddhism, was like Mount Moriah, originally Amour. That the wheel coins of England were symbolic of the Apple Orchard, the Garden of the Rose, or of the Isles called Fortunate is further pointed by the variant here illustrated, which is unmistakeably a *Rosa mystica*.

Fig. 443.—From Evans.

As has been pointed out by Sir George Birdwood it was the Apple Tree of the prehistoric Celtic immigrants that gave to the whole peninsular of the West of England—Gloucestershire, Somersetshire, Dorsetshire, Devonshire, and Cornwall, the mystic name of "Ancient Avalon," or Apple Island :—

> Deep meadowed, happy, fair with orchard lawns,
> And bowery hollows, crowned with summer seas.

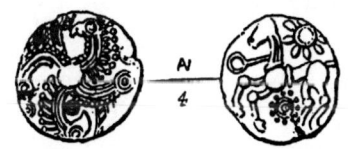

Fig. 443A.—British. From Evans.

CHAPTER XIII.

ENGLISH EDENS

At bottom, a man is what his thinking is, thoughts being the artists who give colour to our days. Optimists and pessimists live in the same world, walk under the same sky, and observe the same facts. Sceptics and believers look up at the same great stars—the stars that shone in Eden, and will flash again in Paradise.—Dr. J. FORT NEWTON.

THE name under which Jupiter was worshipped in Crete is not yet deciphered, but as we are told that the favourite abode of King Jou at Gnossus was on Mount Olympus where in its delightful recesses he held his court, and administered patriarchal justice; and as we are further told by Julius Firmicus that: " vainly the Cretans to this day adore the tumulus of Jou," it is fairly obvious that, however many historic King Jou's there may have been, the archetypal Jou was a lord of the tumulus or dun.

The ancient Irish were accustomed to call *any* hill or artificial mound under which lay vaults, a *shee*, which also is the generic term for fairy: similarly we have noted a connection between the term *rath*—or dun—and *wraith*. Although fairies were partial to banks, braes, purling brooks, brakes, and bracken, they particularly loved to congregate in duns or raths, and their rapid motions to and fro these headquarters were believed to create a noise " somewhat resembling the loud humming of bees when swarming from a hive ". I have little doubt that all hills, *bryns*, or barrows were regarded not only as *bruen*, or

CHAP. XIII.] ENGLISH EDENS 711

breasts, but as ethereal beehives, and the superstitions still associated with bees are evidence that bees themselves were once deemed sacred. There are upwards of a thousand localities in Ireland alone where the word *rath, raw, rah, ray*, or *ra* marks the site of a fairy rath,[1] and without going

FIG. 444.—Birs Nimroud.

so far as to assert that every British *-dun* or *-ton* was a fairy *dun* or *doun* further investigation will probably establish an unsuspected multitude of Dunhills or Edens.

We have seen that in Ireland *fern* meant anciently *anything good*, and also in all probability *fer en* the Fires or Fairies: at the romantic hill of Cnock-Firinn or the *Hill of firinn* was supposed to dwell a fairy chief named Donn

[1] *Irish Folklore*, p. 32.

Firineach, *i.e.*, Donn the Truthful or the Truthteller;[1] evidently, therefore, this Don was a counterpart and consort of Queen Vera, and as he is reputed to have come from Spain his name may be connoted with the Spanish *don* which, like the Phœnician *adon*, is a generic term meaning *the lord*. With "Generous Donn the King of Faery" may be connoted the Jewish Adonai, a plural form of *Adon* "lord" combined with the pronoun of the first person: when reading the Scriptures aloud the Jews rather than utter the super-sacred word Jhuh, substitute Adonai, and in Jewry Adonai is thus a title of the Supreme Being. Among the Phœnicians Adon or *the lord* was specially applied to the King of Heaven or the Sun and that sacred Nineveh was essentially a dunhill is evidenced by Fig. 444.

With Adon may be connoted Adonis, the lovely son of Myrrha and Kinyras, whose name has been absorbed into English as meaning any marvellously well-favoured youth: prior to the festivals of Adonis it was customary to grow forced gardens in earthen or *silver* pots, and there would thus seem to have been a close connection in ideas between our English "*whytepot* queen" or maiden with the pyramid of silver, and with the symbolic Gardens of Adonis or Eden as grown in Phrygia and Egypt.

Skeat connotes the word maiden—which is an earlier form than *maid*—with the Cornish *maw*, a boy: if, however, we read *ma* as *mother* the word *maiden* becomes *Mother Iden*, and I have little doubt that the Maiden of mythology and English harvest-homes was the feminine Adonis. Adonis was hymned as the Shepherd of the Twinkling Stars: I have surmised that Long Meg of the seventy-two

[1] *Irish Folklore*, p. 78.

Daughters was the Mighty Maiden of the Stars, whence it is interesting to find Skeat connoting *maiden* with Anglo-Saxon *magu*, a kinsman: that Long Meg was the All Mother whence *mag* or *mac* came to mean *child of* has already been suggested. Not only does Long Meg of Cumberland stand upon Maiden Way, but there is in the same district a Maidenmoor probably like Maidenhead or Maidenheath, a heath or mead dedicated to the Maid. Our dictionaries define the name May as a contraction of either Mary or Margaret, *i.e.*, Meg: in the immediate neighbourhood of Long Meg is another circle called Mayborough, of which the vallum or enclosure is composed of stones taken from the beds of the Eamount or Eden rivers; in the centre of Mayborough used to stand four magnificent monoliths probably representative of the four *deacons* or Good Kings who supported the Whytepot Queen.

There is a seat called St. Edans in Ireland close to Ferns where, as will be remembered, is St. Mogue's Well: in Lincolnshire is a Maidenwell-*cum-Farworth*, and at Dorchester is a Haydon Hill in the close proximity of Forstone and *Goodman*stone. That this Haydon was the *Good Man* is implied by the stupendous monument near by known as Mew Dun, Mai Dun, or Maiden Castle: this *chef d'œuvre* of prehistoric engineering, generally believed to be the greatest earthwork in Britain, is an oblong camp extending 1000 yards from east to west with a width of 500 yards, and it occupies an area of 120 acres:[1] entered by four gates the work itself is described as puzzling as a series of mazes, and to reach the interior one is compelled to pass through a labyrinth of defences. The name Dorchester suggests a Droia or Troy camp, and I have little doubt that the

---

[1] Heath, F. R. and S., *Dorchester*, p. 40.

labyrinthine Maiden was a colossal Troy Town or Drayton. Among the many Draytons in England is a Drayton-Parslow, which suggests that it stood near or upon a Parr's low or a Parr's lea : out of great Barlow Street, Marylebone, leads Paradise Place and Paradise Passage : there is a Drayton Park at Highbury, and in the immediate proximity an Eden Grove and Paradise Road : there was a Troy Town where Kensington Palace now stands,[1] and in all likelihood there was another one at Drayton near Hanwell and Hounslow. That Hounslow once contained an *onslow* or *ange hill* seems to me more probable than that it was merely the "burial mound" of an imaginary *Hund* or *Hunda* : in Domesday Hounslow figures as Honeslow which may be connoted with Honeybourne at Evesham and Honeychurch in Devon. With regard to the latter it has been observed: " The connection between a church and honey is not very obvious, and this is probably Church of *Huna* " : the official explanation of " Honeybourne " is —" brook with honey sweet water," but it is more probable that Queen Una was reputed to dwell there. That Una was not merely the creation of Spenser is evidenced from the fact that in Ireland " Una is often named by the peasantry as regent of the preternatural *Sheog* tribes " :[2] at St. Mary's-in-the-Marsh, Thanet, is a Honeychild Manor and an Old Honeychild : with the Three White Balls at Iona it may be noted that on the summit of Hydon Heath (Surrey) is a place marked Hydon's Ball.

At a distance of " about 110 yards " from Mayborough is another circle known as Arthur's Round *Table* : a mile from Dunstable is a circular camp known as Maiden Bower,

---

[1] Dorchester stands on the " Ecen Way ".
[2] *Irish Folklore*, p. 79.

whence it is probable that Dunstable meant either Dun staple (market), or that the circular camp there was a "table" of "generous Donn". That the term "Maiden" used here and elsewhere means *maiden* as we now understand it may be implied from the famous Maiden Stone in Scotland: this sculptured Longstone, now measuring 10 feet in height, bears upon it the mirror and comb which were essentially the emblems of the Mairymaid.

There is an eminence called Maiden Bower near Durham which figures alternatively as *Dun*holme; Durham is supposed to mean—"wild beast's home or lair," but I see no more reason to assign this ferocious origin to Durham than, say, to Dorchester or Doracestria: Ma, the mistress of Mount Ida, was like Britomart[1] esteemed to be the Mother of all beasts or *brutes*, and particularly of *deer*; Diana is generally represented with a deer, and the woody glens of many-crested Ida were indubitably a lair of forest brutes—

> Thus Juno spoke, and to her throne return'd,
> While they to spring-abounding Ida's heights,
> Wild nurse of forest beasts, pursued their way.[2]

Yorkshire, or Eboracum and the surrounding district, the habitat of the Brigantes, was known anciently as Deira: by the Romans Doracestria, or Dorchester was named Durnovaria upon which authority comments: "In the

---

[1] In *Crete the Forerunner of Greece*, Mr. and Mrs. Hawes remark that Browning's great monologue corresponds perfectly with all we know of the Minoan goddess—

> I shed in Hell o'er my pale people peace
> On earth, I caring for the creatures guard
> Each pregnant yellow wolf and fox-bitch sleek,
> And every feathered mother's callow brood,
> And all that love green haunts and loneliness.

[2] *Iliad*, xv., 175.

present name there is nothing which represents *varia*, so that it really seems to mean 'fist camp'"; doubtless, fisticuffs, boxing-matches, and many other kind of Trojan game were once held at Doracestria as at every other Troy or Drayton.

King Priam, the Mystic King of Troy, is said to have had fifty sons and daughters: the same family is assigned not only to St. Brychan of Cambria, but also to King Ebor, or Ebrauc of York, whence in all probability the Brigantes who inhabited Yorkshire and Cumberland were followers of one and the same Priam, Prime, Broom, Brahm, or Brahma: the name Abraham or Ibrahim is defined as meaning "father of a multitude". The Kentish Broom Park near Patrixbourne whereby is Hearts Delight, Maydeacon House, and Kingston is on Heden Downs, and immediately adjacent is a Dennehill and Denton: at Dunton Green, near Sevenoaks, the presence of a Mount Pleasant implies that this Dunton was an Eden Town.

There is an Edenkille, or Eden Church at Elgin, and at Dudley is a Haden Cross, supposed to have derived its title "from a family long resident here": it would be preferable and more legitimate to assign this family name to the site and describe them as the "De Haden's". There is a Haddenham at Ely, and at Ely Place, Holborn, opposite St. Andrews, is Hatton Garden: I suggest that Sir Christopher Hatton, like the Hadens of Haden Cross, derived his name from his home, and not *vice versa*.

In the Hibernian county of Clare is an Eden Vale: Clare Market in London before being pulled down was in the parish of St. Clement *Dane*, here also stood Dane's Inn, and within a stone's throw is the church of St. Dunstan. The numerous St. Dunstans were probably once Dane stones, or Dun stanes, and the sprightly story of St. Dunstan seizing the nose of a female temptress with the tongs must be relegated to the Apocrypha. In the opinion of Sir Laurence Gomme the predominant cult in Roman London was undoubtedly that of Diana, for the evidence in favour of this goddess includes not only an altar, but other finds connected with her worship: Sir Laurence goes even further than this, stating his conviction that "Diana practically absorbed the religious expression of London":[1] that London was a *Lunadun* has already been suggested.

It has always been strongly asserted by tradition that St. Paul's occupies the site of a church of Diana: if this were so the Diana stones on the summit of Ludgate Hill would have balanced the Dun stones on the opposing bank of the river Fleet, or Bagnigge. We have seen that *mam* in Gaelic meant a gently sloping hill; the two dunhills rising from the river Fleet, or Bagnigge, were thus probably regarded like the Paps of Anu at Killarney, as twin breasts of the Maiden: there are parallel "Maiden Paps" near Berriedale (Caithness), others near Sunderland, and others at Roxburgh. According to Stow the famous cross at Cheapside was decorated with a statue of Diana, the goddess, to which the adjoining Cathedral had been formerly dedicated: prior to the Reformation, two jets of water—like the jets in Fig. 44 (p. 167)—prilled from Diana's naked breast "but now decayed".

By Claremarket and the church of St. Clement Dane stood Holywell Street, somewhat north of which was yet another well called—according to Stow—Dame Annis the *Clear*, and not far from it, but somewhat West, was also

[1] *London*, p. 59.

one other *clear* water called Perilous Pond. This "perilous" was probably once *peri lass*, *i.e.*, *perry lass*, or *pure lass*, and the neighbouring Clerkenwell (although the city clerks or *clerken* may in all likelihood have congregated there on summer evenings), was once seemingly sacred to the same type of phairy as the Irish call a *cluricanne*.[1] The original Clerken, or Cluricanne, was in all probability the resplendent *clarus*, clear, shining, *Glare* King, or *Glory* King: but it is equally likely that the *-ken* of Clerken was the endearing diminutive *kin*, as in Lambkin. That St. Clare was adored by her disciples is clear from *The Golden Legend*, where among other interesting data we are told: "She was crowned with a crown right clear shining that the obscurity of the night was changed into clearness of midday": we are further told that once upon a time as a certain friar was preaching in her presence: "a right fair child was to fore St Clare, and abode there a great part of the sermon". It is thus permissible to assume that this marvellous holy woman, whose doctrine shall "enlumine all the world," was originally depicted in company of the customary Holy Child, or the Little Glory King.

The original Clerken Well stood in what is now named Ray Street, and quite close to it is Braynes Row; not far distant was Brown's Wood.[2] The name Sinclair implies an order or a tribe of Sinclair followers, and that the St. Dunstan by St. Clement's Dane and Claremarket was something more than a monk is obvious from the tradition that "Our Lord shewed miracles for him *ere he was born*": the marvel in point is that on a certain

---

[1] *Irish Folklore*, p. 34.
[2] Gomme, Sir L., *The Topography of London*, ii., 215.

Candlemas Day the candle of his Mother Quendred[1] miraculously burned full bright so that others came and lighted their tapers at the taper of St. Dunstan's mother; the interpretation placed upon this marvel was that her unborn child should give light to all England by his holy living.[2]

As recorded in *The Golden Legend* the life of poor St. Clare was one long dolorous great moan and sorrow: it is mentioned, however, that she had a sister Agnes and that these two sisters loved marvellously together. We may thus assume that the celestial twins were Ignis, *fire* and Clare, *light* : *Agnes* is the Latin for *lamb*, and this symbol

Fig. 445.—Gaulish. From Akerman.

of Innocence is among the two or three out of lost multitudes which have been preserved by the Christian Church. In the illustration herewith the lambkin, in conjunction with a star, appears upon a coin of the Gaulish people whose chief town was Agatha: its real name, according to Akerman, was Agatha Tyke, and its foundation has been attributed both to the Rhodians and the Phoceans. Agatha is Greek for *good*, and *tyke* meant fortune or good luck: the effigy is described as being a bare head of Diana to the right and without doubt Diana, or the divine Una, was typified both by *ignis* the fire, and by *agnes* the lamb: in India Agni is represented riding on a male *agnes*, and in Christian art the Deity was figured as a ram.

[1] See Cynethryth *post*, p. 761.   [2] *Golden Legend*, iii., 188.

At the Cornish town of St. Enns, St. Anns, or St. Agnes, the name of St. Agnes—a paragon of maiden virtue—is

Fig. 446.—Agni.

coupled with a Giant Bolster, a mighty man who is said to have held possession of a neighbouring hill, sometimes

Fig. 447.—From *Christian Iconography* (Didron).

known as Bury-anack : at the base of this hill exists a very interesting and undoubtedly most ancient earthwork known as " The Bolster ".¹ As Anak meant *giant*,² Bury Anack was seemingly the *abri, brugh, bri*, or fairy palace of this particular Anak, and if we spell Bolster with an *e* he emerges at once into Belstar, the *Beautiful Star* who is represented in association with Agnes on page 719 : probably the maligned Bolster of Cornwall had another of his abris at Bellister Castle on the Tyne, now a crumbling mass of ruins.

Some accounts mention the Clerkenwell pool of Annis the Clear as being that of Agnes the Clear: opposite the famous Angel of this neighbourhood is Claremont Square, and about half a mile eastward is Shepherdess Walk; that the Shepherdess of this walk was Diane, *i.e.*, Sinclair the counterpart of Adonis, the Shepherd of the twinkling stars, is somewhat implied by Peerless Street, which leads into Shepherdess Walk. Perilous Pool at Clerkenwell was sometimes known as Peerless Pool: it has been seen that the hags or fairies were associated with this Islington district which still contains a Paradise Passage, and of both " Perilous " and " Peerless " I think the correct reading should be *peri lass ;* it will be remembered that the peris were quite familiar to England as evidenced by the feathery clouds or " perry dancers," and the numerous Pre Stones and Perry Vales.³ In Red Cross Street, Clerkenwell, are or were Deane's Gardens; at Clarence Street, Islington, the name Danbury Street implies the existence either there or elsewhere of a Dan barrow.

Opposite Clare Market and the churches of St. Dunstan

---

[1] Hunt, R., *Popular Romances of the West of England*, p. 73.
[2] Cf. Numbers xiii. 33.
[3] Adjacent to Perry Mount, Perrivale, Sydenham, are Adamsrill road, Inglemere road, *Allen*by road, and *Ex*bury road.

and St. Clement Dane is situated the Temple of which the circular church, situated in Tanfield Court,[1] is dedicated to St. Anne: St. Anne, the mother of St. Mary, is the patron saint of Brittany, where she has been identified with Ma or Cybele, the Magna Mater of Mount Ida; that Anna was the consort of Joachim or the Joy King I do not doubt, and in her aspect of a Fury or Black Virgin she was in all probability the oak-haunting Black Annis of Leicestershire: "there was one flabby eye, in her head". In view of the famous round church of St. Mary the Virgin it is permissible to speculate whether the "small circular hut of stone," in which Black Mary of Black Mary's Hole was reputed to have dwelt on the banks of the Fleet, Bagnigge or Holeburn (now Holborn) was or was not the original Eye dun of the Pixy, or Big Nikke.

The emblems associated with the Temple and its circular church are three; the Flying Horse or Pegasus; two men or *twain* riding on a single horse (probably the Two Kings) and the Agnus Dei: in the emblem herewith this last is standing on a dun whence are flowing the four rivers of Eden. The lamb was essentially an emblem of St. John who, in Art, is generally represented with it; whence it is significant that in Celtic the word for lamb is identical with the name Ion, the Welsh being *oen*, the Cornish *oin*, the Breton *oan*, the Gaelic *uan*, and the Manx *eayn*. That Sinjohn was always *sunshine* and the *sheen*, never apparently darkness, is implied by the Basque words *egun* meaning *day*, and Agandia or Astartea meaning Sunday.

[1] This Tanfield Court supposedly takes its name from an individual named Tanfield. Wherever the original Tanfield was it was doubtless the scene of many a bonfire or Beltan similar to the joyous "Tan Tads," or "Fire Fathers" of Brittany.

XIII.]   ENGLISH EDENS   723

The Basque for *God* is *jainco*, the Ugrian was *jen*, and the Basque *jain*, meaning *lord* or *master*, is evidently synonymous with the Spanish *don* or *donna*.

In addition to St. Annes opposite St. Dunstans, and St. Clement Dane there is a church of St. Anne in Dean Street, Soho: Anu of Ireland was alternatively Danu, and it is clear from many evidences that the initial *d* or *t* was

FIG. 448.—Divine Lamb, with a Circular Nimbus, not Cruciform, Marked with the Monogram of Christ, and the A and Ω. Sculptured on a Sarcophagus in the Vatican. The earliest ages of Christianity. From *Christian Iconography* (Didron).

generally adjectival. The Cornish for *down* or dune is *oon*, and Duke was largely correct when he surmised in connection with St. Anne's Hill, Avebury: "I cannot help thinking that from Diana and Dian were struck off the appellations Anna and Ann, and that the *feriæ*, or festival of the goddess, was superseded by the fair, as now held, of the saint. I shall now be told that the fane of the hunting goddess would never have been seated on this high and bare hill, that the Romans would have given her a habitation amidst the woods and groves, but here Callimachus comes to my aid. In his beautiful Hymn on Diána he feigns her to entreat her father Jupiter, 'also give me *all* hills and mountains'."

Not only is Diana (Artemis) made to say "give me all hills and mountains," but Callimachus continues, "for rarely will Artemis go down into the cities": hence it is probable that all denes, duns, and downs were dedicated to Diana. In Armenia, Maundeville mentions having visited a city on a mountain seven miles high named Dayne which was founded by Noah; near by is the city of Any or Anni, in which he says were one thousand churches. Among the rock inscriptions here illustrated, which are attributed to the Jews when migrating across Sinai from Egypt, will be noticed the name Aine prefixed by a thau cross: the mountain rocks of the Sinai Peninsular bear thousands of illegible inscriptions which from time to time fall down —as illustrated—in the ravines; by some they are attributed to the race who built Petra.[1] I am unable to offer any suggestion as to how this Roman lettering AINE finds itself in so curious a milieu.

Speaking of the bleak moorlands of Penrith (the *pen ruth?*), where are found the monuments of Long Meg and of Mayborough, Fergusson testily observes: "No one will now probably be found seriously to maintain that the long stone row at Shap was a temple either of the Druids or of anyone else. At least if these ancient people thought a single or even a double row of widely-spaced stones stretching to a mile and a half across a bleak moor was a proper form for a place to worship in, they must have been differ-

[1] *Cf.* Forster, Rev. C., *The One Primeval Language*, 1851.

ENGLISH EDENS

Fig. 449.—View of Wady Mokatteb from the S.E. From *The One Primeval Language* (Forster, C.).

ently constituted from ourselves."[1] Indubitably they were; and so too must have been the ancient Greeks: the far-famed Mount Cynthus, whence Apollo was called Cynthus, is described by travellers as "an ugly hill" which crosses the island of Delos obliquely; it is not even a mountain, but "properly speaking is nothing but a ridge of granite". I am told that Glastonbury—the Avalon, the Apple Orchard, the Sacred Eden of an immeasurable antiquity—is disappointing, and that nowadays little of any interest is to be seen there. "Donn's House," the gorgeous *bri* or palace of generous Donn the King of Faery, is in reality no better than a line of sandhills in the Dingle Peninsula, Kerry; of the inspiring Tipperary I know nothing, but can sympathise with the prosaic Governor of the Isle of Man, who a century or so ago reported that practically every dun in Manxland was crowned with a cairn which seemed "nothing but the rubbish of Nature thrown into barren and unfruitful heaps".

"Miserable churl" sang the wily, enigmatic Bird, whose advice to the rich villein has been previously quoted,[2] "when you held me fast in your rude hand easy was it to know that I was no larger than a sparrow or a finch, and weighed less than half an ounce. How then could a precious stone three ounces in weight be hid in my body? When he had spoken thus he took his flight, and from that hour the orchard knew him no more. *With the ceasing of his song the leaves withered from the pine, the garden became a little dry dust and the fountain forgot to flow.*"

[1] *Rude Stone Monuments*, p. 131.
[2] "His feathers were all ruffled for he had been grossly handled by a glove not of silk, but of wool, so he preened and plumed himself carefully with his beak."

Among the legends of the Middle Ages is one to the effect that Alexander, after conquering the whole world determined to find and compass Paradise. After strenuous navigation the envoys of the great King eventually arrived before a vast city circled by an impenetrable wall: for three days the emissaries sailed along this wall without discovering any entrance, but on the third day a small window was discerned whence one of the inhabitants put out his head, and blandly inquired the purpose of the expedition; on being informed the inhabitant, nowise perturbed, replied: "Cease to worry me with your threats but patiently await my return". After a wait of two hours the denizen of Heaven reappeared at the window and handed the envoys a gem of wonderful brilliance and colour which in size and shape exactly reproduced *the human eye :* [1] Alexander, not being able to make head or tail of these remarkable occurrences, consulted in secret all the wisest of the Jews and Greeks but received no suitable explanation; eventually, however, he found an aged Jew who elucidated the mystery of the hidden Land by this explanation: "O King, the city you saw is the abode of souls freed from their bodies, placed by the Creator in an inaccessible position on the confines of the world. Here they await in peace and quiet the day of their judgment and resurrection, after which they shall reign forever with their Creator. These spirits, anxious for the salvation of humanity, and wishing to preserve your happiness, have destined this stone as a warning to you to curb the unseemly desires of your ambition. Remember that such insatiable desires merely end by enslaving a man, consuming him with cares and depriving him of all peace. Had

[1] *Folklore*, xxix., No. 3, p. 195.

you remained contented with the inheritance of your own kingdom you would have reigned in peace and tranquillity, but now, not even yet satisfied with the conquest of enormous foreign possessions and wealth, you are weighed down with cares and danger."

The name of the aged Jew who furnished Alexander with this information is said to have been Papas, or Papias : Papas was an alternative name for the Phrygian Adonis, whence we may no doubt equate the old Adonis (*i.e.*, Aidoneus, or Pluto ?) with the Aged Jew, or the Wandering Jew. It has been seen that the legend of the Wandering Jew apparently originated at St. Albans : in France *montjoy* was a generic term for herald, and I have little doubt that these Mountjoys were originally so termed as being the denizens of some sacred Mount. There is a Mount Joy near Jerusalem, and there was certainly at least one in France : among the legends recorded in Layamon's *Brut* is one relating to a Mont Giu and a wondrous Star : " From it came gleams terribly shining ; the star is named in Latin, comet. Came from the star a gleam most fierce ; at this gleam's end was a dragon fair ; from this dragon's mouth came gleams enow ! But twain there were mickle, unlike to the others ; the one drew toward France, the other toward Ireland. The gleam that toward France drew, it was itself bright enow ; to *Munt-Giu* was seen the marvellous token ! The gleam that stretched right west, it was disposed in seven beams." [1] It is probable that Chee Tor in the neighbourhood of Buxton, Bakewell,[2] and Haddon Hall, was once just as bogie a Mount as

---

[1] P. 165.

[2] At Bickley in Kent there is a *Shaw*field Park, which may be connoted with the Bagshaw's Cavern at Buxton.

XIII.] ENGLISH EDENS 729

Munt-Giu: at Church*down* in Gloucester is a Chosen Hill, which apparently was sacred to Sen Cho, and this hill was presumably the original church of Down; all sorts of "silly traditions" are said to hang around this spot, and

Fig. 450.—From *The Everyday Book* (Hone, W.).

the natives ludicrously claim themselves to be "the Chosen" People.

Chee Tor at Buxton overlooks the river Wye, a name probably connected with *eye*, and with numerous *Ea*-mounts, *Ey*tons, *Ea*tons, *How*dens, etc.: that Eton in

Bucks was an Eye Dun is inferable from the *ad montem* ceremonies which used until recently to prevail at Salt Hill.[1] In British, *hy* or *ea,* as in Hy Breasil, Batters*ea,* Chels*ea,* etc., meant an island, and the ideal Eden was usually conceived and constructed in island form: if a natural " Eye Town " were not available it was customary to construct an artificial one by running a trench around some natural or artificial barrow. The word *eye* also means a shoot, whence we speak of the eye of a potato, and the standard Eyedun seems always to have possessed an eye of eyes in the form either of a tree, a well, or a tower: it was not unusual to surmount the Beltan fire or Tan-Tad with a tree; the favourite phare tree was a fir tree, in Provence the Yule log was preferably a pear tree. It was anciently supposed that the earth was an island established upon the floods, and Homer preserves the belief of his time by referring to Oceanus as a river-stream :—

> And now, borne seaward from *the river stream*
> *Of the Oceanus*, we plow'd again
> The spacious Deep, and reach'd th' Ææan Isle,
> Where, daughter of the dawn, Aurora takes
> Her choral sports, and whence the sun ascends.[2]

According to Josephus, the Garden of Eden " was watered by one river which ran round about the whole earth,[3] and was parted into four parts," and this immemorial tradition was expressed upon the circular and sacred cakes of ancient nations which were the forerunners of our

---

[1] By Chee Tor is Mon*sal* Dale, and we may reasonably connote *sal* and "*salt*" with Silbury and Sol: into the waters of the Solway Firth flows the river Eden or Ituna, and doubtless the Edinburgh by Salisbury Crags is older than any Saxon Edwin or Scandinavian Odin. (Since writing I find it was originally named Dunedin, *cf.* Morris Jones, Sir G., *Taliesin.*)

[2] *Odyssey*, Book I., 67.   [3] Chapter I.

Good Friday's Hot Cross Buns. Associated with the pagan Eucharists here illustrated [1] will be noted Eros—whose name is at the base of *eucharist*—also what seemingly is the Old Pater. In Egypt the cross cake was a hieroglyph for "civilised land," and was composed of the richest materials including milk and honey, the familiar attributes of Canaan or the Promised Land. The remarkable earthwork cross at Banwell has no doubt some relation to the Alban cross on our Easter *bun*, Greek *boun*, and

FIG. 451.—Love-Feast with Wine and Bread. Relief in the Kircher Museum at Rome, presumably pagan. After Roller, pl. LIV. 7.

the so-termed Pixies' Garden illustrated in Fig. 433 (A), probably was once permeated by the same phairy imagination as perceived Paradise in the dusty "Walls of Heaven," "Peter's Orchard," and "Johanna's Garden".

The name Piccadilly is assumed to have arisen because certain buns called piccadillies were there sold: the greater likelihood is that the bun took its title from Piccadilly. This curious place-name, which commemorates the memory of a Piccadilly Hall, is found elsewhere, and is

[1] From an article by Dr. Paul Carus in *The Open Court*.

probably cognate with Pixey lea, *Poukelay*, and the legend PIXTIL, etc. Opposite Down Street, Piccadilly, or Mayfair, there are still standing in the Green Park the evidences of what may once have been tumuli or duns, and the Buckden Hill by St. Agnes' Well in Hyde Park may, as is supposed, have been a den for bucks, or, as is not more improbable, a dun sacred to Big Adon:[1] leading to Buck Hill and St.

Fig. 452.—A Pagan Love-Feast. Now in the Lateran Museum. From Roller, *Les Cata. de Rome*, pl. LIV. The pagan character is assured by the winged Eros at the left.

Agnes' Well there is still a pathway marked on the Ordnance map Budge Walk, an implication seemingly that Bougie, or Bogie, was not unknown in the district. We have connoted Rotten Row of *Hyde* Park with Rotten Row Tower near Alnwick: this latter is situated on *Aidon* Moor. By *Down* Street, Mayfair, is Hay Hill, at the foot of which flowed the Eye Brook, and this beck no doubt meandered past the modern Brick Street, and through the Brookfield

---

[1] The fine megalith now standing half a mile distant at "The Den" was transported from Devonshire about a century ago—no doubt with the idea of tripping some unwary archæologist.

in the Green Park where the fifteen joyful heydays of the Mayfair were once celebrated: whether the Eye Brook wandered through Eaton Square—the site of St. Peter's Church—I do not know, nor can I trace whether or not the " Eatons " hereabout are merely entitled from Eaton Hall in the Dukeries. Each Eaton or island ton, certainly every sacred island, seems to have been deemed a " central boss of Ocean: that retreat a goddess holds,"[1] and this central boss appears to have been conceived indifferently or comprehensively as either a Cone, a Pyramid, a Beehive, or a Teat. Wyclif, in his translation of the Bible, refers to Jerusalem as "the totehill Zyon," and there is little doubt that all teathills were originally cities or sites of peace: according to Cyprien Roberts: " The first basilicas, *placed generally upon eminences*, were called Domus Columbæ, dwellings of the dove, that is, of the Holy Ghost. They caught the first rays of the dawn, and the last beams of the setting sun."[2] Everywhere in Britain the fays were popularly " gentle people," " good neighbours," and " men of peace": a Scotch name for Fairy dun or High Altar of the Lord of the Mound used to be—*sioth-dhunan*, from *sioth* " peace," and *dun* " a mound ": this name was derived from the practice of the Druids " who were wont occasionally to retire to green eminences to administer justice, establish peace, and compose differences between contending parties. As that venerable order taught a *saogle hal*, or World-beyond-the-present, their followers, when they were no more, fondly imagined that seats where they

---

[1] *Odyssey*, Book I., 67.
[2] *Cours d'Hieroglyphique Chretienne*, in *L'Universite Catholique*, vol. vi., p. 266.

exercised a virtue so beneficial to mankind were still inhabited by them in their disembodied state ".[1]

In Cornwall there is a famous well at Truce which is legendarily connected with Druidism :[2] Irish tradition speaks of a famous Druid named Trosdan; St. Columba is associated with a St. Trosdan ;[3] at St. Vigeans in Scotland there is a stone bearing an inscription which the authorities transcribe "Drosten,"[4] probably all the dwellers on the Truce duns were entitled Trosdan,[5] and it is not unlikely that the romantic Sir Patrise of Westminster was originally Father Truce. It has already been noted that *treus* was Cornish for cross, that children cross their fingers as a sign of fainits or truce, and there is very little doubt that cruciform earthworks, such as Shanid, and cruciform duns such as Hallicondane in Thanet were truce duns. The Tuatha de Danaan, or Children of Donn, who are supposed to have been the introducers of Druidism into Ireland, were said to have transformed into fairies, and the duns or raths of the Danaan are still denominated "gentle places".[6] That the ancient belief in the existence of "gentle people" is still vivid, is demonstrated beyond question by the author of *The Fairy Faith in Celtic Countries,* who writes (1911) : " The description of the

---

[1] *Cf.* Hazlitt, W. C., *Faiths and Folklore*, i., 222.

[2] Hunt, p. 328.

[3] Deer, near Aberdeen, is said to have derived its name from *deur*, the Gaelic for *tear*, because St. Drostan shed tears there. The monkish authority in the Book of Deer says : "Drostan's tears came on parting with Columcille". Said Columcille, "Let Dear be its name henceforward".

[4] Fergusson, p. 273.

[5] The Tuttle family may similarly be assigned to one or other of the innumerable Toothills.

[6] *Irish Folklore*, p. 31.

Tuatha de Danaan in the 'Dialogue of the Elders' as 'sprites or fairies with corporeal or material forms, but endued with immortality,' would stand as an account of prevailing ideas as to the 'good people' of to-day".[1] The generous Donn, the King of Faery, is obviously Danu, or Anu, or Aine, the Irish goddess of prosperity and abundance, for we are told that well she used to cherish the circle of the gods.[2] At Knockainy, or the *Hill of Ainy*, Aine, whose name also occurs constantly on Gaulish inscriptions,[3] was until recent years worshipped by the peasants who rushed about carrying burning torches of hay: that Aine was Aincy, or *dear little aine*, is inferred by the alternative name of her dun Knockain*cy*: "Here," says Mr. Westropp, "a cairn commemorates the cult of the goddess Aine, of the god-race of the Tuatha De Danaan. She was a water-spirit, and has been seen, half raised out of the water, combing her hair. She was a beautiful and gracious spirit, 'the best-natured of women,' and is crowned with meadow-sweet (*spiræa*), to which she gave its sweet smell. She is a powerful tutelary spirit, protector of the sick, and connected with the moon, her hill being sickle-shaped, and men, before performing the ceremonies, used to look for the moon—whether visible or not—lest they should be unable to return."[4] By St. Anne's in Dean Street, Soho, is Dansey Yard, where probably *dancing* took place, and dins of every sort arose.

The original sanctuary at Westminster was evidently associated with a dunhill which seems to have long persisted for Loftie, in his *History of Westminster*, observes:

---

[1] Wentz, W. Y. Evans, p. 404. [2] In Irish *aine* means *circle*.
[3] Westropp, T. J., *Proc. of Royal Irish Academy*.
[4] *Cf. Folklore*, xxix., No. 2, p. 159.

"The *hillock* on which we stand is called Thorn Ey".[1] Tothill Street, Westminster, marks the site of what was probably the teat hill of Sir Patrise: the tothills being centres of neighbourly intercourse a good deal of tittle-tattle doubtless occurred there, and from the toothills watchmen *touted,* the word *tout*[2] really meaning peer about or look out: " How beautiful on the Mounds are the feet of Him that bringeth *tidings*—that publisheth Peace".[3] It has been supposed that certain of the Psalms of David were addressed not to the Jewish Jehovah, but to the Phœnician Adon or Adonis, and it is not an unreasonable assumption that these hymns of immemorial antiquity were first sung in some simple Eyedun similar to the wattled pyreum at Kildare, or that at Avalon or Bride Eye.

The oldest sanctuary in Palestine is a stone circle on the so-called Mount of God, and in Britain there is hardly a commanding eminence which is not crowned with a Carn or the evidences of a circle. The Cities of Refuge and the Horns of the Altar, so constantly mentioned in the Old Testament, may be connoted with the fact that in an island fort at Lough Gur, Limerick, were discovered " two ponderous horns of bronze," which are now in the British Museum: it will be remembered that at Lough Gur is the finest example of Irish stone circles. But stone circles are probably much more modern than the reputed founding of St. Bride's first monastery at Kildare. We are told that Bride the Gentle, the Mary of the Gael, who occasionally hanged her cloak upon a lingering sunbeam, had a great

[1] Quoted from Besant's *Westminster.*
[2] Besant supposes that Tothill Street took its name from watermen outing there for fares.
[3] Ps. lii. 7.

love of flowers, and that once upon a time when wending her way through a field of *clover*[1] she exclaimed, " Were this lovely plain my own how gladly would I offer it to the Lord of Heaven and Earth ". She then begged some sticks from a passing carter, staked and wattled them into a circle, and behold the Monastery was accomplished. The character of this simple edifice reminds one of " that structure neat," to which Homer thus alludes :—

> Unaided by Laertes or the Queen,
> With tangled thorns he fenced it safe around,
> And with contiguous stakes riv'n from the trunks
> Of solid oak black-grain'd hemm'd it without.[2]

The circle of Mayborough originally contained two cairns which are suggestive of Andromache's " turf-built cenotaph with altars twain " : the great bicycle within a monocycle at Avebury is trenched around, and the summit of the circumference is still growing thickly with " tangled thorns ". On the Wrekin there is a St. Hawthorn's Well ; of " Saint " Hawthorn nothing seems to be known, and I strongly suspect that he was originally a sacred thorn or monument bush. The first *haies* or hedges were probably the hawthorn or haw hedges around the sacred Eyes, and the original *ha-has* or sunk ditches were presumably the water trenches which surrounded the same jealously-guarded Eyes: and as *ha-ha* is also defined as " an old woman of surprising ugliness, a caution," it may be suggested that the caretakers or beldames[3] of the awful Eyes were, like

---

[1] In Persia the Shamrakh was held sacred as being emblematical of the Persian triads.

[2] *Odyssey*, xiv., 12.

[3] Skeat comments upon the word *hag* as " perhaps connected with Anglo-Saxon *haga*, a hedge enclosure, but this is uncertain ": this authority's definition of a *ha-ha* is as follows: " Ha-ha, Haw-haw, a sunk fence (F.).

some of the vergers and charwomen of the present day, not usually comely.

The iris-form of the Eye was shown in the ground plan *ante*, page 534, and that this design was maintained even for ages after the first primitive Rock or Tower had given place to statelier edifices might be shown by many more evidences than the design here illustrated: the *maton* of this Trematon Castle was in all probability the same Maiden as the Shee of Maiden Castle, Maiden Paps, and the Maiden Stane. Trematon, in Cornwall, was the site of a Stannary Court, whence arose the proverbial localism "Trematon Law," and there are peculiarities about the Castle which merit more than passing attention. Rising majestically amid the surrounding foliage the keep is described as standing on the summit of a conical mound: Baring-Gould characterises the aspect as being that of a pork pie, whence its windowless walls would seem to bear a resemblance to the massive masonry at Richborough. The Richborough walls now measure 10 feet 8 inches in thickness and nearly 30 feet in height; those at Trematon are stated as being 10 feet thick and 30 feet high. Like Maiden Castle at Dorchester, Trematon is of an oval form

From F. *haha* an interjection of laughter, hence a surprise in the form of an unexpected obstacle (that laughs at one). The French word also means an old woman of surprising ugliness, a 'caution'."

The Celts were conspicuously chivalrous towards women, and I question whether they burst into haw-haws whensoever they met an ill-favoured old dame. As to the ha-has, or "unexpected obstacles," Cæsar has recorded that "the bank also was defended by sharp stakes fixed in front, and stakes of the same kind fixed under the water were covered by the river": if, then, the amiable victim who unexpectedly stumbled upon this obstacle chuckled ha-ha! or haw-haw! as he nursed his wounded limbs, the ancient Britons must have possessed a far finer sense of humour than has usually been assigned to them,

XIII.] ENGLISH EDENS 739

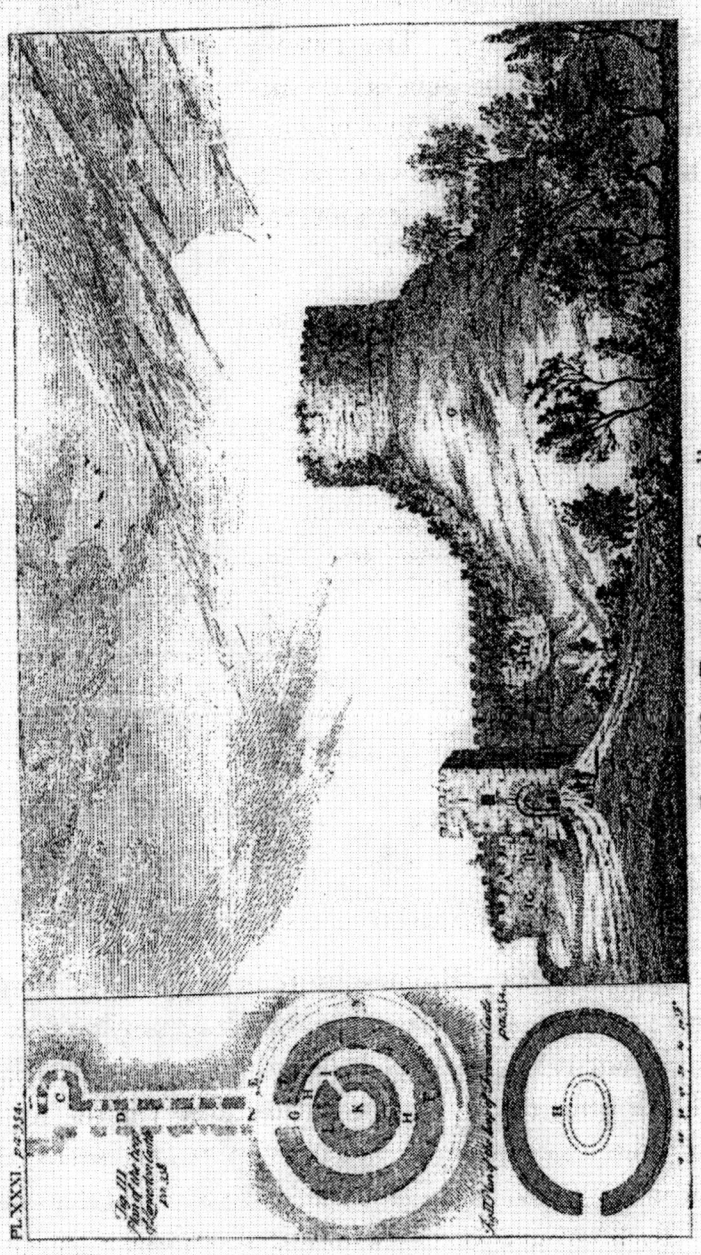

FIG. 453.—Trematon, Cornwall.

and it was formerly divided into apartments, but as there are no marks of windows they would appear to have been lighted from the top.[1] The gateway consisted of three strong arches, and the general arrangements would seem to have resembled those at Chun where, as will be noted, there were three outer chambers encircling about a dozen inner stalls. Chun is cyclopean unmortared stonework; Maiden

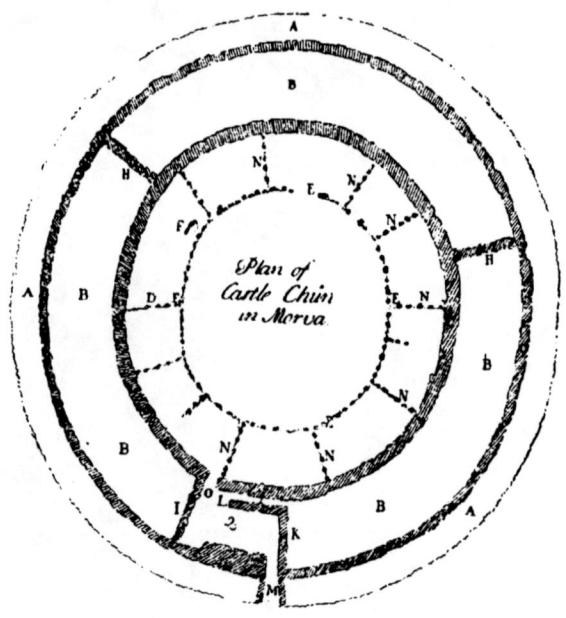

Fig. 454.—Chun Castle.

Castle is earthwork; Richborough is supposedly Roman masonry: of Trematon little is known that may be deemed authentic, but it is generally believed to have been originally erected prior to the Conquest: as, however, the Anglo-Saxons were incapable of masonry it would seem that Trematon might be assigned to an antiquity not less than that of Richborough Castle which it so curiously parallels.

[1] Stockdale, F. W. L., *Excursions Through Cornwall*, 1824, p. 116.

With the various Maiden Lanes of King's Cross, Covent Garden, and elsewhere may be connoted the Mutton Lane of Hackney, which was famous for a bun house which once rivalled that at *Cheynes* Walk, Chelsea: Maiden Lane, Covent Garden, is a continuation of Chandos Street, and it will probably prove that the surname Chandos is ultimately traceable to *Jeanne douce*. In Caledonia *douce* is not necessarily feminine, and the King John tradition, which unaccountably lingered around Canonbury,[1] may be connoted with the John Street and Mutton Hill of Clerkenwell. The sheep or mutton is the proper emblem of St. John, and perhaps the same King John may be further identified with the Goodman of the adjacent Goodman's Fields. We have seen that in Caledonia the gudeman was the devil, whence it becomes interesting to find near Brown's Wood, Islington, stood once a "Duval's (vulgarly called Devil's) Lane".[2]

St. Columba alludes affectionately to—

> My *derry*, my little oak grove,
> My dwelling and my little cell.

The Eye dun illustrated *ante*, page 584, which is described as the strangest, most solitary, most prehistoric-looking of all our motes, is known as *Trow*dale Mote; St. Columba is associated with *Tiree;* he is also said to have been imprisoned at *Tara*, and to have written the book *Durrow* with his own hand: there is thus some ground for tracing the Mote, Maton, Maid or Maiden, *alias* St. Columba, to Droia or Troy. That the dove was pre-eminently a Cretan emblem is well known, and that all derrys or trees were sacred Troys or sanctuaries is further implied by the ancient

---

[1] Gomme, Sir L., *The Topography of London*, ii., 222.
[2] *Ibid.*, ii., 216.

meaning of the adjective *terribilis*, *i.e.*, sacred : thus we find Westminster or Thorn Ey alluded to by old writers as a *locus terribilis*,[1] and it would seem that any awe-inspiring or awful spot was deemed *terrible* or sacred.

In the Celtic Calendar there figures a St. Maidoc or Aidan : Maidoc is *maid high*, and I am afraid St. Aidan was occasionally " a romping girl " or *hoiden*. One does not generally associate Pallas Athene with revelry, and it is difficult to connect with gaiety the grim example of Athene which the present proprietors of *The Athenæum* have adopted as their ideal ; yet, says Plato, " Our virgin Lady, delighting in the sports of the dance, thought it not meet to dance with empty hands ; she must be clothed in full armour, and in this attire go through the dance. And youths and maidens should in every respect imitate her example, honouring the goddess, both with a view to the actual necessities of war and to the festivals." Hoiden or hoyden meant likewise a gypsy—a native of Egypt " the Land of the Eye "—and also a heathen : Athene, who was certainly a heathen maid, may be connoted with Idunn of Scandinavia, who keeps the apples which symbolise the ever-renewing and rejuvenating force of Nature.[2] Tradition persistently associates Eden with an apple, although Holy Writ contains nothing to warrant the connection : similarly tradition says that Eve had a daughter named Ada : as Idunn was said to be the daughter of Ivalde we may equate Idunn, the young and lovely apple-maid, with Ada or Ida, and Ivalde, her mother with the Old *Wife*, or Ive Old.[3]

---

[1] Besant, W., *Westminster*, p. 20.

[2] Rydberg, *Teutonic Mythology*, p. 118.

[3] In the Kentish neighbourhood of Preston, Perry-court, Perry-wood, Holly Hill, Brenley House, and Oversland is an *Old Wives Lees*, and Britton Court Farm.

In an earlier chapter we connected Eve with *happy*, Hob, etc., and there is little doubt that Eve, "the Ivy Girl," was the Greek Hebe who had the power of making old men young again, and filled the goblets of the gods with nectar.

Idunn, "the care-healing maid who understands the renewal of youth," was, we are told, the youthful leader of the *Idunns* or fairies: in present-day Welsh *edyn* means a *winged one*, and *ednyw* a spirit or essence. It is said that from the manes of the horses of the Idunns dropped a celestial dew which filled the goblets and horns of the heroes in Odin's hall; it is also said that the Idunns offer full goblets and horns to mortals, but that these, thankless, usually run away with the beaker after spilling its contents on the ground. There must be an intimate connection between the legend of the fair Idunns, and the fact that at the Caledonian Edenhall, on the river Eden, is preserved an ancient goblet known as The Luck of Edenhall:—

> If this glass do break or fall
> Farewell the luck of Edenhall.

The river Eden flows into the Solway Firth, possibly so named because the Westering Sun must daily have been seen to create a golden track or sun-way over the Solway waters. Ptolemy refers to Solway Firth as Ituna Estuarium, so that seemingly Eden or Ituna may be equated not only with the British rivers Ytene and Aeithon, but also with the Egyptian Aten. According to Prof. Petrie, the cult of Aten "does not, so far, show a single flaw in a purely scientific conception of the source of all life and power upon earth. The Sun is represented as radiating its beams on all things, and every beam ends in a hand which imparts life and power to the king and to all else.

In the hymn to the Aten, the universal scope of this power is proclaimed as the source of all life and action, and every land and people are subject to it, and owe to it their existence and allegiance. No such grand theology had ever appeared in the world before, so far as we know, and it is the forerunner of the later monotheist religions while it is even more abstract and impersonal and may well rank as a scientific theism."

Fig. 455.—British. From Evans.

Egyptian literature tells of a King Pepi questing for the tree of life in company with the Morning Star carrying a spear of Sunbeams.

> Thy rising is beautiful, O living Aton, Lord of Eternity,
> Thou art shining, beautiful, strong,
> Thy love is great and mighty.
> Thy rays are cast into every face
> Thy glowing hue brings life to hearts
> When thou hast filled the two Lands with thy love
> O God, who himself fashioned himself,
> Maker of every land.
> Creator of that which is upon it,
> Men, all cattle, large and small.
> All trees that grow in the soil,
> They live when thou dawnest for them.
> Thou art the mother and the father of all that thou has made.

Yet this resplendent Pair or Parent was also addressed by the Egyptians as the Sea on High and invoked—

> Bow thy head, decline thy arms, O Sea!

The Maiden Morning Star or Stella Maris was imagined as refreshing the heart of King Pepi to life: "She purifies him, she cleanses him, he receives his provision from that which is in the Granary of the Great God, he is clothed by the Imperishable Stars." The intimate connection between Candia and Egypt, the "Land of the Eye" is generally admitted, and as it is an etymological fact that the letters *m* and *n* are almost invariably interchangeable (indeed if language begins with voice and ends with voice it is impossible to suppose that two such similar sounds could have maintained their integrity), it is probable that Candia is radically related to Khem, which seemingly was the most ancient name for Egypt. The celebrated "Maiden Bower," by Mount Pleasant, Dunstable, is believed to be the modern equivalent of magh *din* barr, pronounced mach *dim* barr, and it is decoded as *magh*, a level expanse, *din*, a hill or hill fortress, and *barr*, a summit: I note this derivation —which certainly cannot be applied to the Maiden Stane—as it equates *din* with *dim*, in which connection it is noteworthy that in France and Belgium *Edinburgh* becomes *Edimbourg*. In all probability therefore Adam, the Master of Eden, was originally Adon or "the Lord," and Notre *Dame* of France was equivalent to the Ma*donna* of Italy.

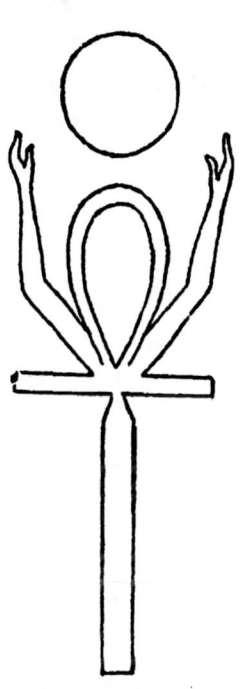

Fig. 456.—From *The Correspondences of Egypt* (Odhner).

In Caledonia the moothills were known alternatively as *Dom*hills, and in the "Chanonry of Aberdeen" was a dun known as Donidon or Dunadon: *doom* still means fate or judgment; in Scots Law giving sentence was formerly called "passing the doeme"; the judge was denominated the Doomster, and the jury the Doomsmen. In the Isle of

Man the judges are termed Deemsters, and in Scandinavia stone circles are known as Doom rings: the Hebrew Dan meant *judgment*, and the English Dinah[1] is interpreted as *one who judges* ; in the Isle of Man the Laws are not legal until they have been proclaimed from the *Tyn*wald Hill. That the Domhills of Britain have largely preserved their physical condition is no doubt due to the doom frequently inflicted on malefactors that they should carry thither a certain quantity of earth and deposit it.[2]

In Europe there are numerous megalithic monuments known popularly as "Adam's Graves," and near Draycott at Avebury the maps mark an Adam's Grave. On the brow of a hill near Heddon (Northumberland) is a trough-like excavation in the solid rock known as the Giant's Grave ; there is a similar Giant's Grave near Edenhall by Penrith, and a neighbouring chasm entitled The Maiden's Step is popularly connected with Giant Torquin: this Torquin suggests Tarquin of Etruria, between which and Egypt there was as close if not a closer connection than that between Candia and Khem.

At Maidstone, originally Maidenstone, there is a *Moat* Park : in Egypt *Mut* was one of the names given to the Queen of Heaven, or Lady of the Sky : Mut was no doubt a variant of Maat, or Maht, the Egyptian Goddess of Truth, for in the worship of the Egyptian Aton "Truth" occupied a pre-eminent position, and the capital of Ikhnaton, the most conspicuous of the Aton-worshipping kings, was called the "Seat of Truth".

Surmounting the Maat here illustrated is a conspicuous *feather* which we have already connoted with *feeder* and

---

[1] A London cockney refers to his sweetheart as his *donah*.
[2] See "Archæologia" (from *The Gentleman's Magazine*), i., 286.

fodder. Maat, the giver of provision from that which is in the granary of the Great God, is thus presumably allied with *meat*, also to *mud*,[1] or liquid earth. The word *mud* is not found in Anglo-Saxon, but is evidently the Phœnician *mot*, and it would be difficult for modern science to add very much to the prehistoric conception of the Phœnicians.

FIG. 457.—Maat.   FIG. 458.—Mut.

According to their great historian Sancaniathon: "The beginning of all things was a condensed, windy air, or a breeze of thick air, and a chaos turbid and black as Erebus. Out of this chaos was generated Môt, which some call Ilus" (*mud*), "but others the putrefaction of a watery mixture. And from this sprang all the seed of the creation, and the generation of the universe. . . . And, when the

[1] The English moot hills are sometimes referred to as *mudes* or *muds*, Johnson, W., *Byways*, p. 67.

air began to send forth light, winds were produced, and clouds, and very great defluxions and torrents of the heavenly waters."[1] It is probable that *Sancaniathon*, the Phœnician sage to whom the above passage is attributed, was radically *Iathon* or *Athene*.

We have connoted the Egyptian sun-god Phra with Pharoah, or Peraa, who was undoubtedly the earthly representative of the same Fire or Phare as was worshipped by the Parsees, or Farsees of Persia: the Persian historians dilate with enthusiasm on the justice, wisdom, and glory of a fabulous Feridoon whose virtues acquired him the appellation of the Fortunate, and it is probable that this Feridoon was the Fair Idoon whose palace, like the Fairy Donn's, was located on some humble fire dun, or peri down. The name Feridoon, or Ferdun (the Fortunate),[2] is translated as meaning *paradisiacal* : Ferdusi is etymologically equivalent to *perdusi*, which is no doubt the same word as *paradise*, and we can almost visualise the term *feridoon* transforming itself into *fairy don*. Nevertheless by one Parthian poet it was maintained —

> The blest Feridoon an angel was not,
> Of musk or of amber, he formed was not;
> By justice and mercy good ends gained he,
> Be just and merciful thou'lt a Feridoon be.[3]

In Germany, Frei or Frey meant a privileged place or sanctuary: in London such a sanctuary until recently existed around the church of St. Mary Offery, or Overy (now St. Saviours, Southwark), and in a subsequent chapter we shall consider certain local traditions which permit the

---

[1] Quoted from Donnelly, I., *Ragnarok*.
[2] Moody, S., *What is Your Name?* p. 266.
[3] Anon, *Secret Societies of the Middle Ages: History of the Assassins*.

equation of St. Mary Overy, and of the Brixton-Camberwell river *Effra*, with the Fairy *Ovary* of the Universe. The Gaelic and Welsh for an opening or *mouth* is *aber*, whence Aberdeen is held to mean the mouth of the Don: but at Loch*aber* or Loch *Apor* this interpretation cannot apply, and it is not improbable that Aberdeen on the river Don was primarily a Pictish Abri town—a Britain or Prydain. As the capital of Caledonia is Edinburgh or Dunedin, it may be suggested that the whole of Caledonia stern and wild was originally a *Kille*, or church of Don.

At Braavalla, in Osturgothland, there are remains of a marvellous "stone town," whence we may assume that this site was originally a Braavalla, or *abri valley* : the chief of the Irish Barony of Barrymore who was entitled "The Barry" is said to have inhabited an enchanted brugh in one of the Nagles Hills. Near New Grange in Ireland there is a remarkable dolmen known locally as the house or tomb of Lady "Vera, or Birra":[1] five miles distant is Bellingham, and I have little doubt that every fairy dun or fairy town, the supposed local home of Bellinga, the Lord Angel or the Beautiful Angel, was synonymously a "Britain"; that Briton and Barton are mere variants of the same word is evident from such place-names as Dumbarton, originally Dunbrettan.

It has been seen that Prydain—of whom it was claimed that before his coming there was little ordinance in these Islands save only a superiority of oppression—was the reputed child of King Aedd: Aedd was one of the titles of Hu, the first of our national Three Pillars, and he was probably identical with Aeddon, a name which, says Davies, "I think was a title of the god himself" : the priests of

[1] Fergusson, J., *Rude Stone Monuments*, p. 231.

750 ARCHAIC ENGLAND [CHAP.

Hu were apparently termed Aeddons, whence like the Mountjoys of France we may assume they were the deni-

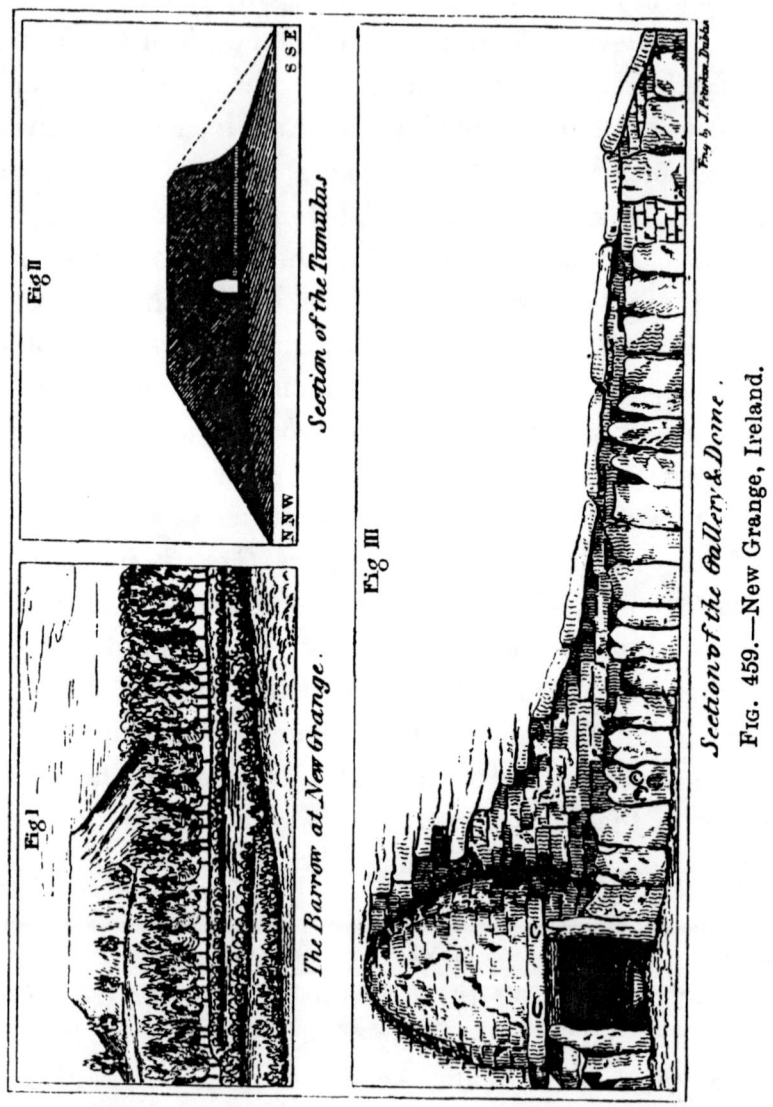

Fig. 459.—New Grange, Ireland.

zens of the Aeddon duns: inquiry will probably establish one of these sanctuaries at Haddington; at Addington (Domesday *Edin*tone) in Kent there are the remains of

Fig. 160.—Kit's Coty, near Maidstone.

[*To face page* 751.

one still standing. With the pagan Aeddons may be connoted the Celtic Saint Aidan, Æden, or Aiden, whose name is associated with Lindis*farne*, also the St. Aidan, or Maidoc of *Ferns*, who among other prodigies is recorded as having driven to and from Rome in twenty-four hours. At *Farn* MacBride in Glencolumkille, there are some cromlechs which exactly resemble in plan the house of Lady Vera, or Birra, at New Grange:[1] at Evora, in *Po*rtugal, situated on bleak heathland, is a similar monument which Borrow described as the most perfect and beautiful of its kind he had ever seen: "It was circular, and consisted of stones immensely large and heavy at the bottom, which towards the top became thinner, having been fashioned by the hand of art to something like the shape of *scallop shells*. . . . Three or four individuals might have taken shelter within the interior in which was growing a small thorn tree."[2] The scallop shell, like the cockle and all coquilles, was obviously an emblem of Evora, the Ovary, the Aber, the opening.

The *Bona dea* of Candia was represented with a headdress in the form of a cat; we shall connote this animal (German *kater*) with St. Caterina or Kate, the immaculate pure one, and it is not unnoteworthy that the Kentish *Kit's* coty, near Maidstone, *vide* the photograph here reproduced, contains what might be a rude much-weathered image of the sacred *cat*, lioness, or *kitten*:[3] In Caledonia is a famous

---

[1] Fergusson, p. 523.   [2] *Ibid.*, p. 390.

[3] Almost immediately above the cromlech is Dan's Hill, and in close neighbourhood are Burham, Borough Court, Preston Hall, Pratling Street, and Bredhurst, *i.e.*, Bred's Wood. That Bred was *San Od* is possibly implied by the adjacent *Snod*hurst and *Snod*land. At Sinodun Hill in Berkshire, Skeat thinks *Synods* may have once been held. The Snodland neighbourhood in Kent abounds in prehistoric remains.

Cat[1] Stane, and the Duchess of Sutherland still bears the honorary title " Lady of the Cat ".[2] The word *kit*ten resolves into Great Itten: the New Forest used to be known as the Forest of Ytene,[3] and I do not think that the great British Forest of Dean has any real connection with the supposition that the Danes may have taken up their residence there: *Dean* was almost a generic name for forest, and we meet with it from Arden to the Ardennes.[4]

For an explication of the word *dawn* Skeat observes: " see day "; it is, however, probable that *dawn* was the little or young Don or Adon. By the Welsh the constellation Cassiopeaia is known under the title of Don's chair. That the Irish Don was Truth is probable from the statement " His blue dome (the sky) was an infallible weather-glass, whence its name the Hill of Truth ".[5]

According to the Edda,[6] a collection of traditions which have been assigned variously by scholars to Norway, Greenland, and the British Isles, the world was created by the sons of Bor, and in the beginning the gods built a citadel in Ida-plain and an age of universal innocence prevailed. Situated on Cockburn Law in Berwickshire—a

[1] The authorities assume that the *cat* is here cath, the Gaelic for *war*. It might equally well be *cad*, the Gaelic for *holy*: in the East a *jehad* is a Holy War.

[2] Lang, A., *Myth, Ritual, and Religion*, i., 72.

[3] *A New Description of England*, 1724.

[4] Sharon Turner informs us, on the authority of Cæsar, Strabo, and Diodorus Siculus, that the Britons " cleared a space in the wood, on which they built their huts and folded their cattle; and they fenced the avenues by ditches and barriers of trees. Such a collection of houses formed one of their towns." *Din* is the root of *dinas*, the Welsh word in actual use for a *town*.

[5] Westropp, T. J., *Proceedings of Royal Irish Academy*, p. 165.

[6] With *Edda*, a general term for the rules and materials for versemaking, may be connoted our *ode*.

wick or fortress of Ber upon which stands the largest of all the brochs—is a prehistoric circle known as Edina or Wodens Hall. The English name Edana or Edna, defined as meaning *perfect happiness* or *rich gift*, is stated to be a variant of Ida or Ada: in Hebrew the name Adah means *beauty*, and Ada, the lovely daughter of Adam, is probably Eda, the "passionately beloved"[1] Breaton princess of Hibernia, or Ma Ida of Tyburnia or Marylebone.

The Garden of Eden has somewhat unsuccessfully, I believe, been located in Mesopotamia: the Jews doubtless

---

[1] According to the original Irish of the story-teller, translated and published for the first time in 1855, Conn, the Consort of Eda, "was a puissant warrior, and no individual was found able to compete with him either on land or sea, or question his right to his conquest. The great King of the West held uncontrolled sway from the island of Rathlin to the mouth of the Shannon by sea, and as far as the glittering length by land. The ancient King of the West, whose name was Conn, was good as well as great, and passionately loved by his people. His Queen (Eda) was a Breaton (British) princess, and was equally beloved and esteemed, because she was the great counterpart of the King in every respect; for whatever good qualification was wanting in the one, the other was certain to indemnify the omission. It was plainly manifest that heaven approved of the career in life of the virtuous couple; for during their reign the earth produced exuberant crops, the trees fruit ninefold commensurate with their usual bearing, the rivers, lakes and surrounding sea teemed with abundance of choice fish, while herds and flocks were unusually prolific, and kine and sheep yielded such abundance of rich milk that they shed it in torrents upon the pastures; and furrows and cavities were filled with the pure lacteal produce of the dairy. All these were blessings heaped by heaven upon the western districts of Innes Fodhla, over which the benignant and just Conn swayed his sceptre, in approbation of the course of government he had marked out for his own guidance. It is needless to state that the people who owned the authority of this great and good sovereign were the happiest on the face of the wide expanse of earth. It was during his reign, and that of his son and successor, that Ireland acquired the title of the 'happy Isle of the West' among foreign nations. Con Mor and his good Queen Eda reigned in great glory during many years."

had their Edens even though Palestine is arid, and the authorities translate the name Adam as having meant *red earth*: according to early Rabbinical writers Adam was a giant; he touched the Arctic pole with one hand and the Antarctic with the other.[1] I have here noted but a handful of the innumerable Edens in Britain which includes five rivers of that name:[2] that the Lady of Britain was Prydain, Brython, or *pure Athene, i.e.*, Wisdom, is a well-recognised tradition, for she is conventionally represented as Athene. In Greece the girl-name Theana meat *Divine Intelligence*,[3] and Ida was interpreted *far seeing*: in Troy the goddess of the city, which originally stood upon a dun hill, was Athene, and the innumerable owl-headed emblems found there by Schliemann were her sign: "Before the human form was adopted her (Athene's) proper symbol was the Owl: a bird which seems to surpass all other creatures in acuteness and refinement, of organic perception; its eyes being calculated to discern objects which to all others are enveloped in darkness; its ear to hear sounds distinctly when no other can perceive them at all, and its

---

[1] Wood, E. J., *Giants and Dwarfs*, p. 11. According to Maundeville in Egypt "they find there also the apple-tree of Adam which has a bite on one side".

[2] There is a conspicuously interesting group of names around the river Eden in Sussex. At Edenbridge is Dencross, and in close neighbourhood Ide Hill, Dane Hill, Paxhill Park, Brown Knoll, St. Piers Farm, Hammerwood, Pippenford Park, Allen Court, Lindfield, Londonderry, and Cinder Hill. With Broadstone Warren and Pippinford Park it is noteworthy that opposite St. Bride's Church, Ludgate Hill, is Poppins Court and Shoe Lane: immediately adjacent is a Punch Tavern, whence I think that Poppins was Punch and *Shoe* was Judy. The gaudy *popinjay*, at which our ancestors used to shoot, may well have stood in Poppins Court: a representation of this brilliant parrot or parrakeet is carved into one of the modern buildings now occupying the site.

[3] Moody, S., *What is Your Name?* p. 257.

nostrils to discriminate effluvia with such nicety that it has been deemed prophetic from discovering the putridity of death even in the first stages of disease."[1]

We have noted the existence of some exclusively British fairies known as Portunes: among the Latins Portunas was a name of *Triton* or Nep*tune*: the Mother of the British Portunes might be termed Phortuna, or, as we should now write the word, Fortuna, and the stone circle at Goodaver in Cornwall might be described as a Wheel of Good Phortune: the Hebrew for *fortune* is *gad*, and it is probable that the famous Gadshill, near Rochester, was at one time a God's Hill; from Kit's Coty on the heights above Rochester it is stated that according to tradition a continuous series of stone monuments once extended to Addington where are still the remains of another coty or cromlech.

There are in England numerous Addingtons or Edintones, and at at least two of these are Druidic remains: the Kentish Addington, near Snodland and Kit's Coty, is dedicated to St. Margaret, and the church itself is situated on a rise or dun. Half a mile from Bacton in Hereford is a small wood known as St. Margaret's Park, and in the centre of this is a cruciform mound, its western arm on the highest ground, its eastern on the lowest: this cruciform mound was described in 1853 as being 15 feet at base,[2] a familiar figure which may be connoted with the statement in *The Golden Legend* that St. Margaret was fifteen years of age. In addition to the cruciform mount at St. Margaret's Park, Bacton, there are further remains of archæologic interest: about 100 years ago nine large yew trees

[1] Knight, R. Payne, *The Symbolic Language of Ancient Art and Mythology*, p. 128.
[2] "Archæologia" (from *The Gentleman's Magazine*), p. 270.

which were surrounding it—one of gigantic size—were felled to the ground, and my authority states that its venerable antiquity was evident from the decayed stumps of *oaks* still visible felled ages ago together with more recent ones.[1] In addition to the cross in this prehistoric Oak grove of the Lady Margaret there are three curious cavities, two of them circular, the third oval or egg-shaped: the ancient veneration for the *oeuf*, or egg, has degenerated to the Easter egg, and in Ireland the Dummy's Hill,[2] associated with egg-trundling may, I think, be equated with Donna or the Dame.

[1] "Archæologia" (from *The Gentleman's Magazine*), p. 270.

[2] "When I was a child I would no more have thought of going out on Easter morning without a real Easter egg than I would have thought of leaving my stocking unsuspended from the foot of my bed on Christmas Eve. A few days before Easter I used to go out to the park, where there were a great many whin bushes, and gather whinblossoms, which I carried home to my mother, who put two eggs in a tin, one for me and one for my sister, and added the whinblossoms and water to them, and set them to boil together until the eggs were hard and the shells were stained a pretty brown hue.

"On Easter Monday my sister and I would carry our eggs to a mound in the park called 'The Dummy's Hill,' and would trundle them down the slope. All the boys and girls we knew used to trundle their eggs on Easter Monday. We called it 'trundling'. The egg-shell generally cracked during the operation of 'trundling,' and then the owner of it solemnly sat down and ate the hard-boiled egg, which, of course, tasted very much better than an egg eaten in the ordinary way. 'The Dummy's Hill' was sadly soiled with egg-shells at the end of Easter Monday morning.

"My uncle, who was a learned man, said that this custom of 'trundling' eggs was a survival of an old Druidical rite. It seems to me to be queer that we in the North of Ireland should still be practising that ancient ceremony when English children should have completely forgotten it, and should think of an Easter egg, not as a real thing laid by hens and related to the ancient religion of these islands, but as a piece of confectionery turned out by machinery and having no ancient significance whatever."
—Ervine, St. John, *The Daily Chronicle*, 4th April, 1919.

The Cretan Britomart in Greek was understood to mean *sweet maiden;* in Welsh *pryd* meant precious, dear, fair, beautiful; Eda of Ireland was "passionately beloved," and to the Britons the sweet maiden was inferentially Britan*nia*, the *new* pure Athene, Ma Ida the Maid or Maiden whose character is summed up in the words *prude, proud, pride,* and *pretty.* In Ireland we may trace her as Meave, *alias* Queen Mab, and the headquarters of this Maiden were either at Tara or at Moytura: the latter written sometimes Magh Tuireadh, probably meant the plain of Troy, for there are still all the evidences here of a megalithic Troy town. The probabilities are that Stanton Drew in Somerset, like Drewsteignton in Devon, with which tradition connects St. Keyna, was another Dru stonetown for here are a cromlech, a logan stone, two circles, some traces of the Via Sacra or Druid Way and an ancient British camp: in Aberdeen there are circles at *Tyre*bagger, Dun*adeer,* and at Deer.

Among other so-called monuments of the Brugh at Moytura recorded in the old annalists are "the Two Paps of the Morrigan," "The Mound of the Morrigan," *i.e.,* the Mound of the Great Queen, also a "Bed of the Daughter of Forann":[1] Forann herself was doubtless the Hag whose weirdly-sculptured chair exists at Lough Crew in Meath: *Meath* was esteemed the *mid, middle,* or *midst,* of Ireland, and here as we have seen existed the central stone at Birr. There is a celebrated Hag's Bed at Fermoy, doubtless the same Hag as the "Old Woman of Beare," whose seven periods of youth necessitated all who lived with her to die of old age: this Old Woman's grandsons and great grandsons were, we are told, tribes and races, and in several

[1] Fergusson, J., *Rude Stone Monuments,* p. 191.

stories she appears to the hero as a repulsive hag who suddenly transforms herself into a beautiful Maid. At Moytura—with which tradition intimately associates the Children of Don—is a cairn called to this day the "cairn of the One Man": with this One Man we may connote Un Khan or Prester John, of whose mystic Kingdom so many marvellous legends circulated during the Middle Ages.

Among the miracles attributed to St. Patrick is one to the effect that by the commandment of God he "made in the earth a great circle with his staff": this might be described as a *byre*, *i.e.*, an enclosure or bower, and we may connote the word with the stone circle in Westmoreland, at Brackenbyr, *i.e.*, the byre of Brecon, Brechin, or the Paragon? The husband of Idunn was entitled Brage, whose name *inter alia* meant King: Brage was the god of poetry and eloquence; a superfluity of prating, pride, and eloquence is nowadays termed *brag*.

The burial place of St. Patrick, St. Bride, and Columba the Mild, is alleged to be at Duno in Ulster: "In Duno," says *The Golden Legend*, "these three be buried all in one sepulchre": the word Duno is *d'uno*, the divine Uno, and the spot was no doubt an Eden of "the One Man": Honeyman[1] is a fairly common English surname, and although this family may have been dealers in honey, it is more probable that they are descendants of the One Man's ministers: in Friesland are megalithic Hunnebeds, or Giant's Beds, and I have little doubt that the marvellously scooped stone at Hoy in the Hebrides[2]—the parallel of

[1] The surname Honeywell found at Kingston implies either there or somewhere a Honeywell. There are several St. Euny Wells in Cornwall.

[2] It measures 36 feet × 18 feet 9 inches, see *ante*, p. 9.

which existed in Egypt, the Land of the Eye—was originally a Hunne Bed or *grotte des fees*.

"Of Paradise," says Maundeville, " I cannot speak for I have not been there ": nevertheless this traveller—who was not necessarily the arch liar of popular assumption—has recorded many artificial paradises which he was permitted to explore: the word *paradise* is the Persian *pairidaeza*, which means an enclosure, or place walled in: it is thus cognate with our *park*, and the first parks were probably sanctuaries of the divine Pair. Nowhere that I know of is the place-name Paradise [1] more persistent than in Thanet or Tanet, a name supposed by the authorities to be Celtic for *fire*: at the nose of the North Foreland old maps mark Faire Ness, and I have little doubt that

---

[1] At Margate are Paradise Hill, Dane Park, Addington Street leading to Dane Hill, and Fort Paragon: at Ramsgate is also a Fort Paragon, and a four-crossed dun called Hallicondane. There used to be a Paradise near Beachy (Bougie, or Biga Head (?)): by Broadstairs or Bridestowe which contains a shrine to St. Mary to which all passing vessels used to doff their sails, is Bromstone, and a Dane Court by Fairfield, all of which are in St. Peter's Parish. By the Sister Towers of Reculver are Eddington, Love Street, Hawthorn Corner, and Honey Hill: in Thanet, Paramour is a common surname. By Minster is Mount Pleasant and Eden Farm: by Richborough is Hoaden House and Paramore Street. To Reculver as to Broadstairs passing mariners used customarily to doff their sails:—

> Great gods, whom Earth and Sea and Storms obey,
> Breathe fair, and waft us smoothly o'er the main.
> Fresh blows the breeze, and broader grows the bay,
> And on the cliffs is seen Minerva's fane.
> We furl the sails, and shoreward row amain
> Eastward the harbour arches, scarce descried,
> Two jutting rocks, by billows lashed in vain,
> Stretch out their arms the narrow mouth to hide.
> Far back the temple stands and seems to shun the tide.
> —*Æneid*, Bk. III., lxviii.

Thanet, " by some called Athanaton and Thanaton,"[1] was originally sacred to Athene. In Suffolk is a Thingoe, which is understood to mean "how, or mound of the *thing*, or provincial assembly": the chief Cantian *thing* or folkmoot was probably held at the Dane John at Cantuarbig or Durovernon; the word *think* implies that Athene was a personification of Reason or Holy Rhea, and the equivalence of the words *remercie* and *thank*, suggest that all dons, donatives, and donations were deemed to have come from the Madonna or Queen Mercy, to whom thanks or remerciements were rendered by the utterance of her name. In the North of England there are numerous places named Unthank, which seemingly is ancient Thank: the Deity is still thanked for *meat, i.e., fare*, or *forage; free*, according to Pearsall, " comes from an Aryan root meaning *dear* (whence also our word *friend*), and meant in old Teutonic times those who are *dear* to the head of the household—that is connected with him by ties of friendship, and not slaves, or in bondage ".[2] The word *dear*, French *adore*, connects *tre* or abode with Droia or Troy: yet the *Sweet Maiden* of Crete could at times show dour displeasure, and one of her best known representations is thus described: " The pose of the little figure is dignified and firm, the side face is even winning, but the eyes are fierce, and the outstretched hands holding the heads of the snakes are so tense and show such strength that we instinctively feel this was no person to be played with ".[3] The connection at Edanhall of The Maiden's Step with Giant Torquin establishes a probability that the Maid or the Maiden was either the

---

[1] *A New Description of England and Wales*, 1724, p. 84.
[2] *The English Language*, p. 141.
[3] Mr. and Mrs. Hawes, *Crete the Forerunner of Greece*, p. 123.

Troy Queen or the Eternal Queen, or *dur queen*, the hard Queen, at times a little dragon, oftener a *dear Queen, i.e.*, Britomart, the Sweet Maiden, or Eda, the passionately beloved, the *Adorée*. "Bride, the *gentle*" is an epithet traditionally applied to St. Bride, St. Brigit, or St. Brig; in Welsh, *brig* and *brigant* mean *tip top* or *summit*, and these terms may be connoted with the Irish *brig* meaning pre-eminent power, influence, authority, and high esteem. At Chester, or Deva, there has been found an inscription to the "Nymph-Goddess Brig," and at Berrens in Scotland has been found an altar to the Goddess of Brigantia, which exhibits a winged deity holding a spear in one hand, and a globe in the other.

In the British Museum is a coin lettered CYNETHRYTH REGINA: this lady, who is described as the widow of Offa, is portrayed "in long curls, behind head long cross": assuredly there were numerous Queen Cynethryths, but the original Cynethryth was equally probably Queen Truth, and in view of the fact that the motto of Bardic Druidism was "the Truth against the world," we may perhaps assume that the Druid was a follower of Truth or Troth.

In the opinion of the learned Borlase the sculpture illustrated on page 485 represents the six progressive orders of Druidism contemplating Truth, the younger men on the right viewing the Maiden draped in the garb of convention, the older ones on the left beholding her nude in her symbolic aspect as the feeder of two serpents: it is not improbable that Quendred, the miraculous light-bearing Mother of St. Dunstan, was a variant of the name Cynethryth, at times Queen Dread, at times Queen Truth.

The frequent discovery of coins—Roman and otherwise —within cromlechs such as Kit's Coty and other sacred

Fig. 461.—Britannia, A.D. 1919.
By permission of the Proprietors of "Punch".

sites appears to me to prove nothing in respect of age, but rather a survival of the ancient superstition that the fairies possessed from time immemorial certain fields which could not be taken away or appropriated without gratifying the pixy proprietors by a piece of money:[1] the land-grabber is no novelty, nor seemingly is conscience money. That important battles occurred at such sites as Moytura and Braavalla is no argument that those fantastic Troy Towns or Drewsteigntons were, as Fergusson laboriously maintained, monuments to commemorate slaughter. According to Homer—

> Before the city stands a lofty mound,
> In the mid plain, by open space enclos'd;
> Men call it Batiæa; but the Gods
> The tomb of swift Myrinna; muster'd *there*
> *The Trojans and Allies their troops array'd*.[2]

Nothing is more certain than that with the exception of a negligible number of conscientious objectors, a chivalrous people would defend its Eyedun to the death, and that the last array against invaders would almost invariably occur in or around the local Sanctuarie or Perry dun.

It is a wholly unheard of thing for the British to think or speak of Britain as "the Fatherland": the Cretans, according to Plutarch, spoke of Crete as their Motherland, and not as the Fatherland: "*At first*," says Mackenzie, "the Cretan Earth Mother was the *culture deity* who instructed mankind . . . in Crete she was well developed before the earliest island settlers began to carve her images on gems and seals or depict them in frescoes. She symbolised the island and its social life and organisation."[3]

[1] Hazlitt, W. Carew, *Faiths and Folklore*, i., 222.   [2] *Iliad*, ii., 940.
[3] *Myths of Crete and Pre-Hellenic Europe*, pp. 70, 190. The italics are mine.

CHAPTER XIV.

DOWN UNDER.

"It is our duty to begin research even if we have to penetrate many a labyrinth leading to nowhere and to lament the loss of many a plausible system. A false theory negatived is a positive result."—THOS. J. WESTROPP.

IN the year 1585 a curious occurrence happened at the small hamlet of Mottingham in Kent: betimes in the morning of 4th August the ground began to sink, so much so that three great elm trees in a certain field were swallowed up into a pit of about 80 yards in circumference and by ten o'clock no part of them could be seen. This cavity then filled with water of such depth that a sounding line of 50 fathoms could hardly find or feel any bottom: still more alarming grew the situation when in an adjacent field another piece of ground sunk in like manner near the highway and " so nigh a dwelling house that the inhabitants were greatly terrified therewith ".[1]

To account for a subsidence much deeper than an elm tree one must postulate a correspondingly lofty *souterrain* : the precise spot at Mottingham where these subsidences are recorded was known as Fairy Hill, and I have little doubt that like many other Dunhills this particular Fairy Hill was honeycombed or hollowed. Almost every Mottingham [2] or Maiden's Home consisted not only of the

[1] Walford, E., *Greater London*, ii., 95.

[2] Mottingham, anciently Modingham, is supposed to be from Saxon *modig*, proud or lofty, and *ham*, a dwelling. Johnstone derives it as, " Enclosure

characteristic surface features noted in the preceding chapter, but in addition the thoroughly ideal Maiden's Home went down deep into the earth: in Ireland the children of Don were popularly reputed to dwell in palaces *underground;* similarly in Crete the Great Mother—the Earth Mother associated with circles and caves, the goddess of birth and death, of fertility and fate, the ancestress of all mankind—was assumed to gather the ghosts of her progeny to her abode in the Underworld.[1]

Caves and caverns play a prime and elementary part in the mythologies of the world: their rôle is literally vital, for it was believed that the Life of the World, in the form of the Young Sun, was born yearly anew on 25th December, always in a cave: thus caves were invariably sacred to the Dawn or God of Light, and only secondarily to the engulfing powers of Darkness; from the simple cell, *kille,* or little church gradually evolved the labyrinthine catacomb and the stupendous rock-temple.

The County of Kent is curiously rich in caves which range in importance from the mysterious single *Dene* Hole to the amazing honeycomb of caverns which underlie Chislehurst and Blackheath: a network of caves exists beneath Trinity Church, Margate; moreover, in Margate is a serpentine grotto decorated with a wonderful mosaic of shell-work which, so far as I am able to ascertain, is unique and unparalleled. The grotto at Margate is situated in the Dene or Valley underneath an eminence now termed *Dane* Hill: one of the best known of the Cornish so-called

of Moding," or " of the Sons of Mod or Mot ". We may assume these people were followers of the Maid, and that Mottingham was equivalent to Maiden's Home.

[1] Mackenzie, D. A., *Myths of Crete,* p. xlvi.

Giant's Holts is that situated in the grounds of the Manor House of Pen*deen*, not in a dene or valley, but on the high ground at Pendeen Point. In Cornish *pen* meant head or point, whence Pendeen means *Deen Headland*, and one again encounters the word *dene* in the mysterious Dene holes or Dane holes found so plentifully in Kent: these are supposed to have been places of refuge from the Danes, but they certainly never were built for that purpose, for the discovery within them of flint, bone, and bronze relics proves them to be of neolithic antiquity.

There must be some close connection in idea between the serpentine grotto in The *Dane*, Margate, the subterranean chamber at Pen*deen*, Cornwall, the Kentish *Dene* Holes and the mysterious tunnellings in the neighbourhood of County *Down*, Ireland: these last were described by Borlase as follows: "All this part of Ireland abounds with Caves not only under mounts, forts, and castles, but under plain fields, some winding into little hills and risings like a volute or ram's horn, others run in zigzag like a serpent; others again right forward connecting cell with cell. The common Irish think they are skulking holes of the Danes after they had lost their superiority in that Island."[1] They may conceivably have served this purpose, but it is more probable that these mysterious tunnellings were the supposed habitations of the subterranean Tuatha te Danaan, *i.e.*, the Children of *Don* or *Danu*.

In County Down we have a labyrinthine connection of cell with cell, and in some parts of Kent the same principle appears to have been at work culminating in the extraordinary subterranean labyrinth known as "The Chislehurst Caves": these quarryings, hewn out of the chalk,

[1] Borlase. Wm., *Antiquities of Cornwall*, p. 296.

XIV.] DOWN UNDER 767

cover in seemingly unbroken sequence—superposed layer

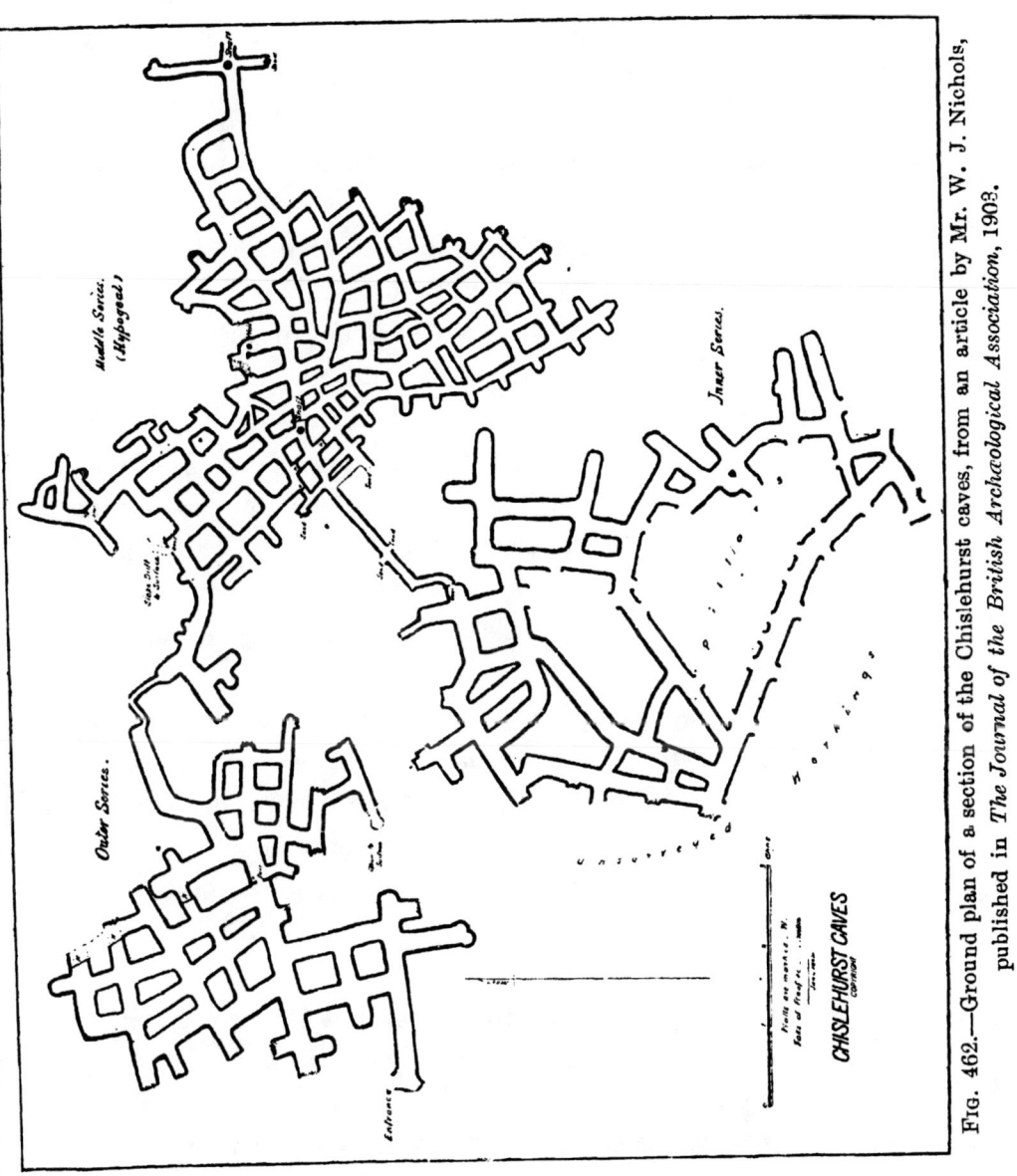

FIG. 462.—Ground plan of a section of the Chislehurst caves, from an article by Mr. W. J. Nichols, published in *The Journal of the British Archæological Association*, 1903.

upon layer—an enormous area, under the Chislehurst district: between 20 and 30 miles of extended burrowings have, it is said, already been located, yet it is suspected that more remain to be discovered. Commenting upon this extraordinary labyrinth Mr. W. J. Nichols, a Vice-President of the British Archæological Association, has observed: "Not far from this shaft we see one of the most interesting sights that these caves can show us: a series of galleries, with rectangular crossings, containing many chambers of semicircular, or apsidal form, to the number of thirty or more—some having altar-tables formed in the chalk, within a point or two of true orientation. This may be accidental, but the fact remains; and the theory is supported by the discovery of an adjoining chamber, apparently intended for the officiating priest. There is an air of profound mystery pervading the place: a hundred indications suggest that it was a subterranean Stonehenge; and one is struck with a sense of wonder, and even of awe, as the dim lamplight reveals the extraordinary works which surround us."

In the caverns of Mithra twelve apses corresponding to the twelve signs of the Zodiac used to be customary: the *thirty* apses at Chislehurst may have had some relation to the thirty dies or days, and if the number of niches extended to thirty-three this total should be connoted with the thirty-three elementary giants considered in an earlier chapter.

There are no signs of the Chislehurst Caverns having at any time been used systematically as human abodes, but in other parts of the world similar sites have been converted into villages: one such existing at Troo in France is thus described by Baring-Gould: "What makes Troo specially interesting is that the whole height is like a sponge perforated with passages giving access to halls, some of which are circular and lead into stone chambers; and most of the houses are wholly or in part underground. The caves that are inhabited are staged one above another, some reached by stairs that are little better than ladders, and the subterranean passages leading from them form a labyrinth within the bowels of the hill and run in superposed stories."[1] The name of this subterranean city of Troo may be connected with *trou*, the French generic term for a hole or pit: the Provençal form of *trou* is *trauc*, which etymologists identify with *traugum*, the Latin for a cave or den. The Latin *traugum* (origin unknown) is radically the same as *troglos*, the Greek for a cave, whence the modern term *troglodite* or cave dweller, and it is not unlikely that the *dene* of *denehole* is the same word as *den*: the Provençal *trauc* may be connoted with the English place-name Thurrock, which is on the Essex side of the river Thames, and is famous for the large number of deneholes that still exist there.

The place-name Thurrock and the word *trauc*, meaning a cave, may evidently be equated with the two first syllables of *traugum* and *troglos*. According to my theories the primitive meaning of *tur og* was Eternal, or *Enduring Og*, and it is thus a felicitous coincidence that Og, the famous King of Bashan, was a troglodite: the ruins of his capital named Edrei, which was situated in the Zanite Hills, still exist, and are thus described by a modern explorer: "We took with us a box of matches and two candles. After we had gone down the slope for some time, we came to a dozen rooms which, at present, are used as goat stalls and store-rooms for straw. The passage became gradually smaller, until at last we were compelled to lie down flat

[1] *Cliff Castles*, p. 33.

and creep along. This extremely difficult and uncomfortable progress lasted for about eight minutes, when we were obliged to jump down a steep well, several feet in depth. Here I noticed that the younger of my two attendants had remained behind, being afraid to follow us; but probably it was more from fear of the unknown European, than of the dark and winding passages before us. We now found ourselves in a broad street, which had dwellings on both sides, whose height and width left nothing to be desired. The temperature was mild, the air free from unpleasant odours, and I felt not the smallest difficulty in breathing. Further along there were several cross-streets, and my guide called my attention to a hole in the ceiling for air, like three others which I afterwards saw, now closed from above. Soon after we came to a market-place, where, for a long distance, on both sides of the pretty broad street were numerous shops in the walls, exactly in the style of the shops seen in Syrian cities. After a while we turned into a side street, where a great hall, whose roof was supported by four pillars, attracted my attention. The roof, or ceiling, was formed of a single slab of jasper, perfectly smooth and of immense size, in which I was unable to perceive the slightest crack."[1] The here-described holes in the ceiling for air " now closed from above " correspond very closely to the shafts running up here and there from the Chislehurst caves to the private gardens overhead.

In connection with the troglodite town of Troo, and with the French word *trou* meaning a hole, it is worthy of note that a subterranean chamber or " Giant's Holt," exists at *Trew* in Cornwall, and a similar one at the village of

[1] *Cf.* Baring-Gould, *Cliff Castles.*

*Trew*oofe: the name Trewoofe suggests the word *trough*, a generic term for a scooped or hollowed-out receptacle: we have already noted that in the west of England a small ship is still called a *trow;* the Anglo-Saxon for a trough was *troh*, the German is *trog*, the Danish is *trug*, and the Swedish *trag*.

The artificial cave at *Trewoofe* also suggests a connection with the famous Cave-oracle in Livadia known as the Den of *Trophonius*: this celebrated oracle contained small niches for the reception of gift-offerings and there are curious little wall-holes in some of the Cornish *souterrains* which cannot, so far as one can judge, have filled any other purpose than that served by the niches in the Cave of Trophonius. The calcareous mountain in which the oracle of Trophonius was situated is tunnelled by a number of other excavations, but over the entrance to what is believed to be the veritable prophetic grotto is graved the mysterious word CHIBOLET, or, according to others, ZEUS BOULAIOZ, meaning ZEUS THE COUNSELLOR. The Greek for *counsellor* is *bouleutes*, and the radical *bouleut* of this term is curiously suggestive of Bolleit, the name applied to *two* of the Cornish subterranean chambers, *i.e.*, the Bolleit Cave in the parish of St. Eval and the Bolleit Cave near St. Buryan: the latter of these sites includes a stone circle and other monolithic remains which are believed by antiquarians to mark the site of some battle; whence the name Bolleit is by modern etymologers interpreted as having meant *field of blood*, but it exceeds the bounds of coincidence that there should also be a Bolleit cave elsewhere, and the greater probability would seem that these Cornish *souterrains* were sacred spots serving among other uses the purposes of Oracle and Counsel Chambers. If the disputed inscription over the Trophonian Den really read CHIBOLET it would decode agreeably in accordance with my theories into CHI or Jou the COUNSELLOR; but I am unaware that the Greek Zeus was ever known locally as Chi.[1]

The celebrated Blue John cave of Derbyshire—where we have noted Chee Dale—is situated in *Tray* Cliff, and in the neighbouring "Thor's Cave" have been found the remains of prehistoric man: similar remains have been unearthed at Thurrock where the dene holes are conspicuously abundant, and in view of the persistent recurrence of the cave-root *tur* or *trou* it is worth noting that cave making was a marked characteristic of the people of *Tyre*: "Wherever the Tyrians penetrated, to Malta, Sicily, Sardinia, similar burial places have been discovered."[2] According to Baring-Gould all the subterranean dwellings of Europe bear a marked resemblance to the troglodite town of King Og at Edrei—a veritable Tartarus or Underworld—and the *drei* of Edrei is no doubt a variant of trou, Troo, Trew or Troy, for, as already seen, in the Welsh language "Troy town" is Caer *Droia* or Caer *Drei*.

One has to consider three forms or amplifications of the same phenomenon: (1) the single cave; (2) several caves connected to one another by serpentine tunnels; (3) a labyrinth or honeycomb of caves leading one out of the other and ranged layer upon layer. Etymology and mythology alike point to the probability, if not the certainty,

---

[1] Chislehurst is supposed to mean the pebble hurst or wood, but Chislehurst is on chalk and is less pebbly than many places adjacent: at Chislehurst is White Horse Hill: Nantjizzel or *jizzle valley*, in Cornwall, is close to Carn Voel, *alias* the Diamond House, and thus, I am inclined to think that Chislehurst was a selhurst or selli's wood sacred to Chi the great Jehu.

[2] Adams, W. H. A., *Famous Caves and Catacombs*, p. 90.

XIV.]   DOWN UNDER   773

that among the ancients a cave, natural or artificial, was regarded as the symbol of, and to some extent a facsimile of the intricate Womb of Creation, or of Mother Nature. "Man in his primitive state," says a recent writer, "considers himself to have emerged from some cave; in fact,

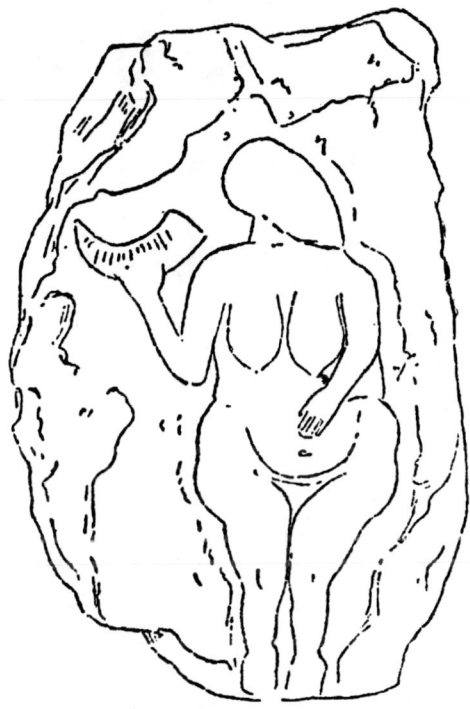

FIG. 463.

from the entrails of the Earth. Nearly all American creation-myths regard men as thus emanating from the bowels of the great terrestrial mother."[1]

Fig. 463, evidently representative of the Great terrestrial Mother holding in her hand a simple horn, the fore-runner of the later *cornu copia* or horn of abundance, is the outline sketch of a rock-carved statue, 2 feet in height,

[1] Spence, L., *Myths of Mexico and Peru*, p. 293.

discovered on the rubble-covered face of a rock cliff in the *Dordogne*: this has been proved to be of Aurignacian age

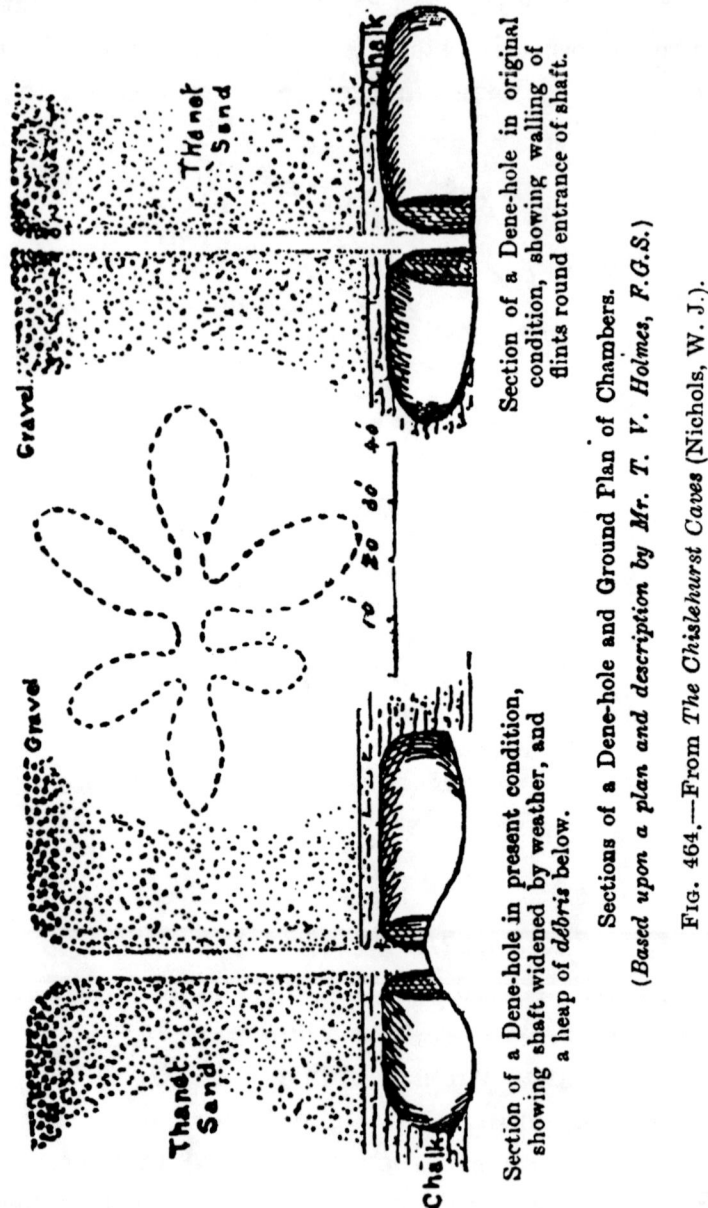

Fig. 464.—From *The Chislehurst Caves* (Nichols, W. J.).

and is the only yet discovered statue of any size executed by the so-called Reindeer men; in the Chislehurst caves

XIV.] DOWN UNDER 775

have been discovered the deer horn picks of the primeval men who apparently first made them.

The Kentish Dene hole is never an aimless quarrying; on the contrary it always has a curiously specific form,

Fig. 465.—Ground plan of a group of Dene Holes in Hangman's Wood Kent. From a plan by Mr. A. R. Goddard, F.S.A.

dropping about 100 feet as a narrow shaft approximately 3 feet in diameter and then opening out into a six-fold chamber, *vide* the plans[1] herewith. This is not a rational

[1] In 1867 Mr. Roach Smith published the following description: "The ground plan of the caves was like a six-leaved flower diverging from the central cup which is represented by the shaft. The central cave of each

or business-like form of chalk quarry, and it must have been very difficult indeed to bucket up the output in small driblets, transport it from the tangled heart of woods, and pack-horse it on to galleys in the Thames: nevertheless something similar seems to have been the procedure in Pliny's time for he tells that white chalk, or *argentaria*, "is obtained by means of pits sunk like wells with narrow mouths to the depth sometimes of 100 feet, when they branch out like the veins of mines and this kind is chiefly used in Britain".[1]

In view of the fact that either chalk or flints could have been had conveniently in unlimited quantities for shipment, either from the coast cliffs of Albion, or if inland from the commonsense everyday form of chalk quarry, it is difficult to suppose otherwise than that the Deneholes —which do *not* branch out indiscriminately like ordinary mine-veins—were dug under superstitious or ecclesiastical control. Of this system perhaps a parallel instance may be found in the remarkable turquoise mines recently explored at Maghara near Sinai: "These mines," says a writer in *Ancient Egypt*,[2] "lie in the vicinity of two adjacent

three is about 14 yards long and about 6 yards high. The side caves are smaller, about 7 yards long and 2 yards wide. The section is rather singular: taken from end to end the roof line is horizontal: but the floor rises at the end of the cave so that a sketch of the section from end to end of the two principal caves is like the outline of a boat, the shaft being in the position of the mainmast. The section across the cave is like the outline of an egg made to stand on its broader end. They are all hewn out of the chalk, the tool marks, like those which would be made by a pick, being still visible."—*Archæologia*, i., 32.

Dr. Munro states: "They are usually found on the higher ground of the lower reaches of the Thames . . . in fact, North Kent and South Essex appear to be studded with them."—*Prehistoric Britain*, p. 222.

[1] *Nat. Hist.*, lib. xvii., cap. viii.   [2] Part I.

caves facing an extensive site of burning, which has the peculiarities of the high-places of which we hear so much in the Bible. These caves formed a sanctuary which, judging from what is known of ancient sanctuaries in Arabia generally, was at once a shrine and a store house, presumably in the possession of a priesthood or clan, who, in return for offerings brought to the shrine, gave either turquoise itself, or the permission to mine it in the surrounding district. The sanctuary, like other sanctuaries in Arabia, was under the patronage of a female divinity, the representative of nature-worship, and one of the numerous forms of Ishthar."

The name of this Istar-like or Star Deity is not recorded, but in this description she is alluded to as *Mistress of the Turquoise Country*, and later simply as *Mistress of Turquoise*. We may possibly arrive at the name of the British Lady of the star-shaped dene holes by reference to a votive tablet which was unearthed in 1647 near Zeeland: this is to the following effect :—

> To the Goddess Nehalennia—
> For his goods well preserved—
>   Secundus Silvanius
>   A chalk Merchant
>   Of Britain
> Willingly performed his merited vow.

I am acquainted with no allusions in British mythology to Nehalennia, but she is recognisable in the St. Newlyna of Newlyn, near Penzance, and of Noualen in Brittany: it is not an unreasonable conjecture that St. Nehalennia of the Thames was a relative of Great St. Helen, and she was probably the little, young, or *new Ellen*. At Dunstable, where also there are dene holes, we find a Dame

Ellen's Wood, and it may be surmised that *Nelly* was originally a *diminutive* of Ellen.

Among the Bretons as among the Britons precisely the same mania for burrowing seems at one period to have prevailed, and in an essay on *The Origin of Dene Holes*, Mr. A. R. Goddard pertinently inquires: "What, then, were these great excavations so carefully concealed in the midst of lone forests?" Mr. Goddard points out that an interesting account of the use made of very similar places in Brittany by the peasant armies, during the war in La Vendee, is to be found in Victor Hugo's *Ninety Three*, and that that narrative is partially historic, for it ends, "In that war my father fought, and I can speak advisedly thereof". Victor Hugo writes: "It is difficult to picture to oneself what these Breton forests really were. They were towns. Nothing could be more secret, more silent, and more savage. There were wells, round and narrow, masked by coverings of stones and branches; the interior at first vertical, then horizontal, spreading out underground like funnels, and ending in dark chambers." These excavations, he states, had been there from time immemorial, and he continues: "One of the wildest glades of the wood of Misdon, perforated by galleries and cells, out of which came and went a mysterious society, was called The Great City. The gloomy Breton forests were servants and accomplices of the rebellion. The subsoil of every forest was a sort of *madrepore*, pierced and traversed in all directions by a secret highway of mines, cells, and galleries. Each of these blind cells could shelter five or six men."

The notion that the dene holes of Kent were built as refuges from the Danes, and that the tortuous *souterrains* of County Down were constructed by the defeated Danes as skulking holes is on a par with the supposition that the *souterrains* of La Vendee were built as an annoyance to the French Republic; and the idea that the solitary or combined dene holes situated in the heart of lone, dense, and inaccessible forests were due to action of the sea, or mere shafts sunk by local farmers simply for the purpose of obtaining chalk seems to me irrational and inadequate. It is still customary for hermits to dwell in caves, and in Tibet there are Buddist Monasteries "where the inmates enter as little children, and grow up with the prospect of being literally immured in a cave from which the light of day is excluded as well as the society of their fellow-men, there to spend the rest of their life till they rot": it is thus not impossible that each dene hole in Britain was originally the abode of a hermit or holy man, and that clusters of these sacred caves constituted the earliest monasteries. In Egypt near Antinoe there is a rock-hewn church known as *Dayn* Aboo Hannes, which is rendered by Baring-Gould as meaning "The Convent of Father John": it would thus appear that in that part of the world *dayn* was the generic term for *convent*, and it is not unlikely that the ecclesiastical *dean* of to-day does not owe his title to the Greek word *diaconus*, but that the original deaneries were congeries of dene holes or dens. The mountains and deserts of Upper Egypt used to be infested with ascetics known as Therapeutæ who dwelt in caves, and the immense amount of stone which the extensive excavations provided served secondarily as material for building the pyramids and neighbouring towns: the word Therapeut, sometimes translated to mean "holy man," and sometimes as "healer," is radically *thera* or *tera*, and one of the most remarkable of the Egyptian cave temples is that situated at *Derr* or *Derri*.

In addition to dene holes on the coast of *Dur*ham and at *Dun*stable there are dene holes in the *dun, down*, or hill overlooking Kit's Coty: it may reasonably be surmised that the latter were inhabited by the *drui* or wise men who constructed not only Kit's Coty but also the other extensive megalithic remains which exist in the neighbourhood. The well-known cave at St. Andrews contains many curious Pictish sculptures, and the connection between *antrou* (or *Andrew*), a cave, and *trou*, a hole, extends to the words *entrails, intricate,* and *under*. Practically all the "Mighty Childs" of mythology are represented as having sprung from caves or underground: Jupiter or Chi (the *chi* or χ is the cross of *Andrew*[1]) was cave-born and worshipped in a cave; Dionysos was said to have been nurtured in a cave; Hermes was born at the mouth of a cave, and it is remarkable that, whereas a cave is still shown as the birthplace of Jesus Christ at Bethlehem, St. Jerome complained that in his day the pagans celebrated the worship of Thammuz, or Adonis, *i.e.*, Adon, *at that very cave*.

Etymology everywhere confirms the supposition that underlying cave construction and governing worship within caves was a connection, in idea, between the cave and the Mother of Existence or the Womb of Nature. The

---

[1] One of the most characteristic symbols of the Ægean is St. Andrew's Cross: I have suggested that the Scotch Hendrie meant *ancient drie* or *drew*, and it is not without significance that tradition closely connects St. Andrews in Scotland with the Ægean. The legend runs that St. Rule arrived at St. Andrews bringing with him a precious relic—no less than Sanct Androwis Arme. "This Reule," continues the annalist, "was ane monk of Grece born in Achaia and abbot in the town of Patras".—Simpkins, J. E., *Fife*, Country Folklore, vol. vii., p. 243.

"Womb of Being" is a common phrase applied to Divinity, and in Scotland the little pits which were constructed by the aborigines are still known as *weems*, from *wamha*, meaning a cave. In Lowland Scotch *wame* meant *womb*, and *wamha*, a cave, is obviously akin not only to *wame* but also to *womb*, Old English *wambe*; indeed the cave was considered so necessary a feature of Mithra-worship that where natural cavities did not exist artificial ones were constructed. The standard reason given for Mithraic cave-worship was that the cave mystically signified "the descent of the soul into the sublunary regions and its regression thence". Doubtless this sophisticated notion at one period prevailed: that all sorts of Mysteries were enacted within caves is too well known to need emphasis, and I think that the seemingly unaccountable apses within the Chislehurst labyrinth may have served a serious and important purpose in troglodite philosophy.

The celebrated cave at Royston is remarkably bell-shaped; many of the barrows at Stonehenge were *bell*-formed, and in Ceylon the gigantic bell-formed pyramids there known as Dagobas are connected by etymologists with *gabba*, which means not only *shrine* but also *womb*. In the design on p. 783, Isis, the Great Mother, is surrounded by a cartouche or halo of bell-like objects : the sistrum of Isis which was a symbol of the Gate of Life was decorated with bells ; bells formed an essential element of the sacerdotal vestments of the Israelites ; bells are a characteristic of modern Oriental religious usage, and in Celtic Christianity the bell was regarded—according to C. W. King—as "the actual type of the Godhead".[1]

The Royston Cave is said to be an exact counterpart to

---

[1] *The Gnostics and their Remains*, p. 72.

certain caves in Palestine,[1] which are described as "tall

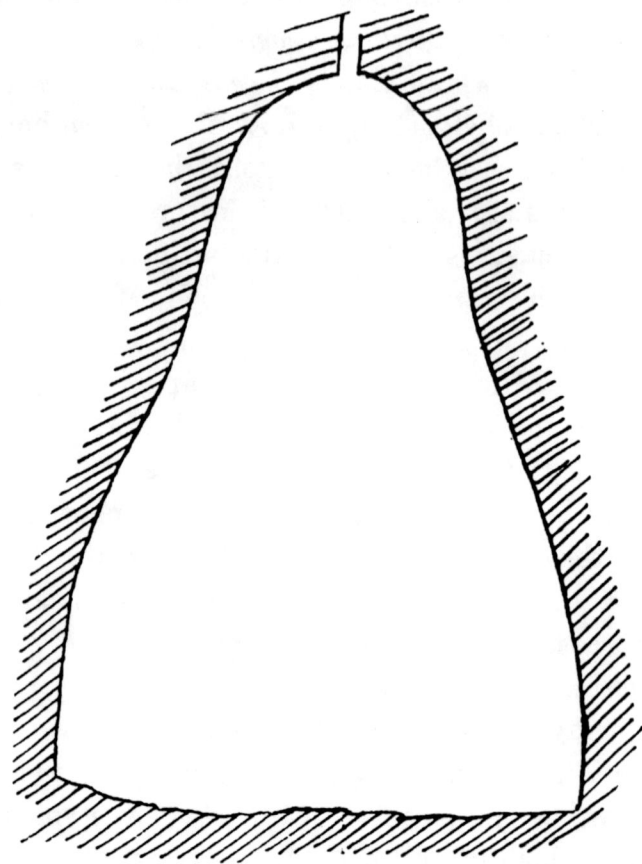

Fig. 466.—Section of Royston Cave traced from a drawing in *Cliff Castles and Cliff Dwellings of Europe* (Baring-Gould, S.).

[1] "It is certain that ancient caves do exist in Palestine which in form and circumstance, and to some extent also in decoration, approximate so nearly to the Royston Cave that if any historical connection could be established between them, it would scarcely seem doubtful that the one is a copy of the other."—Beldam, J., *The Royston Cave*, p. 24. According to the same authority there are indications at the Royston Cave "of an extreme and primeval antiquity," and he adds, "it bears, indeed, a strong resemblance in form and dimension to the ancient British habitation; and certain marks and decorations in its oldest parts such as indentations and punctures, giving a diapered appearance to the surface, are very similar to what is seen in confessedly Druidical and Phœnician structures," p. 22.

Fig. 468. [*To face page* 783.

domes or bell-shaped apartments ranging in height from 20 to 30 feet, and in diameter from 10 to 12 to 20 or 30 feet, or more. The top of these domes usually terminates in a small circular opening for the admission of light and air. These dome-shaped caverns are mostly in clusters three or four together. They are all hewn regularly. Some of them are ornamented either near the bottom or high up, or both with rows of small holes or niches like pigeon holes extending quite round."[1] It was customary to sell pigeons in the Temple at Jerusalem: there is a prehistoric cave in Dordogne on the river Dronne which *vide*, Fig. 468 is distinguished by pigeon holes. This sacred cave is still used as a pigeonry, and in

FIG. 467.—From *Ancient Pagan and Modern Christian Symbolism* (Inman, C. W.).

view of the mass of evidence connecting doves with prehistoric caves and Diana worship, I should not be surprised if the pigeons which congregate to-day around St. Paul's are the direct descendants of the Diana's Doves of the prehistoric *domus columbae*.[2] At *Chadwell* in Essex are ordinary dene holes, and at Tilbury there were "several spacious caverns in a chalky cliff built artificially of stone to the height of 10 fathoms and somewhat straight at the top": I derive this information, as also the illustrations

[1] Beldam, J., *The Royston Cave*, p. 24.

[2] In Caledonia dovecots or *doocats* are still superstitiously maintained: there may be a connection between *doocat* and the "Dowgate" Hill which neighbours the present Cathedral of St. Paul.

here reproduced, from the anonymous *New Description of England and Wales*, published in 1724.

Both St. Kit and St. Kate figure on the walls of the bell-shaped cave situated beneath Mercat House at the cross roads at Royston; and thus the name Mercat may here well have meant Big Kit or Kate: close by was an

Figs. 469 and 470.—From *A New Description of England* (Anon, 1724).

ancient inn known as the Catherine Wheel. We shall probably be safe not only in assigning Kit's Coty to Kate or Ked "the most generous and most beauteous of ladies," but also in assigning to her the Kyd brook, on the right bank of which the Chislehurst caves are situated: "It is somewhat remarkable," says Mr. Nichols, "that the archæological discoveries hitherto made have been for the

FIG. 171.—Sculpturings from the interior of Royston Cave.

[To face page 784.

most part on the line of this stream ". The Kyd brook rises in what is now known as the Hawkwood, which was perhaps once equivalent to the Og from whom the King of Edrei took his title.

Following the course of the Kyd brook—in the neighbourhood of which the Ordnance Map records a "Cadlands"—there exists to this day within Elmstead Woods a sunken road, a third of a mile in length, now covered with venerable oaks: three miles southward are the great earthworks at Keston, the supposed site of the Roman station of Noviomagus, " with its temple tombs and massive foundations of flint buildings scattered through the fields and woodland in the valley below ".[1]

The name Noviomagus meant seemingly New Magus; that Keston was a seat of the Magi is implied by the fact that the ruins in question are situated in Holwood Park: whether this meant Holywood Park, or whether it was so known because there were holes in it, is not of essential importance; it is sufficiently interesting to note that there are legends at Keston that two subterranean passages once ran from the ruins, the one to Coney Hall Hill adjoining Hayes Common, the other towards Castle Hill at Addington.[2] These burrows have not been explored within living memory, but at Addington itself near the remains of a monastery which stand upon an eminence "a subterranean passage communicates which even now is penetrable for a considerable distance ".[3] At Addington are not only numerous tumuli, but it is a tradition among the inhabitants that the place was formerly of much greater extent than at present, and we are told that timbers and other

[1] Nichols, W. J., *The Chislehurst Caves and Dene Holes*, p. 5.
[2] Walford, E., *Greater London*. ii.; 127.   [3] *Ibid.*, p. 131.

50

material of ruined buildings are occasionally turned up by the plough: here also is an oak of which the trunk measures nearly 36 feet in girth, and in the churchyard is a yew which from the great circumference of its trunk must be of very great antiquity; that Addington was once a seat of the Aeddons or Magi, is an inference of high probability.

Addington is situated in what is now Surrey, and is in close proximity to a place named Sanderstead: the Sander whose stead or enclosure here stood may be connoted with the French Santerre, which district abounds with *souterrains:* in the valley of the Somme alone there are at least thirty "singular excavations" which *communicate with parish churches:* [1] these Santerre and Sanderstead similarities may be connoted with the fact that on the coast of Du*r*ham are caverns hewn in the limestone and known as Dane's holes.

In the forest of Tournehem near St. Omer are some curious square and circular *fosses* known locally as Fosses, Sarrasines, or Fosses des Inglais: [2] saracens is the name under which the Jews or Phœnicians are still known in Cornwall, and in view of the Tyrians love of burrowing or making trous, Tournehem may here perhaps be identified with Tyre, or the Tyrrhenians of Etruria. The Inglais can hardly be the modern English, but are more probably the prehistoric Ingles whose marvellous monument stands today at Mount Ingleborough in Yorkshire, or ancient Deira: this must have been a perfect Angel borough, or Eden, for not only is it a majestic hill crowned by a tower called the

---

[1] Goddard, A. R., *Essex Archæological Society's Transactions*, vol. vii., 1899.

[2] Courtois, *Dictionaire Geographique de l'Arrondissement de Saint Omer*, p. 156.

Hospice, and with other relics previously noted, but it also contains one of the most magnificent caverns in the kingdom. This is entered by a low wide arch and consists for the first 600 feet, or thereabouts, of a mere tunnel which varies in height from 5 to 15 feet: one then enters "a spacious chamber with surface all elaborated in a manner resembling the work of a Gothic cathedral in limestone formations of endless variety of form and size, and proceeds thence into a series of chambers, corridors, first made accessible in 1838, said to have an aggregate extent of about 2000 feet, and displaying a marvellous and most beautiful variety of stalactites and stalagmites. A streamlet runs through the whole, and helps to give purity to the air."[1] This description is curiously reminiscent of the famous and gigantic Han Grotto near Dinant: with the Han Grotto, through which run the rivers Lesse and Tamise, may be connoted the Blue John Cavern in Derbyshire, and I have little doubt that Han or Blue John, or Tarchon was the Giant originally worshipped by the Chouans or Jacks, who inhabited the terrible recesses of La Vendee. The name Joynson which occurs in the Kentish dene hole district implies possibly the son of a Giant, or a son of Sinjohn: it is not unlikely that the "Hangman's" Wood, in which the group of dene holes here planned occur, was originally the Han, Hun, giant, or Hahnemann's Wood. At Tilbury the spacious caverns were adjacent to *Shen*field, in the neighbourhood of Downs Farm: at Dunstable is a little St. John's Wood, a Kensworth, and a Mount Pleasant; this district is dotted with "wells," and the adjacent Caddington is interpreted as having meant "the hill meadow of Cedd or Ceadda".

[1] Wilson, J. G., *Gazetteer*, i., 1044.

Dinant or Deonant is generally supposed to derive its name from Diana, and we are told that the town originally possessed "*onze* eglises paroissales". Whether these eleven parishes were due to chance or whether they were originally sacred to an elphin eleven must remain a matter of conjecture: at the entry to the Grotto in Dane Hill, Margate (Thanet), is a shell-mosaic *yoni* surmounted by an eleven-rayed star.

The association of "les Inglais" with the fosses in the forest of Tournehem may possibly throw some light upon the curiously persistent sixfold form in which our British dene holes seem invariably to have been constructed. Engelland as we have seen was the mystic Angel Land in which the unborn children of the future were awaiting incarnation: that six was for some reason associated with birth and creation is evident from the six days of Jewish tradition, and from the corresponding 6000 years of Etrurian belief. The connection between six and creation is even more pointed in the Druidic chant still current in Brittany, part of which has already been quoted:—

> Beautiful child of the Druid, answer me right well.
> What would'st thou that I should sing?
> Sing to me the series of number one that I may learn it this very day.
> There is no series for one, for One is Necessity alone.
> The father of death, there is nothing before and nothing after.

Nevertheless the Druid or Instructor runs through a sequence expounding three as the three Kingdoms of Merlin, five as the terrestrial zones, or the divisions of time, and *six* as "*babes of wax quickened into life through the power of the moon*":[1] the moon which periodically wanes and waxes like a matron, was of course Diana,

---

[1] Eckenstein, L., *Comparative Studies in Nursery Rhymes*, p. 154.

whence possibly the sixfold form of the dene or Dane holes.

In the Caucasus—the land of the Kimbry, *don* was a generic term for water and for river:[1] we have a river *Dane* in Cheshire, a river *Dean* in Nottinghamshire, a river *Dean* in Forfarshire, a river *Dun* in Lincolnshire, a river *Dun* in Ayrshire, and a river *Don* in Yorkshire, Aberdeen, and Antrim. There is a river Don in Normandy, and elsewhere in France there is a river Madon which is suggestive of the *Madonna :* the root of all these terms is seemingly Diane, Diana, or Dione, and it may reasonably be suggested that the dene or Dane holes of this country, like many other dens, were originally shrines dedicated to the prehistoric Madonna.

The fact that the subsidence at Modingham immediately filled up with water is presumptive evidence not only of a vast cavern, but also of a subterranean river, or perhaps a lake. That such spots were sacrosanct is implied by numerous references such as that quoted by Herbert wherein an Italian poet describes a visit of King Arthur to a small mount situated in a plain, and covered with stones: into that mount the King followed a hind he was chasing, tracking her through subterranean passages until he reached a cavern where "he saw the preparations for earthquakes and volcanic fires. He saw the flux and reflux of the sea."

Among the poems of Taliesin is one entitled *The Spoils of Hades*, wherein the mystic Arthur is figured as the retriever of a magic cauldron, no doubt the sun or else

---

[1] Dan or Don is one of the main European root river names; it occurs notably in the story of the *Dan*aides who carried water in broken urns to fill a bottomless vessel, and again in *Dan*aus who is said to have relieved Argos from drought.

the *pair dadeni*, or cauldron of new birth: "It commences," says Herbert, "with reference to the prison-sepulchre of Arthur describing in all *six* such sanctuaries; though I should rather say one such under *six* titles". This mysterious *six* is suggestive of the *six*fold dene holes, and that this six was for some reason associated with the Madonna is obvious from the Christian emblem here illustrated. According to the theories of the author of *L'Antre*

Thirteenth Century Window from Chartres.
Fig. 472.—From *Christian Iconography* (Didron).

des Nymphes, "the cave was considered in ancient times as the universal matrix from which the world and men, light and the heavenly bodies, alike have sprung, and the initiation into ancient mysteries always took place in a cave". I have not read this work, and am unacquainted with the facts upon which M. Saintyves bases his conclusions: these, however, coincide precisely with my own. It will not escape the reader's attention that Fig. 472 is taken from Chartres, the *central* site of Gaul, to which as Cæsar recorded the Druids annually congregated.

Layamon in his *Brut* recounts that Arthur took counsel with his knights on a spot exceeding fair, " beside the water that Albe was named ":[1] I am unable to trace any water now existing of that name which, however, is curiously reminiscent of Coleridge's romantic Alph :—

> In Xanadu did Kubla Khan
> A stately pleasure-dome decree,
> Where Alph, the sacred river, ran
> Through caverns measureless to man
> Down to a sunless sea.

It has already been noted that the Saxon monks filled up passages at St. Albans which ran even under the river: that similar constructions existed elsewhere is clear from the Brut of Kings where it is stated that Lear was buried by his daughter Cordelia in a vault under the river Soar in Leicestershire : " a place originally built in honour of the god Janus, and in which all the workmen of the city used to hold a solemn ceremony before they began upon the new year ".[2] That the Druids worshipped and taught in caves is a fact well attested ; that solemn ceremonies were enacted at Chislehurst is probable ; that they were enacted in Ireland at what was known as Patrick's Purgatory even to comparatively modern times is practically certain. This famous subterranean Purgatory, which Faber describes as a " celebrated engine of papal imposture," flourished amazingly until 1632, when the Lords Justices of Ireland ordered

[1] P. 242.   [2] Herbert, A., *Cyclops*, p. 154.

it to be utterly broken down, defaced, and demolished; and prohibited any convent to be kept there for the time to come, or any person to go into the said island on a superstitious account.[1] The popularity of Patrick's Purgatory, to which immense numbers of pilgrims until recently resorted, is connected with a local tradition that Christ once appeared to St. Patrick, and having led him to a desert place showed him a deep hole: He then proceeded to inform him that whoever entered into that pit and continued there a day and a night, having previously repented and being armed with the true faith, should be purged from all his sins, and He further added that during the penitent's abode there he should behold both the torments of the damned, and the joyful blisses of the blessed. That both these experiences were dramatically represented is not open to doubt, and that the actors were the drui or magi is equally likely: Lough *Derg*, the site of the Purgatory, is suggestive of drui, and also of Thurrock where, as we have seen, still exist the dene holes of troglodites.

On page 558 was reproduced a coin representing the Maiden in connection with a right angle, and there may be some connection between this emblem and the form of Patrick's Purgatory: "Its shape," says Faber, "resembles that of an L, excepting only that the angle is more obtuse, and it is formed by two parallel walls covered with large stones and sods, its floor being the natural rock. Its length is $16\frac{1}{2}$ feet, and its width 2 feet, but the building is so low that a tall man cannot stand erect in it. It holds nine persons, and a tenth could not remain in it without considerable inconvenience."[2] This Irish chapel to hold nine may be connoted with Bishop Arculf's description in A.D.

---

[1] Wright, T., *Patrick's Purgatory*, p. 162. [2] *Ibid.*, p. 231.

700 of the Holy Sepulchre at Jerusalem. He describes this church as very large and round, encompassed with three walls, with a broad space between each, and containing three altars of wonderful workmanship, in the middle wall, at three different points; on the south, the north, and the west. "It is supported by twelve stone columns of extraordinary magnitude; and it has eight doors or entrances through the three opposite walls, four fronting the north-east, and four to the south-east. In the middle space of the inner circle is a *round grotto cut in the solid rock*, the interior of which is *large enough to allow nine men to pray standing*, and the roof of which is about a foot and a half higher than a man of ordinary stature."[1] To the above particulars Arculf adds the interesting information that: " On the side of Mount Olivet there is a cave not far from the church of St. Mary,[2] on an eminence looking towards the valley of Jehoshaphat, in which are two very deep pits. One of these extends under the mountain to a vast depth; the other is sunk straight down from the pavement of the cavern, and is said to be of great extent. These pits are always closed above. In this cavern are four stone tables; one, near the entrance, is that of our Lord Jesus, whose seat is attached to it, and who,

---

[1] *Travels in the East*, p. 2.

[2] " This was the *round* church of St. Mary, divided into two stories by slabs of stone; in the upper part are four altars; on the eastern side below there is another, and to the right of it an empty tomb of stone, in which the Virgin Mary is said to have been buried; but who moved her body, or when this took place, no one can say. On entering this chamber, you see on the right-hand side a stone inserted in the wall, on which Christ knelt when He prayed on the night in which He was betrayed; and the marks of His knees are still seen on the stone, as if it had been as soft as wax."

doubtless, rested Himself here while His twelve apostles sat at the other tables."[1]

Jerusalem was for many centuries regarded as the admeasured centre of the whole earth, and doubtless every saintuaire was originally the local *centre*: in Crete there has been discovered a small shrine at Gournia "situated in the very centre of the town," and with the mysterious pits of elsewhere may be connoted the "three walled pits," nearly 25 feet deep, which remain at the northern entrance of Knossus: the only explanation which has been suggested for these constructions is that "they may have been oubliettes".

Around Patrick's Purgatory in Lough Derg were built seven chapels, and it is evident that at or near the site were many other objects of interest: Giraldus Cambrensis says there were nine caves there,[2] another account states that an adventurer—a venerable hermit, Patrick by name—"one day lighted on this cave which is *of vast extent*. He entered it and wandering on in the dark lost his way so that he could no more find how to return to the light of day. After long rambling through the gloomy passages he fell upon his knees and besought Almighty God if it were His will to deliver him from the great peril wherein he lay."[3] This adventure doubtless actually befell an adventurous Patrick, and before starting on his foolhardy expedition he would have been well advised to have consulted some such experienced Bard as the Taliesin who—

---

[1] Wright comments upon this: "Dr. Clarke is the only modern traveller who has given any notice of these subterranean chambers or pits, which he supposes to have been ancient places of idolatrous worship".

[2] *Cf.* Baring-Gould, *Curious Legends*, p. 238.

[3] *Mysteries of the Cabiri*, ii., 393.

claiming himself to be born of nine constituents—wrote—

> I know every pillar in the Cavern of the West.

Similarly the author of *The Incantation of Cunvelyn* maintained :—

> With the habituated to song (Bard)
> Are flashes of light to lead the tumult
> In ability to descend
> Through spikes along brinks
> Through the opening of trapdoors.[1]

This same poet speaks of the furze or broom bush in blossom as being a talisman: "The furzebush is it not radiance in the gloom?" and he adds "of the sanctity of the winding refuge they (the enemy) have possessed themselves". Upon this Herbert very pertinently observes: "This sounds as if the possessors of the secret had an advantage over their opponents from their faculty of descending into chambers and galleries cunningly contrived, and artfully obscured and illuminated. . . . I think there was somewhere a system of chambers, galleries, etc.,[2] approaching to the labyrinthine character."[3]

The Purgatory of St. Patrick was once called *Uamh Treibb Oin*, the *wame*, or cave of the tribe of Oin or Owen, upon which Faber comments: "Owen, in short, was no other than the Great God of the Ark, and the same as Oan, Oannes, or Dagon": he was also in all probability the *Janus* of the river Soar, the *Shony* of the Hebrides, the Blue *John* of Buxton, the Tar*chon* of Etruria, and the St.

---

[1] *Cf.* Herbert, A., *Cyclops*, p. 155.   [2] *Ibid.*, p. 154.
[3] It is not improbable that the Pied Piper incident was actually enacted annually at the Koppenburg, and that the children of Hamelyn were given the treat of being taken through some brilliantly lit cavern "joining the town and close at hand". Whether the Koppenburg contains any grottos I am unable to say.

Patrick on whose festival and before whose altar all the fishes of the sea rose and passed by in procession. After expressing the opinion "I am persuaded that Owen was the very same person as Patrick," Faber notes the tradition, no doubt a very ancient one among the Irish, that Patrick was likewise called Tailgean or Tailgin: there is a celebrated Mote in Ireland named Dun*dalgan*, and the Glen*dalgeon*, to which the miraculous Bird of St. Bridget is said to have taken its flight, was presumably a glen once sacred to the same Tall John, or Chief King, or Tall Khan, or High Priest, as was worshipped at the Pictish town of Delginross in Caledonia; we have already considered this term in connection with the Telchines of Telchinia, Khandia, or Crete.

That Lough *Derg* was associated with Drei, Droia, or Troy, and with the *drui* or Druids, is further implied by its ancient name Lough *Chre*, said to mean lake of the *soothsayers*. Sooth is Truth and the Hibernian *chre* may be connoted with the "Cray," which occurs so persistently in the Kentish dene hole district, *e.g.*, Foots Cray, St. Mary Cray, and St. Paul's Cray: the Paul of this last name may be equated with the Poole of the celebrated Buxton Poole's Cavern, Old Poole's Saddle, and Pell's Well: the "bogie" of Buxton was no doubt the same Puck, Pooka, or Bwcca, as that of the Kentish Bexley, Bickley, and Boxley at each of which places are dene holes.

The cauldron of British mythology was known occasionally as Pwyll's Cauldron, Pwyll, the chief of the Underworld, being the infernal or Plutonic form of the Three Apollos. Referring to the Italian tale of King Arthur's entrance into the innermost caverns of the earth, Herbert observes: "Valvasone's account of this place is a just

Fig. 473.—Sculpture on the Wall of St. Clement's Cave, Hastings.

[*To face page* 797.

description of the Cor upon Mount Ambri, and goes to identify it with the mystical Ynys Avallon (Island of Apples). All that he says of it is in wide departure from the tales which he might have read in Galfridus and Giraldus. But when we further see that he places within its recesses the cauldron of deified nature or Keridwen, it truly moves our wonder whence this matter can have come into his pages."[1] Doubtless Herbert would have puzzled still more in view of what is apparently the same mystic cauldron, bowl, or tureen carved upon the walls of St. Clement's Caves at Hastings.[2]

Presumably the St. Clement of these caves which have been variously ascribed to the Romans and the Danes, was a relative of St. Clement Dane in London by St. Dunstan in the West: the Hastings Caves are situated over what is marked on the Ordnance map as Torfield, and as this is immediately adjacent to a St. Andrew it is probable that the Anderida range, which commences hereby and terminates at the Chislehurst Caves, was all once dedicated to the ancient and eternal Ida. *Antre* is a generic term for cave, and as *trou* means hole, the word *antrou* is also equivalent to *old hole*. When first visiting the famous Merlin's Cave at Tintagel or Dunechein, where it is said that Arth*ur*

---

[1] *Cyclops*, p. 156.

[2] The authorities connect the surnames Kettle and Chettle with the Kettle or Cauldron of Norse mythology, whence Prof. Weekley writes: " The renowned Captain Kettle, described by his creator as a Welshman, must have descended from some hardy Norse pirate ". Why Norse? The word *kettle*, Gaelic *cadhal*, is supposedly borrowed from the Latin *catillus*, a small bowl: the Greek for cup is *kotulos*, and it is probable that *kettle* and *cotyledon* are alike radically Ket, Cot, or Cad. In Scotland *adhan* meant cauldron, whence Rust thinks that Edinbro or Dunedin was once a cauldron hill.

or Ar*tur*, the mystic Mighty Child, was cast up by the ninth wave into the arms of the Great Magician, my companion's sense of romance received a nasty jar on learning that Merlin's Cave was known locally as "The Old Hole": it may be, however, that this term was an exact rendering of the older Keltic *antrou*, which is literally *old hole*: the Tray Cliff in Derbyshire, where is situated the Blue John Mine, may well have been the *trou* cliff.

The highest point of the highland covering St. Clement's Caves is known as "The Ladies' Parlour"; at the foot of this is Sandringham Hotel, whence—in view of the neighbouring St. Andrew and Tor field—it is possible that "Sandringham"[1] was here, as elsewhere, a *home of the children of Sander*: immediately adjacent is a Braybrook, and a Bromsgrove Road. Near Reigate is a Broome Park which we are told " in the romantic era rejoiced in the name of Tranquil Dale ":[2] the neighbouring Buckland, Boxhill, and Pixhome Lane may be connoted with Bexhill by Hastings, and there are further traditional connections between the two localities. Under the dun upon which stand the remains of Reigate Castle are a series of caves, and besides the series of caves under the castle there are many others of much greater dimensions to the east, west, and south sides:[3] my authority continues, "Here many of the side tunnels are sealed up; one of these is said to go to Reigate Priory—which is possible—but another which is *reputed to go to Hastings*, impels one to draw the line somewhere ".[4]

[1] Sandringham, near King's Lynn, appeared in Domesday as Sandersincham: upon this Johnston comments, "Curious corruption. This is 'Holy Dersingham,' as compared with the next parish Dersingham. French *saint*, Latin *sanctus*, Holy."

[2] Ogilvie, J. S., *A Pilgrimage in Surrey*, ii., 183.

[3] *Ibid.*, p. 166. [4] *Ibid.*, p. 167. The italics are mine.

We have seen that Brom and Bron were obviously once one and the same, and there is very little doubt that the Bromme of Broompark or Tranquil Dale was the same Peri or Power as was presumably connected with Purley, and as the Bourne or Baron associated with Reigate. In one of the Reigate caverns is a large pool of clear water which is said to appear once in seven years, and is still known as Bourne water:[1] under the castle is a so-called Baron's Cave which is about 150 feet long, with a vaulted roof and a circular end with a ledge or seat around it. In popular estimation this is where the Barons met prior to the signing of Magna Charta: possibly they did, and without doubt many representatives of *The* Baron—good, bad, bold, and indifferent—from time to time sat and conferred upon the same ledge. From the Baron's Cave a long inclined plane led to a stairway of masonwork which extended to the top of the mound.

Reigate now consists of a pair of ancient Manors, of which one was Howleigh; the adjacent A*g*land Moor, as also O*x*ted, suggests the troglodyte King Og of Edrei.

[1] "The old Bourne stream, generally known as the 'Surrey Woe Water,' has already commenced to flow through Caterham Valley, and at the moment there is quite a strong current of water rushing through an outlet at Purley.

"There are also pools along its course through Kenley, Whyteleafe, and Warlingham, which suggest that the stream is rising at its principal source, in the hills around Woldingham and Oxted, where it is thought there exists a huge natural underground reservoir, which, when full, syphons itself out at certain periods about every seven years.

"Tradition says that when the Bourne flows 'out of season' or at irregular times it foretells some great calamity. It certainly made its appearance in a fairly heavy flow in three of the years of the war, but last year, which will always be historical for the declaration of the armistice and the prelude of peace, there was no flow at all."—*The Star*, 15th March, 1919.

Among the Reigate caves is one denominated "The Dungeon": *Tin*tagel was known alternatively not only as *Dun*dagel, but also as *Dune*chein, evidently the same word as the great *Dane* John tumulus at Canterbury. The meaning of this term depends like every other word upon its context; a *dungeon* is a down-under or dene hole, the keep or *donjon* of a castle is its main tower or summit: similarly the word dunhill is identical with dene hole; *abyss* now means a yawning depth, but on page 224 Abyss was represented as a dunhill.

From the cavern at Pentonville, known as Merlin's Cave, used to run a subterranean passage: modern Pentonville takes its title from a ground landlord named Penton, a tenant who presumably derived his patronymic either from that particular *penton* or from one elsewhere. In connection with the term *pen* it is curious to find that at Penselwood in Somerset there are what were estimated to be 22,000 "pen pits": these pits are described as being in general of the form which mathematicians term the frustrum of a cone, not of like size one with another, but from 10 to 50 feet over at top and from 5 to 20 feet in the bottom.[1] I have already surmised that the various Selwoods, Selgroves, and Selhursts were so named because they contained the cells of the austere *selli*: by Penselwood is Wincanton, a place supposed to have derived its title from "probably a man's name; nasalised form of *Hwicca*, *cf.* Whixley, and see *ton*"; but in view of the innumerable *cone*-shaped cells hereabout, it would seem more feasible that *canton* meant *cone town*. We have already illustrated the marvellous cone tomb said to have once existed in Etruria: in connection with this it is

---

[1] "Archæologia" (from *The Gentleman's Magazine*), i., 283.

further recorded that within the basement King Porsenna made an inextricable labyrinth, into which if one ventured without a clue, there he must remain for he never could find the way out again; according to Mrs. Hamilton Gray the labyrinth of a counterpart of this tomb still exists, "but its locality is unascertained".

There are said to be pits similar to the Wincanton pen pits in Berkshire, there known as Coles pits: we have already connoted St. Nichol of the tub-miracle, likewise King Cole of the Great Bowl with Yule the Wheel or Whole. The Bowl of Cole was without doubt the same as the *pair dadeni*, or Magic Cauldron of *Pwyll* which Arthur "spoiled" from Hades: with *Paul's* Cray may be connoted the not-far-distant Pol Hill overlooking Sevenoaks. Otford, originally Ottanford, underlies Pol Hill, which was no doubt a dun of the celestial Pol, *alias* Pluto, or Aidoneus: in the graveyard at Ottanford may be seen memorials of the Polhill family, a name evidently analogous to Penton of Pentonville.

The memory of our ancestors dwelling habitually in either pen pits, dene holes, or cole pits, has been preserved in Layamon's *Brut*, where it is recorded: "At Totnes, Constantin the fair and all his host came ashore; thither came the bold man—well was he brave!—and with him 2000 knights such as no king possessed. Forth they gan march into London, and sent after knights over all the kingdom, and every brave man, that speedily he should come anon. The Britons heard that, *where they dwelt in the pits*, in earth and in stocks they hid them (like) badgers, in wood and in wilderness, in heath and in fen, so that well nigh no man might find any Briton, except they were in castle, or in burgh inclosed fast. When they heard of this word, that Constantin was in the land, *then came out of the mounts* many thousand men; they leapt out of the wood as if it were deer. Many hundred thousand marched toward London, by street and by weald all it forth pressed; and the brave women put on them men's clothes, and they forth journeyed toward the army."

It has been assumed that the means of exit from the dene holes, and from the subterranean city with which they communicated, was a notched pole, and it is difficult to see how any other method was feasible: in this connection the Mandan Indians of North America have a curious legend suggestive of the idea that they must have sprung from some troglodite race. The whole Mandan nation, it is said, once resided in one large village underground near a subterranean lake; a grape-vine extended its roots down to their habitation and gave them a view of the light. Some of the most adventurous climbed up the vine and were delighted with the sight of the earth which they found covered with buffalo and rich with every kind of fruit: men, women, and children ascended by means of the vine (the notched pole?), but when about half the nation had attained the surface of the earth a big or buxom woman, who was clambering up the vine, broke it with her weight and closed upon herself and the rest the light of the Sun. There is seemingly some like relation between this legend and the tradition held by certain hill tribes of the old Konkan kingdom in India, who have a belief that their ancestors came out of a cave in the earth. In connection with this Konkan tale, and with the fact that the Concanii of Spain fed on horses, it may here be noted that not only do traces of the horse occur in the most ancient caves, but that vast deposits of horse bones point to the probability that horses were eaten sacrificially in caves.¹ In the Baron's Cave at Reigate, "There are many bas relief sculptures, Roman soldiers' heads, grotesque masks of monks, horses' heads and other subjects which can only be guessed at":² these idle scribblings have been assigned to the Roman soldiery, who are supposed at one time to have garrisoned the castle, and the explanation is not improbable: the favourite divinity of the Roman soldiery was Mithra, the Invincible White Horse, and several admittedly Mithraic Caves have been identified in Britain.³ It has

¹ *Cf.* Johnson, W., *Byeways*, pp. 411, 417.
² Ogilvy, J. S., *A Pilgrimage in Surrey*, ii., 164.
³ That the solar horse was sacred among the Ganganoi of Hibernia is probable, for: " On that great festival of the peasantry, St. John's Eve, it is the custom, at sunset on that evening, to kindle immense fires throughout the country, built like our bonfires, to a great height, the pile being composed of turf, bogwood, and such other combustibles as they can gather. The turf yields a steady, substantial body of fire, the bogwood a most brilliant flame; and the effect of these great beacons blazing on every hill, sending up volumes of smoke from every part of the horizon, is very remarkable. Early in the evening the peasants began to assemble, all habited in their best array, glowing with health, every countenance full of that sparkling animation and excess of enjoyment that characterise the enthusiastic people of the land. I had never seen anything resembling it; and was exceedingly delighted with their handsome, intelligent, merry faces; the bold bearing of the men, and the playful, but really modest deportment of the maidens; the vivacity of the aged people, and the wild glee of the children. The fire being kindled, a splendid blaze shot up; and for a while they stood contemplating it, with faces strangely disfigured by the peculiar light first emitted when the bogwood is thrown on. After a short pause, the ground was cleared in front of an old blind piper, the very beau-ideal of energy, drollery, and shrewdness, who, seated on a low chair, with a well-plenished jug within his reach, screwed his pipes to the liveliest tunes and the endless jig began.

" But something was to follow that puzzled me not a little. When the fire burned for some hours, and got low, an indispensable part of the ceremony commenced. Every one present of the peasantry passed through

always been supposed that these were the work of Roman invaders, and in this connection it should be noted that deep in the bowels of the Chislehurst labyrinth there is a clean-cut well about 70 feet deep lined with Roman cement: but granting that the Romans made use of a ready-made cave, it is improbable that they were responsible for the vast net-work of passages which are known to extend under that part of Kent. There is—I believe—a well in the heart of the Great Pyramid; a deep subterranean well exists in one of the series of caves at Reigate.

In his article on the Chislehurst Caves Mr. Nichols inquires, "might not the shafts of these dene holes have lent themselves to the study of the heavenly bodies?" That the Druids were adepts at astronomy is testified by various classical writers, and according to Dr. Smith there are sites in Anglesey still known in Welsh as "the city of

---

it, and several children were thrown across the sparkling embers; while a wooden frame of some 8 feet long, with a horse's head fixed to one end, and a large white sheet thrown over it, concealing the wood and the man on whose head it was carried, made its appearance. This was greeted with loud shouts as the '*white horse*'; and having been safely carried by the skill of its bearer several times through the fire with a bold leap, it pursued the people, who ran screaming and laughing in every direction. I asked what the horse was meant for, and was told it represented all cattle.

"Here was the old pagan worship of Baal, if not of Moloch too, carried on openly and universally in the heart of a nominally Christian country, and by millions professing the Christian name! I was confounded; for I did not then know that Popery is only a crafty adaptation of pagan idolatries to its own scheme; and while I looked upon the now wildly excited people, with their children and, in a figure, all their cattle passing again and again through the fire, I almost questioned in my own mind the lawfulness of the spectacle, considered in the light that the Bible must, even to the natural heart, exhibit it in to those who confess the true God."—Elizabeth, Charlotte, *Personal Recollections*, quoted from "S.M." *Sketches of Irish History*, 1845.

the Astronomers," the Place of Studies, and the Astronomers' Circle.[1] There was a famous Holy Well in Dean's Yard, Westminster, and it would almost seem that a well was an integral adjunct of the sacred duns: according to Miss Gordon "there is a well of unknown antiquity at Pentonville under Sadlers Wells Theatre (Clerkenwell), lined with masonry of ancient date throughout its entire depth, similar to the prehistoric wells we have already mentioned in the Windsor Table Mound, on the Wallingford Mound, and the Well used by the first Astronomer Royal at Greenwich".[2] But masonry-lined wells situated in the very bowels of the earth as at Chislehurst and Reigate cannot have served any astronomic purpose; they must, one would think, have been constructed principally for ritualistic reasons. At Sewell, near Dunstable, immediately next to Maiden Bower there once existed a very remarkable dene hole: this is marked on the Ordnance Maps as "site of well," but in the opinion of Worthington Smith, "this dene hole was never meant for a well". It was recently destroyed by railway constructors who explored it to the depth of 116 feet; but, says Worthington Smith, "amateur excavators afterwards excavated the hole to a much greater depth and found more bones and broken pots. The base has never been reached. The work was on the top of a very steep and high bank."[3] On Mount Pleasant at Dunstable was a well 350 feet deep,[4] and any people capable of sinking a narrow shaft to this depth must obviously have been far removed from the savagery of the prime.

[1] *The Religion of Ancient Britain*, p. 28.
[2] *Prehistoric London*, p. 137.
[3] *Man the Primeval Savage*, p. 328.   [4] *Ibid.*, p. 66.

In 1835 at *Tin*well, in Rutlandshire, the singular discovery was made of a large subterranean cavern supported in the centre by a stone pillar: this chamber proved on investigation to be "an oblong square extending in length to between 30 and 40 yards, and in breadth to about 8 feet. The sides are of stone, the ceiling is flat, and at one end are two doorways bricked up."[1] About forty years ago, at Donseil in France—or rather in a field belonging to the commune of Saint Sulpice le *Don*seil[2]—a ploughman's horse sank suddenly into a hole: the grotto which this accident revealed was found to have been cut out from soft grey granite in an excellent state of preservation and is thus described: "After passing through the narrow entrance, you make your way with some difficulty down a sloping gallery some 15 yards in length, to a depth beneath the surface of nearly 20 feet; this portion is in the worst condition. Then you find yourself in a *circular gallery* measuring about 65 feet in circumference, *with the roof supported by a huge pillar*, 18 feet in diameter. It is worth noticing that the walls, which are hewn out of the granite, are not vertical, but convex like an egg. At 19 feet to the left of the inclined corridor, and at an elevation of 30 inches above the level of the soil of the circular gallery, we come upon a small opening, through which it is just possible for a man to squeeze himself: it gives access to a gallery *thirty-three* feet long, at the bottom of which a loftier and more spacious gallery has been begun, but, apparently, not completed."[3]

[1] *Archæologia*, i., 29.

[2] *Le donseil* probably here means *donsol*, or *lord sun*. Adonis and all the other Sun lords were supposed to have been born in a cave on 25th December. We have seen that Michael's Mount (family name St. Levan), was known alternatively as *dinsol*.

[3] Adams, W. H. D., *Famous Caves and Catacombs*, p. 183.

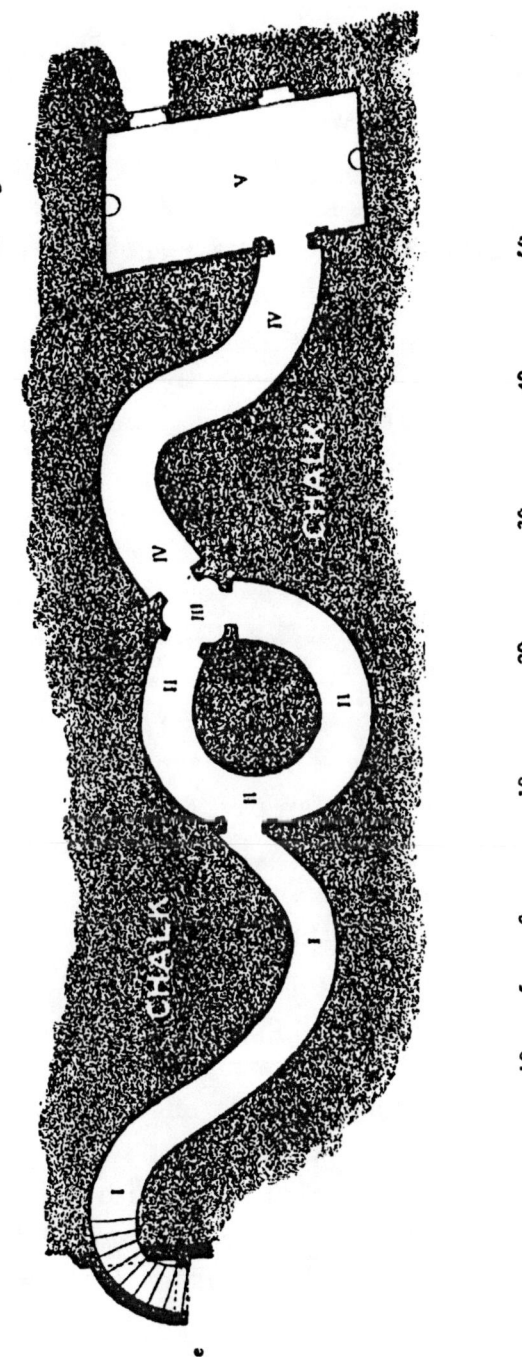

Fig. 474.—Plan of the Grotto at Margate.

I. Rough Chalk Passage.
II. Rotunda.
III. Dome.
IV. Serpentine Passage.
V. Rectangular Chamber.

I invite the reader to note the significance of these measurements and to compare the general design of the Donseil *souterrain* with the form of Fig. 474: this is the ground plan of a grotto which was accidentally discovered by some schoolboys in 1835, and exists to-day in the side of *Dane* Hill, Margate. Its form is very similar to the apparent design of the great two-mile Sanctuary at Avebury, see page 351, and its situation—a dene or valley on the side of a hill—coincides exactly with that of the small Candian cave-shrines dedicated to the serpent goddess. In Candia no temples have been discovered but only small and insignificant household shrines: "It is possible," says Mr. Hall, "that the worship of the gods on a great scale was only carried out in the open air, or the palace court, or in a grave or cave not far distant. Certainly the sacred places to which pilgrimage was made and at which votive offerings were presented, were such groves, rocky gorges, and caves."[1]

The sanctity of Cretan caves is indisputably proved by the immense number of votive offerings therein found, in many cases encrusted and preserved by stalagmites and stalactites. Among the house shrines of the Mother Goddess and her Son remain pathetic relics of the adoration paid by her worshippers: one of these saved almost intact by Sir Arthur Evans is described as a small room or cell, smaller even than the tiny chapels that dot the hills of Crete to-day—a place where one or two might pray, leave an offering and enjoy community with the divinity rudely represented on the altar . . . one-third of the space was for the worshipper, another third for the gifts, the last third for the goddess.[2]

[1] *Ægean Archæologia*, p. 156.
[2] Mr. and Mrs. Hawes, *Crete the Forerunner of Greece*, p. 65.

There are diminutive *souterrains* in Cornwall notably at St. Euny in the parish of Sancreed where the gift niches still remain intact: in many instances these "Giants Holts" are in serpentine form, and the serpentine form of the Margate Grotto is unmistakable. The Mother Goddess of Crete has been found figured with serpents in her hands and coiling round her shoulders: according to Mr.

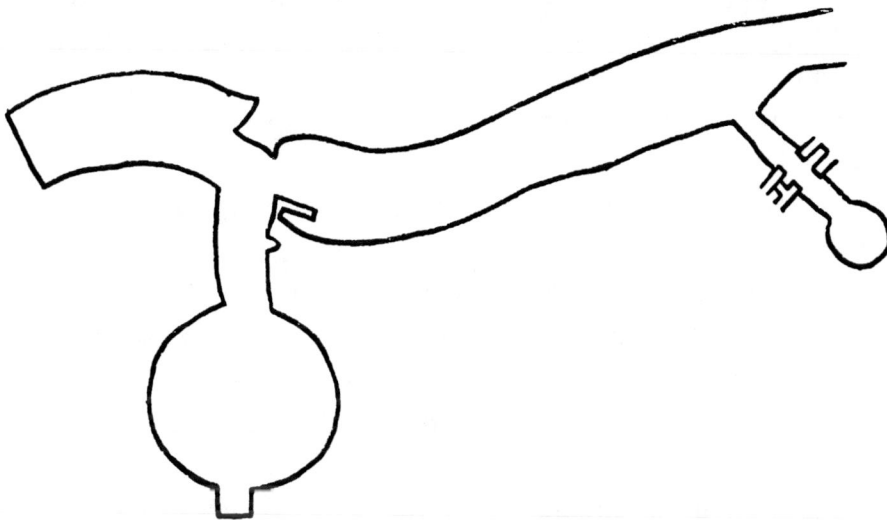

Fig. 475.—Ground plan of *Souterrain* at St. Euny's, Sancreed, Cornwall.

Mackenzie: "Her mysteries were performed in caves as were also the Paleolithic mysteries. In the caves there were sacred serpents, and it may be that the prophetic priestesses who entered them were serpent charmers: cave worship was of immense antiquity. The cave was evidently regarded as the door of the Underworld in which dwelt the snake-form of Mother Earth."[1]

It has been seen that the serpent because of sloughing its skin was the emblem of rejuvenescence, regeneration,

[1] *Myths of Crete and Pre-Hellenic Europe*, p. 183.

and New Birth; it is likely that the word *sanctus* is radically the same as *snag*, meaning a short branch, and as *snake*, which in Anglo-Saxon was *snaca*: it is certain that the *snake trou* or snake cave was one of the most primitive sanctuaries.[1] Not only is the Margate Grotto constructed in serpentine form, but upon one of the panels of its walls is a Tree of Life, of which two of the scrolls consist of horned serpents: these are most skilfully worked in shells, and from the mouth of each serpent is emerging the triple tongue of Good Thought, Good Deed, Good Word.

The word dean, French *doyen*, is supposed to be the Latin *decanum* the accusative of decanus, one set over ten soldiers or ten monks: it is, as already suggested, more probable that the original deans were the priests of Diane, and that they worshipped in dene holes, in dens, in denes, on downs, and at dunhills. The word *grot* is probably the same as *kirit*, the Turkish form of Crete, and as the *Keridwen* or *Kerid Holy* of Britain. The ministers of the Cretan Magna Mater were entitled *curetes*, and the modern curate may in all likelihood claim a verbal descent from the Keridwen or Sancreed whose name is behind our *great*, *crude*, and *cradle*. The Magna Mater of Kirid or Crete was sometimes as already mentioned depicted with a cat upon her head: I have equated the word *cat* with Kate, Kitty, or Ked, and in all probability the catacombs of Rome anciently Janicula were originally built in her honour. In Scotland *souterrains* are termed *weems*, a word which

---

[1] "Herodotus in *Book VIII.* says that the ancients worshipped the Gods and Genii of any place under the form of serpents. 'Set up,' says some one in Persius' *Satires* (No. 1), 'some marks of reverence such as the painting of two serpents to let boys know that the place is sacred.'"—Seymour, F., *Up Hill and Down Dale in Ancient Etruria*, p. 237.

is undoubtedly affiliated both in form and idea with womb, tomb, and coombe: the British bards allude frequently to the grave as being the matrix or womb of Ked; as archæologists are well aware, primitive burials frequently consisted of contracting the body into the form of the fœtus, depositing it thus in a stone cist, chest, or "coty": and there is little doubt that the St. Anne who figures so prolifically in the catacombs of Janicula, was like St. Anne of Brittany the pre-Christian Anne, Jana, or Diane.

At Caddington by Dunstable there is a Dame Ellen's Wood; Caddington itself is understood to have meant—"the hill meadow of Cedd or Ceadda," and among the prehistoric tombs found in this neighbourhood was the interment illustrated on page 64. It has been cheerily suggested that "the child may have been buried alive with its mother": it may, but it equally may not; the pathetic surround of sea-urchins or popularly-called fairy loaves points to sentiment of some sort, particularly in view of the tradition that whoso keeps a specimen of the fairy loaf in his house shall never lack bread.[1] *Echinus*, the Latin for sea-urchin, is radically the same word as Janus; in the Margate grotto an echinus forms the centre of most of the conchological suns or stars with which the walls are decorated, and a large echinus appears in each of the four top corners of the oblong chamber.

I have suggested that the Kentish Rye, a town which once stood on a conical islet and near to which is an earthwork known nowadays as Rhee wall, was once dedicated to Rhea or Maria, and that Margate owes its designation to the same Ma Rhea or Mother Queen. According to "Morien" *Rhi* was a Celtic title of the Almighty, and is

[1] Johnson, W., *Byways*, p. 304.

the root of the word *rhinwedd* (Virtue): according to Rhys *rhi* meant *queen*, and was a poetic term for a lady: according to Thomas *Rhea* is the feminine noun of *rhi*, prince or king; it would thence follow that *regina*, like the French name Rejane, meant originally Queen Gyne, either Queen Woman or Royal Jeanne. There are numerous Ryhalls, Ryhills, and in Durham is a Ryton which figured anciently as Ruyton, Rutune, and *Ruginton*: near Kingston is Raynes Park, and at Hackney, in the neighbourhood of the Seven Sisters and Kingsland Roads, is Wren's Park.

That the Candians colonised the North of Africa is generally supposed, whence it becomes likely that the marvellous excavations at *Rua* were related to the worship of the serpentine *Rhea*: these are mentioned by Livingstone who wrote: "Tribes live in underground houses in Rua. Some excavations are said to be 30 miles long, and have running rills in them; a whole district can stand a siege in them. The 'writings' therein, I have been told by some of the people, are drawings of animals and not letters, otherwise I should have gone to see them."[1]

The word grotesque admittedly originated from the fantastic designs found so frequently within grottos or grots, and if the natives of Rua could construct a *souterrain* 30 miles in extent, I see no reason to doubt the accuracy of the tradition that the natives of Reigate had run a tunnel towards Rye which is within a few miles of St. Clement's Caves at Hastings. The *gate* of Margate and Reigate means *opening*; *wry* means awry or twisting, and we may probably find the original name of Reigate in the neighbouring place-name Wray Common.

The Snake grotto at Margate, which is situated almost

[1] *Proceedings of the Royal Geographical Society*, 1869.

below a small house named "Rosanna Lodge," is decorated throughout with a most marvellous and beautiful mosaic of shellwork, the like of which certainly exists nowhere else in Britain : the dominant notes of this decoration are roses or rosettes, and raisins or grapes ; over the small altar in the oblong chamber, at the extremity, are rising the rays of the Sun. The shells used as a groundwork for this decorative scheme were the yellow periwinkle now naturally grey with antiquity but which, when fresh, must, when illuminated, have produced an effect of golden and surpassing beauty. In the shrines of Candia large numbers of sea-shells, artificially tinted in various colours, have come to light :[1] that the altar at the Cantian Margate grotto was constructed to hold a lamp or a candle cannot be doubted, in which connection one may connote a statement by "Morien" that "All shell grottos with a candle in it (*sic*) were a symbol of the cave of the sun near the margin of the ocean with the soul of the sun in it".[2] There is indeed little doubt that the snake trou under Rosanna Lodge was, like the grotto at St. Sulpice le Donseil, dedicated to le Donseil or *donna sol*. At the mouth of the shrine is a figurine seated, of which, unfortunately, the head is missing, but the right hand is still holding a cup : in Fig. 44 *ante*, page 167, Reason is holding a similar cup into which is distilling *la rosee*, or the dew of Heaven —doubtless the same goblet as was said to be offered to mortals by the fairy Idunns ; their earthly representatives, the Aeddons, may be assumed once to have dwelt in the Dane Park or at Addington Street, now leading to Dane Hill where the grotto remains.

[1] MacKenzie, D. A., *Myths of Crete*, p. 138.
[2] *Light of Britannia*, p. 200.

We have connected the Cup of Reason with the mystic Cauldron of Keridwen, or "cauldron of four spaces," and have noted among the recipe "the liquor that bees have collected *and resin*," to be prepared "when there is a calm dew falling": another Bard alludes to "the gold-encircled liquor contained in the golden cup," and I have little doubt that resin, rosin, or rosine was valued and venerated as being, like amber, the petrified tears of Apollo. I do not suggest that the Rosanna Lodge in the dene at Margate has any direct relation to the grotto of Reason beneath, but there is evidently a close connection with the small figurine holding a cup and the Lady Rosamond of Rosamond's Well at Woodstock. "There was," says Herbert, "a popular notion of an infernal maze extending from the bottom of Rosamond's Well": this labyrinth almost certainly once existed, for as late as 1718 there were to be seen by the pool at Woodstock the foundations of a very large building which were believed to be the remains of Rosamond's Labyrinth.[1]

The story of Fair Rosamond being compelled to swallow poison is precisely on a par with the monkish legend that St. George was "tortured by being forced to drink a poisoned cup," and how the Rosamond story originated is fairly obvious from the fact that on her alleged tombstone, "among other fine sculptures was engraven the figure of a cup. This, which perhaps at first was an accidental ornament (perhaps only the chalice), might in aftertimes suggest the notion that she was poisoned; at least this construction was put upon it when the stone came to be demolished after the nunnery was dissolved." The above is the opinion of an archæologist who died in 1632, and it

[1] *Cf. Percy Reliques* (Everyman's Library), p. 21.

is in all probability sound: the actual site of Rosamond's Bower at Woodstock seems to have been known as Godstone, and it was presumably the ancient Ked Stone that gave birth to the distorted legend. According to the Ballad of Fair Rosamond, that maiden was a ladye brighte, and most peerlesse was her beautye founde:—

> Her crisped locks like threads of gold
> Appeared to each man's sighte,
> Her sparkling eyes like Orient pearls
> Did cast a heavenlye light.
>
> The blood within her crystal cheekes
> Did such a colour drive
> As though the lillye and the rose
> For mastership did strive.

The ballad continues that the enamoured King—

> At Woodstock builded such a bower
> The like was never seene,
> Most curiously that bower was built
> Of stone and timber strong
> An hundered and fifty doors [1]
> Did to this bower belong,
> And they so cunninglye contrived
> With turnings round about,
> That none but with a clue of thread
> Could enter in or out.

According to Drayton, Rosamond's Bower consisted of vaults underground arched and walled with brick and stone: Stow in his *Annals* quotes an obituary stone reading, *Hic jacet in tumba Rosa Mundi; non Rosa Munda, non redolet sed olet*, which may be Anglicised into, Here lies entombed a mundane Rosa not the Rose of the World; she is not redolent, but "foully doth she stinke". I am inclined, however, to believe that the traditional Rosamond

---

[1] The Baron's Cave at Reigate is "about 150 feet long" (*ante*, p. 799).

was really and indeed the "cleane flower" and that the ignorant monks added calumny to their other perversions. History frigidly but very fortunately relates that "the tombstone of Rosamond Clifford was taken up at Godstone and broken in pieces, and that upon it were interchangeable weavings drawn out and decked with roses red and green and the picture of the cup, out of which she drank the poison given her by the Queen, carved in stone".[1] At the Cornish village of Sancreed, *i.e.*, San Kerid or St. Ked, engraved upon the famous nine foot cross is a similar cup or chalice, out of which rises a tapering fleur de lys: with the word *creed* may be connoted the fact that the artist of Kirid or Crete, "with a true instinct for beauty, chose as his favourite flowers the lovely lily and iris, the wild gladiolus and crocus, all natives of the Mediterranean basin, and the last three, if not the lily, of his own soil".[2] Opinions differ as to whether the Sancreed lily is a spear head or a fleur de lys: they also differ as to the precise meaning of the cup: in the opinion of Mr. J. Harris Stone, "the vessel or chalice is roughly heart-shaped—that is the main body of it—and the head of the so-called spear is distinctly divided and has cross-pieces which, being recurved, doubtless gave rise to the lily theory of the origin. Now there was an ancient Egyptian cross of the Latin variety rising out of a heart like the mediæval emblem of *Cor in Cruce, Crux in Corde*, and this is irresistibly brought to my mind when looking at this Sancreed cross. The emblem I am alluding to is that of Goodness."[3]

With this theory I am in sympathy, and it may be

---

[1] *Percy Reliques*, p. 20.
[2] Hawes, *Crete the Forerunner of Greece*, p. 125.
[3] *The Cornish Riviera*, p. 265.

Fig. 476.—The famous Sancreed Cross. From *The Cornish Riviera* (Stone, J. Harris). [*To face page* 816.

reasonably suggested that the alleged "tombstone" of Rosamond at Godstone was actually a carved megalith analogous to that at Sancreed: the carving on the latter may be comparatively modern, but in all probability the rock itself is the original *crude* Creed stone, Ked stone, or Good stone, touched up and partly recut.

The Rose is the familiar emblem of St. George or Oros who, according to some accounts, was the son of Princess Sophia the Wise: his legs were of massive silver up to the knees, and his arms were of pure gold from the elbows to the wrists. According to other traditions George was born at Coventry, and "is reported to have been marked at his birth (forsooth!) with a red bloody cross on his right hand".[1] The first adventure of St. George was the salvation of a fair and precious princess named Sabra from a foul dragon who venomed the people with his breath, and this adventure is located at Silene: with this Sil*ene* may be connoted the innocent Una, who in some accounts occupies the position of the Lady Sabra: Sabra is suggestive of Sabrina, the little Goddess of the river Severn, whose name we have connected with the soft, gentle, pleasing and propitious Brina: that St. Burinea, the pretty daughter of Angus whose memory is sanctified as the patron of St Burian's or Eglos*berrie*, was originally *pure* Una is more likely than that this alleged Maiden was an historic personage of the sixth century.

The series of excavations at Reigate, of which the principal is the Baron's Cave, extends to a Red Cross Inn which marks the vicinity where stood the chapel of the Holy Cross, belonging to the Priory of the Virgin and Holy Cross: about a mile from Reigate in a little brook (the

---

[1] H. O. F., *St. George for England*, p. 15.

Bourne Water) used to stand a great stone stained red by the victims of a water Kelpie, who had his lair beneath. The Kelpie was exorcised by a vicar of Buckland: nevertheless the stone remained an object of awe to the people, which, says Mr. Ogilvie, " was regarded as a vile superstition by a late vicar who had the stone removed to demonstrate to his parishioners that there was nothing under it, but some of the old folks remember the story yet ".[1] Part of Reigate is known as Red Hill, obviously from the red sandstone which abounds there: at Bristol or Bristowe, *i.e.*, the Stockade of Bri, the most famous church is that of St. Mary Redcliffe: the Mew stone off Devonshire is red cliff, the inscriptions at Sinai are always on red stone, and there is little doubt that red rock was particularly esteemed to be the symbol of gracious Aine, the Love Mother. In Domesday the Redcliff of St. Mary appears as Redeclive,[2] and may thus also have meant Rood Cleeve: in London we have a Ratcliffe Highway, and in Kensington a Redcliffe Square.

In what is now the Green Park, Mayfair, used to be a Rosamond's Pool: with Rosamond, the Rose of the World, and Rosanna—whose name may be connoted with the inscription RU NHO or QUEEN NEW,[3] which occurs on one

[1] *A Pilgrimage in Surrey*, ii., 177.   [2] At Bristol is White Lady's Road.

[3] The curious name Newlove occurs as one of the erstwhile owners of the Margate grotto: the Lovelace family, for whose name the authorities offer no suggestions except that it is a corruption of the depressing Loveless, probably either once worshipped or acted the Lovelass. This conjecture has in its favour the fact that " many of our surnames are undoubtedly derived from characters assumed in dramatic performances and popular festivities ".—Weekley, A. B., *The Romance of Names*, p. 197. " To this class belong many surnames which have the form of abstract nouns, *e.g.*, *charity, verity, virtue, vice*. Of similar origin are perhaps, *bliss, chance, luck*, and *goodluck*."—*Ibid.*, p. 197.

of the Sancreed crosses—may also be connoted St. Rosalie of Sicily or Hypereia, whose grotto and fete still excite "an almost incredible enthusiasm". The legend of St. Rosalie represents her as—

> Something much too fair and good
> For human nature's daily food,

and her mysterious evanishment is accounted for by the tradition that, disgusted by the frivolous life and empty gaiety of courts, she voluntarily retired herself into an obscure cavern, where her remains are now supposed to be buried under wreaths of imperishable roses which are deposited by angels.[1]

According to ecclesiastical legend the beloved St. Rosalie—whose fete is celebrated in Sicily on the day of St. Januarius—was the daughter of a certain Tancred, the first King of Sicily: it is not unlikely that this Tancred was Don Cred or Lord Cred, a relation of the Cornish Sancreed. Sancreed is supposed to derive its name as being "an abstract dedication to the Holy Creed": but it is alternatively known as Sancris: the Cretans, or Kiridians, or Eteocretes claimed Cres the Son of Jupiter by the nymph

---

[1] With the old English custom of burying the dead in roses, and with the tradition that at times a white lady with a red rose in her mouth used to appear at Pen*deen* cave (Courtney, Miss M. L., *Cornish Feasts and Folklore*, p. 9), in Cornwall may be connoted the statement of Bunsen: "The Phœnicians had a grand flower show in which they hung chaplets and bunches of roses in their temples, and *on the statue of the goddess Athena* which is only a feminine form of Then or Thorn" (*cf.* Theta, *The Thorn Tree*, p. 40. The probability is that not only was the rose sacred to Athene but that Danes Elder (*Sambucus ebulus*), and Danes flower (*Anemone pulsatilla*) had no original reference to the Danes, but to the far older Dane, or donna, the white Lady. Both *don* and *dan* are used in English, as the equivalent of *dominus*, whence Shakespeare's reference to Dan Cupid.

[2] Adams, W. H. D., *Famous Caves and Catacombs*, p. 177.

Idea as their first King, and they traced their descent from Cres. In a subsequent volume we shall consider this Cres at greater length, and shall track him to India in the form of Kristna, to whose grace the subterranean cross at Madura

FIG. 477.—Iberian. From Akerman.

seems to have been dedicated. In Celtic *cris* meant pure, holy; *crios* meant the Sun:[1] the principal site of Apollo-worship was the island of Crissa; in England Christy[2] is a familiar surname, and I am convinced that the

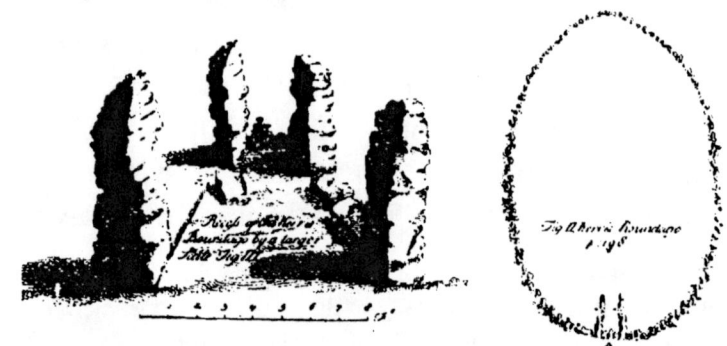

FIG. 478.—Kerris Roundago. From *Antiquities of Cornwall*.

Christ tradition in Britain owed little to the Roman mission of Augustine, but was of far older origin. We may perhaps trace the original transit of Cris to Sancris at Carissa, now Carixa, in Spain: among the numerous coins of this district some as figured herewith bear the legend

[1] Davidson, P., *The Mistletoe and its Philosophy*, p. 51.
[2] The term Christ is interpreted as " the anointed ".

Caris, some bear the head of the young Hercules, others a female head.[1] As in classic Latin *C* was invariably pronounced hard, it is probable that the maiden Caris was Ceres, and that the Cretan pair are responsible for Kerris Roundago, an egg-like monument near Sancreed; also for Cresswell in Durham where is the famous Robin Hood Cave:[2] one may further trace Caris at Carisbrook near Ryde, at the diminutive Criss Brook near Maidstone, and at the streamlet Crise in Santerre.

The town of Carissa, now Carixa, may be connoted with the synonymous *cross* or *crux*: the Cornish for *cross* was *crows*, and at Crows-an-Rha, near St. Buryans, there is a celebrated wayside cross or crouch.[3] That Caris was *carus* or *dear*, and that he was the inception of *charis* or charity will also eventually be seen: I have elsewhere suggested that *charis*, or *love*, was originally 'k Eros or Great Eros; in the Christian emblem here illustrated Christ is associated with a rose cross, which is fabricated from the four hearts, and thus constitutes the *Rosa mystica*. At Kerris Roundago are four megaliths.

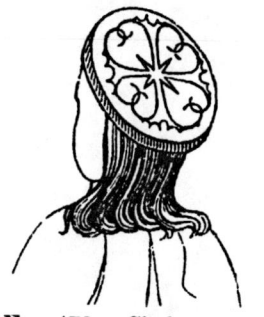

FIG. 479.—Christ, with a Nimbus Resembling a Flat Cap, or Casquette. From a Carving on Wood in the Stalls of Notre Dame d'Amiens. XVI. Cent. From Didron.

[1] Akerman, J. Y., *Ancient Coins*, p. 25.

[2] We shall consider Robin Hood whom the authorities already equate with Odin in a subsequent chapter. In Robin Hood's Cave have been discovered remains of paleolithic Art representing a horse's head. In Kent the ceremony of the Hooden Horse used until recently to survive, and the same Hood or Odin may possibly be responsible for "*Woodstock*".

[3] Crutched Friars in London marks the site of a priory of the freres of the Crutch or Crouch.

822 ARCHAIC ENGLAND [CHAP.

The Sancris cup or chalice [1] might legitimately be termed a *cruse*: Christ's first miracle was the conversion of a

Fig. 480.   Fig. 481.

cruse or can of water into wine, and the site of this miracle was Cana. The *souterrain* of St. Sulpice le Donseil is situated in a district known as La Creuse, and the solitary

[1] The San*creed* chalice may be connoted ideally and philologically with the San*graal*, Provençal *gradal*: the apparition of a child in connection with the graal or gradal also permits the equation *gradal = cradle*. At Llandudno is the stone entitled *cryd Tudno*, i.e., the cradle of Tudno.

pillar in the heart of this grotto, as also that in the Margate grotto, and that in the *souterrain* at Tinwell, were probably symbols of what the British Bard describes as "Christ the concealed pillar of peace". The Celtic Christs here reproduced from an article in *The Open Court* by Dr. Paul Carus are probably developments of ancient Prestons or Jupiter Stones: the connection between these crude Christs and Cres, the Son of Jupiter, by the nymph Idea, is probably continuous and unbroken.

A cruse corresponds symbolically to a cauldron or a cup: according to Herbert, "The Cauldron of the Bards was connected by them with Mary in that particular capacity which forms the portentous feature in St. Brighid (*viz.*, her *being Christ's Mother*) to the verge of identification. The reason was that divine objects considered by them essentially, and, as it were, sacramentally as being Christ, were prepared within and produced out of that sacred and womb-like receptacle." He then quotes two bardic extracts to the following effect:—

(1) The One Man and our Cauldron,
And our deed, and our word,
With the bright pure Mary daughter of Anne.

(2) Christ, Creator, Emperor and our Mead,
Christ the Concealed, pillar of peace,
Christ, Son of Mary and of my Cauldron, a pure pedigree![1]

The likelihood is that the solitary great Jasper stone in the roof of the four-columned hall at Edrei, the Capital of King Og, was similarly a symbol of the ideal Corner Stone or the Concealed Pillar of Peace.

At Mykenae the celebrated titanic gateway is ornamented by two lions guarding or supporting a solitary

[1] *Cyclops*, p. 137.

pillar or numeral 1 : at other times a figure of the Magna Mater takes the place of this ONE, and it is probable that the Io of Mykenae was originally My Kene, *i.e.*, Mother Queen or, more radically, Mother Great One. That Io was represented by the horns or crescent moon is obvious from the innumerable idols in the form of cows horns found at Mykenae: we have already connected Cain, Cann, and Kenna with the moon or *choon*, Latin *luna*, French *lune*, otherwise Cynthia or Diana.

Not only was Crete or Candia essentially an island of caves, but the district of the British Cantii seems if anything to have been even more riddled: *canteen* is a generic term for cellar or cool cave, and the origin of this word is not known. In Mexico *cun* meant *pudenda muliebris*, in London *cunny* and *cunt* carry the same meaning, and with *cenote*, the Mexican for *cistern*, may be connoted our English rivers Kennet and Kent. Dr. Guest refers to the cauldron of *Cend*wen (Kerid wen): according to Davidson the magic cup of the Cabiri corresponded to the *Condy* Cup[1] of the Gnostics which is the same as that in which *Guion* (Mercury) made his beverage—the beverage of knowledge or divine Kenning, the philosophical Mercury of the mediæval alchemists. Sometimes the Egg or Cup was encircled by two serpents said to represent the Igneous and Humid principles of Nature in conjunction: it is not improbable that the spirals found alike at Mykenae and New Grange represented this dual coil, spire, or maze of Life, and the Coil Dance or the Snail's Creep, which was until recently executed in Cornwall, may have borne some relation to this notion.[2]

[1] *The Mistletoe and its Philosophy*, p. 31.

[2] " The young people being all assembled in a large meadow, the village band strikes up a simple but lively air, and marches forward, followed by

XIV.] DOWN UNDER 825

In the neighbourhood of Totnes and the river Teign is the world-famous Kent's Cavern,[1] whence has emanated evidence that man was living in what is now Devonshire,

Fig. 482.—Entry to New Grange.

contemporaneously with the mammoth, the cave-lion, the woolly rhinoceros, the bison, and other animals which are now extinct. Kent's Cavern is in a hill, *dun, tun*, or

the whole assemblage, leading hand-in-hand (or more closely linked in case of engaged couples) the whole keeping time to the tune with a lively step. The band or head of the serpent keeps marching in an ever-narrowing circle, whilst its train of dancing followers becomes coiled around it in circle after circle. It is now that the most interesting part of the dance commences, for the band, taking a sharp turn about, begins to retrace the circle, still followed as before, and a number of young men with long, leafy branches in their hands as standards, direct this counter-movement with almost military precision."—*Cf.* Courtney, Miss M. L., *Cornish Feasts and Folklore*, p. 39.

[1] The name Kent here appears to be of immemorial antiquity, and was apparently first printed in a 1769 map which shows "Kent's Hole Field".

what the Bretons term a *torgen*, and the *torgen* containing Kent's Cavern is situated in the Manor of Torwood in the parish of Tor, whence Torbay, Torquay, etc.: in Cornwall *tor*, or *tur*, meant belly, and *tor* may be equated with *door*, Latin *janua*.

The entrance to Kent's Hole is in the face of a cliff, and the people mentioned in the Old Testament as the *Kenites* were evidently cliff-cave dwellers, for it is related that Balaam looked on the Kenites and said: " Strong is thy dwelling-place, and thou puttest thy nest in a rock ":[1] Kent is the same word as *kind*, meaning *genus*; also as *kind*, meaning affectionate and well-disposed, and it is worthy of note that the cave-dwelling Kenites of the Old Testament were evidently a kindly people for the record reads: "Saul said unto the Kenites 'Go, depart, get you down from among the Amalekites, lest I destroy you with them: for *ye shewed kindness to all the children of Israel when they came up* out of Egypt'.[2] So the Kenites departed from among the Amalekites."[3]

There is evidence that Thor's Cavern in Derbyshire was inhabited by prehistoric troglodites; the most high summit in the Peak District is named Kinder Scout, and in the southern side of Kinder Scout is the celebrated Kinderton Cavern: at Kinver in Staffordshire there are prehistoric caves still being lived in by modern troglodites, and at Cantal in France there are similar cave dwellings.

In Derbyshire are the celebrated Canholes and at Cannes, by Maestricht, is an entrance to the amazing grottos of St. Peter: this subterranean quarry is described as a

---

[1] Num. xxiv. 21.
[2] In modern Egyptian *kunjey* means *kinship*.
[3] 1 Sam. xv. 6.

succession of long horizontal galleries supported by an immense number of square pillars whose height is generally from 10 to 20 feet: the number of these vast subterranean alleys which cross each other and are prolonged in every direction cannot be estimated at less than 2000, the direct line from the built up entrance near Fort St. Peter to the exit on the side of the Meuse measures one league and a half. That these works were at one time in the occupation of the Romans, is proved by Latin inscriptions, but evidently the Romans did not do the building for, " underneath these inscriptions you can trace some ill-formed characters traditionally attributed to the Huns; which is ridiculous since the Huns did not build, and therefore had no need of quarries, and moreover were ignorant of the art of writing ".[1] In view of the fact that the gigantic cavern farther up the Meuse, is entitled the Han Grotto, this tradition of Hun " writing " is not necessarily ridiculous: the Huns in question, whoever they were, probably were the people who built the Hun's beds and were worshippers of " the One Man and our Cauldron ".

The Peter Mount now under consideration does not appear to have been such a Peter's Purgatory as found on "the island of the tribe of Oin": on the contrary its galleries, based on pillars about 16 feet high, are traced on a regular plan. These cross one another at right angles, and their most noticeable feature is the extreme regularity and perfect level of the roof which is enriched with a kind of cornice—a cornice of the severest possible outline, but with a noble simplicity which gives to the galleries a certain monumental aspect.

Within the criss-cross bowels of the Peter Mount is

[1] Adam, W. H. D., *Famous Caves and Catacombs*, p. 167.

another very remarkable curiosity—a small basin filled with water called Springbronnen ("source of living water") which is incessantly renewed, thanks to the drops falling from the upper portion of a fossil tree fixed in the roof.[1] The modern showman does not vaunt among his attractions a "source of living water," and we may reasonably assume that this appellation belongs to an older and more poetic age: the Hebrew for "fountain of living waters" is *ain*, a word to be connoted with Hun, Han, and St. Anne of the Catacombs: St. Anne is the patron of all springs and wells; at Sancreed is a St. Eunys Well, and the word *aune* or *avon* was a generic term for any *gentle flowing* stream.

It is reasonable to equate St. Anne of the Catacombs with "Pope Joan" of Engelheim, and it is probable that the original Vatican was the terrestrial seat of the celestial Peter, the Fate Queen or Fate King: with St. Peter's Mount may be connoted the Arabian City of Petra which is entirely hewn out of the solid rock. The connection between the Irish Owen, or Oin, and the Patrick of Patrick's Purgatory has already been considered, and that Janus or Janicula was the St. Peter of the Vatican is very generally admitted: we shall subsequently consider Janus in connection with St. Januarius or January; at Naples there are upwards of two miles of catacombs, and the Capo di *Chino*, under which these occur, may probably be identified with the St. Januarius whose name they bear.

That Janus, the janitor of the Gates of Heaven and of all other gates, was a personification of immortal Time is sufficiently obvious from the attributes which were assigned to him; that the Patrick of Ireland was also the Lord of the 365 days is to be implied from the statement of Nennius

[1] Adams, W. H. D., *Famous Caves and Catacombs*, p. 163.

that St. Patrick "at the beginning" founded 365 churches and ordained 365 bishops.[1] I was recently accosted in the street by a North-Briton who inquired "what *dame* is it?": on my failure to catch his meaning his companion pointed to my watch chain and repeated the inquiry "what *time* is it"; but even without such vivid evidence it is clear that *dame* and *time* are mere variants of the same word. It is

FIG. 483.—Seventeenth Century Printer's Mark.

proverbial that Truth, *alias* Una, *alias* Vera, is the daughter of Time: that Time is also the custodian of Truth is a similar commonplace: Time is the same word as Tom, and Tom is a contracted form of Thomas which the dictionaries define as meaning *twin, i.e., twain*: Thomas is the same name as Tammuz, a Phrygian title of Adonis, and in Fig. 404 (*ante*, p. 639), Time was emblemised as the Twain or Pair; in Fig. 483, Father Time is identified

[1] Usher, Dr. J., *A Discourse on the Religion Anciently Professed by the Irish and British*, p. 77.

with Veritas or Truth, for the legend runs, " Truth in time brings hidden things to light ".[1] The Lady Cynethryth, who dwells proverbially at the bottom of a well, is, of course, daily being brought to light; it is, however, unusual to find her thus depicted clambering from a dene hole or a den. In all probability the " Sir Thomas " who figures in the ballad as Fair Rosamond's custodian was originally Sir Tammuz, Tom, or Time—

> And you Sir Thomas whom I truste
> To bee my loves defence,
> Be careful of my gallant Rose
> When I am parted hence.

The relentless Queen who appears so prominently in the story may be connoted with the cruel Stepmother who figures in the Cinderella cycle of tales—a ruthless lady whom I have considered elsewhere. The silken thread by which the Queen reached Rosamond—to whose foot, like Jupiter's chain, it was attached—is paralleled by the thread with which Ariadne guided the fickle Theseus. In an unhappy hour the Queen overcomes the trusty Thomas, and guided by the silken thread—

> Went where the Ladye Rosamonde
> Was like an Angel sette.

> But when the Queen with steadfast eye
> Beheld her beauteous face
> She was amazed in her minde
> At her exceeding grace.

The word *grace* is the same as *cross*, and grace is the interpretation given by all dictionaries of the name John or Ian: the red cross was originally termed the Jack, and

---

[1] At the foot of this emblem the designer has introduced an intreccia or Solomon's knot between his initials R. S.

to the Jack, without doubt, was once assigned the meaning " Infinite in the East, Infinite in the West, Infinite in the South. Thus it is said, He who is in the fire, He who is in the heart, He who is in the Sun, they are *One* and the same:" in *China* the Svastika is known as the *Wan*.

CONCLUSIONS.

"I can affirm that I have brought it from an utter darknesse to a thin mist, and have gonne further than any man before me."—JOHN AUBREY.

"But for my part I freely declare myself at a loss what to say to things so much obscured by their distant antiquity; and you, when you read these conjectures, will plainly perceive that I have only groped in the dark."—CAMDEN.

ONE may perhaps get a further sidelight on the marvellous labyrinthic cave temples of the ancients by a reference to the so-called worm-knots or cup-and-ring markings on cromlechs and menhirs. With regard to these sculptures Mr. T. W. Rolleston writes: "Another singular emblem, upon the meaning of which no light has yet been thrown, occurs frequently in connection with megalithic monuments. The accompanying illustrations show examples of it. Cup-shaped hollows are made in the surface of the stone, these are often surrounded with concentric rings, and from the cup one or more radial lines are drawn to a point outside the circumference of the rings. Occasionally a system of cups are joined by these lines, but more frequently they end a little way outside the widest of the rings. These strange markings are found in Great Britain and Ireland, in Brittany, and at various places in India, where they are called *mahadeos*. I have also found a curious example—for such it appears to be—in Dupaix' *Monuments of New Spain*. It is reproduced in Lord Kingsborough's *Antiquities of Mexico*, vol. lv. On the circular top of a cylindrical stone, known as the Triumphal

CONCLUSIONS

Stone, is carved a central cup, with nine concentric circles round it, and a duct or channel cut straight from the cup

Fig. 484.—From *Mythology of the Celtic Races* (Rolleston, T. W.).

through all the circles to the rim. Except that the design here is richly decorated and accurately drawn, it closely

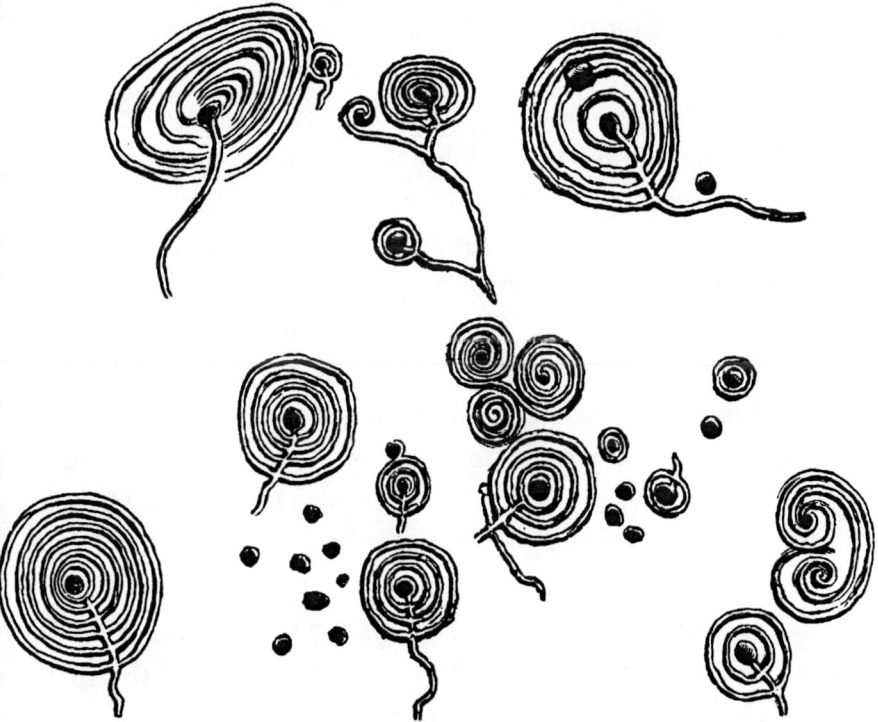

Fig. 485.—*Ibid.*

resembles a typical European cup-and-ring marking. That these markings mean something, and that wherever they are found they mean the same thing, can hardly be doubted, but what that meaning is remains yet a puzzle to antiquarians. The guess may perhaps be hazarded that they are diagrams or plans of a megalithic sepulchre. The central hollow represents the actual burial-place. The circles are the standing stones, fosses, and ramparts which often surrounded it: and the line or duct drawn from the centre outwards represents the subterranean approach to the sepulchre. The apparent avenue intention of the duct is clearly brought out in the varieties given herewith, which I take from Simpson. As the sepulchre was also a holy place or shrine, the occurrence of a representation of it among other carvings of a sacred character is natural enough; it would seem symbolically to indicate that the place was holy ground. How far this suggestion might apply to the Mexican example I am unable to say." [1]

Mr. Rolleston is partially right in his idea that the designs are as it were ground plans of monuments, but that theory merely carries the point a step backward and the question remains—Why were monuments constructed in so involved and seemingly absurd a form? I hazard the conjecture that the Triumphal Stone with its central cup and *nine* concentric circles was a symbol of Life, and of the *nine* months requisite for the production of Human Life; that the duct or channel straight from the cup through all the circles to the rim implied the mystery of creation; and that the seemingly senseless meander of long passages was intended as a representation of the maw or stomach. That the Druids were practised physiologists is deducible from the complaint made against one of them, that he had dissected 600 bodies: the ancient anatomists might quite reasonably have traced Life to a

[1] *Mythology of the Celtic Races*, p. 68.

germ or cell lying within a mazy and seemingly unending coil of viscera: we know that auguries were drawn from the condition of the entrails of sacrificial victims, whence originally the entrails were in all probability regarded as the seat of Life. *Mahadeo*, the Indian term for a worm-knot or cup-marking, resolves as it stands into *maha*, great ; and *deo*, Goddess : our English word *maw*, meaning stomach, is evidently allied to the Hebrew *moi*, meaning bowels ; with *moeder*, the Dutch for womb, may be connoted Mitra or Mithra, and perhaps Madura. It is well known that the chief Festival celebrated in the Indian cave temples at Madura and elsewhere is associated with the *lingam*, or emblem of sex, and it may be assumed that the invariable sixfold form of the Kentish dene holes was connected in some way with sex worship. The word *six* is for some reason, which I am unable to surmise, identical with the word *sex* : the Chaldees—who were probably not unconnected with the " pure Culdees " of Caledonia—taught that Man, male and female, was formed upon the *sixth* day: Orpheus calls the number *six*, " Father of the celestial and mortal powers," and, says Davidson, " these considerations are derived from the doctrine of Numbers which was highly venerated by the Druids ".[1] Six columbas centring in the womb of the Virgin Mary were illustrated on page 790, and it will probably prove that *columba* meant holy womb, just as *culver* seemingly meant holy ovary.

The sixfold marigold or wheel was used not infrequently as an emblem during the Middle Ages: in Fig. 504—a mediæval paper-mark—this design is sanctified by a cross, and the centre of Fig. 486 consists of the circle and Serpent.

[1] *The Mistletoe*. p. 30.

Figs. 486 to 491.—Paper-marked Mediæval Emblems, Showing the Combination Serpent, Circle, and Six Lobes. From *Les Filigranes* (Briquet, C. M.).

FIGS. 492 to 502.—Paper-marked Mediæval Emblems, Showing Circle and Serpent "like the intestines". From *Les Filigranes* (Briquet, C. M.).

Figs. 492 to 502 exhibit further varieties of this circle and Serpent design—the symbol of fructifying Life—and some of these examples bear a curious resemblance to the twists and convolutions of the entrails. In Egypt, Apep, the Giant Serpent, was said to have—" resembled the intestines ":[1] the word Apep is apparently related to *pepsis*. the Greek for *digestion*, as likewise to our *pipe*, meaning a long tube.

Prof. Elliot Smith, who has recently published some lectures entitled *The Evolution of the Dragon*, sums up his conclusions as follows: " The dragon was originally a concrete expression of the divine powers of life-giving; but with the development of a higher conception of religious ideals it became relegated to a baser rôle, and eventually became the symbol of the powers of evil ".[2] I have elsewhere illustrated a mediæval dragon-mark which was sanctified by a cross, and it is a highly remarkable fact that the papermakers of the Middle Ages were evidently *au fait* with the ancient meaning of this sign. Several of their multifarious serpent designs are associated with the small circle or pearl, in which connection it is noteworthy that not only had pearls the reputation of being givers of Life, but that *margan*, the ancient Persian word for pearl, is officially interpreted as meaning *mar*,

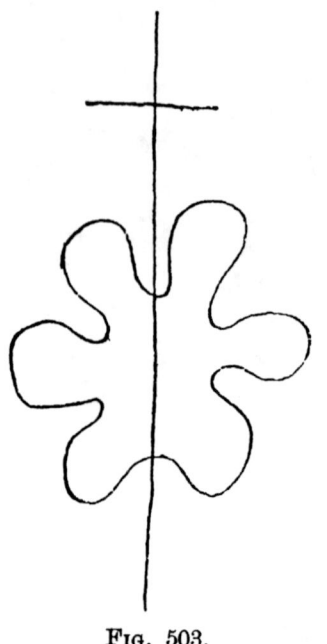

Fig. 503.

[1] Budge, W., *Legends of the Gods*, lxxii.   [2] P. 234.

"giver," and *gan*, "life". This word, says Prof. Elliot Smith, has been borrowed in all the Turanian languages ranging from Hungary to Kamchatka, also in the non-Turanian speech of Western Asia, thence through Greek and Latin (*margarita*) to European languages.[1] The Persian *gan*, in Zend *yan*, seeming corresponds to the European John, or Ian; and it is evident that Figs. 486 to 491 might justly be termed marguerites.

One of the most favourite decorations amongst Cretan artists is the eight-limbed octopus, and it is believed that the Mykenian volute or spiral is a variant of this emblem. According to Prof. Elliot Smith the evidence provided by Minoan paintings, and Mykenian decorative art, demonstrates that the spiral as a symbol of life-giving was definitely derived from the octopus.[2] Other authorities believe that the octopus symbolised "the fertilising watery principle," and that the svastika is a conventionalised form of this creature. In the light of these considerations it would thus seem highly probable that the knot, maze, Troy Town, or trou town, primarily was emblematic of the Maze or Womb of Life, conceived either physically or etherially in accord with the spirit of the time and people.

There is a certain amount of testimony to the fact that the Druids taught and worshipped within caves, and there is some reason to suppose that the Druids had a knowledge, not only of the lense, telescope, or Speculum of the Pervading Glance, but also of gunpowder, for Lucan, writing of a grove near Marseilles, remarks: "There is a report that the grove is often shaken and strangely moved, and that dreadful sounds are heard from its caverns; and that it is sometimes in a blaze without being consumed".

---

[1] Smith, Prof. Elliot, *The Evolution of the Dragon*, p. 157.
[2] *Ibid.*, p. 176.

That abominations were committed in these eerie places I do not doubt: that animals were maintained in them there is good reason to suppose; and in all probability the story of the Cretan Minotaur, to whom Athenian youths were annually sacrificed, was based on a certain amount of fact. The Bull being the symbol of life and fecundity, there would have been peculiar propriety in maintaining a bull or *toro*, Celtic *tarw*, within the *trou*, labyrinth, or maze of life: upon two of the British coins here illustrated the Mithraic

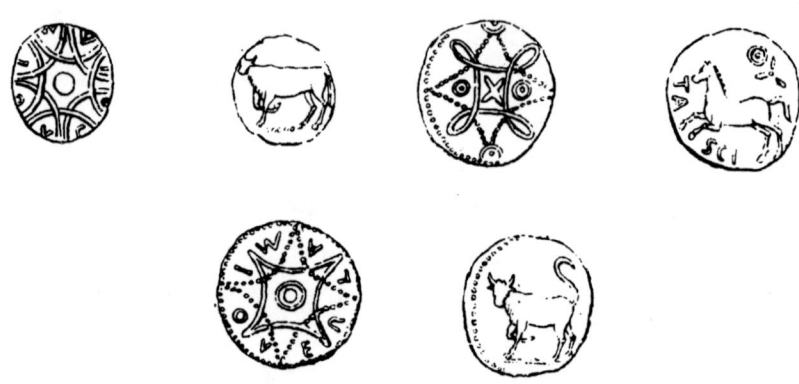

FIGS. 504 to 506.—British. From Akerman.

Bull appears in combination with an intreccia. The colossal labyrinths built in Egypt to the honour of the sacred toro are well known: in Europe remains of the horse are constantly discovered within caves,[1] and it is a cognate fact that in Mexico a tapir—the nearest approach Mexico could seemingly show to a horse—was maintained in the subterranean temple of the god Votan.

This Votan of South America is an interesting personality: according to the native traditions of the Chiapenese Indians—there was once a man named Votan, who was the grandson of the man who built the ark to save himself

---

[1] Notably at Solutre—*the Sol uter?*

and family from the Deluge. Votan was ordered by the Lord to people America and "He came *from the East*" bringing with him seven families: Votan, we are further told, was of the race of Chan, and built a city in America named Nachan, after Chan his family name. The name Votan is seemingly a variant of Wotan, the Scandinavian All Father, and also of Wootton, which is a common Kentish family name: Wotan of *Wednesday* was, it is believed, once widely worshipped in Kent, notably at *Woodnes*borough, which is particularly associated with the tradition: on Christmas Eve Thanet used to celebrate a festival called *Hooden*ing which consisted of decorating either the skull of a horse, or the wooden figure of a horse's head, which then was perambulated on a pole by a man hidden beneath a sheet.[1]

In Central America *chan* meant serpent, in which connection it is noteworthy that in Scandinavian mythology Wotan presides over the great world snake coiled at the roots of the mighty Ash Tree, named Iggdrasil. This word may, I think, be resolved into *igg dra sil*, or High Tree Holy, and the Ash of our innumerable Ashdowns, Ashtons, Ashleys, Ashursts, etc., may in all probability be equated not only with *aes*, the Welsh for *tree*, but also with *oes*, the Welsh for *life*. That Janus, whose coin was entitled the *as*, was King As has already been suggested, and that As or Ash[2] was Odin is hardly open to doubt. According to Borlase (W. C.): "There is reason to believe that the Sun was a principal divinity worshipped under the name of Fal, Phol, Bel, Beli, Balor, and Balder, all synonymous terms in the

---

[1] Wright, Miss E. M., *Rustic Speech and Folklore*, p. 303.

[2] Odin was essentially a *Wind* God: in Rutlandshire gales are termed *Ash* winds. *N. and Q.*, 1876, p. 363.

comparative mythology of the Germanic peoples whether Celtic or Teutonic in speech. A curious passage in Johannes Cornubiensis permits us to equate this deity with Asch or As, one name of Odin. The more deeply we study this portion of the subject the more certain becomes the identity of the members of the pantheon of the two western branches of the Aryan-speaking peoples."[1]

The word *Kent* or Cantium is, I think, connected with Candia, but whether Votan of the race of Chan came from Candia, Cantium, or Scandinavia is a discussion which must be reserved for a subsequent volume: it is sufficient here to note in passing that one-third of the language of the Mayas is said to be pure Greek, whence the question has very pertinently been raised, "Who brought the dialect of Homer to America? or who took to Greece that of the Mayas?"

It is now well known that there was communication between the East and West long before America was rediscovered by Columbus, and there is nothing therefore improbable in the Chiapenese tradition that their Votan, after settling affairs in the West, visited Spain and Rome. The legend relates that Votan "went by the road which his brethren, the Culebres, had bored," these Culebres being presumably either the inhabitants of Calabar in Africa now embraced in the Niger Protectorate, or of Calabria, the southernmost province of Italy. The allusion to a road which the Culebres had bored might be dismissed as a fiction were it not for the curious fact mentioned by Livingstone that tribes lived underground in Rua: "Some excavations are said to be thirty miles long and have running rills in them; a whole district can stand a siege

[1] *The Age of the Saints.* p. xxvii.

in them. The 'writings' therein I have been told by some of the people are drawings of animals and not letters, otherwise I should have gone to see them." The primitive but, in many respects, advanced culture of Mykenae and of Troy does not seem to have possessed the art of writing, and contemporary ideas must thus necessarily have been expressed by symbols akin to the multifarious animal-hieroglyphics of ancient Candia: it would even seem possible that the writings of underground Rua were parallel to the records of Egypt alleged in the following passage: "It is affirmed that the Egyptian priests, versed in all the branches of religious knowledge, and apprised of the approach of the Deluge, were fearful lest the divine worship should be effaced from the memory of man. To preserve the memory of it, therefore, they dug in various parts of the kingdom subterranean winding passages, on the walls of which they engraved their knowledge, under different forms of animals and birds, which they call hieroglyphics, and which are unintelligible to the Romans." [1]

The existence of underground ways seems to be not infrequent in Africa, for Captain Grant, who accompanied Captain Speke in his exploration for the source of the Nile, tells of a colossal tunnel or subway bored under the river Kaoma. Grant asked his native guide whether he had ever seen anything like it elsewhere and the guide replied, "This country reminds me of what I saw in the country to the south of Lake Tanganyika": he then described a tunnel or subway under another river named also Kaoma, a tunnel so lengthy that it took the caravan from sunrise to noon to pass through. This was said to be so lofty that if mounted upon camels the top could not

[1] *Cf.* Christmas, H. C., *Universal Mythology*, p. 43.

be touched: "Tall reeds the thickness of a walking-stick grew inside; the road was strewed with white pebbles, and so wide—400 yards—that they could see their way tolerably well while passing through it. The rocks looked as if they had been planed by artificial means." The guide added that the people of Wambeh Lake shelter in this tunnel,[1] and live there with their families and cattle.[2]

In view of these Rider-Haggard-like facts it is unnecessary to discredit the tradition that the South American Votan of the tribe of Chan visited his kinsmen the Culebres, by the road which the Culebres had bored. The journey is said to have taken place in the year 3000 of the world or 1000 B.C., and among the spots alleged to have been visited was the city of Rome where Votan "saw the house of God building". It is well known that great cities almost invariably exhibit traces of previous cities on the same site: Schliemann's excavations at Troy proved the pre-existence of a succession of cities on the site of Troy, and the same fact has recently been established at Seville and elsewhere. The city of Rome is famous for a labyrinth of catacombs, the building of which has always been a mystery: the catacombs abound in pagan emblems, and it is, I believe, now generally supposed that they are of pre-Christian origin.

A correspondent of *Notes and Queries* suggested in 1876 that the Roman Catacombs were the work of the prehistoric Cimmerii who notoriously dwelt *in subterraneis domiciliis*. The rocks of the Crimea, notably at Inkerman, are honeycombed with caverns; in fact the burrowing proclivities of the Kymbri are proverbialised in the expres-

---

[1] In *Wambeh* we again seem to detect *womb*.
[2] Quoted from Donnelly, I., *Atlantis*.

sion "Cimmerian darkness". The same correspondent of *Notes and Queries*[1] further drew attention to the remarkable fact that in the year 1770 coal mining operations in Ireland, at Fair Head, near The Giant's Causeway, disclosed prehistoric quarryings together with stone hammers "of the rudest and most ancient form". It is difficult to believe that prehistoric man, surrounded by inexhaustible supplies of fuel in the form of forest and peat, found it necessary to mine, with his poor implements, for coal fuel, and the description of the supposedly prehistoric mine—"wrought in the most expert manner, the chambers regularly dressed and pillars left at proper intervals to support the roof"—arouses not only a strong suspicion that the *souterrain* in question was actually a shrine, but also that the place-name Antrim—where these quarryings occur—may be connected with *antre*, a cave. When the Fair Head labyrinth was accidentally disclosed we are told that two lads were sent forward who soon found themselves in "numerous apartments in the mazes and windings of which they were completely bewildered and were finally extricated, not without some difficulty".

With Joun of Etruria, and Janus of Janicula may be connoted the Ogane of Africa, whose toe, like that of Peter, was reverently kissed: that Northern Africa, Etruria, and Dodona were once peopled by a kindred race is one of the commonplaces of anthropology, and these Iberian people are, I think, traceable not only in Britain and Hibernia, but in the actual names *Berat*, *Britain*, *Aparica* (now Africa), *Barbary*, *Berber* or *Barabbra*, *Epirus*, *Hebrew*, *Culebre*, *Calabria*, and *Celtiberia*. Tacitus, who describes

---

[1] Henry Kilgour, *Notes and Queries*, 8th January and 19th February, 1876.

the ancient Britons as being dark complexioned and curly haired, adds: "that portion of Spain in front of Britain encourages the belief that the ancient Iberians had come over and colonised this district—the Gauls took possession of the adjacent coast". According to Huxley and Laing the aboriginal inhabitants of Caledonia were from—"the great Iberian family, the same stock as the Berbers of North Africa":[1] the prehistoric inhabitants of Wales similarly belonged to the Iberian stock and—"no other race of men existed in Wales until the neolithic period".[2]

In Cornwall the persisting Iberian type is popularly supposed to be the offspring of Spanish sailors wrecked at the time of the Armada, but this theory is not countenanced by anthropologists. Speaking of the short natives of the Hebridean island of Barra—a significant name—Campbell, in his *West Highland Tales*, observes: "Behind the fire sat a girl with one of these strange foreign faces which are occasionally to be seen in the Western Isles, a face which reminded me of the Nineveh sculptures, and of faces seen in St. Sebastian. Her hair was as black as night, her clear eyes glittered through the peat smoke. Her complexion was dark and her features so unlike those who sat about her, that I asked if she were a native of the island, and learned that she was a Highland girl."

Whether this Barra maiden was a persistent type of Hebrew may be questioned: she was certainly not Mongolian, the other great family whose traces still persist here. The Hebrews traditionally came from Candia, and the Candians or Cretans are universally described as diminutive and dark-haired: according to Prof. Keith the

[1] *The Prehistoric Remains of Caithness*, pp. 70, 71.
[2] Macnamara, N. C., *Origin and Character of the British People*, p. 179.

typical Bronze Age man was narrow-faced, round-headed, handsome, and about 5 feet 8 inches in height. "It is curious," he says, "that men of this type are playing leading parts in large proportion to the number living."

The antithesis to the round-headed Gael, and the oval-headed Cynbro is the square-headed Teuton, Finn, or Mongol. While the Cretan was essentially creative and artistic, we are told on the other hand that "it must always be remembered that the Phœnicians were only intermediaries and created no art of their own ".[1] The same verity is still curiously true of the modern Jew who almost invariably is an intermediary, rarely if ever a producer: neither in Caledonia, Cambria, or Hibernia does one often find a Jewish nose, and the craftsmen-artists of the primeval world were, I think, not the Jews of Tyre, but the older Jous of Candia or Crete. In the name Drew, translated to have meant *skilful*, we have apparently a true tradition of the Jous of Cornwall and the Jous of Droia, or Troy.

It is presumably the Mongolian influence in Prussia, the home of the square-headed, that justified Matthew Arnold in writing: "The universal dead-level of plainness and homeliness, the lack of all beauty and distinction in form and feature, the slowness and clumsiness of the language, the eternal beer, sausages, and bad tobacco, the blank commonness everywhere pressing at last like a weight on the spirits of the traveller in Northern Germany, and making him impatient to be gone—this is the weak side, the industry, the well-doing, the patient, steady elaboration of things, the idea of science governing all departments of

[1] Read, Sir H., *A Guide to Antiquities of Bronze Age*, p. 17.

human activity—this is the strong side; and through this side of her genius, Germany has already obtained excellent results."

The unimaginative and plodding German is the antithesis to the impressionable, poetic, and romantic Celt, as probably were the loathed Magogei to the chic Cretans whose national characteristics are commemorated in their frescoes and vases. I have already suggested that the same antipathies existed between the ugsome Mongolians and the swarthy slim Iberians of Epirus or Albania. Descendants of both Mongolians and Jous undoubtedly exist to-day in Britain, particularly in Cornwall, where Dr. Beddoe notes and comments upon the slanting Ugrian or Mongolian eye. The same authority observes that anthropologists had long been calling out for the remains of an Iberian, or pre-Celtic, language in the British Isles before their philological brethren awoke to the consciousness of their existence. "Mongolian or Ugrian types have been recognised though less distinctly; and now Ugrian grammatical forms are being dimly discerned in the Welsh and Irish languages."[1] In Ireland only two Iberian words are known to have survived, one of which, as we have seen, was *fern*, meaning *anything good*. In view of the fact that the Celtiberians were also known as Virones,[2] and as the Berones (these last named neighbouring the Pyrenees), it would seem possible that the Iberians were the Hibernians, and had originally a first-class reputation. As already noted our records state of Prydain, the son of Aedd, that before his advent there was little gentleness in Britain, and only a superiority in oppression.

It is probable that the Iberians were the original builders

[1] *Races of Britain*, p. 46.   [2] *Strabo*, III., lv., 5.

CONCLUSIONS 849

of *barrows*, and the excavators of the stupendous *burrows*, found from Burmah to Peru, and from Aparica to Barra: in which direction the Iberian culture flowed it would be premature at present to discuss, but the question will ultimately be settled by an exercise of the perfectly sound canon of etymology, that in comparing two words a and b belonging to the same language, of which a contains a lesser number of syllables, a must be taken to be a more original word unless there be evidence of contractions or other corruption. The theory of a generation ago that our innumerable British monosyllables are testimonies of phonetic decay is probably as false as many similar notions that have recently been relegated to limbo. In a paroxysm of enthusiasm for the German-made Science of Language, and for the theory that sound etymology has nothing to do with sound, one of the disciples of Max Müller has observed that unless *every letter* in a modern word can be scientifically accounted for according to rule the derivation and definition cannot be accepted. The Dictionaries now prove that spelling was a whimsical, temporary, shallow thing, and it will, I am confident, be an accepted axiom in the future that "Language begins with voice, language ends with voice". If the present book fails to add any weight to this dictum of Latham the evidence is none the less everywhere, and is merely awaiting the shaping hand of a stronger, more competent, and more influential workman than the present writer.

Whether or not the radicals I have used will prove to be chips of Iberian speech remains to be further tested, but in any case, the official contention that the language we speak to-day is, " of course, in no sense native to England but was brought thither by the German tribes who conquered the island in the fifth and sixth centuries "[1] may be confidently impugned : Prof. Smith is, however, doubtless correct in his statement that when our Anglo-Saxon ancestors came first to ravage Britain, and finally to settle there, they found the island inhabited by a people " weaker, indeed, but infinitely more civilised than themselves ".

The present essay will not have been published in vain if to any extent it discredits the dull contempt in which our traditions and ancient coinage are now held ; still less if it negatives the offensive supposition that England was " the one purely German nation which arose out of the wreck of Rome," and that practically all our English place-names are of German origin.

On re-reading my MSS. in as far as possible a detached and impartial spirit, there would appear to be much *prima facie* evidence in favour of the traditional belief that these islands once possessed a very ancient culture, and that the Kimbri, or followers of Brute, were originally pirates or adventurers who reached these shores " over the hazy sea from the summer country which is called Deffrobani, that is where Constantinoblys now stands ".[2] Constantinople—originally the Greek colony of Byzantium—is the city nearest the site of Troy ; Ægean influences have long been recognised in Britain, and the accepted theory is that these influences penetrated overland via Gaul. This supposition seems, however, to be strikingly negatived in a fact noted recently by Prof. Macalister, who, speaking of the spiral decoration found alike at Mykenae and New Grange, observes : " But spirals cannot travel through the air ; they must be depicted on some portable object in order to find their way from Orchomenos to the neighbourhood of

[1] Smith, L. P., *The English Language*, p. 1.   [2] Triad, 4.

Drogheda. The lines of the trade routes connecting these distant places ought to be peppered with objects of late Minoan Art-bearing spirals. Even a few painted potsherds would be sufficient. But there is no such thing. The media through which the spiral patterns were *ex hypothesi* carried to the north have totally disappeared."[1] We have seen a similar lack of connective evidence in the case of the British spearhead, which seemingly either evolved independently in this country, or was brought hither by sea from the Ægean.

With regard to Celtic and Ægean spiral decoration, Prof. Macalister writes: "People in the cultural stage of the builders of New Grange do not cultivate Art for Art's sake. Some simple religious or magical significance must lie hidden in these patterns. . . . Therefore, if we are to suppose that the barbarians acquired the spiral patterns from the Ægean merchants we must once more postulate the enthusiastic trading missionary who taught them how to draw spirals in the intervals of business. I, for one, cannot believe in that engaging altruist. I prefer to believe that the spirals at New Grange are not derived from the Ægean at all, but that they are an independent growth."[2]

The Trojans were proverbially a pious race, and personally I should prefer the theory of enthusiastic (sea) trading missionaries to the painfully overworked hypothesis of independent growth.

According to Mr. Donald A. Mackenzie the process of developing symbols from natural objects can be traced even in the Paleolithic Age:[3] the earliest town at Troy which

---

[1] *Proceedings of Royal Irish Academy*, xxxiv., C. 10, 11, p. 387.
[2] *Ibid.*
[3] *Myths of Crete and Pre-Hellenic Europe*, p. 235.

was built in the Neolithic Age existed on a hillock and has been likened to the ubiquitous hill fort of Caledonia; seemingly Troy was originally a Dunhill and it was not until about 2500 B.C. that the original hillock, dunhill, or Athene Hill,[1] was levelled. It is a most remarkable fact that, according to Prof. Virchow, " the few skulls which were saved out of the lower cities have this in common, that without exception they present the character of a more civilised people: all savage peculiarities in the stricter sense are entirely wanting in them ".[2] So far, then, as the testimony of anthropology carries weight, the Trojan fell from a high state of grace, and neolithic Man was quite as capable of the fair humanities as any modern Doctor of Divinity.

If, as I now suggest, the Iberians, the Hebrews, and the British or Kimbry were originally one and the same race, and if, as I further suggest, fragments of the " British " language are recoverable, it follows that the same words will unlock doors in every direction where Iberian or Kimbrian influence permeated: this in a subsequent volume I shall endeavour to show is actually the case, from Burmah to Peru.[3]

Schliemann mentions in connection with Mykenae a small stream known nowadays as the Perseia, and as Mykenae was said to have been founded by Perseus, the stream Perseia was presumably connected with the ancient pherepolis. The survival of this fairy name is the more remarkable as Mykenae itself was utterly destroyed, buried, and lost sight of, yet the title of this rivulet survived: is there any valid reason to deny a similar vitality and anti-

---

[1] *Myths of Crete and Pre-Hellenic Europe*, p. 232.   [2] *Ilios*, p. xii.
[3] There were peoples in the Caucasus known as the Britani or Burtani.

quity to the brook- and river-names of Britain? Most of these have been complacently ascribed to German settlers, others to Keltic words, but some are admittedly pre-Keltic. Amongst the group of "rare insolubles" occurs the river Kennet which flows past Abury, and may be connoted with the river Kent in the Kendal district. Apart from the Kentish Cantii Herodotus speaks of a race called Kynetes or Kynesii, both of which terms, as Sir John Rhys says, " have a look of Greek words meaning dogmen": according to Herodotus, " the Celts are outside the Pillars of Hercules and they border on the Kynetii, who dwell the farthest away towards the west of the inhabitants of Europe". Ancient writers locate the Kynetes in the west of Spain which, according to Rhys, " suggests a still more important inference—namely, that there existed in Herodotus' time a continental people of the same origin and habits as the non-Celtic aborigines of these islands".[1] *Kennet*, as we have seen, was a British word meaning Greyhound; I think the Kynetes were probably worshippers of every variety of *chien*, and that dog-headed St. Christopher, the kindly giant of Canaan, was the jackalheaded "Mercury" of the track-making merchants of Candia.[2] In Ireland there figures in the Pantheon a Caindea, whose name is understood to mean the *gentle goddess*: the fact of the dove being held in such high estimation in Candia,[3] as elsewhere, is presumptive evidence of the Candian goddess being fundamentally regarded

---

[1] *Celtic Britain*, p. 268.

[2] In a subsequent volume I shall trace the Iberian *perro* or dog to *Peru*, where the perro or dog was the supreme object of devotion.

[3] The capital of old Ceylon was Candy: I am unable to trace the origin of the port of Colombo.

as gentle, and that Candian adventurers were gentlemen. That Crete or Candia was an Idaeal, Idyllic, and an Aerial island is implied not only by its titles Idaea, Doliche, and Aeria, but also by the characteristics of its Art.

Etymology—by which I mean a Science that does not quibble at everything beyond the view of Mrs. Markham as being out of bounds—permits us to assume that the faith of the Iberii was belief in the Iberian *peyrou*, the Parthian *peri*, the British *perry*, *phairy*, or *fairy*. Anthropologists patronisingly describe the creed of primitive man as being animism by which they mean that an anima or soul was attributed to everything on earth: this may be a credulous and degraded faith, or it may be sublimated into the conception of the Egyptian philosophers of whom it has been said: "In their view the earth was a mirror of the heavens, and celestial intelligences were represented by beasts, birds, fishes, gems, and even by rocks, metals, and plants. The harmony of the spheres was answered by the music of the temples, and the world beheld nothing that was not a type of something divine."

Speaking of the fairy tales of Ireland W. B. Yeats characterises them as full of simplicity and musical occurrences: "They are," he adds, "the literature of a class for whom every incident in the old rut of birth, love, pain, and death, has cropped up unchanged for centuries; who have steeped everything in the heart *to whom everything is a symbol*". It is generally supposed that fairy tales are of a higher antiquity than cromlechs and stone avenues, and anthropologists have not hesitated to extract from them incidents of crude character as evidence of the barbarous and objectionable period in which they originated. With a curious perversity Anthropology has, however, ignored the fair humanities of phairie, while eagerly seizing upon its crudities: in view of the prophet Micah's environment there seems to me to be no justification for such prejudice, and if fairy-tale is really archaic its beauties may quite well be coeval with its horrors.

In his booklet on *Folklore* Mr. Sydney Hartland observes: " Turning from savage nations to the peasantry of civilised Europe, you will be still more astonished to learn that up to the present time the very same conditions of thought are discernible wherever they are untouched by modern education and the industrial and commercial revolution of the last hundred years. There can only be one interpretation of this. The human mind, alike in Europe and in America, in Africa and in the South Seas, works in the same way, according to the same laws." This one and only permissible theory of independent evolution is daily losing ground, and in any case it can hardly be pushed to such extremes as identity of words and place-names.

But while I am convinced that Crete was a culture-centre of immense importance, this bright and particular star, was, one must think, too small a place to account for the vast influence apparently traceable to it. Schliemann, whom nobody now ridicules, claimed to have discovered at Troy a bronze vase inscribed in Phœnicean characters with the words: " From King Chronos of Atlantis," and in a paper opened after his death he expressed his belief: " I have come to the conclusion that Atlantis was not only a great territory between America and the West Coast of Africa, but the cradle of all our civilisation as well ". The anonymous suggestion which appeared a few years ago in the columns of *The Times*, that Crete was the reality of the wonderful island "fabled" by Plato, seems to me to have nothing to support it, and I would commend to the attention of those interested the facts collected by Ignatius Donnelly in *Atlantis*, and by others elsewhere. Personally I incline to the opinion that Plato's story was well founded, and that the identities found in Peru and Mexico, Britain, the Iberian Peninsula, and Northern Africa are due to these countries, like the Isles of the Mediterranean, being situated in the full sweep of Atlantean influence.

According to Plato, the inhabitants of Atlantis (" an island situated in front of the straits which you call the columns of Hercules: the island was larger than Libya and Asia put together and was the way to other islands ") were not only highly civilised, but they "despised everything but virtue not caring for their present state of life and thinking lightly on the possession of gold and other property". It is thus quite possible that the Atlanteans and not the pious Trojans were the enthusiastic and altruistic missionaries who carried the spiral ornament to Mykenae as to New Grange. Prof. Macalister finds it difficult to believe in the existence of such a frame of mind, but it seems to accord very closely to that of the hypothetical peace-loving Aryans or " noble nations " which etymologists have already been compelled to postulate, and which my own findings both herein and elsewhere endorse: the semi-supernaturalness of the Idaens has already been noted, as likewise has that of the ancient Britons and of the modern Bretons.

In the year 1508 a French vessel met with a boat full of American Indians not far from the English coast,[1] and there is thus one historic warrant for the possibility of

[1] Baring-Gould, S., *Curious Myths*, p. 527.

very ancient maritime contact between Europe and America. The Maoris of New Zealand emigrated from Polynesia in frail canoes during the historic period, and I have little doubt that the Maoris of to-day, who tattoo themselves with spirals similar to those found upon the prehistoric monuments of Britain, were cognate with the woad-tattoed Britons, who opposed their naked bodies to the invincible legends of Cæsar. One can best account for the many and close connections between the South Sea islands and elsewhere by the supposition that some of these islands were colonised by Atlantis, Lyonesse, or whatever the traditional lost island was entitled: and as many of the maritime Atlanteans must have been at sea when the alleged catastrophe occurred, these survivors would have carried the dire news to many distant lands: whence perhaps the almost universal tradition of a Flood, and the salvation of only one boat load of people.

It has been said that the chief thing which makes Japan so fascinating a land to dwell in is the consciousness that you are there living in an atmosphere of universal kindliness and courtesy. There are still to-day races in Polynesia who display the same kindly and almost angelic dispositions,[1] whence there is nothing ridiculous in the

[1] The inhabitants of Tukopia are described as: "Tall, light-coloured men with thick manes of long, golden hair . . . wonderful giants, with soft dark eyes, kind smiles, and child-like countenances". The surroundings of the villages of this Polynesian island were like well-tended parks, all brushwood having been carefully removed. "They presented sights so different in blissful simplicity from what were to be seen in Melanesia, they all looked so happy, gay, and alluring, that it hardly needed the invitations of the kind people, without weapons or suspicion, and with wreaths of sweet-scented flowers round their heads and bodies, to incline us to stay." This exquisite morsel of Arcadia was, like other parts of pure

supposition that Peru, whose natives claimed to be children of the Sun, was associated with peyrou, the Iberian for phairy, or that the original Angles were deemed to be angels, and England or Inghilterra their country.

One of the most noted beliefs of all races, whether civilised or savage, is the erstwhile existence of a Golden Age when all men were well happified, and if existence to primitive man was merely the hideous and protracted nightmare which anthropologists assume, it is difficult to see at what period of his upward climb this curiously idyllic story came into existence: it would be simpler to assume that the tradition had some foundation in fact, and was not merely the frenzied invention of a dreamer. No race possesses more beautiful traditions of the Adamic Age than the British, and I have little doubt that the four quarters of the Holy Rood or Wheel are connected with the four fabulous Cities of Enchantment which figure in Keltic imagination. According to Irish MSS. the Tuatha de Danaan, or Tribe of the Children of Don, after suffering a terrible defeat at the hands of the Fomorians, quitted Ireland, returned to Thebes, and gave themselves up to the study of Magic: leaving Greece they next went to Denmark (named after them) where they founded four great schools of diabolical learning—the Four Cities of Keltic imagination. It would thus seem possible that the Children of Don were the fabricators of the Eden, or Adam, tradition, and that they may be connoted with the Danoi under which name Homer habitually refers to the Greeks: with these Danoi or Danaia, Dr. Latham connotes the

Polynesia, governed by a dynasty of hereditary chieftains, who were looked up to with the greatest respect, and to whom honours were paid almost as to demi-gods.—*Cf.* Sir Harry Johnston in *The Westminster Gazette.*

Hebrew tribe of Dan, supposing that both these peoples traced their origin to the same culture-hero.[1] That Gardens of Eden were frequent in these islands has been evidenced in a preceding chapter, and in Asia the custom of constructing Edens or Terrestrial Paradises was equally prevalent: Maundeville and other travellers have left detailed accounts of these *abris,* all of which seem to have been constructed more or less to the standard design of the Garden of Eden, watered by four rivers, with a Tree or Fountain in the midst.

It is supposed that the celebrated Epistle of Prester John was a malicious antepapal concoction of the Gnostic Troubadours, or Servants of Love: these were certainly the shuttles that disseminated it over Europe. I have elsewhere endeavoured to show the rôle played in mediæval Europe by the Troubadours and Minnesingers (*Love Singers*), and the subject might be infinitely extended. The derivation of *trouvere,* or *troubadour,* from *trouver* to find, is probably too superficial, and if the matter were more fully investigated it is probable that, like the Merry Andrew, these mystic singers and philanderers originated from some Troy or Ancient Troy. Whether the *drui* or *druids* are similarly traceable to the same root is debatable, but that the bards of Britain were depositaries and disseminators of the Gnosis I do not doubt: the evidence on that point is not only the testimony of outsiders, but it is inherent in the literature itself, and whether this literature was committed to writing in the sixth, twelfth, or

[1] "I think that the Eponymus of the Argive Danaia was no other than that of the Israelite Tribe of Dan; only we are so used to confine ourselves to the soil of Palestine in our consideration of the Israelites that we treat them as if they were adscriptigleboe, and ignore the share they may have taken in the history of the world."—*Ethnology of Europe,* p. 137.

eighteenth century is immaterial. There are in existence many unquestionably prehistoric tales and ideas which have been handed down verbally, and committed to writing for the first time only within the past few years: many more are living *viva voce*, and are not yet registered. The Welsh bards, like the bards of other races, were a recognised class, graduates in a particular Art, and were strictly and definitely trained in the traditional lore of their profession. This hereditary order which was known to the Romans certainly as early as 200 B.C., like the bards of other countries, almost unquestionably transmitted an enormous literature solely by word of mouth.[1] If the feats of even the modern human memory were not well vouched for they would not be credited: in the past, the Zend Avesta, the Kalevala, the Popul Vuh, Homer, much of the Old Testament, and in fact all very ancient literature has come down to us simply by memory alone.

To an inquirer such as myself, incompetent to criticise Welsh literature, yet hesitating to accept the once current theories of fabrication, forgery, and deception, it is peculiarly gratifying to find so distinguished a scholar as Sir John Morris-Jones vindicating at any rate some portion of the suspect literature. In his study *Taliesin*, Sir John grinds detractors past and present into as fine and small a powder as that to which Spedding imperturbably reduced the flashy superficialities of Macaulay,[2] and I confess it has caused me most agreeable emotions to find Sir John alluding to a certain truculent D.Litt. as " that naïve type of mind which naturally assumes that what it does not

---

[1] Cæsar says it took twenty years' study to acquire: other writers say the Druids taught 20,000 verses.

[2] *Cf. Evenings with a Reviewer.*

understand is mere silliness ":[1] it is even more stimulating to witness the iconoclastic and dogmatic Nash rolled in the dust for his "unparalleled impudence" in laying down the law of antiquity in language.

Among the fragments of Welsh poetry occurs the claim " Bardism or Druidism originated in Britain—pure Bardism was never well understood in other countries—of whatever country they might be, they are entitled Bards according to the rights and institutes of the Bards of the Island of Britain."[2] Before superciliously dismissing the high claims of British Bardism it would be well to consider not only the recent findings of Prof. Sir John Morris-Jones, but to bear steadily in mind the following points: (1) The cultured shape of the extraordinarily ancient British skull: (2) Avebury, the strangest megalithic monument in the world : (3) Stonehenge, a unique and most developed form of stone circle: (4) that England was the principal home of stone circles: (5) that England not only possessed the greatest earth-pyramid in the world, but that Britain was peculiarly the home of the barrow, and that there is no word *barrow* in either Greek or Latin, thus seeming to have been essentially British: (6) that in Cæsar's time the youth of the Continent were sent to Britain to study the Druidic philosophy which was believed to have originated there: (7) the remarkable character of the English coinage which dates back admittedly to 200 B.C., and for aught one knows much earlier: (8) that the art of enamelling on bronze probably originated in Britain, and the craft of spear-making evolved there.

In *Earthwork of England* Mr. Allcroft observes: " Of

[1] *Y Cymmroder*, xxiii.
[2] *Cf.* Davies, E., *Celtic Researches*, p. 183.

all the many thousands of earth-works of various kinds to be found in England, those about which anything is known are very few, those of which there remains nothing more to be known scarcely exist. Each individual example is in itself a new problem in history, chronology, ethnology, and anthropology; within every one lie the hidden possibilities of a revolution in knowledge. We are proud of a history of nearly twenty centuries: we have the materials for a history which goes back beyond that time to centuries as yet undated. The testimony of records carries the tale back to a certain point: beyond that point is only the testimony of archæology, and of all the manifold branches of archæology none is so practicable, so promising, yet so little explored, as that which is concerned with earthworks. Within them lie hidden all the secrets of time before history begins, and by their means only can that history be put into writing: they are the back numbers of the island's story, as yet unread, much less indexed."

The prehistoric building here illustrated might be any age: it is standing to-day in a remote corner of Britain, and, so far as I am able to trace, has been hitherto uncharted and unrecognised. Whether it were a temple or the compound of a chieftain, the authorities to whom it has been referred are unable to say: my brother, to whom its discovery was due, is of the opinion that it was a temple, and on a subsequent occasion we hope—after digging—to publish a more detailed account of it, merely now noting it as an example of the innumerable objects of interest which exist in this country at present unrecognised, unconsidered, and unvalued.

Evidence has been forthcoming that a cave in Oban was occupied by human beings, at an epoch when the sea was 30 feet higher than its present level, and it is now generally admitted that humanity existed in these islands

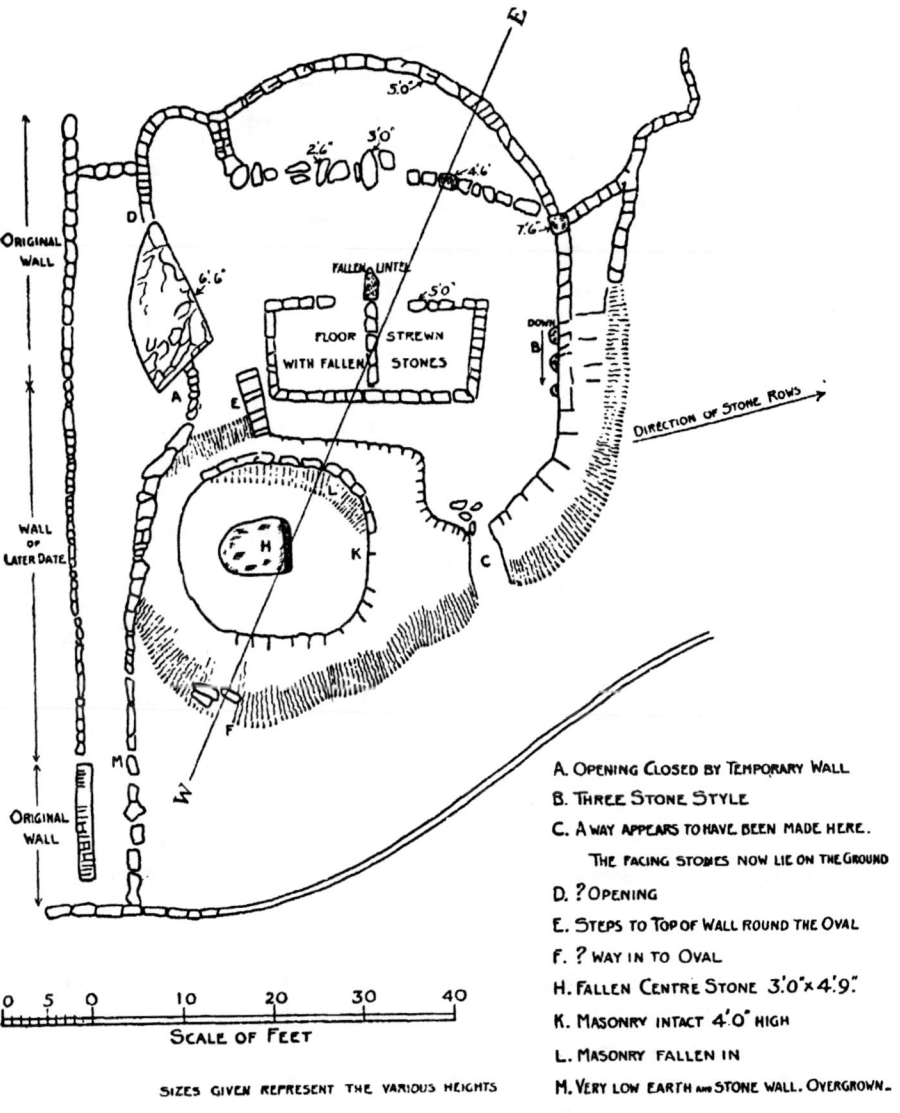

Fig. 507.—Ground plan of a hitherto Uncharted English Edifice.

A. Opening closed by Temporary Wall.
B. Three Stone Style.
C. A way appears to have been made here. The facing stones now lie on the ground.
D. ? Opening
E. Steps to Top of Wall round the Oval
F. ? Way in to Oval
H. Fallen Centre Stone 3′0″ × 4′9″.
K. Masonry intact 4′0″ high
L. Masonry fallen in
M. Very low earth and Stone Wall. Overgrown.

Sizes given represent the various heights

prior to the Glacial Period. Archæology of the future will provide strong wine of astonishment to her followers: she will prove beyond question that mythology is not merely fossil philosophy, but is likewise to a large extent fossil history, and that the records may be pieced together from the traditionary blissful Tertiary Period to that time and onwards when a perilous torrent-fire struck the earth, resulting in sequent horrors, and the slow replenishment of the world.[1] She will prove, I think, further that the land

[1] In *Ragnarok* Donnelly argues that the glacial epoch and the "drift" were due to the earth's collision with one of the many million comets which are careering through the solar universe. It would certainly appear probable that such abnormous masses of ice as are evidenced by the Glacial Period, must have been the result of abnormous heat first sucking up the lakes and rivers, and then returning them in the form of clouds, rain, and snow. Practically all mythologies contain an account of some unparalleled catastrophe, and in the opinion of Donnelly the widespread story of man's progenitors emerging from a cave is based upon the literal probability of man—if he survived at all—surviving in caverns. Among the numerous myths which Donnelly cites in support of his ingenious theory is the following British one: "The profligacy of mankind had provoked the great Supreme to send a pestilential wind upon the earth. A pure poison descended, every blast was death. At this time the patriarch, distinguished for his integrity, was shut up, together with his select company, in the inclosure with the strong door (the cave?). Here the just ones were safe from injury. Presently a tempest of fire arose. It split the earth asunder to the great deep. The lake Llion burst its bounds, and the waves of the sea lifted themselves on high around the borders of Britain, the rain poured down from heaven, and the waters covered the earth." Donnelly believes that comets were the origin of the world-wide fiery-dragon myth. In support of this theory he might have instanced the following Scotch legend: "There lived once upon a time in Sutherland a great dragon, very fierce and strong. It was this dragon that burnt all the fir woods in Ross, Sutherland, and the Reay country, of which the remains charred, blackened, and half-decayed may be found in every moss. Magnificent forests they must have been, but the dragon set fire to them with his fiery breath and rolled over the whole land. Men fled from before his face and women fainted when his shadow crossed the sky-line. He made the whole land desert."—(Henderson, Dr. G. H., Intro. to *The Celtic Dragon Myth*, p. xxii.) The burnt forests found in Ireland were noted on p. 21.

now called England possesses a documentary record, and an intellectual ancestry which is practically beyond computation, and if History shies at her findings she will instance Brandon as a typical example of continuous occupation and unbroken sequence from the Stone Age to to-day. Further, she will in all probability prove that in either Crete or England the main doctrines of Christianity were practically indigenous. The version of Christianity which returned to us about 1500 years ago is now generally attributed to the mystic Therapeuts of Egypt: from the time it was officially adopted by the temporal powers the materialising process seems almost steadily to have progressed, notwithstanding the allegorising teaching of the Troubadours and kindred Gnostics who claimed really to know.[1] Happily petrifaction is a preservative, and it

---

[1] All these "heretics" claimed to be the real possessors of the true Christian doctrine, and they charged Rome with being *Mère sotte*, an ignorant and blatant usurper: the incessant and insidious conflict which was carried on between Gnosticism and Rome has been considered in *A New Light on the Renaissance*, also in *The Lost Language of Symbolism*, and with the exception of a few surface errors there is little in those volumes which I should now rewrite. The murderous campaign which was launched against the Albigenses not only failed seemingly to stamp them out, but if Baring-Gould's opinion is valid the descendants of the Albigenses are even to-day not extinct. In *Cliff Castles* he writes as follows: "There was a curious statement made in a work by E. Bosc and L. Bonnemere in 1882, which if true would show that a lingering paganism is to be found among these people. It is to this effect: 'What is unknown to most is that at the present day there exist adepts of the worship (of the Celts) as practised before the Roman invasion, with the sole exception of human sacrifices, which they have been forcibly obliged to renounce. They are to be found on the two banks of the Loire, on the confines of the departments of Allier and Saone-et-Loire, where they are still tolerably numerous, especially in the latter department. They are designated in the country as Les Blancs, because that in their ceremonies they cover their heads with a white hood,

may be doubted whether when Comparative Archæology has finished her researches any of the prehistoric Christianity preached by the Celtic Christies will prove actually lost, and whether the supposedly impassable gulf of ages which separates the earliest literature from the testimony of the Stones may not practically be bridged. That our popular customs were the detrita of dramatised mythology, and that many of these customs evidence an astonishing beauty of imagination and depth of thought, will not be questioned except by those unfamiliar with English folklore. In many cases the quaint customs which still linger in the countryside, and the cults which underlie them are, as Dr. Rendel Harris has recently observed, those of misunderstood rituals and lost divinities, and thus embalmed like flies in the amber of unchanging habit turn out to be the very earliest beliefs and the most primitive religious acts of the human race: " Every surviving fragment of

and their priests are vested like the Druids in a long robe of the same colour. They surround their proceedings with profound mystery; their gatherings take place at night in the heart of large forests, about an old oak, and as they are dispersed through the country over a great extent of land, they have to start for the assembly from different points at close of day so as to be able to reach home again before daybreak. They have four meetings in the year, but one, the most solemn, is held near the town of La Clayette under the presidence of the high priest. Those who come from the greatest distance do not reach their homes till the second night, and their absence during the intervening day alone reveals to the neighbours that they have attended an assembly of the Whites. Their priests are known, and are vulgarly designated as the bishops or archbishops of the Whites; they are actually druids or archdruids. . . . We have been able to verify these interesting facts brought to our notice by M. Parent, and our personal investigations into the matter enable us to affirm the exactitude of what has been advanced.' If there be any truth in this strange story we are much more disposed to consider the Whites as relics of a Manichæan or Albigensian sect than as a survival of Druidism." P. 46.

such a ritual is as valuable to us as a page of an early Gospel which time has blurred or whose first hand has been overwritten ".[1]

Few nowadays have any sympathy with the theories which a generation ago autocratically ascribed Myth to a Disease of Language ; still less is it possible to accept the more modern supposition that Mythology is merely the gross growth of disgusting savagery! There is more truth in Bacon's dictum that in the first ages when such inventions and conclusions of the human reason as are now trite and common were new, and little known, all things abounded with fables, parables, similes, comparisons, and illusions which were not intended to conceal, but to inform and teach. Research tends more and more to justify Bacon in his penetrating judgment: " And this principally raises my esteem of these fables, which I receive not as the product of the age or invention of the poets, but as sacred relics, gentle whispers, and the breath of better times, that from the traditions of more ancient nations came at length into the flutes and trumpets of the Greeks ". Whence these sacred relics came, whether from Atlantis, Crete, or Britain,[2] we are not yet in a position to assert, but eventually the Comparative Method will decide this point. Dr.

---

[1] *Origin and Meaning of Apple Cults.*

[2] " Lords and Commons of England—Consider what nation whereof ye are, and whereof ye are the Governors: a nation not slow and dull, but of a quick, ingenious and piercing spirit; acute to invent, subtle and sinewy to discourse, not beneath the reach of any point the highest that human capacity can soar to. Therefore, the studies of learning in her deepest sciences have been so ancient and so eminent among us, that writers of good antiquity and able judgment have been persuaded that the School of Pythagoras, and the Persian Wisdom, took beginning from the old philosophy of this Island, Britain.'—Milton.

Rendel Harris who has, to quote his own words, "audaciously affirmed that Apollo was only our *apple* in disguise,"[1] further concludes: "It is tolerably certain that Apollo in the Greek religion is a migration from the more northerly regions and his mythical home is somewhere at the back of the north wind".[2] While I am in sympathy with many of Dr. Harris' findings, it is, however, difficult to accept his conclusions that the Olympian divinities were merely "personifications of, or projections from the vegetable word": the greater probability seems to me that the Apple was named after Apollo rather than Apollo from the Apple: similarly the mandrake was in greater likelihood an emblem of Venus rather than Aphrodite a projection from the Mandrake. The Venus of the Gael was Bride or Brigit, "The Presiding Care," who was represented with a brat in her arms: there is an old Spanish proverb to the effect that "An ounce of Mother is worth a ton of Priest"; nowhere was Woman more devoutly idealised than among the Celts, and it is more probable that the conception of an immaculate Great Mother originated somewhere in Europe rather than in the sensuous and woman-degrading East. Of the legends of Ireland Mr. Westropp has recently observed: "When we have removed the strata of euhemerist fiction and rubbish from the ruin, the foundations and beautiful fragments of the once noble fane of Irish mythology will stand clear to the sun":[3] "Whether," said Squire, "the great edifice of

---

[1] In *The Lost Language of Symbolism* I anticipated this opinion.

[2] Writing of the Pied Piper story Mr. Ernest Rhys observes: "There is every reason to believe that Hamelin was as near home as Newton, Isle of Wight, and that the Weser, deep and wide, was the Solent".—Preamble to *Fairy Gold* (Ev. Library).

[3] *Proc. of Royal Irish Academy*, xxxiv., C., No. 8, p. 140.

Celtic mythology will ever be wholly restored one can at present only speculate. Its colossal fragments are perhaps too deeply buried and too widely scattered. But even as it stands ruined it is a mighty quarry from which poets yet unborn will hew spiritual marble for houses not made with hands."

FINIS

British. From Akerman.

APPENDIX A.

IRELAND AND PHŒNICIA.

The following extract is taken from *Britain and the Gael: or Notices of Old and Successive Races; but with special reference to the Ancient Men of Britain and its Isles.*—Wm. Beal, London, 1860.

PLAUTUS, a dramatic writer, and one of the great poets of antiquity, who lived from one to two centuries before the Christian era; was mentioned in the last section. In his Pænulus, is the tale of some young persons said to have been stolen from Carthage, by pirates, taken to Calydonia, and there sold; one of these was Agorastocles, a young man; the others were two daughters of Hanno, and Giddeneme, their nurse. Hanno, after long search, discovered the place where his daughters were concealed, and by the help of servants who understood the Punic language, rescued his children from captivity. Plautus gives the supposed appeal of Hanno, to the gods of the country for help, and his conversations with servants in the Punic language, are accompanied with a Latin translation. The Punic, as a language, is lost, and those long noticed, but strange lines had long defied the skill of learned men. But at length, by attending to their vocal formation (and all language, Wills states, is addressed to the ear). It was discovered by O'Neachtan, or some Irish scholar, that they were resolvable into words, which exhibited but slight differences from the language of Keltic Ireland. The words were put into syllables, then translated by several persons, and these translations not only accorded with the drama, but also, with the Plautine Latin version. The lines were put to the test of more rigid examination, placed in the hands of different persons one of whom was Dr. Percy, bishop of Dromore. They were also given to different Irish scholars for translation, to persons who had no correspondence with each other on this subject, nor knew the principal object in view; and by the whole the same meaning was given.

Bohn's edition, by H. T. Riley, B.A., is before the writer; but from the edition used by the late Sir W. Betham, some few lines from Plautus, with the Gaelic or Irish underneath, are given, and the eye will at once perceive how closely the one resembles the other. Milphio, the servant of Agorastocles, addressed Hanno and his servants in Punic, and asked them "of what country aré you, or from what city?"

The following is the reply, and the supposed appeal of Hanno to the god, or gods of the country:—

Plautus. Hanno Muthumballe bi Chaedreanech.
Irish. Hanno Muthumbal bi Chathar dreannad.
English. I am Hanno Muthumbal dwelling at Carthage.

Plautus. Nyth al O Nim ua-lonuth sicorathissi me com syth.
Irish. N'iaith all O Nimh uath-lonnaithe socruidhse me comsith.
English. Omnipotent much dreaded Deity of this country, assuage my troubled mind.

Plautus. Chim lach chumyth mum ys tyal mycthi barii im schi.
Irish. Chimi lach chuinigh muini is toil miocht beiridh iar mo scith.
English. Thou the support of feeble captives, being now exhausted with fatigue, of thy free will guide me to my children.

Plautus. Lipho can ethyth by mithii ad ædan binuthi.
Irish. Liomtha can ati bi mitche ad eadan beannaithe.
English. O let my prayers be perfectly acceptable in thy sight.

Plautus. Byr nar ob syllo homal O Nim! Ubymis isyrthoho.
Irish. Bior nar ob siladh umhal O Nimh! ibhim A frotha.
English. An inexhaustible fountain to the humble; O Deity! Let me drink of its streams.

Plautus. Byth lym mo thym noctothii nel ech an ti daisc machon.
Irish. Beith liom mo thime noctaithe, neil ach tanti daisic mac coinne.
English. Forsake me not! my earnest desire is now disclosed, which is only that of recovering my daughters.

Plautus. Uesptis Aod eanec Lic Tor bo desiughim lim Nim co lus.
Irish. Is bidis Aodh eineac Lic Tor bo desiussum le mo Nimh co lus.
English. And grateful Fires on Stone Towers will I ordain to blaze to Heaven.

Plautus. Gan ebel Balsameni ar a san.
Irish. Guna bil Bal-samen ar a san.
English. O that the good Bal-samhen (*i.e.* Beal the sun) may favour them. Act v. scene 1 and 2.

This alleged work of Plautus, and these strange lines, have long been before the world, and under the notice of men of letters. Is there any reason to doubt whether it is genuine? If not, can it be supposed that the writer purposely placed some strange jargon before his readers to bewilder them ! and if so, by what singular hazzard should it so closely resemble the language of the Gael. Plautus avers, that Milphio addressed the strangers (Hanno and servants), in Punic, and declared to Agorastocles, his master, that "no Punic or Carthaginian man speaks Punic better than I". Unless these statements can be proved to be worthless, will they not as connecting links appear to say, probably the Gaels of Britain, and the Punic people of Carthage, were branches of the old and once celebrated race, known as Phenicians?

APPENDIX B.

PERRY-DANCERS AND PERRY STONES.

ON page 312 I stated that in Kent the light cloudlets of a summer day were known as "Perry-dancers": as I am unable to trace any printed authority for this statement it is possible that it was a mis-remembrance of the following passage from Ritson's "Dissertation on Fairies," prefacing *English Folklore and Legends*, London, 1890: "Le Grand is of opinion that what is called Fairy comes to us from the Orientals, and that it is their genies which have produced our fairies . . . whether this be so or not, it is certain that we call the auroræ boreales, or active clouds in the night, perry-dancers."

In connection with my suggestion that Stonehengles, now Stonehenge, of which the outer circle consists of thirty stones, meant *Stone Angels*, may be considered the repeated statements of Pausanias that the oldest gods of all were rude stones in the temple, or the temple precincts. In Achaean *Pharae* he found some thirty squared stones *named each after a god:* obviously these were phairy or peri stones, and the chief stone presumably stood for the *pherepolis.*

That *ange* or *inge* varied into *ink* is implied not only by *Ink*pen Beacon figuring in old records as *Inge*penne and *Hinge*pene, but also by Ritson's statement : "In days of yore, when the church at *Ink-berrow* was taken down and rebuilt upon a new site, the fairies, *whose haunt was near the latter place*, took offence at the change". The following passage quoted by Keightley from Aubrey's *Natural History of Surrey* is of interest apart from the significant names : " In the vestry of Frensham Church, in Surrey, on the north side of the chancel is an extraordinary great kettle or cauldron, which the inhabitants say, by tradition, was brought hither by the fairies, time out of mind, from Borough-hill about a mile hence. To this place, if anyone went to borrow a yoke of oxen, money, etc., he might have it for a year or longer, so he kept his word to return it. There is a cave where some have fancied to hear music. In this Borough-hill is a great stone lying along of the length of about 6 feet. They went to this stone and knocked at it, and declared what they would borrow, and when they would repay, and a voice would answer when they should come, and that they should find what they desired to borrow at that stone. This cauldron, with the trivet, was borrowed here, after the manner aforesaid, and not returned according to promise ; and though the cauldron was afterwards carried to the stone, it could not be received, and ever since that time no borrowing there."

APPENDIX C.

BRITISH SYMBOLS.

IN *Wookey Hole* Mr. H. E. Balch quotes the following important passage from Gildas : "A blind people [the Britons], they paid divine honour to the mountains, wells, and streams. Their altars were pillars of stone inscribed with emblems of the sun and moon, or of a beast or bird *which symbolised some force of nature*". This passage justifies the supposition that the inscribed "barnacles," elephants. etc., were symbolic, and supports the contention that a people using such subtleties were far from "blind". The Museum at Glastonbury contains a bronze ring about 3 inches in diameter, in the form of a serpent with its tail in its mouth. Obviously this object, which was found at Stanton Drew, *i.e., the stone town of the Druids*, was symbolic, probably, of the Eternal Wisdom.

APPENDIX D.

GLASTONBURY.

In view of the fact that Halifax claimed to possess the Holy Face of St. John, and that four roads centred there in the form of a cross at the chapel of St. John, it is interesting to note that the four cross-roads of Glastonbury are similarly associated with St. John. In the words of a local guidebook, " From the Tor, a walk will bring you to Weary-All Hill to view the town, and it is curious to note that from this hill it seems to be laid out as a perfect cross, St. John's Church being the central point ".

The probability is that there was some connection between the St. John of modern Glastonbury and the Fairy King Gwyn who was exorcised from the neighbouring Tor by a certain St. Collen.

APPENDIX E.

THE DRUIDS AND CRETE.

Since the preceding pages were in the press I have come into the possession of *La Religion des Gaulois* by Jacques Martin (Paris, 1727). This standard writer favours the idea that *druid* is derived from the Celtic *deru*, meaning an oak, but he also makes a remarkable statement to the following effect : " If the opinion of P. Pezron was well founded one should also say that certain people of Crete whom one called *Druites*, because their country was full of oaks, made a trade of magic and enchantment, which is far removed from the truth and perhaps also from good sense " (vol. i., p. 176). In the same volume (pp. 406-7) Martin illustrates a Gaulish god whose name Dolichenius is curiously suggestive of Dalgeon, Telchin, Talgean, and Telchinea.

L'ENVOI.

Now if any brother or well-wisher shall conscientiously doubt or be dissatisfied, touching any particular point contained in this treatise, because of my speaking to many things in a little room : and if he or they shall be serious in so doing, and will befriend me so far, and do me that courtesy, to send to me before they condemn me, and let me know their scruples in a few words of writing, I shall look upon myself obliged both in affection and reason, to endeavour to give them full satisfaction.

H. B.

OVERBYE,
  CHURCH COBHAM,
    SURREY.

INDEX

Abar, 325
Abaris, 325, 330, 377
Abb, St., 617
Abbey, 515
Abchurch, 513, 518
Abdera, 296
Abdy, 526
Aber, 310
Aber! 310, 325
Aber, Loch, 670, 749
Aberdeen, 749
Aberfield, 664
Aberystwyth, 194
Abhras, 325
Abonde, 165, 216
— La Dame, 557
Abra, 328
Abracadabra, 325
Abraham, 227
Abraham, 716
Abri, 289
Abroad, 369
Abundance, 216
Abundia, 165
Abyss, 224
Ac, 48
Ache, 200
Achil, 280
Achill, 82
Achilles, 82
Acorn, 227
Ada, 455, 742
Ada, 753
Adad, 508
Adam, 745, 754
Adam and Eve, 495, 501, 589
Adam Cædmon, 110
Adam's Dances, 589
— Graves, 746
— Peak, 546
Addington, 750. 755, 785, 813
Addy, 509
Adelphi, 365
Adisham, 560
Adkin, 509
Adon, 712
Adonai, 712
Adonis, 46, 112, 153, 605, 712
Aedd, K., 309, 749
Aeddon, 749
Aeddons, The, 750
Ægean influences, 850
— The, 81, 93
Ægeon, 402
Ægina, 399

Aeithon, R., 743
Aeon, 203, 652
Aeons, 204
Aeria, 76
Africa, 375
Agatha, 719
— St., 253
Agland Moor, 799
Agglestone, 280
Agnes, St., 591
Agnes, St., Well, 732
— the Clear, 721
Agni, 591, 719
Ague, 200
Aidan, St., 742, 751
Aidon Moor, 732
Aine, 288, 368, 544, 724
Aion, 321
Aitkin, 509
Akeman, St., 38, 200
Alas! 412
Alava, 322
Alban, 251
Alban, St., 129
Albani! 125
Albania, 84, 86, 112, 261
Albano, 89, 112
Albans. St., 107, 208, 268, 523, 791
Albanus, R., 89
Albany, The, 162
Alberic, 342
Alberich, 510
Albi, 377
Albigenses, 865
Albine, St., 148
Albinia, R., 97
Albinus, 321
Albion, 124
Albion, Prince, 162, 317
Albiorix, 301
Albon, 247
Al Borak, 347, 468
Albs, 342
Albury, 342
Alcmena, 140, 200
Alcantara, 290
Alef, 240
Alexander, 727
Alf, 559
Alfred, 153
Alibone, 131
Alipius, St., 321
Allah, 581
Allan apples, 696
— St. 696

Allantide, 698
Allan Water, 103
Allen, 104
Allen, St., 132
All Hallows, 244, 288
All-Heal, 181, 681
Allington, 290
"All is one," 133
Allistone, 318
Alma, 136
Alma Mater, 258
Alma Mater Cantabrigia, 167
Almaquah, 136
Almo R., 136
Almond, R., 137
Aln, R., 417
Alne, R., 103, 697
Alnwick, 417
Aloft, 165
Alone, R., 103, 417
Alp, 127
Alpha, 152, 363, 653
Alphabet, 12, 13
— Bardic, 14
— Celtiberian, 14
Alphage, St., 154
Alpha Place, 288
Alph, R., 791
Alpheus, 288
Alphey, 154
Alphian Rock, 153, 548
Alphin, 284
Alphington, 548
Aluph, 165
Alva, Lady, 153
Alvastone, 318
Alvechurch, 524
Alvescott, 153
Amber, 565
— R., 569
— Stone, 566
Amberstone, 568
Amberwood, etc., 569
Ambresbury, 554, 569
Ambrose, St., 565
Ambrosden, 569
Ambrosia, 567, 688
Ambrosius aurelius, 565
Amergin, 326, 327, 665
Amicable, 249
Amor, 225, 287
Amoretti, 381-3
Amour, 604
Ana, 282, 288
Ancaster, 444

878 ARCHAIC ENGLAND

Anchetil, 557
Anchor, 496
Ancient One, 577
Anderida, 797
Andrew, 117, 122
Andrew, St., 117, 163, 319, 443, 471, 780
Andrews, St., 160
Androgynous, 122
Ange, 217, 556
Angel, 305
Angel Christopher, 262
Angel Inn, 588
— The, 667, 685
Angel, 552
Angels, 175
Angle, 552, 558, 792
Angle, 556
Anglesea, 492, 560
Anglo-Saxon, 60
Anglo-Saxons, 22, 85, 107
Angus Og, 661
Angus, 266
Angus Mac Oge, 397
Anlaf, St., 154
Anne, St., 722, 811, 828
Annesbury, 565
Annis, Dame, 717
— the clear, 721
Anses, 473
Antiquity of European habitation,
Antlers, 257
Antony, St., 242
Antre, 797
Antrim, 845
Anu, 197, 722
— Paps of, 717
Anubis, 111
Any, 724
Apep, 836
Apex, 292
Apheia, 426, 532
Apsley, 529
Apt, 526
Apollo, 71, 104, 134, 242, 320, 324, 508 562, 867
Apollo, 673
Apor, Loch, 749
Appear, 367
Apple, 674, 742
Apple, 674, 867
Apple of Adam, 754
— village, 678
Appleby, 674
Appledore, 675
Appledurwell, 675
Apples, Three, 181
Appleton, 675
Archdruid of Tara, 563
Archery, 508
Arethusa, 398
Argonauts, 84
Arianrod, 438
Ark, 56, 158, 450, 653
Arrow, 325
Arrow-Elf, 306
Artemis, 258, 724
Arthur, K., 62, 798
Aryans, 10, 168
Asch, 841

Ash, 841
Ass, 114, 212
Astarte, 646
Astronomy, 167
— Druidic, 804
Aten, 743
Athenæum, 742
Athene, 323, 461, 584, 742, 819
Athens, 322
Atlantis, 19, 855
Attire, 100
Aubers Ridge, 289
Auborn, R., 664
Aubrey Walk, 289, 439
Auburn, 507, 572
Aubury, 335
Aught, 655
Aulph, 165
Aumbrey, 569
Aunt, 597
Aunt Judy, 225
— Mary, 220
— Mary's Tree, 597
Austerfield, 645
Aust on Severn, 645
Austreclive, 645
Alvington, 349
Avagddu, 158
Avalon, 289, 682
Avebury, 27, 335, 351, 368, 475, 498, 518, 808
Avebury, 403
Averroes, 378
Avery, 601
Avereberie, 342
Avon, 425
— R., 828
"Awd Goggie," 189
Axe, 643
Aylesbury, 481
Aylesford, 480, 481
Ayliffe, 162

BABCHILD, 356
Babe, 653
Babes of wax, 788
Babette, 356
Babs, 356
— Cairn, 589
Baccho, St., 240
Bacchus, 240
Bach Camp, 246
Backbone, 254
Bacon, 240
Bacon, 246
Bacton, 755
bad, 372
Badcock, 195
Bagden, 232
Baggy Point, 238
Bagnigge, R., 722
— Wells, 618
Bagshaw, 448, 728
Bain, R., 137
bairn, 325
bake, 245
Balder, 71, 76, 473, 841
Bald one, 640
Baldwin, 154
Ball, 182

Balor, 192, 841
Balls, Three, 181
Bana, R., 137
Banac, R., 137
Bancroft, 138
Bandog, 112
Bandon, R., 137
Banney, R., 137
Bannockburn, 137
Banon, R., 137
Banstead, 445
Banwell, 445
Bara, Feast of, 320
Baranton, 676
Barbara, 329, 473
Barbara, 353
Barbara, St., 354
Barbarie, The Town of, 353
barbaroi, 369
barbes, 377
Barbe, St., 377
Barbury, 353
Bardic Triads, 177, 181, 184, 185
Bardism, 860
Bardon, 350
Barea, 329
Bargeist, 346
Barle, R., 348
Barlow, 678, 714
Bark, R., 348
Barnabas, St., 553
Barnabas, 507
Barnacles, 346
Barnebas, 509
Barneby Bright, 507
Barnwell, 572
Baroc, 468
baron, 319
Baron's Cave, 799
Barra, I., 661, 846
Barri, I., 467
Barrow, R., 510
barrow, 319
Barrows, 333
Barry, 329
Barry, 508
Barry, I., 348
— The, 749
Bashan, 194
Basilica Ulpia, 296
Basinghall, 511
Basques, 648
Battersea, 464, 669
Baucis, 227, 291
Beads, 82, 579
Beaker, 302
Beane R., 110, 137
Bean-setting dance, 539
Bear, 72
Beard, 373
Beare, Old Woman of, 757
Beccles, 299
Beckjay, 282
Becky, R., 246
Bee, 46
Beech, 387, 569
Beeg, R., 246
Beelzebub, 222
Beer Head, 349
Bees, 567

INDEX 879

Bega, St., 238
Bekesbourne, 670
Bel, 46, 841
bel, 248
Belerium, 193
Belgrave, 347
Beli, 841
Belin, 241
Belindi, 241
Bell, 445, 781
— Giant, 347
Belleros, 193
Bellingham, 749
Bellister, 721
Bellona, 647
Bel's Fires, 612
Ben, R., 137
Beneficia R., 110
Beltan, 730
Beltane, 169
Beltan fires, 611
Berat, 460, 467
Berbers, 205, 375, 846
Berberis, 385
Berea, 341
Bergyon, Giant, 331
Berith, 460
Berkeley, 666
Berkhampstead, 666
Berkshire, 664
Berkswell, 666
Berne, 329
Bernesbeg, 507
Beroë, 460, 484
Berrens, 761
Berries, Three, 181
Berry, 345
Bertha, 362
Bertinny, 334
Bertram, 507
Bewl Bri, 350
Beyrout, 460
Beyrut, 134
Bickley, 448
Biddenden, 589
— Maids, 371
Biddy, 372
Bifrons, 670
big, 238
Bigbury, 238
Bigha, 238
Bigness, 238
Billing-, 658, 668
Birbeck, 667
Bird of Fire, 691
Birds, 326, 691
Bird-wheel, 691
Birmingham, 431, 437
Birr, 335
Birra, Lady, 749
Birrenswork, 387
Bishop, The, 590
bishop, 577
Black, 475
— Annis, 722
— and White Dove, 486
Blackfriars, 467
Black Mary, 598, 722
— Mary's Hole, 619
Blackthorn, 419, 677
Blaze, St., 244, 602

Blban, 248
bleary, 193
Blind Fiddler, The, 226
— Man's Buff, 425
Blue, 270, 273, 579
— John, 795
— — Cavern, 787
— Stones, 587
Boar, 58, 241, 242, 329
Bocock, 195
Boduo, 276
Boduoc, 277
boer, 242
Bog, 233
bogel, 233
Boggart, 232
Bogle, 518
Bohemia, 307
Bolerium, 193
Bolingbroke, 658
Bolleit caves, 771
Bolster, Giant, 720
Bonchurch, 163
Bond, 162
Bonfire, 169, 245
Bookham, 231, 667, 686
Bor, 752
Boreas, 422
Boreland Mote, 533
borough, 312
Borr, 471
Borrowdale, 682
Boskenna, 510
bosom, 509
Bosomzeal, 349
Bosow, Giant, 613
boss, 529
Bosse Alley, 509
Bossenden Woods, 510
Boston, 248, 510
both, 372
bouche, 293
Boudicca, 519
Boulogne, 210, 647
Bourdon, 601
Bourjo, 644
Bournemouth, 551
Bourne Water, 799, 818
Bowl, 615
Box-, 246
Boxhill, 231
Box Hill, 386
— tree, 665
Boy Bishop, 590, 616
Boyne R., 110
Braavalla, 749
Bracken, 385
Brackenbyr, 758
Bradford, 82
Bradmore, 432
Bradstone, 312
Brage, 758
Brahan Stone, 530
Brahma, 145, 161, 223
Brahma, 716
Brahmins, 168
Brahan Wood, 317
Brain, 378, 574
brain, 320, 324
Braintree, 430
Bramble, 159

Branch, Silver, 679
— The Divine, 660
Bran Ditch, 387
Brandon, 36, 349
— St., 679
Brangwyn, 572
Branksea, 551
Bran, the Blessed, 379
— Voyage of, 679
Brantome Cave, 783
brass, 467
brat, 458
Bratton, 402
Brawn, St., 317
Bray, 406, 664
— Down, 704
— R., 348
Braybroke, 798
Braynes Row, 718
bread, 460
Bread and Cheese Lands, 371, 589
breath, 460
Brecan's Cauldron, 689
Breceliande, 676
Brecon, 380
Brede Place, 460
Bredon, 350
Breeches, 377
breed, 458
Brehon Laws, 318, 333
Brennos, 379
Brent, R., 609
Brentford, 609, 617, 668
Breock, St., 666
Bress, 46, 389, 467
Bretons, 575
Breton souterrains, 778
Brewer, 295
Brew King, 689
Brian, 379, 389
— Boru, 380
Briancon, 379
Briareus, 82, 402
Brickel's Lane, 510
Bride Eye, 682
— St., 119, 327, 458, 552, 603, 663, 686, 736, 761, 823
Bridewell, 458
Bride's Fire, St., 472
Bridget, St., 169
Bridlington, 492
Brig, 761
Brigan, 379
Brigantes, 715
Brightlingsea, 119, 312, 343
Brigid, 459, 467
Brigit, 388
Brigit's Bird, 433
Bri Leith, 397
Brimham Rocks, 602
brimstone, 477
Brinsmead, 317
Brinsmead, 602
Brisen, Dame, 343
Brisons, The, 336, 343
Bristol, 818
Britani, 852
Britannia, 118, 461
British character, 122
Britomart, 118, 460, 715, 757

Briton, 100, 377
Brittany, 44
Brixham, 343
Brixton, 343
Broad arrow, 363, 534, 629
— Sanctuary, 660
Broadstairs, 95, 119
Broad, The, 121, 337
Brochs, 343
Brockhurst, 343
Brockley, 343, 666
Brodhulls, 119
broglodite, 769
brok, 347
Brok, 471
Broken Wf., 510
Bromfield, 419
Bromley, 602
Bromley's, etc., 419
Brompton, 419
Brondesbury, 419, 602
Bronwen, 334
Bronze, 463
bronze, 467
Brooch, 348
brood, 458
brook, 510
Brookland, 343
Broom, 419, 602, 795
Broome Park, 716, 798, 799
brow, 324
Browne, 317
Brownies, 620
Brownie Stone, 316
Brownlows, 318
Brown Willy, 387
Brown's Well, 609
— Wood, 718, 741
Browny, 315
Bru, 311, 348, 349
Brue, R., 289, 348
Bruin, 329
Brun, R., 387
Bruno, St., 317
Brunswick, 402
Brute, 124
Brutes, Mistress of, 715
Bruton, St., 601
Brutus, 83, 119, 186, 681
— Stone, 312, 350
Bryan, 577
Bryanstone, 314, 507, 530, 601, 678
— Sq., 317
Brychan, St., 379, 716
bryony, 328
Brython, 100
bubs, 374
Bubwood, 374
Bucato, 305
Bucca Dhu, 231
— Gwidden, 231
Buck, 239
Buckaboo, 578
Buckden, 732
Bucket, 294, 474, 479, 481
Buckingham, 387
Buckland, 231, 246
Bucklersbury, 518
Buckwheat, 254
Bug, 255

Bugbear, 232
Buggaboo, 232
Buggy, 405
Bukephalus, 280
Bulinga Fen, 658
Bull, 46, 119, 259, 265, 328, 336, 414, 604, 840
Bun, 261, 515
— Hot cross, 731
Bungen, 303
Bunhill, 155
Buratys, 331
Burchun, 331
Burdock, 385
Burfield, 664
Burford, 386
Burgate, 510
burgeon, 484
Burgoyne, 380
Burinea, St., 817
Burkenning, 666
burn, 510, 572
Burn, R., 387
Burnebishop, 590
Burnham, 387
Burnie Bee, 507
Burnsall, 402
Burrian, 327
Burry, R., 348, 387
Burtani, 852
Burtree, 576
Burwood, 601
bury, 319
Buryan, St., 345, 510
Buryan's St., 817
Buryanack, 720
bush, 293
Bush, 612
Bushey Park, 612
Butterfly, 46, 176
— idols, 380
Buxton, 291, 796
Buzza's Hill, 613
Byron, 317
Byzantium, 362, 516
Byzing Wood, 510

CAB, 504
Cabala, 577
Cabalists, 135
Cabiri, 493
Cabura, 493
Cac Horse, 453
cackle, 243
Cacus, 478
caddie, 642
Caddington, 787, 811
Cadi, 138, 234, 641
Cadlands, 785
Cadman, 110
Caenwood, 151
Cain, 149
— and Abel, 503
Caindea, 151, 319, 537
Cairn Voel, 424
Caistor, 443
cake, 245
calander, 341
Caleb, 150
Calne, 342

Calpe, 283
Camber, K., 681
Camberwell, 705
Cambrai, 406, 617
Cambre Castle, 396
Cambria, 310
Cambourne, 222, 397
Camperdizıl, 586
Can, 310, 650
Can-, 826
Can, R., 221, 667
Canaan, 150
Canbury, 349, 607
Cancan, 412
candescent, 212
Candia, 151, 319
candid, 212
Candle, 171
— in cave, 813
candour, 212
Candour, British, 101
Cane Goose, 223
Cangians, 519
Canhole, 448
Canna, R., 261
— St., 649
Cannibalism, Jewish, 185
Cannon, 274
— St., 666
canny, 212
Canonbie Lea, 666
Canonbury, 667
Cantabria, 322
Cantabres, 323
canteen, 824
canter, 409
Canterbury, 87, 90, 168, 239, 409
Cantii, 411, 519
Cantorix, 410
Cape Wrath, 574
Caphira, 494
Cardia, 556
Cardinal, 555
Carfax, 514
Caris, 820
Carisbroke, 821
Carnac, 217, 642
Carn Bre, 396
Cars, 503
Cart-wheeling, 164
Cass, 243
Cassock, 234
Castor and Pollux, 354, 475
castra, 477
Cat, 58, 751
— Lady of, 752
— Stane, 752
Catacombs, 810, 844
Catchpole, 446
Cathay, 191
Catherine, 243
Catherine, St., 784
Caucasus, 852
Cauchemar, 477
Cauldron, 615, 637, 797, 823, 875
— of Pwyll, 801
cause, 224
Causeway, 439
Cave, 765, 773, 780

INDEX

Cave, at Bethlehem, 780
Cave = matrix, 790
Caverns, 193, 194
Celi, 224
celibate, 340
Celtiberia, 12
Celtiberians, 323
Celtic words, 61
Celts, 116, 228
Cendwen, 651, 824
Cenimagni, 283
Cenomagni, 411
Cenomani, 329
Centaur, 305, 424
Centaurs, 409
Centre, 794
Ceres, 402, 821
Chac, 161
Chad, St., 288
Chadfish, 212
Chadwell, 288, 783
Chain, 482
Chairs, Stone, 545
Chalice, 167
Chalk pits, 776
Chandos, 741
change, 146
Chaos, 224, 225, 292, 490, 507
Chariot, 435, 470, 517
— of Jehovah, 503
Charis, 469
Charon, 262
Chartres, 791
Chastity, 457
Chee Dale, 447
— Tor, 728
Chei, St., 447
Cheiran, St., 409
Chemin des Dames, 439
Chester, 444, 445
Chester, 447
Chevauchée, 511
— de St. Michael, 420
Chew Magna, 447
Cheyne, 93, 741
Cheyneys, 670
Chi, 772, 780
Chi (X), 385, 446
Chiana, R., 97
chic, 97
Chichester, 445
Children in Hell, 558
Chilperic, 342
Chin, 161
China, 191, 216, 272, 292
chink, 400
Chios, 225
Chiron, 409
Chisbury Camp, 446
Chislehurst, 766, 772
Chiun, 140
Choir, Gawr, 561
Chosen Hill, 729
Christ, 178, 206, 211, 214, 250, 264, 265, 487, 537, 574
Christ, 820
Christianity, 31, 864
Christian "tortures," 107
Christine, St., 486
Christmas, 257

Christofer, The, 270
Christopher, St., 54, 107, 112, 151, 164, 204, 264, 267, 299, 640, 853
Chuckhurst, 372
chuckle, 471
chun, 92
Chun, 649, 740
— Castle, 90
Chwyvan Cross, 708
Chyandour, 97
Ciconians, 192
Cimmerians, 844
Cingen, 412
Circle, 604
— and Triangle, 571, 573
Circles, 499, 503
— Stone, 543
Cirencester, 453
Cissbury Ring, 446
Cities of Refuge, 736
Clare, St., 718
Claus, 140
Clement, St., 716, 797
Clerkenwell, 718
Clover, 737
Clowes, 299
Club, 663, 666
Cluricanne, 718
coach, 468
Coal-mining, prehistoric, 845
cock, 195
Cock, 196, 197, 361, 620
— R., 197
Cockayne, 190, 195, 196
Cockburn Law, 752
Cockchafer, 255
Cocker, R., 198
Cockey, 197
Cock horse, 444
— Law, 197
Cockle, 245, 385, 473
— bread, 248
Cockles, Hot, 248
Cocknage, 197
Cockney, 190
— dialect, 529
Cockshott, 197
Cocks Tor, 197
Codfish, 213
cog, 195
Cogenhoe, 197
Coggeshall, 197, 639
Coggo, 197
Cogidumnus, 446
Cogs, 195
Cogynos, 197
Cohen, 112
Coil Dance, 824
coin, 397
Coinage, 394
— British, 24-
Coins, 763
Coke hill, 197
Coldharbour, 299
Cole Abbey, 615
— Old King, 103
Coleman, 155
Coles pits, 801
Colman, St., 43
Colne, R., 342

Cologne, 216
Columb, R., 661
Columba, St., 43, 552, 660
Columbine, 93, 669
— St., 93, 669
com, 310
Com, 330
Comb, 715
Combarelles, 402
Comber, 310
Comberton, 586
Comet, 864
commère, 330
common, 440
Comparative method, 75
compère, 330
Conan, 649
Conann, 192
Concangi, 411
Concanni, 411, 667
Concord, St., 141
Condy Cup, 824
cone, 236
Cone, 398, 800
Coney Hall Hill, 785
Conical cap, 669
Coniston, 151
Conn, 753
— K., 151, 512
Connaught, 151, 182, 512
Conneda, 182, 753
Constantine, 226, 365, 566
Constantinople, 84
Conyers, 272
Cook, 195, 196, 245
Cooknoe, 197
Cook's Kitchen Mine, 222
Coquet, R., 197
Coquille, 248
Cormac, 517
Cornish types, 848
Cos, 510
Coundon, 435
Counter Earth, 580
Coveney, 430
Covent Garden, 428
Coventina, 427
Coventry, 427, 435
Cox, 195
cradle, 810
Cranbrook, 427
Cray, 796
Cres, 105, 819
Crescent, 254, 286, 390, 392, 528
Crescents, 492, 704
Cresswell Crags, 402
Cretan Caves, 808
— Horse, 407
— Maze Coins, 87
— Ship, 491
Cretans, 846
Crete, 11, 76, 104, 182, 192, 493, 687, 855
Crew, Lough, 200
Crimea, 844
Crissa, 820
Cromlechs, 17
Cronus, 82
Cross, 104, 106, 286, 296, 441, 445, 560, 561, 683

cross, 107, 821
Cross of St. John, 104
— — — George, 104
— Red, 270
crude, 810
Cruse, 822
Cuchulainn, 278
Cuckmere, R., 452
Cuckoo, 197
Cuin, 290
— coin, 397
Culdees, 835
Culebres, 842
Cullompton, 661
cumber, 569
Cumberland, 682
cun, 92
Cun-, 235
Cunbaria, 330
Cunegonde, 412
Cuneval, 318
cunning, 212, 280
CUNO
Cuno, 279, 305
Cunob, 528
Cunobeline, 241
Cup, 813
— and Ring markings, 833
Cupid, 225, 231, 233, 304, 326, 494, 594
Cupra, 493
curate, 810
Cuthbert, St., 362
Cuthbert's beads, St., 248
Cyclops, 192
Cymbeline, 241
Cymner, 310
Cymry, 310
Cynethryth, 761
Cynopolis, 54
Cynthia, 151, 213
Cynthus, Mt., 726

da, 320
Dactyli, 574
Dad-, 256
dad, 509
daddy, 209, 256
Daddy, 263
Daddy's Hole, 349
Dagda Mor, 169, 389, 397, 512
Daisy, 169, 210, 216, 233, 384
Dalston, 285
dame, 745
Danaan, Tuatha te. 766
Danbury, 721
Dancing, 540
Dandelion, 169
Dane Hill, 765
— John, 90, 683, 800
— R., 789
Dane's Inn, 716
Danoi, 858
Dansey, 735
Daphnephoria, 541
Darbies, 227
Darby, 227
Darkness, 625
Date palm, 258
Dava, Flood of, 641
David, St., 625

Davy Jones, 641
dawn, 752
day, 320
Day, St., 320
Dayne, 724
dazzle, 591
deacon, 687
dean, 779, 810
Dean, Forest of, 752
— R., 789
Deane's Gardens, 721
Dear, 734
dear, 760
Death, 263, 264, 307
— disregarded, 173
Deberry, 345
Deemster, 746
Dee, R., 320
Deer, 257, 405, 599, 715
Deffrobani, 84
Delginross, 605, 796
Delphi, 653
Demijohn, 302, 687
Denbies, 613
Deneholes, 765-74
Denmark, 690
Dennehill, 716
Derbyshire, 401
Derg, L., 792, 796
derry, 86
Deucalion, 337
Devil's Dyke, 519
Dew, 167
dextra, 477
Dhia, 319
Diamond Horse, The, 424
Diana, 134, 135, 239, 258, 444, 475, 717, 788
Dianthus, 169
Digits, 575
Diminutives, 619
di, 319
dieu, 319
Dinant, 788
Dingwall, 317
Dinsul, 208
Dioscoros, 366
Dioscorus, 354
Dioscuri, 354, 512
Dionysus, 71
Divinity of Kings, 172
Dod-, 256
Dodbrook, 349
Doddington, 262
Dodecans, 207, 700
Dodman, The, 263, 349
Dodona, 89, 92, 133, 260, 273, 339
Dog, 54, 57, 111, 112, 121, 150, 152, 155, 264, 293, 329, 346, 853
Doliche, 76
Dolmen chapel, 30
Dolphin, 653
Domhills, 745
Don, 664
Doncaster, 444
Donidon, 745
donjon, 800
Donn, 712
— Children of, 734

Don, R., 749, 789
Don's Chair, 752
Donseil cave, 806
Donn's House, 726
Doo Cave, 494
Doom Rings, 746
Doomster, 745
Dorchester, 713, 715
Dordogne, 406, 774
Dorking, 386
Dot and Circle, 276, 547
Dots, 105, 250
Double Disc, 494
dour, 119
Dove, 92, 144, 486, 624, 627, 652, 853
dove, 625
Dove Cots, 733
Dover, 95
Doves, 790
Dowgate Hill, 783
Dowdeswell, 262
Dowdy, 640
Down, County, 766
Dragon, 208, 242, 250, 270, 272, 274, 655, 836
— guards, 274
— slayer, 651
Drainage, 103
Dray, River, 87
Drayton, 714
Dress, 100, 122
Drew, 471
Drewsteignton, 757
droit, 101
Drosten, 734
Drucca coin, 483
Druid, 761
Druidesses, 570
Druidic Creeds, 536
— Fairy tale, 166
— Music, 582
— Remains in Spain, 324
Druidism, 6-9, 66, 87, 167, 171, 393, 488, 544
Druid Physiologists, 834
Druids, 554
— caves, 791
— circles, 544
— Town, 572
Druids = *brans*, 679
ducat, 397
Dudsbury, 263
due, 223
Dumbarton, 472, 523
Dummy's Hill, 756
Dun, R., 789
Duncannon, 274
Dundalgan, 796
Dunechein, 90
Dunence, 552
dungeon, 800
Dunodon, 745
Duno, 758
Dunstable, 714, 745, 777
— grave, 64, 65
Dunstan, St., 716
Dunton, 716
Durham, 715
Durovern, 268
Duval, 741

EAGLE, 280
Earthwork, 862
Easter, 608
— dancing, 540
Eaton, 733
ebb, 524
Bbbe, R., 524
Ebchester, 431
Ebgate, 513
Ebony, 165
Ebor, R., 370
Bbora, 328, 329
Ebrington, 349
Ebro, R., 323, 370
Ebur, 329
Ebury, 601, 621
Bceni, 411
Echo, 226
Eclipse, 167
Ecne, 390
Eda, 455, 753
— good Queen. 151
— Queen, 512
Edans, St., 713
Edda, The, 752
Eden, 683, 730, 858
Edenhall, 743
Edenkille, 716
Eden, R., 713
— Vale, 716
Edimbourg, 745
Edina Hall, 753
Edinburgh, 730
Edinburgh, 797
Edmonton, 679
Edna, 753
Edrei, 194, 769
Effingham, 430
Effra, R., 749
Egg, 223, 226, 276, 532, 756
Egypt, 9, 46, 69, 135, 166, 189, 252, 254, 414, 475, 577, 843
Egypt, 534
Eight, 188, 189, 204, 636, 642
eight, 655
Eight Bishops, 659
Eighteen, 206, 207, 588
El, 132, 135
Elaine, 103
Elbarrow, 133
Elbe, R., 558
El Borak, 635, 664
Elboton, 154
elder, 153
Elen, 103, 221, 285
— R., 103
Elens Ways, 519
Elephant, 160
Eleven, 214, 421, 548, 557, 574, 581, 593, 633, 788
eleven, 217
Eleven Blindfolded Men, 577
— curtains, 576
— feet longstones, 548. 552
— foot grave, 560
— hundred, 214
— Loch, 219
— thousand, 214
elf, 153
Elfe, 153
Elfland, 559

Elgin, 450
Elijah, 147
Blini Cunob, 528
Elisha, 147
Blk, 289
Ellan, 133
Ellen, Dame, 778
Ellendown, 565
Ellendune, 133
Elles, The, 154
Ellesmere, 439
Ellingfort, 285
Ellistone, 318
Elmo's Fires, St., 475
Elphin, 158, 664
— Horses, 281, 287
Elphinstone, 318
Elphinstone, 548
Elphinstones, 217
Elven, 217
Blwyn St., 132
Ely, 716
Ember Days, 572
emerge, 219
Empire, 570
Empyrean, 570
enceinte, 220
Engelheim, 359, 591
Engelland, 558, 788
Englefield, 588
Englewood, 553
Englysshe Wood, 588
Ennis, 557
Enns, St., 720
Ep, 430
Ep, 523
Epeur, 326
Ephesus, 598
Ephialtes, 478
Epirus, 322
epo, 430
Epona, 284, 445
Epora, 328
Eppi, 523
Eppilos, 430
Eppilus, 280
Epping, 445
Epsom, 430
equity, 332
Eros, 158, 604
Esclairmond, 683
Eseye, 531
Esus, 278
Ethereal Plant, 181
Ethereus, 215
Bthne, 461
ethnic, 462
Eton, 730
Etruria, 17, 89, 139, 145, 148, 217, 236, 475
Eubonia, 163, 165, 216, 346
Eubury, 335
Buchar, 389
Euny, St., 261. 828
Eure, R., 370
Europa, 265
Europe, 525
Eve, 152, 403, 500, 742,
Eve, 496
Evesham, 430
Evora. 329. 751

Exton, 685, 697
exuberance, 328
Eye, 251, 252, 282, 532, 538, 604, 727
— ball, 579
— of Christ, 384
— of Heaven, 195, 216
— of Horus, 122
— Land of the, 252
— of S'iva, 526
— Towns, 730
Eyes, 499, 539, 624

F, 497
Fabell, Peter, 679
Fainites ! 117
Fainits ! 616
Fairbank, 667, 686
Fairmead, 569
Fairs, 572
Fairy Family, 522
— Hill, 764,
— Hills, 552
— leaves, 65
— Queen, 308
fake, 206
Fal, 424, 450, 841
— R., 424
Falcon, 426
Faraday, 508
Farandole, 412
farisees, 619
Farn, 751
Faroe Islands, 507
Farringdon, 466
Fata, 202
Fate, 593
— Tree, 322
fay, 153
Fearbal, 679
Feather, 160, 258. 366, 746
Feathers, 496
Fechan, St., 672
feckless, 206
fecuud, 206
Fées, 165
Felikovesi, 423
Felixstowe, 423, 426
Fen, 426
Ferdinand, 507
Feridoon, 748
fern, 266
Fern, 260 267, 385
— Islands, 206, 209
Fernacre 550
Ferns, 266
Feron, 266
Feronia, 572
Ferriby, 495
Ferry, St., 672
Fiddler, The, 225
Field-names, 41
Fiery cross, 107
Fife, 153, 201
Fifteen, 206, 598, 601, 633, 755, 806
Fifty Sons, 716
Fig, 206
— Sunday, 500
Fingers, 574
Finwell cave, 806
fir = quercus

884 ARCHAIC ENGLAND

Fir Tree, 730
fire, 467
Fire 72, 166, 167, 618
— Halo, 571
— Insurance, 705
— of Heaven, 164
Fish, 247, 254, 286, 296
five, 363
Five, 238, 437, 513, 503, 689,
— acres, 372
— grains, 517
— islands, 517
— king's, 262
— peaks, 518
— roads, 516
— streams, 517
— wells, 261
Flamborough, 492
Fleur de lys, 816
Fleur de lys, 242
Flint Knapping, 349
Flokton, 435
Flood, 857
— The, 20
Flora dance, 486
Flounders Field, 419
Flower names, 68
Fly, 221
Foal, 422
fog, 211
Foleshill, 435
Folkestone, 423, 426, 432
Font de Gaune, 402
Footprints, 546
Forbury, The, 438
Fore, 672
Forfar, 368, 495
Fortunate Isles, 683, 690
Fortune, 489
— Wheel of, 537
Fosses des Inglais, 786
— Sarrasins, 786
Fossils in tomb, 65
Fountain of Knowledge, 689
Four Cities, 853
— Kings, 687
— Quarters, 188
— Rivers, 722
— Roads, 515
— -streamed Mount, 130
— -teated Horse, 284
Fox, 263
Fraid, St., 459
Frederick the Great, 462
free, 760
Freemasonry, 296
Frei, 748
Freisingen, 700
Freya, 572
Friday, 572
Fulham, 422, 426
fun, 57
Furry dance, 271, 274, 412, 486
Furze, 602, 795

gad, 143
Gaddesden, 673
Gadfly, 282
Gadshill, 755
Gaelic, 79
— regrets, 69

Gaelic tenderness, 43
gagga, 478
Galva, Carn, 318
Gancanagh, 412
Gander, 223
Ganesa, 160, 280
Gangani, 411
Ganganoi, 54, 702
Ganging Day, 246
Gangrad, 143
Garden of the Rose, 683
Gardens of Adonis, 712
gas, 225
gauche, 477
Gauls and Britons, same speech, 91
Gaurs, 561
Gayhurst, 288
Gedge, 471
Gee, 91
Gee, 282
Geecross, 446
Geho, 282
Gemini, 475
general, 146
generate, 145
Genesis, 145
Geneva, 329
geniality, 140
genie, 146
genital, 145
genius, 146
gennet, 285
"Gentle People," 733
"Gentle Places," 734
Gentry, The, 146
genus, 145
George, 272
George, St., 242, 268, 271, 304, 614, 642, 695, 817
Gerberta, 362
Germans, 525
Germany, 74
Gest, 272
gewgaw, 448
Geyser, 243
ghost, 231
Gian Ben Gian, 140, 304
Giant's Beds, 758
— civic, 188
— grave, 746
— graves, 191
— hedges, 17
Giants = Dwarfs, 233
Gig, 453, 471
gigantic, 195
giggle, 190
Gigglewick, 189
Giggy's, St., 190
Giglet Fair, 194
Gig na Gog, 190
Gigonian Rock, 194
gigue, 195
Gilbey, 284
Givendale, 429
Givon's grove, 430
Glastonbury, 289, 682
Gnosis, 76, 279, 859
Gnossus, 76, 794
Gnostic gems, 108, 112
Gnostics, 135, 361

Goat, 57, 361, 504
Goblet, 813
god, 178
Godber, 572
Gode, 220
Godiva, 41, 403, 475, 598
Godmanham, 550
Godolcan, 285
Godolphin, 284
— Hill, 668
Godrevy, 531
God's Acre, 673
Godstone, 815
Godstones, etc., 673
Goemagog, 186-8
Gofannon, 432
Gog, 188, 478
Gog, 194
goggle, 189
Goginan, 194
Gogmagog, 83, 639
Golden Age, 858
— Ball Bar, 590
Golden Bough, The, 71, 74
Goldhawk, 433
Gooch, 195
good, 178
Goodge, 195, 477
Goodman, 741
Goodmanstone, 713
"Good Neighbours," 733
Good People, 556
— — The, 174
Goodwood, 446
Goose, 223, 228, 243, 276, 346, 512, 661
goose, 224, 225, 231
Goosegog, 345
Goosey, 447
Goostrey, 447
Gorhambury, 111, 562
Gorsedd, 564
— prayer, 181
Gosh, 195
Gospel oak, 228
Goss, 243
Goswell, 243
Govan, 426
Govannon, 426
Gowk, 198
Grace, 830
Graces, Three, 181
Great, 810
Great Bear, 216
Greek, 81
— in Mexico, 842
Green, 268
Greengoose Fair, 243
Green Man, 268
— — and Still, 270
Gretchen, 302, 362
Greyhound bitch, 36
Grimm's Law, , 60
grot, 810
grotesque, 812
Gudeman, The, 109
Guedienus, 325
guess, 273
Guinea, 400

INDEX   885

Guion, 824
Gun, 274
Gunpowder, 839
Gur, Lough, 736
gush, 273
gust, 243, 272
Gwenevere, 389
Gwennap, 531
gyne, 511
Gyre, 562

HABONDE, 165
Hack, 283
Hackington, 411
Hackney, 283
hackney, 392
Hackney, 285, 287, 699
Haddenham, 716
Haddington, 750
Haden Cross, 716
Hag, 737
Hagbourne, 38
Hagman, 199
Hag tracks, 200, 283
Hags, 685
— chair, 200
Haha, 58
Haha, 737
Haig, 199
Hailsham, 568
Hakon, 235
Halcyon, 290
Half moon, 490
Halifax, 514
Hallicondane, 290, 412, 734
Hamelyn, 867
Hammer, 270, 355
— of Thor, 706
Hammersmith, 431
Hand, 744
Hangman's Wood, 787
Han Grotto, 787, 827
Hannafore, 275
Hanover, 275, 695
Happy Valley, 523
Harp, 562
Harper, 305
Harpocrates, 118
Hastings, 95, 798
Hathor, 46
Hatton Garden, 716
Hawk, 205
hawker, 205
Hawthorn, 152, 159
— St., 737
Haxa, 644
haycock, 198
Haydon, 713
Hay Hill, 421
Haymarket, 421
Heart, 158, 287, 595, 816
— Cross, 105
Heart's Delight, 350, 687
Heathen chant, 373
Heaven's Walls, 672, 683
Hebe, 743
Heber, 310
Hebrew, 79
Hebrew, 191, 369
Hebrews, 184
Hebrews, 502

Hebrides, 165
Hebrides, 315
Hebron, 34, 370
Heck! 283
Heddon, 746
Helen, 103, 221, 286, 477
Helena, 104
Helen, St., 456, 587
Helen's day, St., 478
Helens, St., 95, 103
Helicon, 289
Heligan Hill, 289
Helios, 103, 104, 135
Hellana, 103
Hellas, 133, 412
Hellen, 337
Hellenes, 103, 412
Hellingy, 588
Helston, 271, 412
Hen, 197, 653
Hengist, 275
— and Horsa, 85
Hengston Hill, 554
Hensor, 386
Hepburn, 526
Hephaestus, 426
Hepworth, 527
Herculaneum and Pompei
Hercules, 97, 114, 139, 200 666, 668
Hermes, 116
Herne's Oak, 239
Herring-bone-walls, 91
Hesy, Tel el, 531
Hewson, 450
Hexe, 644
Hibera, 323
Hibernia, 310
Hidden One, 577
Hide and Seek, 578
Hieroglyphics, 114
high, 125
Highbury, 667
Himbra, Pt., 586
Hindus, 168
hinge, 556
Hiniver, 695
Hinover, 275, 452
hip, 524
Hip! Hip! Hip! 526
Hipperholme, 514
hips, 526
Hipswell, 513
Hive, 710
Hivites, 497
Hob, 165, 513
Hobany, 216, 284
Hobby, 423
— Horse, 268, 275, 527
Hobday, 526
Hobredy, 165
hoch, 125
Hogg, 199
Hogmanay, 199
Hoketide, 244
Holborn, 722
Holda, 220
Holed stone, 538
Holiburn, Giant, 318
Holland House, 422
Hollantide, 245

Holle, 220
Holloway, 517, 521
Holly, 40, 140, 417, 597
Hollybush, 155
Hollyhock, 204
Holly tree, 220
Holofernes, 266
holy, 140
Holy Ghost, 487
— Holy Vale, 586
— Sepulchre, 793
Holvear Hill, 590
Holwood Park, 785
Homer, 63, 99, 225, 326, 327
Homerton, 287
Honeybourne, 261, 714
Honeybrooke, 38
Honey Child, 261, 714
Honeychurch, 714, 261
Honeycrock, 568
Honeydew, 623
Honeyman, 758
Honeysuckle, 258
Honor Oak, 228, 231, 666
Honover, 695
Hoodening, 841
Hoodown, 350
Hoof, 573
Hoop, 542
hoop, 525
Hooper, 425
Hooper's Blind, 311
— Hide, 578
Hop, 523
Hop o' my Thumb, 524
— Queen, 540
Hope, 523
hope, 524
Hopkin, 540
Hoppyland, 523
hops, 524
Horn, 286
Horns of Altar, 736
Horsa, 275
Horse, 241, 274, 389, 615, 623, 840
— Eye, 282
— Eye Level, 568
— flesh, 478
— hair wig, 332
— = Liberty, 328
Horselydown, 38
Horse-ornaments, 286
— ship, 654
Horseshoe, 572
Horus, 46
Hospitality, 227
Hounds, 461
Hounslow, 714
Howel, 104
Hoxton, 285, 685
Hoy, 758
Hoy obelisk, 9
Hoyden, 742
Hu, 84, 214, 320, 311, 327, 349, 386, 450, 586, 749
hubbub, 525
Hube, Mt., 542
Hudkin, 509
huge, 198
Huggen Lane, 511

Huggins Hall, 350
Hugh, 320
Hugh Town, 586
humane, 695
Humber, R., 569
Hun, 234
Hun, 827
Huns, 216
Hunsonby, 220
Hyde, 473, 455, 621
Hydon's Ball, 714
Hyperboreans, 324, 370, 562
Hypereia, 320, 346
Hyperion, 328
Hymn of Hate, 525

IBAR, St., 311, 326
Iberian coin, 292, 322, 397
— coins, 247, 254, 265, 297, 231, 386
— language, 266
Iberians, 451
Iceni, 248
Icenians, 451.
Ichnield, 519
Ichnield way, 248, 411, 518, 520
Ickanhoe, 248
Ida, 742
Ida, 754
— Mt., 574, 715, 455
— plain, 752
— plains, 473
Idaeians, 456
Ideia, 76
Idle, R., 462
Idle's Bush, 462
Idunn, 742
Ieithon, 461
Iffley, 40
Iggdrasil, 841
Ikeni, 283, 519
Iliberi, 322
Ilibiris, 330
Iliffe, 162
Ilkley, 290
Illtyd, St., 257
Illtyds House, 257
Ilma, 136
Ilmatar, 137
Imp Stone, 623
Inachus, 266, 282
inane, 201
inch, 556
Inch, 557
Inchbrayock, 495
inept, 526
Ing, 556
Inga, 556
Inge, 556
Ingene Lane, 511
ingle, 552
Ingleborough, 587, 786
Inghilterra, 557
Inglesham, etc., 659
Ingletons, etc., 588
Inkberrow, 874
Inkpen, 659
Inn, 294, 298
Inquisition, 549
Intoxication, 688
Intreccia, 706, 840

Intreccia coins, 491
Invicta, 275
Invictus, 210
Io, 282, 362, 399
Iona, 627, 651, 670, 714
Ionia, 92
Ipareo, 320
Ippi, 523
Ireland, 182, 193
Iris, 265
Irish circles, 545
Iron, 574
Isaac, 471
Isle of Dogs, 38, 113
Islington, 685
Issey, St., 531
Istar, 608, 644
Ith, Plain of, 473
Ivalde, 742
Ives, St., 41, 425, 427, 430, 531
Ivy, 498
— Bridge, 427
— Girl, The, 40, 540
Ixion, 163
Iysse, St., 531

JACK, 97, 195, 417
Jack a lantern, 152
— in green, 268
— The, 270, 273,
— the Giant Killer's well, 212
— up the orchard, 447
Jackal, 111, 263
jackass, 212
Jah, 161
Jaina cross, 105
Jana, 97
Jane, 447
Janicula, 828
Janina, 261, 460
janitor, 146
Januarius, St., 828
January, 140, 146
— 1st, 650
Janus, 92, 141, 203, 140, 213, 241, 399, 490, 555, 626, 670, 795, 828, 841
— of Sicily, 143
Japan, 216, 857
Jason, 82
jaunty, 143
Jay, 91
Jay, 283
Jehovah, 184, 502, 508
Jehu, 282
jennet, 285
jenny, 212
Jenny, Aunt, 228
Jerusalem, 296, 794
Jesus, 214
jeu, 106, 448
Jew, 91
Jew, Eternal, 203
Jews, 502
Jews, 456
— Garden, 468
— in Cornwall, 80
— Harp, 448
— Lane, 697
— The Everlasting, 196

Jews, Walk, 439
— Wandering, 448, 663, 696, 728
jig, 195
jingle, 400
jinn, 146
Jinn, 166
Jo, 644
Joan, 227
— Pope, 357
Joan's Pitcher, 190, 301
Jock, 106
Jockey, 444
jocund, 106
Johanna, 213
Johanna's garden, 703
John, 830
John, 53
— of Gaunt, 648
— of Perugia, 326
— St., 165, 268, 449, 514, 537, 539, 636
— the Baptist, 448
Johnstone, 53
Johnstone's Inn, 331
John's Wood, St., 151
Jonah, 652
Jones, 92
Jonn, 91
jonnock, 97, 236
Joseph, 147
Joseph's Rod, 629
Jou, 91, 147, 151, 456, 508, 710
Jove, 140, 257
— androgynous, 233
— coin, 282
joviality, 140
Joy, 91
joy, 106, 147
Juda, 362
Jude, St., 287
Judge, 447
Judge's bough, 691
— walk, 439
Judson, 447
Judy, 362, 754
Jug, 295, 301
Jug, 447
Jugantes, 453
Juggling, 563
Juktas, Mt., 471
June, 146
junior, 146
Juno, 144, 146, 223, 243, 407, 493, 715
Jupiter, 311
Jupiter, 142, 227, 283, 362, 386, 458, 508
— Ammon, 578
Jupiter's Chain, 581, 830
Just, St., 563
Jutt, 359
Juxon, 446

KAADMAN, 109, 204, 249, 288
Kalbion, 125
Kate Kennedy, 319
— St., 784
Katherine Wheel, 107
Kayne, St., 212, 221, 649
Keach, 471
Kean, 212

INDEX

Ked, 242
Kelpie, 283, 818
Kember, 310
Ken, 212
Ken, R., 221
— wood, 151, 649
Kendal, 221, 411, 667
Kenia, Mt., 236
Kenna, 213, 261, 317
— Princess, 162
— St., 649
Kennet, R., 853
Kenites, 826
Kennington, 292
Kenny, 212, 649
Kensington, 317
— Gore, 420
— Hippodrome, 449
Kent, 95, 411
— R., 667
Kent's Cavern, 4, 401, 825
— Copse, 349
Keridwen, 158, 651
Keridwen, 157
Kerris Roundago, 820
Keston, 785
Kettle, 797
Keyna, St., 757
Keynsham, 212
Khan, 234, 310
Khem, 745
Kid, 504
Kigbear, 194
Kilburn, 155
Kildare, 603
Kilkenny, 290
Kilkenny, etc., 340
Killbye, 284
Kilts, 98
Kimball, 39
Kimbdton, 39
Kind, 826
King, 234, 342
King Charles' Wain, 406
— of Cockney's, 617
— of the May, 527
King's cross, 288
— Lynn, 697
Kingston, 548, 606
Kingston, 349
Kingstons, etc., 606
Kinross, 605
Kinyras, 605
Kintyre, 409
Kio, 282
— eye coin, 253
Kirkcudbright, 362
Kirkmabreck, 579
Kit, St., 784
— with a canstick, 152
Kit's Coty, 153, 750, 751, 780
Knap Hill, 528
— well, 528
Knave, 529
Knightsbridge, 621
Knockainy, 288, 735
Knocking Stone, 317
Knop, 528
Knot, 707
Know, 280
Konah, 236

Konkan, 412
Konken, 412
Koppenburg, 303
Kostey, 226, 231
Kristna, 105, 820
Kun, Mt., 236
Kunnan, Island of, 157
Kwan yon, 216
Kyd brook, 784, 785
Kymbri, 16, 330
Kymbri, 310
Kymbric, 79
Kynetii, 853

L, 792
labour, 322
Labyrinth, 706
Labyrinths, 107
Lac d'Amour, 707
Ladies Walk, 439
lady, 512
Ladybird, 507
Lady Bird, 591
Lamb, 719, 722
Land's End, 193
Language, poetic element
lanky, 285
Lanky man, 337
Lansdown, 342
Lansdowne, 417
Latin cross, 105
Laurel-Bearer, 541
Leaf, 427
— Man, Little, 305
Leaper, 568
Lear, K., 791
Leda, 354, 512
Leen, R., 697
Legs, 346
Leinster, 661
Len, R., 697
Lense, 839
Lenthall, 285
Leprechaun, 330
Levan, St., 212, 703
Leven, Loch, 219
Levens, 221
Leviathan, 162
Lewes, 416
Lewis, 432
liberal, 322
Liberini, 322
liberty, 322
Libora, 328
Liege, 330
Lieven, 217, 224
Lif and Lifthraser, 558
life, 153
Life Tree, 322
Lily, 242
Lily, 633
Linden, 154, 228
Linscott, 285
Lion, 57, 578
Lissom Grove, 623
Little Bird, Lay of, 692
— Britain, 522
— Leaf Man, 577
— London, 292
"Little Mothers," 174
Livingstone, 318

Lizard, 284
Llan, 103
Llandrindod, 367
Llandudno, 256, 272, 552
Llanfairfechan, 672
Llangan-, 261
loaf, 253
Londesborough, 285
London, 104
London, 103, 521, 522, 717
— Bridge, 575
— Fields, 285
— Stone, 513, 518
Lone, R., 221, 697
long, 285
Long Man, 337
— Meg, 206, 209, 266, 588, 646, 713
Lonsdale, 221
Lord of Misrule, 617
Lothbury, 470
Lough Gur, 562
love, 153
Love, 168, 225, 275
Lovekyn, 607
Lovelace, 818
Lucifer, 222
Luna, 234
Lune, R., 221, 697
Lunus, 234
Lyne grove, 285
Lyn, R., 697

M, 678
m and *n*, 745
ma, 136
Ma, 136, 258
Maat, 746
Mab, Queen, 556, 757
Mabon, 163
Mabonogi, 557
Mac, 375
Mc, 205
McAlpine laws, 172
McAuliffe, 205
Macclesfield, 511
Macedonian stater, 394
Macha, 512
Madeira, 89
Madon, R., 789
Madonna, 745
Madonna, 790
Madura, 104
Maga, 202
magazine, 205
Maggie Figgie, 205, 211
— Figgy, 500
— Witch, 219
Maggots, 222
Magi, 181, 413, 544, 702
magic, 202
magna mater, medals, 128
Magog, 188
magog, 194
Magogoei, 191
Magon, 674
Magonius, 674
Magpie, 656
Magu, 436
magus, 202
Magus, 203, 436, 702

Magusae, 436
Mahadeo, 835
Mahadeos, 832
Maht, 746
Maia, 606
maid, 458
Maida, 151, 456
maiden, 712
Maiden Bower, 714, 745,
— Castle, 713
— Lane, 428
— Paps, 209, 717
— Stane, 745
— Stone, 715
— Way, 206
Maidenhead, 660
Maidoc, St., 742, 751
Mairae, 594
maisie, 211
Mama Allpa, 135
— Cocha, 196
mamma, 136
Mammoth dugger, 599
Man in the Moon, 149, 161, 293
— Isle of, 163, 205, 320, 346, 556
— in the Oak, 230, 240
Manorbeer, 468
Manston, 96
Maoris, 579, 857
Mara, 600
Marazion, 91
Mare, 615, 653
Mare Street, 285
Maree, Loch, 604
Margaret, St., 208, 219, 220, 275, 647, 660, 755
Margate, 91
— Grotto, 765, 807
Margery Daw, 219
— Hall, 208
margot, 220
Marguerite, 210, 216
Marguerite, 839
Maria, 91, 301
Marian, Maid, 268
Marigold, 210, 607, 636
Marine, St., 607
Marion, 270
Market Jew, 91
Marlow, 660
Marne, 406
marrain, 330
marry, 601
Marseilles, 81
Martha's, St., 585
Martin, St., 274
Mary, 201, 604
Mary, 201
— Ambree, 648, 657
— Morgan, 201, 626
— St., 287, 590, 595, 793
Mary's Island, St., 586
Materialism, 74
Math, 432
Matterhorn, 147
Maur, St., 217, 578
Maurus, 217
Maurice, St., 217, 224
Mawgan, St., 674

May, 606, 713
May doll, 542
— Queen, 308, 686
Maya, 606
Mayas, 842
Mayborough, 713
Maycock, 195
Mayday, 268, 287
Maydeacon, 687
— House, 350
Mayfair, 601
Maypole, 260, 438, 684
mazes, 87, 585
Meacock, 195
Mead, 688
mead, 473
Meadows, 568
Meantol, 226
meat, 747
Meath, 757
Meave, 757
Meek, The, 660
meek, 211
Meg, 208
Megale, 223
Megalopolis, 362
Megstone, 206, 266
Meigle, 505
"Men of Peace," 733
mer, 91
merchant, 97
Mercury, 85, 97, 111, 134, 140, 195, 227, 262, 269, 347
mère, 91
Merlin's Cave, 797, 800
Merritot, 447
merry, 590, 600
Merry Andrews, 701
— Maidens, 206, 549
Meru, Mt., 708
Mesembria, 691
Metal inlay, 464
Mexico, 105, 161
Mirror, 251, 700, 715
Micah, 111, 184
Michal, 208
Michael, St., 111, 207, 245, 271, 287, 304, 416, 420, 504, 511, 557, 661
Michael's Mount, 208
Michaelmas, 245
— Day, 213
Michelet, 212
Mickleham, 208
Mihangel, 557
Mildmay, 287
Milkmaids, 603
Minerva, 139
Minnis Bay, 94
— Rock, 94
Minos, 333, 440
— King, 95
Minotaur, 840
Minster, 95
minster, 96
Mist, 211
Mistletoe, 181, 681
Mithra, 121, 768, 781, 835
Mithras, 413
mo, 234
Moccus, 240

Mogadur, 208
Mogounus, 202
Mogue, St., 266
moke, 211
Moirae, 594
Mona, 391
monastery, 96
Mongols, 191, 847
Mont Giu, 728
montjoy, 728
Moon, 149, 234
Moot hills, 209, 747
morbid, 600
Morgan, 201
Morgana, 317
Moria, 597, 322
Moriah, Mt., 633, 708
Morln, 275
Morning Star, R., 68
morose, 600
Morrigan, 757
Morris dance, 606
Mother Goose, 223, 225
"Mother Margarets," 222
Mother Ross, 604
"Mothers' Blessings," 174, 230
Mottingham, 764, 789
mouche, 221
Mound, 448
— of Peace, 733
Mounds, 171
Mount Pleasant, 288, 716, 745
Mountain tops, 171
mouth, 293
Mowrie, 604
Moytura, 757
mud, 747
Mudes, 747
muggy, 211
Mug's well, 208
Muire, 604
Mulberry, 596
murder, 600
Mushroom, 261
Music of Spheres, 67
Mut, 746
Mutton, 741
Mykale, 261
Mykenae, 258, 383, 430, 843, 850
mykenae, 824
Myrrh, 601
Myrrha, 605
Mysteries, The.

NAG, 622
Nag's Head, 589
Name, Sacred, 535
Nat, 621
naught, 655
naughty, 656
Necessity, 489
neck, 614
Neck Day, 614
nectar, 656
Nectar, 688
Nehelennia, 456, 777
Nehellenia, 697
neigh, 279
Neith, 621

INDEX 889

Nelly, 697, 777
Nelly, 456
Neot, St., 621
new, 257
New Grange, 9, 166, 258, 266, 561, 750, 850
New Jerusalem, 702
New Year's Gifts, 141
Newark, 450
Newbon, 162
Newcastle, 700
Newmarket, 450
Newington, 450
Newlands Corner, 387
Newlove, 818
Newlyn, 697
Neyte, 621
nice, 620
niche, 622
Nicholas, 613
Nicholas, 478
— St., 140, 239, 507, 563, 614, 663
Nicolette, 633
Night, 621
night, 620
Nina, 46
Nine, 72, 94, 194, 214, 537, 549, 588, 609, 642, 664, 792, 834
Nine maids, 549
Nine men's morris, 585, 609
Nine Worthies, 609
Nineteen, 169, 472, 587, 806
Nineveh, 93
Nisses, 620
Nixy, 619
Noah, 152, 450
Noe, R., 450
Nonnon, 625
Norway, 96
November, 244
Noviomagus, 785
Nox, 225
nucleus, 614
Nut, 621
Nutria, 622
Nymph Stone, 623

Oaf, 524
Oak, 73, 87, 133, 226, 228, 370, 393, 665
Oannes, 201
Oats, 663, 680
Oberland, 329
Oberon, 317, 320, 570, 588, 683
ocean, 142
Oceanus, 142
— R., 730
Ock, R., 198
Ockbrook, 198
Ockham, 231
Ockley, 672
Octopus, 839
Oddendale, 461
Odestone, 461
Odin, 157, 461, 743, 842
Odstone, 509
Oendia, 537
Oengus, 266, 512
Offa, 524

Offham Hill, 416
Offida, 474
Og, 194, 195, 243
Og, 194, 76 9
— R., 198
Ogane, 400, 845
Ogbury, 198
Ogdoad, 189
Ogle, 190
Ogmios, 114, 148, 195, 201, 304, 663
Ogmore, R., 198
ogre, 198
Ogwell, 198
Ogygia, 193
Ohio, 535
Oin, 795
Oisin, 175
Ok, 126
Okehampton, 194
Okement, R., 194
Okenbury, 349
Olaf's Beard, St., 267
Olantigh Park, 292
Olave St., 155, 285
Olcan, R., 239
Old Cider, 677
— Davy, 641
— Harry, 199
— Hob, 527
— Joan, 90, 227
— King, The, 152
— man, The, 152, 225, 666, 668, 675
— Moore, 225, 327
— Nick, 140, 478, 620
— Parr, 327, 668
— Poole's Saddle, 796
— Shock, 447
— Surrender, 374
— Wife, 742
Olen, 566
Oliff, 162
Olinda Rd., 285
Oliphaunt, 159
Olive, 155, 427
— tree, 322
Oliver, 601
Olivet, Mt., 793
Oluf, St., 157
Omar, St., 225
On, 450
Ona, 282
One, 489, 537, 547
"One and All," 132
— Essence, 229
— Man, 758
— Man, The, 826
Onslow, 550
ope, 525
Ophites, 496
opine, 285
oppidum, 523
Orand, 572
Oratory of Gallerus, 450
Orchard, 671
Orme's Head, 272
Osmund, 267
osmunda, 267
Ossian, 177, 225
Ostara, 608, 646

Osterley, 608
ounce, 556
Ouphes, 524
Ovary, St., Mary, 748
over, 329
Oving, 419
Ovington Sq., 419
Overkirkhope, 495
Overton, 500
Owen, 795
Owl, 754
Oxford, 514
Oxted, 799
Oyster Hills, 608, 646

pa, 135
Pachevesham, 430
Padstow, 273, 669
Paddington, 151, 456
Pair, 354
pair, 458
Paleolithic symbol, 254
Palm, 278, 390
Palm leaf, 247, 255, 258
— of Paradise, 612
Palmette, 258
Palmtree, 256
Pan, 134, 137, 206, 250, 448
Pankhurst, 137
Panku, 137
Pann, 162
Pans, 169
Pansy, 169, 182
pantaloon, 377
papa, 126, 136
PapaStour, etc., 339
Papas, 728
Papermarks, 365, 381, 503
Pappas, 136
Paps, 209, 757
— of Anu, 334
Paradise, 759
Paradise, 517, 667, 678, 683, 697, 699, 701, 714
— Celtic, 174
Paragon, 759
Parcae, 595
Pardenic, 424
Pardon churchyard, 472
parent, 323
Paris, 412
parish, 312
Parisii, 493
parrain, 330
parricides, 323
parrot, 327
Parsees, 412, 748
Parslow, 714
Parsons, 343
Parthenon, 207
Partholon, 337
Parton, 533, 572
Patera, 674
Patrick, 794
— St., 42, 113, 175, 182, 202, 552, 671, 758, 829
Patrick's Purgatory, 791, 794
Patrise, Sir, 674, 734
Patrixbourne, 670, 687, 716
Paul, St., 342, 346
Paul's, St., 239, 472

890 ARCHAIC ENGLAND

Paul's Stump, 509, 542
paunch, 139
pawky, 231
Paxhill, 754
Peaceful immigrations, 85
Peace Mounds, 736
Peak, 291
— Hill, 440
Pear, 691
— Tree, 730
Pearce, 707
Pearl, 660, 836
Pechs, 244
Peck, 294
Peckham, 231, 373, 670
Pedlar of Swaffham, 575
Pedrolino, 668
peer, 319
Peerless Pool, 721
Peg, 232
Pegasus, 276, 277, 278, 287, 295, 305, 722
Peggy, 233
Peirun, 338
Pelagienne, St., 626
Pelasgi, 92
Pelasgian Heresy, 178
Pell's Well, 796
Pendeen, 766
Pennefather, 137
Penny, 169
penny, 397
Pennyfields, 169
Pennyroyal, 169, 267
Pen pits, 800
Penrith, 724
Penselwood, 800
Pentagon, 77
Pentargon, 90
Pentecost, 243
Penton, 800
Pentonville, 800
Pepi, King, 744
Pera, 702
pere, 323
Perigord, 402
Perilous Pool, 721
— Pond, 718
periphery, 368
Periwinkle, 384, 385
Perkunas, 431
Peronne, 406
Peroon, 358, 431
Perran Round, 387
Perranzabuloe, 316
Perriwiggen, 320
Perriwinkle, 320 384, 385
Perro, 329
Perron du Roy, 315, 420
Perry Court, 313
— dancers, 312, 874
— Stones, 874
— Woods, 313
Perseia, R., 852
Persia, 168, 412
Persians, 171, 181, 182, 183, 322, 544, 570
person, 367
Perth, 461
Peru, 135, 196, 858
Perugia, 326

Perun, 316
Peter, 669
Peter Mount, 826
— St., 127, 249, 478, 613, 668
— the Poor, St., 502
Peter's Hill, 472
— Orchard, 671, 683
— Purgatory, 827
Peterill, R., 675
Peterkin, 668
Petersham, 674
Petra, 724
Petrockstow, 671
Petrocorii, 402
Petronius quoted, 73
Phaëton, 504
Pharoah, 242
Pharoah, 507
Pherepolis, 313
Phial, 427
Philemon, 227
philosophy, 394
Phocean Greeks, 507
Phœbus, 111
Phœnicians, 13, 78, 99, 871
Phol, 424, 841
phooka, 206
Phoroneus, 266
Phra, 507, 748
Phrygia, 227, 326, 574
Phrygians, 164
Picardy, 381
Piccadilly, 731
Pichtil, 305
Pickhill, 231
Pickmere, 231
Pickthorne, 231
Picktree, 231
Pickwell, 231
Pictish sculptures, 381
Pictones, 244
Picts, 244
Pied Piper, 303, 700, 795
Piepowder, 698
Pierre, 668
Pierrot, 138, 668
Piers, 707
Pig, 240, 406
Pigdon, 231
pigeon, 144
Pigeon caves, 783
Pilgrim's Way, 520
Pillar, 241, 255, 269, 384, 481, 823
— palm, 258
Pillars, 297, 309
Pink, 169, 182
Pipbrook, 386
Piper, 305
Pipes of Pan, 158
Piran, St., 316
pirate, 526
Pisgies, 176
Pitcher, 300, 302, 570
Pixham, 231
Pixie's Garden, 703
Pixtil, 284, 305, 557
pixy, 230
Place-name persistences, 34
Plan au guare, 561
planta genista, 419

Pleasant, Mt., 759
Plough Monday, 227, 271, 272
Plutarch quoted, 75
pock, 290
Pocock, 195
Pol Hill, 801
pollute, 426
Polyphemus, 193
Pontiff, 701
pony, 284, 445
Pooctika, 305
Poole's cavern, 796
Poor John Alone, 696
pope, 126
Pope, 357-9
— Joan, 626, 703
Pope's Hole, 589
Popinjay, 754
Poppy, 245, 385
Population, density,
Porsenna's Tomb, 236
Portreath, 574
Portunes, 489, 755
Poseidon, 440
Pot of Treasure, 576
Poukelays, 231, 316
Power, 458
prad, 402
prate, 327
Prechaun, 330
Precious Gem, The, 660
Prehistoric edifice, 863
presbyter, 330
Presteign, 319
Prester, John, 699, 858
Preston, 312, 313, 349, 372, 402, 416
Prestonbury Rings, 332
pretty, 458
Pria, 328
Priam, 716
Prickle, 292
Priest, 330
pride, 119
Prime, 602
Primrose, 182
— Hill, 602
prince, 318
Prince of Purpool, 617
Prize Ring, 563
Proboscis deities, 161
Prometheus, 153
Proserpine, 484
Proteus, 507
proud, 458
Provence, 170
Prow, 399
prude, 119, 458
Prujean, Sq., 331
Prussia, 847
Prydain, 118, 309, 311, 749
Prydwen, 548
Psyche, 177
Puck, 230, 280, 320
Puckstone, 552
Puckstones, 231, 316
pun, 592
Punch, 138, 754
Punchinello, 138
Punning, 54
Purbeck, 551

INDEX 891

Pure, 458
Purfleet, 349
Purgatory, 175
Purity, Hymn to, 183
Purley, 664
Purple, 617
Pwll, 477
Pwyll, 796
Pydar, 698
— Hundred of, 669
Pyrenees, 323
Pyrrha, 337
Pythagoras, 180

QUEAN, 511
queen, 235
Quendred, 719, 761
Quick, 153
quick, 245
Quimper, 310
Quinipily, 531

RA, 152
Racing, Etrurian, 409
Radipole, 684
— rood, 438
Radwell, 470
Rainbow, 265
Rath, 711
rath, 574
Rawdikes, 434
Rayed Fingers, 356
Rayham, 93
Raynes Park, 812
Reading, 437
— St., 443
Rea, R., 436
reason, 437
Reason, 690, 695, 813
Reculver, 95, 661, 759
Red cliff, 818
— Cross, 104, 438, 171
— Horse, 278
— Rood, 555
Reddanick, 438
Redon, 434
Redones, 435
Redruth, 396, 438
regina, 812
Regni, 445
Reigate, 798
Reigate, 812
Reindeer, 622
Resin, 689, 814
rex, 300
Rey cross, 437
Rhadamanthus, 440
Rhea, 301
Rhea, 92, 493
rhetoric, 574
rhi, 300
rhoda, 338
Rhoda coin, 339
Rhode, 440
Rhodesminnis, 440
Rhodians, 683
Rialobran, 314, 318
Richborough, 441, 567, 738
ride, 435
rigan, 301
Ripon, 437

river, 437
River God, 142
Roads, 517
Roas Bank, 93
Robin Goodfellow, 230, 284
— Hood, 509
Rochester, 87, 443
Rock, 73, 127, 129, 207
— Monday, 127
— of Moses, 671
Rodau's Town, 339 350, 435, 683
Roden, R., 435
Roding, R., 435
roi, 300
Romans, 26, 520
Rome, 17
roue, 436
Rood, 437
Rosalie, St., 819
Rosa mystica, 709
Rosamond, 683, 814, 830
Rosanna, 813
Rose, 604
Rose, 442, 610, 626, 669, 672, 817, 819
— coins, 683
Ross, 605
Rota coins, 683
Rothwell, 438
Rotomagi, 436
Rotten Row, 418, 732
Rottenrow, 433
Rottingdean, 443
Rotuna, 443
Round Table, 683
Row Tor, 550
Royal Bright Star, The, 660
Royston, 640, 641, 672, 673, 683, 781
Ruadan, St., 434
Rua excavations, 812
Rudra, 526
Rudstone, 435
rue, 436
Rule, cave of St., 160
Rule, St., 780
Ruthen, 443
Rutland, 434
Rutupiae, 442
Rye, 811

SABRA, Lady, 817
Sabrina, 622, 817
Saffron Walden, 260
Saint's, bisexual, 234
St., John and Father, 165
— Nicholas Acon, 650
Salakee, 589
Salisbury, 340
— Crags, 730
— Seal, 659
Salla Key, 538
Sampson, St., 313
Sancreed, 538, 549, 816
— cross, 816
Sanctuary, 810
Sanderstead, 786
Sandringham, 798
Sangraal, 822
Sanscrit, 49

Santa Claus, 140
Santones, 244
Saturn, 140
Saul, 208
Saxons, 452, 481, 553
Scales, 218
Scandinavians, 471, 558
Scarab, 122
Scarabeus, 256
Scarf, 264
Sceattae, 364, 506
Scilly, Islands, 340, 585
Scroll coins, 252
Seal, 224, 506
Sea Urchins, 811
Secrecy, 118
Seeley, 213
Selby, 340
Selena, 213
Selenus, 688
Selgrove, etc., 340
Sellinger's Round, 685
Selli, The, 339
Selly Oak, 340
Selsea, 340
Semele, 257
Sence, R., 437
Sengann, 411, 512
Senile, 146
Sennen, 425
Sentry Field, 660
Serapis, 497
Serpent, 204, 351, 352, 483, 486, 495, 500, 838
— Shrines, 809
Seven, 495, 657
— Barrows, 416
— Kings, 228, 547
Sevenoaks, 228
Seventy-two, 206, 597, 700
Severn, R., 622
Shadwell, 288
Shah, 696
Shaman, 699
Shamrock, 101, 182, 737
Shandy's Hill, 349
Shanid, 53, 411, 734
Shannon, 53, 411, 512
Shawfield, 448
Shec, 195
Sheen, 674
Sheep, 213
shekel, 400
Shells, 247, 248, 813
Shên jên, 517
Shened, Castle, 703
Shenstone, 53
Shepherdess, 657, 662
— walk, 721
Shick Shack Day, 447
Shield, 548
Ship, 166
— of Isis, 450
Shobrook, R., 447
Shock, Old, 272
Shoe Lane, 754
Shoes, 269
Shony, 142, 201, 671, 699, 795
Shuck, 447
Shuckborough, 447
Shuggy Shaw, 447

Sicily, 320
Sickles, 492, 705
Sid, 440
Silbury, 340, 352
— Hill, 341
Silenus, 213
Silgrave, 432
Silly, 213
Silus Stone, 359
Silver, 439, 512
— plate, 603
— St., 590
— wheel, 438
Silverhills, etc., 439
Sinann, 512
Sinclair, 718
Sindre, 471
Sindry Island, 96
sinister, 477
Sinjohn, 201, 722
Sinodun, 751
S'iva, 526
Six, 487, 490, 624, 788, 790, 835
Six-winged Dove, 486
sleep, 537
Sleep Bringer, 537
Slee, R., 298
Smile Bringer, 537
smite, 467
smith, 432
Smith, Big, 591
— -brethren, 471
Smithfield, 466
Snail's creep, 824
Snake, 841
Snape, 568
Snapson's Drove, 568
Snave, 568
snob, 529
Snodland, 751
Soar, R., 791
Sockburn, 272
Soho, 722
Solar chariot, 495
— cross, 55
— faces, 381
solemn, 297
Soles Court, 292
Solmariaca, 296
Solomon, 296, 298
Solomon's Knot, 706
— Seal, 77
Solutre, 840
Solway, 340, 730, 743
Sophia, 817
— St., 487
Soul, 148, 173
— fivefold, 437
Soul, 172
Spain, 549
Sparrow, 623
— hawk, 433
speak, 251
Spearheads, 465
Specks, 250
Spectacle ornament, 381
Spectral Horse, 294, 300
Speculum, 251
Sphinx, 306, 320, 321
Spike, 253
spike, 293

Spiked chariots, 404
Spindle Whorls, 534, 582
Spine, 254
Spirals, 825, 850
Spirit, St., 624
Splendid Mane, 348
spook, 230, 293
Spots, 250
Spotted Beast, 655
— coins, 249
Sprig, 260, 689
Spring Festival, 307
Sprout, 260
SS, 479, 483
Stag, 257
Stanhope, 529
Stanton Drew, 757, 874
Star, 384, 612, 633, 744, 788
Statuettes, 645
Stella Maris, 607
Stone, 129
— circles, 8
— mortars, 17
— of Fruitful Fairy, 462
Stonehenge, 8, 18, 133, 403, 518, 553, 561, 688, 874
Stork, 46
Stour, R., 608
Sulli, Isle, 348
sulphur, 477
Sun, 166, 167, 195
— and Fire symbols, 690
— god, 134
Sunning, 659
svastika, 230
Svastika, 18, 106, 117, 345, 361, 690, 704, 706, 831, 839
Swan, 224, 225, 243, 512
swan, 240
Sweet Sis, 453
swine, 240
Swine, 240
sy, 230
Sydenham, 440
Symbols, antiquity of, 851
Symbolism, 54, 56, 66, 854, 874
Synagogue, 222

T, 705
ta, 320
Table, 714
Taddington, 261
Taddy, 509
Tailgean, 796
Talavera, 329
Talchin, 493
Talchon, 113
Taliesin, 83, 180, 324, 325, 378, 664
tall, 113
Tallstones, 547
Tammuz, 271
Tanfield, 722
Tapir, 840
Tara, 101, 182, 290, 424, 757
Tarchon, 89, 270, 795
tariff, 98
Tarquin, 90
Tarragona, 89, 278
Tarshish, 96
Tartan, 98

Tartars, 96, 253, 411
Tartary, 700
Tat, 256
Tattooing, 249
Tau, 392
Tear Bringer, 537
Tears of Apollo, 566
teat, 260
Tegid, 157
— Voel, 424
Telchines, 493
Telescope, 839
Telmo's Fires, St., 478
Temple, 296, 328
Ten Lights, 577
Terebinth, 227
Termagol, 192
terre, 99
terrible, 742
terror, 100
Teut or Teutates, 226
Teutons, 558
Thadee, 288
Thane Stone, 461
Thanet, 759
thank, 760
Theana, 754
Therapeuts, 779
theta, 250
Thing, 760
Thirty, 198, 199, 204, 242, 434
— and Eleven, 567
— by Eleven, 738
— three, 192, 198, 204, 214, 226, 641, 768, 806
Thistle, 328
Thopas, Sir, 159
Thor, 102, 355, 384, 674
Thorgut, 221
Thorn, 292, 553, 676
— bush, 152, 293
Thors Cavern, 826
Thoth, 251, 256
Thought, 264
Thread, 830
three, 182
Three Apples, 632, 675
— balls, 632
— basins, 634
— -berried branch, 327
— breasts, 632
— chained whip, 273
— circles, 367, 381
— crescents, 286
— eyes, 102, 632
— fates, 594
— feathers, 366
— fiddlers, 610, 615
— fountains, 346
— fronds, 258
— Graces, 594
— grooves, 579
— hearts, 286
— holy hills, 708
— hundred and thirty, 205, 214
— kings, 228, 632
— legs, 163, 345
— -One, 662
— paps, 367
— peaks, 257

INDEX

Three rays, 535
— springs, 257
— stone balls, 670
— twigged apple, 680
— windows, 366
Threeleo cross, 350
Thurgut, 675,
Thuringia, 305
Thurrock, 769
Thursday, 102
Ticehurst, 350
Tideswell, 448
Time, 829
Time, 639
— Three faced, 143
Tin, 611
Tino, 611
Tintagel, 90, 800
tired, 123
Tirre, Sir, 104
Titan, 263
Titans, 206
Titania, 261, 159
Tithonus, 263
Tiw, 319
Toadstool, 261
toddy, 367
token, 400
Tom-Tit-Tot, 263
Toothill, 733
Toothills, 209
Torfield, 797
Torquay, 95
Torquay, etc., 826
Torquin, 760
Torrent-fire, 20, 864
Tory Hill, 290
— Island, 96, 192, 355
Tot, 256
— Hill, 209
— Hill, St., 209
Totnes, 312, 849
Tottenham, 261
Touriacks, 376
Tours, 355
tout, 226
Toutiorix, 301
Tower, 355
Tra mor, tra Brython, 122
Tradition, 19, 27
Tranquil Dale, 798
Tray Cliff, 798
tre, 86
Trebiggan, Giant, 247
tree, 86
Tree, 96, 363
— Crystal, 181
— of Fate, 322
— of Life, 495, 500-2
Trefoil, 182
Trefoil, 286
Treleven, 214
Trematon, 738
Trendia, 537
Trendle Hills, 578
Treport, 96
Trevarren, 660
Trew, 770
Trewa Witcher, 584
Triangle, 571
— of Downs, 352

Trinacria, 320, 345
Trinidad, 256
Trinity, 101, 256, 499, 535
— in moon, 150
— of Evil, 356
Trinovantes, 86
Triple-tongued Serpent, 810
Triton, 247
Troglodites, 191
Trojan, 123
— Horse, 408
Trojans, 186, 309, 312, 319
"Trojan's or Jew's Hall," 91
Troo, 768
Trophonius, Den of, 771
Trosdan, 734
trou, 86
Troubadours, 701, 858
trough, 771
trow, 98
Trowdale, 741
— mote, 584
Troy, 584
Troy, 16, 19, 44, 49, 79, 83, 86, 102, 118, 227, 238, 399, 406, 411, 466, 534, 707, 852
— Game, 87, 215
— goddess, 754
— Town, 292, 443, 585, 714
— Towns, 87, 581
— weight, 104
Troynovant, 83, 86, 123
truce, 117
Truce, 734
true, 86
True, St., 349
Truth, 752, 761, 830
— and Righteousness, 166
try, 101, 122
Tryamour, 247, 594
Tuatha de Danaan, 858
Tudas, 205
Tudno, St., 256
Tuesday, 102
Tunnel, 843
tur, 90
turn, tourney, 88
Turones, 300
Turquoise mines, 776
Tuttle, 734
Twelve Old men, 698
Twickenham, 610
Twin Brethren, 473
— children, 474
— Mounds, 417
— Sisters, 589
Twinlaw cairns, 417
Two breasts, 253
— cakes, 610
— circles, 367, 475, 495
— cups, 268
— eyes, etc., 546
— horses, 479, 546
— Kings, 610
— miles, 416
— mounts, 209
— necks, 243
— pigeons, 628
— pits, 793
— racehorses, 478
— rocks, 207, 212

Two serpents, 824
— stags, 258
— stars, 476
— tumuli, 208
— virgins, 603
Tyburn, 678
Tynwald, 746
Tyr, 102
tyrant, 100
Tyre, 79, 96
Tyrians, 89, 508, 772

Uar, 389
Uber, Mount, 191
Uffington, 275, 403
Uffingham, 416
Uglow, 685
ugly, 201
Ugrians, 848
Uig, 198
Uist, Island, 661
Ule! 131
Ulysses, 193
Umbria, 569
Umpire, 570
Una, 261, 714
Uncumber, St., 373
unique, 614
up, 525
upper, 328
Upsall, 576
Upwell, 513
Urn, 300, 301, 797
Ursula, St., 266, 214, 643
Uther, and Ambrosie, 656

V = W, 422
vague, 206
Valencia, 188
Vandalisms, 551
Varnians, 658
Varuna, 316
Varvara, 329, 368
Vatican, 828
Vedas, 168
Veil, upon veil, 576
Velchanos, 426
Ver, 267
ver, 266
Vera, 329, 362, 484
— Lady, 749
Verbal tradition, 180, 860
Verdun, 282
Ver Galant, 268, 270
Vergingetorix, 300
Vernon, 440
Verray, 484
Verulam, 608
Veryan, St., 345
Via Egnatio, 519
Vidforull, 203, 227
Vigeans, 327
Village Stone, 312
Vine, 499, 500
virgin, 484
Virgin as Cone, 398
— Mary, 206, 320
— Sisters, 549
— six-breasted, 296
virtue, 609
. Virtues, 640

Virtues, Cardinal, 547
Vol coins, 423
Vorenn, 266
Votan, 840
Vulcan, 426, 469, 478

W = V, 422
Wakes, 323
Walbrook, 510
Walham, 422, 426
Wallands Park, 416
wallow, 422
Wambeh, Lake, 844
Wand, 545
Wanderer, the, 143
War Boys, 612
War treasures, 564
Water, 425, 650
— horse, 284
Wayland, 426, 439
Wayzgoose, 243
Well, 130, 804
Welland, R., 434
welkin, 438
Welsh language, 374
Werra, 485
Westminster Abbey, 673
Whale, 162, 651
Wheatear, 255, 287
Wheel, 164, 269, 276, 282, 438, 482, 574, 578
— cross, 490, 515
— — coins, 491
— of Fortune, 506
whirligig, 195

Whitby, 95
White, 148, 475
— Horse, 273-5, 695, 803
— — Hill, 403
— — Stone, 481
— — Vale of, 272
— Lady, 676
— thorn, 677
Whit Monday, 420
Whorls, 407
Whylepot Queen, 687, 712
Wicker monsters, 407
Wiggonholt, 402
Wilton, 424
Will o' the Wisp, 152
willow, 426
Winander Mere, 221
Wincanton, 800
Winchelsea, 91
Windsor, 273
Winged genii, 326
— wheels, 499
Wisdom, 625
Wise, The, 660
Woden's Hall, 753
Woe Water, 799
Wolf, 148, 373, 661
Womb, 781
Woodnesborough, 841
Woodpecker, 283
word, 390
worthy, 609
Wotan, 841
wraith, 574
Wreath, 573

Wreath, giant, 574
Wren's Park, 812
Wrestling, 186
Writing, 13
Wye, 292, 450
— R., 729

Xidd, 653

Yankee, 97
Yankeeisms, 405
yell, 131
yellow, 131
Yeoman, 508
Yeo, R., 151
Yew, 385
— barrow, 151
Yokhanan, 196
Yole! 131
York, 370, 667, 681, 715
Young Man, the, 668
Ypres Hall, 472
Ytene, 752
— R., 743
Ythan, R., 461
Yule, 124, 131

Zeal, 172
— Monachorum, 340
Zed, 495
Zendavesta, 695
Zennon, 424, 584
Zeus, 444, 472, 771
Zodiac, 207

Printed in the United States
96892LV00005BA/14/A